Ministry with Youth in Crisis

Ministry with Youth in Crisis

Revised Edition

Harley T. Atkinson
W. Lee Barnett
Mike Severe

CASCADE *Books* · Eugene, Oregon

MINISTRY WITH YOUTH IN CRISIS
Revised Edition

Copyright © 2016 Harley T. Atkinson, W. Lee Barnett, and Mike Severe. All rights reserved. Except for brief quotations in critical publications or reviews, no part of this book may be reproduced in any manner without prior written permission from the publisher. Write: Permissions, Wipf and Stock Publishers, 199 W. 8th Ave., Suite 3, Eugene, OR 97401.

Cascade Books
An Imprint of Wipf and Stock Publishers
199 W. 8th Ave., Suite 3
Eugene, OR 97401

www.wipfandstock.com

PAPERBACK ISBN: 978-1-4982-2562-5
HARDCOVER ISBN: 978-1-4982-2564-9
EBOOK ISBN: 978-1-4982-2563-2

Cataloguing-in-Publication data:

Names: Atkinson, Harley. | Barnett, W. Lee. | Severe, Mike.

Title: Ministry with youth in crisis / Harley T. Atkinson, W. Lee Barnett, and Mike Severe.

Description: Eugene, OR: Cascade Books, 2016. | Includes bibliographical references and indexes.

Identifiers: ISBN 978-1-4982-2562-5 (paperback). | ISBN 978-1-4982-2564-9 (hardcover). | ISBN 978-1-4982-2563-2 (ebook).

Subjects: LSCH: Church work with teenagers. | Teenagers—United States. | Teenagers—Canada.

Classification: BV4447 A85 2016 (print) | BV4447 (ebook)

Manufactured in the U.S.A.   11/08/16

Scripture marked (NIV) is taken from Scripture taken from the Holy Bible, NEW INTERNATIONAL VERSION®, NIV® Copyright © 1973, 1978, 1984, 2011 by Biblica, Inc.® Used by permission. All rights reserved worldwide.

We would like to dedicate this book to the hundreds of students we have taught in our youth ministry courses or who have majored in the discipline of Youth Ministry at Toccoa Falls College, Taylor University, and Legacy Christian University.

Contents

Tables and Figures

Preface to the Revised Edition

Since *Ministry with Youth in Crisis* was first published in 1997 much has changed in youth culture and the world of adolescents. We now talk about living in a postmodern world characterized by an eroded system of morality, a blurring of values, and diminished understanding of right and wrong. While adolescents, youth culture, and the issues they face remain constant in some ways, in other ways we have seen radical changes. The technological revolution of the 1990s brought us the personal computer and cell phone, as well as all the platforms and applications that come with them. Teenagers thus discovered new ways of communicating with each other, accessing information, and entertaining themselves, and cell phones and various personal devices became almost universal with youth. New disorders also emerged such as cutting and Facebook depression. Furthermore, the rates of incidence of at-risk behaviors such as drug and alcohol use and abuse, teen pregnancies and abortions, and sexual activity were in constant flux. With the dramatic cultural changes and ever-changing demographics it was a given that an updated version of the book was in order.

When I first wrote the book, I had been fairly recently involved in ministry with youth and was teaching college-level courses related to youth ministry. As time marched on, I became less involved with middle-school (junior-high) and high-school teens, and my teaching responsibilities shifted from an emphasis in youth ministry to a broader focus on Christian education and ministry leadership. In other words, youth culture and the world of adolescents had passed me by. I was well aware that any effort to revise and update *Ministry with Youth in Crisis* necessitated the enlistment of one or more individuals who were younger and currently or very recently involved in youth ministry and more mindful of the issues facing contemporary youth. Joining me, then, in the work of revising the book are Mike Severe and Lee Barnett, both veteran youth workers and professors of youth ministry. With their expertise and insights, considerable changes were in order. We expanded from eight chapters in the first edition to eleven in the new one. The chapter on adolescent identity was divided into two chapters, a chapter dedicated to faith development also emerged out of the material on identity formation, a section on at-risk behaviors and health issues became its own chapter, and a completely new chapter on social media and technology was added. In the revised edition we have added new subject matter related to family-based youth ministry, self-abusive behaviors such as cutting and burning, school shootings, and social media.

There is one notable difference between the first edition and the current one. As mentioned elsewhere, the original edition was edited and published by James Michael Lee of Religious Education Press. Dr. Lee's philosophy was such that he wanted all of his books to appeal to a broad audience of readers—evangelicals, Catholics, mainline Christians, liberals, or anyone else who might be interested in reading about youth in crisis. Thus the language (beyond the title) he insisted upon included terms such as "religious education" and "youth religious educator." We have altered the terminology to be more narrow but more accurate in the language used in most Christian denominations and movements—terms such as "youth ministry," "youth pastors" or "youth ministers," and "youth workers."

Like the first, this edition is both descriptive and prescriptive. It is descriptive in that we purpose to describe the problems and critical issues facing contemporary youth. In so doing we do much to integrate the social sciences—statistical data, theories, and definitions. It is prescriptive in that it endeavors to provide strategies and procedures for providing ministry to youth in crisis from a biblical perspective. Our prayer is that this book will serve as an orientation to the complex world and needs of adolescents, as a reference for those studying youth ministry, and as an effective tool for those ministering in the local church.

Harley T. Atkinson

Preface to the First Edition

In the early 1980s, I was a youth pastor in a midsized church in western Canada. The teenagers with whom I had contact over the few years I was there struggled with typical adolescent issues—career choice, difficulties with parents, peer pressure, indifference to the church, and so forth. Yes, we had our moments, like the time a couple of the boys came to a youth function with alcohol on their breath. But, for the most part, the teenagers I encountered were interested in spiritual matters, were cooperative, and were reasonably well-behaved.

A decade later, I did volunteer youth work in a small congregation and the issues I encountered were much different—open rebellion and insolence, severe family dysfunction, sexual molestation, and trouble with the law. I am not so naïve as to think that these things did not occur prior to the 1990s, nor do I believe all youth today are engaging in at-risk behaviors or encountering crises that threaten their well-being. But the two contrasting experiences do illustrate the fact, in my mind at least, that life is considerably more difficult, dangerous, and complex for teenagers today than it ever has been.

The stress, struggles, and crises that characterize the lives of contemporary youth make the task of the youth religious educator much more difficult as well. This book is designed to be a source of help for the youth worker who is working with teenagers in crisis. It is both descriptive and prescriptive. It is descriptive in that it endeavors to portray the problems and critical issues facing contemporary youth. It is prescriptive in that it endeavors to provide strategies and procedures for providing religious education to youth in crisis.

I am grateful to a number of individuals who have made the writing of this book a possibility. James Michael Lee, my publisher and editor, in his meticulous and thorough critique of my rather rough original manuscript has taught me much about writing.

Appreciation is offered to Jon Harris and Don Ratcliff, my colleagues at Toccoa Falls College, for their insights and suggestions for improvement. I am especially grateful to Suzanne Rich for her careful editing of the manuscript. I want to express my deepest gratitude to my wife, Shirley, and my daughters, Sarah and Hannah, for allowing me to spend many hours at my computer and in my office, even to the point of agreeing to shorten a summer trip.

Finally, I am indebted to a man who was my first adult youth leader. In the days when full-time professional youth ministers were rare, Bob Davison took it upon himself to shepherd the teenagers in our small church in Vernon, British Columbia. Without any formal training in youth ministry and with little understanding of adolescent development, theories of learning, or strategizing for long-term effectiveness, he positively impacted the lives of many teenagers like Dennis, Joe, Walter, Janice, Jim, June, Doug, Jake, and me Bob assisted us through the turbulent years of adolescence and helped prepare us for adulthood. To Bob Davison and countless other youth workers who often receive little recognition for their labors I dedicate this book.

Harley Atkinson

Acknowledgments

In a collaborative project such as this, it goes without saying that many people are involved in the outcome of the final creation. Several individuals provided help with the manuscript by proofreading, editing, and researching. Mike would like to thank Karen Windle and Maddie Gold for tracking down hundreds of citations and sources. Harley expresses appreciation to three of his colleagues: Dr. Donald Williams, for editing and proofreading several chapters; Dr. Phil Howard, for proofing the front matter; and Rick Thomas, MD, for examining the chapter on "Adolescent At-Risk Behaviors and Health Issues." Lee would like to thank his colleague Tim Payne for proofreading several chapters, and his current youth ministry students for their feedback.

We are grateful to the staff at Cascade Books for accepting our manuscript and then working with us throughout the project. Brian Palmer and Matthew Wimer assisted us in the initial stages of the proposal and submission while Dr. K. C. Hanson aided us as editor of the manuscript.

I (Harley) would like to once again acknowledge the input of James Michael (Jim) Lee, editor and publisher of the first edition. He took a chance on me as an unknown writer, and it is he to whom I must give much credit for my writing achievements. Dr. Lee passed away in 2004, a few days after he was involved in a car accident.

Finally we would like to acknowledge our families for their support as we worked on this project. Special thanks to Leeann Severe (wife), and to Malaysia, Hope, Maleiyah, and Dacovin Severe (children); as well as to Shirley Atkinson (wife); and to Robyn Barnett (wife), and Bekah, Hannah, Emily, and Malcolm Barnett (children).

Introduction

As we were working on the front matter for this book (including acknowledgments, preface, and introduction), an announcement came across the news channel—a seventeen-year-old student went on a shooting spree, first killing a pair of teenage brothers in a residence, then killing two adults in the school while injuring seven others. The shooting happened in a small community in northern Saskatchewan—yet another bleak and urgent reminder that youth in Canada and the United States live in a perilous world. Not all the crises are as devastating or life-threatening as a school shooting. Some are a normal part of the growing pains of adolescence such as struggles with academics, conflict with parents, and crises of faith. Youth pastors and volunteers are reminded at each incidence of crisis of the importance of being equipped to assist the adolescents they work with.

We would like to take this opportunity to tell you, the youth worker, a little bit about *Ministry with Youth in Crisis*. First, we want to advise you that this book is academic in nature. In a critique of the initial edition, the reviewer indicated that he felt as if he were back in college reading a textbook. We do not apologize for the academic tone. In reality, one of our primary audiences is the student of youth ministry, be it college or graduate school. Another significant audience, however is made up of practitioners—youth pastors and volunteer workers. We are convinced that in the repertoire of readings for youth workers there is a place for something more than how-to books, as helpful as they are.

Second, we want to underscore the important principle that theory precedes practice. All too many youth workers wade into youth ministry without paying attention to theory (as well as philosophy and theology) that informs why we do what we do. As a result, they tend to "shoot from the hip" without serious reflection, going from workshop to workshop or conference to conference in order to find out what is working across the nation, often learning or adopting faddish or region-specific strategies and techniques.[1] Adolescents in crisis are rarely helped by poor preparation or refusal to engage core issues facing teens today.

Third, with our concern for theoretical foundations, it is important to state our own philosophical underpinning that "all truth is God's Truth." We believe that truth is found not only in the Scriptures (special revelation) but in the created world as well (natural revelation). Thus we carefully embrace and integrate the social sciences and social-science research with what the Bible says about values, morality, and ministry. For example we look to James Fowler for a structural theory of adolescent faith development, with which we integrate what the authoritative Scriptures tell us about Christian formation. We investigate and consider countless research endeavors to better understand the nature and pervasiveness of teen at-risk behaviors such as acts of violence, alcohol use and abuse, sexual activity, and use of media technology.

Fourth, we are struck by the vastness of the issues of adolescence, and by the magnitude of research available in helping us understand these issues. When we add the ministry responses to the immensity of the issues, we are overwhelmed to the point of realizing that we could easily write a book for each chapter theme. The challenge of a project of this nature is to know what to include and not to include, as well as how extensive to be in incorporating the preponderance of research available to us. We pray that the orientation to these critical topics gives a structure to explore the many resources contained in the footnotes.

Fifth, we want to remind those who are sometimes frustrated with the seeming futility of their efforts that their labors do produce results. In virtually every at-risk behavior, the research indicates that there is a positive correlation between church or youth group involvement and godly behavior. The impact may not always be as strong or immediate as we would like, but nonetheless the evidence is clear that lives are changed through the diligent ministry of youth pastors and volunteers.

Finally, we believe in the indwelling power of the Holy Spirit to enable youth workers to be used by God to impact the lives of teens, as well as to heal hurting teens and reconcile them to a loving God. While not a

---

1. We want to make it clear that we encourage youth workers to learn all they can from workshops and conferences. However, these often provide only the nuts and bolts of youth ministry rather than theory and philosophy.

topic of the book, we start with the assumption that youth ministry will not happen unless the worker is filled and empowered by the Holy Spirit (Ephesians 5:18) and teenage lives will not be changed but for the work of the Spirit.

Harley T. Atkinson
W. Lee Barnett
Mike Severe

1

Youth in Crisis

Jeremy is sixteen years old and will be graduating in another year. For some time, he has been considering his future and what he will do upon finishing high school. His parents want him to go to medical school and become a doctor like his father, but Jeremy has a strong desire to go to Bible college. Jeremy has always been a good kid and has never given his parents any serious problems, but now feels trapped by their expectations. Recently, discussions have become heated over this issue, and relations have been strained between Jeremy and his parents.

James is 17 years old and dropped out of school when he was 15. Although he has a good mind, school always bored him, and he was a constant source of trouble and concern to his teachers. Over the past year, James has run away from home twice, been kicked out once, and most recently had a minor run-in with the law. James is from a good Christian home, and his parents are left wondering what went wrong.

It was a year ago today that Brandon's father took a twenty-two-caliber rifle, went out to the barn, and took his own life. Brandon comes from a family with a long history of farming, but in recent years farming had not been good to them. After three straight years of failed crops and significant financial losses, his father could take no more. For several days now Brandon has been in a state of depression as he is reminded of his father's suicide and the possibility that his family could lose their farm. As he stares at the closet where his own gun is stored, he wonders if suicide is not the best alternative for him as well.

By age 11 Joni was already talking about her weight and looks. As she moved into her early teen years, she became increasingly conscious of her appearance and desired to have the body and looks of the models in the teen magazines she so admired. While family and friends insisted she was not overweight, perhaps even a little thin, she felt she was fat and ugly. In the past year her dieting has become more intense. Her weight has dropped far below normal, and her mother cannot get her to eat on a regular basis.

Brad is 13 years old and has just begun junior high school. He had been excited, though slightly nervous, about moving up to junior high, and his parents had anticipated no major problems with this significant change in his life. But after three days of classes, Brad was dragging his feet and showing resistance to going to school. Finally, the issue came to a confrontation, and Brad ran to his room crying, insisting he would never go back to that school. Sensitive and insightful probing by his father revealed that Brad was in a PE class that required the boys to shower after class. Changing and sharing the shower with twenty other boys frightened and intimidated the shy and body-sensitive boy. The fact that some of the bolder and more aggressive boys teased the others and made crude jokes about the body made it especially difficult for Brad.

What is common to the stories above? In each case, the teenager is experiencing a crisis or a crisis situation. It might be something as simple as a confrontation with a parent or as complex as an attempted suicide. It seems that there is no limit to the number of crises adolescents can go through: experiencing a separation or divorce of parents, failing a class, getting kicked out of school, witnessing a school shooting, deciding on a career, experiencing an unwanted pregnancy, undergoing an abortion, losing a part-time job, or moving to a new town and school. While some crises may be brushed off as a normal part of "growing up," each is significant and powerful in the life of the teen. Many teens are not equipped socially, emotionally, or mentally to navigate the weight or scale of the issues. An ever-increasing body of research and statistics indicates that in every area of life, adolescents and their families are experiencing more crises in their lives than did any previous generation.

Scott Larson and Larry Brendtro rightly remind us that teenagers of the twenty-first century are worlds apart from youth of a century earlier.[1] Many sociologists now claim that high school is fundamentally and qualitatively different than just ten years ago. Christian Smith, the foremost researcher on adolescent spirituality, states that adolescence and young adulthood has, "morphed into a different experience from that of previous generations."[2] Chap Clark entered the world of teens and for a full year and talked with them as a part of his research on adolescence. He noticed that while there were positive elements, much was terribly wrong: "I also witnessed palpable darkness. I heard vicious and vile conversations. I saw new levels of vulgarity that I found astonishing. I saw tremendous pain masked by obnoxious defiance, an insatiable selfishness, and indescribable cruelty. Even with all the good, the world beneath is filled with dark corners and hidden crevices."[3] Doing youth ministry in the twenty-first century means working with adolescents who are experiencing life difficulties at unprecedented levels and rates. Unfortunately, many youth workers, whether volunteer or professional, are ill-equipped to deal with the critical issues today's adolescents face. Unawareness of or obliviousness to youth and their experiences leads us to trivialize their adolescent experience. There is nothing either trivial or fake about the crisis facing teens today. This book is designed to help prepare the youth worker, church leader, and church body to better assist members of emerging generations to successfully survive the turbulent and stressful years of adolescence.

WHAT IS A CRISIS?

The notion of crisis became especially apparent in popular developmental literature of the 1970s. Gail Sheehy's best seller *Passages* created a wave of public interest in its description of developmental crises or "passages" through predictable life events. Shortly after, Roger Gould likewise described the predictable crises and changes in adult life in his popular book *Transformations*. Perhaps the most definitive book related to developmental crises across the life cycle was Daniel Levinson's *Seasons of a Man's Life*. In this research publication, Levinson made popular the phrase *male midlife crisis* and suggested that a man experiences a crisis when he finds his current life structure intolerable yet seems unable to

1. Larson and Brendtro, *Reclaiming Our Prodigal Sons and Daughters*, 5.
2. Smith and Snell, *Souls in Transition*, 6.
3. Clark, *Hurt 2.0*, 70.

construct a better one. In a severe crisis life itself is threatened, and he experiences the danger of chaos and dissolution, and the loss of hope for the future.[4]

The popular works of the 1970s, however, were preceded by the theoretical study of life-cycle development by Erik Erikson. Erikson proposed eight stages of life, each presenting a new challenge (crisis). His theory assumed that each stage of life is characterized by turning points or crises. Erikson's concept of *identity crisis* is considered critical to the understanding of adolescent development. He originally coined the phrase to describe the breakdown of inner controls of psychiatric patients. Psychologists eventually used the phrase to describe adolescents when similar characteristics were found in young people who suffered disturbances and conflict. For Erikson, a crisis does not mean catastrophe or complete breakdown but rather a critical period when the individual must move one way or another, and when the view of oneself is no longer appropriate to the life-changing setting.[5]

James Fowler is a widely regarded researcher in the psychology of religion and is best known for his theory of faith development. Building on the works of Jean Piaget, Erikson, and Lawrence Kohlberg, he describes life crises as challenges and disruptions that bring disequilibrium or imbalance to one's life and therefore require changes in the ways of seeing and being. These crises can result in growth and development, as change of some sort is required.[6]

For developmentalists, a crisis is a turning point, the result of a struggle or threat to one's emotional security or physical safety. But crisis can bring opportunity for growth or change, as well as danger or destruction. When doctors talk about a crisis, they are referring to the point in the course of a disease when a change for better or worse occurs. When counselors talk about a marital crisis, they are speaking of turning points when the marriage can go either way.[7] Thus an individual experiencing a crisis can never remain completely static. Gary Collins gives a simple and straightforward definition of *crisis* as any event or series of circumstances that endangers a person's well-being and hinders his or her daily routine of living.[8]

4. Levinson et al., *Seasons of a Man's Life*, 58.

5. Erikson, *Identity, Youth, and Crisis*.

6. Fowler, *Stages of Faith*, 100–101.

7. Wright, *Crisis Counseling*, 20.

8. Collins, *How to Be a People Helper*, 71.

Crises that teenagers experience might be considered one of two types: situational or developmental. *Situational crises* are precipitated by traumatic events that have a significant impact on the teenager's life: for example, losing a loved one, experiencing the breakup of a relationship, going through parents' divorce, moving to a new city and school, becoming pregnant, getting raped, or being involved in an accident. Usually crises of this nature occur with little or no warning, catching the adolescent totally off guard. In the words of adolescent psychologist David Elkind, they are neither foreseeable nor avoidable and can lead to guilt, self-punishment, depression, or denial in the teen.[9] The chief characteristics of situational life crises may be summarized as follows:

- *Sudden onset:* They seem to strike from nowhere. What prepares a girl for date rape? What student at Columbine High School anticipated such a massacre in 1999?

- *Unexpectedness:* Few adolescents prepare for or believe that these crises will happen to them. In fact, adolescents are generally naïve about their own vulnerability to accidents and dangerous situations.

- *Emergency quality:* Many situational crises threaten physical or psychological well-being.

- *Danger and opportunity:* While danger may be the watchword of situational crises, some sort of reorganization or recovery must eventually begin. The good news is that since these events call for coping and resolve to overcome the adversity, it is possible for a teenager to emerge from the crises better equipped to face life in the future.[10]

Developmental crises tend to be a natural or an expected part of growing, or going through transitions: for example, gaining independence from parents, developing peer relationships, dating, undergoing pubescent changes, and entering high school.[11] In each case the teenager reaches a stress point where the demands push the individual close to or beyond the limit of being able to cope effectively. Developmental crises often cause less pain and anxiety than situational crises because they are generally predictable. However, researchers document that teens

---

9. Elkind, *All Grown Up & No Place to Go.*

10. Slaikeu, *Crisis Intervention,* 64–93.

11. Olson, *Counseling Teenagers,* 282–83.

experience a greater level of disruption in reaction to stressful stimuli compared to adults.[12] In some cases, the coping mechanisms continue to function well during developmental crises. In other cases, such as when a teen doubts his or her ability to navigate the crisis, special support and help are necessary. The common theme in developmental crises is that the precipitating events are strongly embedded in the life-maturation process.[13]

Again, there is a positive side to experiencing crises. The ancient Greek word for crisis means a decision-making time that could turn out for better or for worse. A crisis is dangerous because an individual may not be able to cope effectively with the situation in a positive manner. It is an opportunity because in crisis situations people are given an occasion, or are even forced, to grow and change. Consequently the youth worker is in an ideal position to help adolescents turn crises, or what appear to be negative situations, into opportunities for transformation and spiritual growth.

UNDERSTANDING ADOLESCENCE

Before any effort is made to address the critical issues that adolescents encounter, a discussion of the psychology of adolescence is in order. Adolescence is a transitional stage of life where the individual is considered to be neither child nor adult. Unfortunately, the boundaries for adolescence are unclear, and in contemporary Western culture there is no single rite of passage that defines entry into this phase, nor are there identifiable criteria that clearly signal an exit from adolescence.

The term "adolescence" is derived from the Latin word *adolescere,* meaning "to grow into maturity." It is a critical period of human development lying between childhood and adulthood, roughly the ages eleven and twenty. The beginning of adolescence is often identified with the onset of puberty, which for a girl begins with breast development, and for a boy with an increase in the size of the testicles. Boys and girls experience puberty at ages younger than previous generations. In general, children begin pubertal changes between eight and fourteen, with hormonal changes beginning a year or two earlier for girls than for boys.[14]

12. Herrman, "Teen Brain as a Work in Progress," 144–48.

13. Slaikeu, *Crisis Intervention*, 42.

14. Berger, *Developing Person*, 381–5.

When adolescence ends is not so easily determined. A number of criteria, however, help signal termination.

- *Legally:* when one reaches the age of majority. In the United States this is eighteen years of age.

- *Biologically:* when physical maturity is achieved; when the teenager is finished growing.

- *Socially:* when the teenager has successfully passed through certain social institutions. Finishing high school and gaining economic and emotional independence from parents are two examples of key social transformations.

- *Psychologically:* when the teenager has completed certain developmental tasks such as achieving identity and gaining skills for coping with demands of society.

Unfortunately, the existence of multiple criteria makes it difficult to come to a consensus on the completion of adolescence. For example, while a young person may be eighteen (the legal age for adulthood), he may live with his parents, have his mother wash his clothes, and not yet have his own bank account. Some observers speak of an extended adolescence where young Americans remain adolescents well into their twenties[15]—not yet willing to make full commitments to primary social institutions such as vocation, marriage, and family.[16]

Other terms used to describe this transition period are improperly used as synonyms for *adolescence*. While describing the approximate age group and capturing certain aspects of the concept of adolescence, they sometimes exclude essential qualities or include peripheral connotations. The term *juvenile* is often used for this age span but should be limited to matters of law violations and enforcement: for example, *juvenile court* or *juvenile delinquency*.[17]

The term *teenager* is perhaps the most popular word used in referring to young people in Canada and the United States. While it refers to a specific age bracket (thirteen to nineteen), its connotation suggests a stereotypical behavior that is immature and many times less valued by the adult population. Sociologist Hans Sebald suggests that the terms

15. Arnett, *Emerging Adulthood,* 4.
16. Sebald, *Adolescence,* 9.
17. Ibid., 8.

teenager and *adolescent* are closely related yet slightly different. Referring to a person as an adolescent means that we emphasize the particular time of life between childhood and adulthood. On the other hand, referring to a person as a "teenager calls attention to age and the tendency to associate with peers and subcultural activities."[18]

The term *youth* is generally used in a broader and nonspecific manner. It can refer to the younger generation, including children, teenagers, and young adults.[19] In the context of working with teenagers in the church context, however, *youth* ministry generally refers to work done with young people in secondary school. In this book the three terms *adolescent, teenager,* and *youth* will be used interchangeably, even though each carries with it a slightly different connotation. Unless otherwise noted, each term will refer to young people approximately between the ages of thirteen and eighteen.

Developmental Changes

Teenagers are especially vulnerable to crises given that during the adolescent years rapid and dramatic change occurs in so many areas of life. An awareness of these developmental changes can help youth workers understand what adolescence is all about. With such an understanding, they are better prepared to nurture teenagers through these critical and tumultuous years.

Physical Changes

The physical development that adolescents experience is second only to that which occurs in the earliest years of life. But while infants are unable to ponder the metamorphosis they are going through, adolescents have the intellectual capacity to reflect on the changes that are occurring. This awareness of what is happening to the body is often a major cause of anxiety, frustration, and, at times, embarrassment.

For both boys and girls, a rapid growth spurt characterizes the preadolescent and early adolescent years, with girls maturing about two years earlier than boys. For girls their first menstruation, or menarche, marks the beginning of puberty. Along with menarche, the development

18. Ibid., 10.
19. Ibid., 8.

of pubic hair, the enlargement of breasts, and the widening of hips are among the physical changes taking place. The emergence of facial and pubic hair, the deepening of the voice, and the enlargement of genitalia mark this rapid growth period for boys.

Physical development can be the source of much worry, anxiety, and frustration to teenagers, especially if there is delayed development or unusual spurts of growth. Problems such as clumsiness, body odor, acne, and voice cracks are also related to puberty, and are additional sources of anxiety. As the body takes on new shapes and characteristics, the teenager suddenly becomes aware of his or her sexuality. New thoughts, feelings, and experiences related to sexual maturation often confuse and concern the young adolescent.

Social Change

Coinciding with physical changes are dramatic social changes. The strong, dependent relationship the preadolescent had with his or her family begins to change. While they are still physically dependent on parents, gradually teens depend more on peers for emotional support. Parents are still the main source of guidance and support for moral decisions, but even this pattern shifts as adolescents assume more and more personal responsibility for decision making.

Peer relationships will change over the adolescent years as well. Initially, same-sex relationships will predominate, but gradually interest in the opposite sex will precipitate more boy-girl relationships. As a general rule, dating will become increasingly important but will not totally replace peer group relationships and friendships. Without proper instruction and supervision, heterosexual relationships can be a primary source of sexual crises when temptations and feelings are allowed to get out of control.

Significant social change also takes place in the school environment. Fifth- or sixth-graders move from the safe haven of a smaller elementary school to the much larger and impersonal junior high or middle school. Likewise eighth- or ninth-grade students move into the even more threatening senior high school.

Intellectual Change

Cognitive skills are changing as well. Young adolescents move into a stage of life where their thinking capacity becomes more abstract and less concrete. Teenagers can engage in debate with others because their advanced thinking skills allow them to anticipate the arguments of their opponents and prepare in advance to counter them.[20] Abstract thinking skills allow adolescents to imagine the ideal and to compare reality with the imagined world. Usually, reality does not meet the standards of fantasized perfection. As a result, adolescents may question or challenge their parents and may become skeptical of religious beliefs and practices such as prayer or church attendance.

Schoolteachers may also come under the critical eye of the teenager. While children may not like a teacher, they are rarely critical of his or her teaching skills. The adolescent, on the other hand, may be very disparaging of the teacher's competence and knowledge. Toward the middle adolescent years, youth become a little less critical of parents and teachers, and turn their critical eye on government, the church, and other social institutions. They become more concerned with social issues and may criticize other countries and societies as well.[21]

At times the newly discovered thinking skills cause adolescents to challenge much of what they previously believed or were taught. They may doubt the existence of God, question the teachings of their church, or reject (or at least seriously challenge) the values and mores with which they have been brought up. Such relativistic thinking often creates conflict and interpersonal problems between teenagers and their parents.[22]

A Tumultuous Stage of Life

Many psychologists and researchers have characterized adolescence as an extremely difficult and tumultuous period of one's life. For example, Norm Wright says that for some, "adolescence is a time of continual crisis with a few respites in between. For others, their development is a bit smoother. But overall, adolescence is one of the most difficult transitions of life. It

20. Elkind, *Sympathetic Understanding of the Child,* 220.

21. Ibid., 224.

22. For an extensive study of adolescents and religious development see Hyde, *Religion in Childhood and Adolescence.*

is a roller-coaster experience, a time of stress and storm."[23] In reference to this stage of life, Christian psychology professor Ronald Koteskey says Western culture has created a monster and is now having trouble controlling it.[24] At the turn of the twentieth century, American psychologist G. Stanley Hall, the first to write on the psychology of adolescence, characterized these years as *Sturm und Drang*—storm and stress.[25]

The phase of life we now identify as adolescence has always been considered somewhat turbulent. Socrates and Aristotle described youth and young men as having contempt for authority and disrespect for elders and teachers, as having strong passions, and as thinking they know everything. However, even in the recent past most teenagers were expected to successfully ride out the turbulence of youth relatively unscathed. Certainly there were those who stumbled and fell or in some way became casualties, but they were the exception. Now each generation of adolescents seems to face an increasingly complex, stressful, and confusing world.

Many of the experts who work with youth or those who study and research adolescence and youth culture are concerned about the difficulty many contemporary teenagers are experiencing in getting through this phase of life. One source says, "Unfortunately, too many of our young people are not doing well. Too many are falling by the wayside. In fact, so many are falling away—so many are at risk—that we might conclude that our society itself is at risk."[26] Peter Benson of Search Institute, an organization that conducts extensive empirical research on adolescents, says, "It is not clear whether growing up now is riskier business than it once was, or whether we are simply doing a better job of naming and counting the problems that have existed before. It does not really matter. What does matter is that there are too many casualties, too many wounded, too many close calls."[27] Chap Clark summarizes his research as follows: "As I studied students and culture, I came to believe that we as a society have allowed the institutions and systems originally designed to nurture children and adolescents to lose their missional mandate. In other words, society has systemically abandoned the young."[28]

23. Wright, *Crisis Counseling*, 228.

24. Koteskey, *Understanding Adolescence*, 16.

25. Hall, *Adolescence*.

26. McWhirter et al., *At-Risk Youth*, 4.

27. Benson et al., *Troubled Journey*, 1.

28. Clark, *Hurt 2.0*, 27.

Growing up is clearly a risky business today. Issues such as sexuality, dating, self-image, peer pressure, vocational decisions, school, and parents still typify the worries of teenagers. But a host of new concerns frighten and bring anxiety to many adolescents. The quality of family life is negatively impacting this generation of young people, as a majority of them are growing up in broken homes or dysfunctional families. Child abuse, date rape, AIDS, school shootings, suicide, self-harm, and substance abuse are a few of the additional issues many of today's youth face. Furthermore, broader domestic and worldwide concerns, such as war, global warming, world hunger, economic instability, homelessness, and other injustices burden teenagers.

For a number of years, observers of youth and youth culture have noticed a significant growth in the severity and frequency of youth crises. For example, in 1989 seminary professor Wade Rowatt reported that "perhaps as many as 30 to 50 percent of the current teen population will experience a major crisis before reaching the age of eighteen. They will be hospitalized, appear in court, have major parental conflicts, attempt suicide, abuse alcohol or drugs, drop out of school, get pregnant, pay for or have an abortion, or something else of this magnitude. Many will experience multiple crises!"[29]

Then in 1995, a youth pastor in North Carolina observed that the gravity and regularity of youth crises were increasing in this generation. He reported that the youth "I work with are becoming more sophisticated at an earlier age, so they are dealing with more sophisticated and complex problems. Their crises are dramatic—and often fatal. In my ministry I continually confront crises of teen depression, preoccupation with death, suicidal impulses and families in which a teen suicide has occurred."[30] In 2005, Ron Luce likened contemporary youth to someone trapped in a burning car: "The car is on fire and the youth of America are trapped inside. Suicide, abortion, alcohol, drug abuse, and violence are fiery flames licking at the wreckage of many young lives."[31]

Indeed, in a world that is experiencing change and transformation at a breathtaking rate, teenagers are suffering the stressful and often damaging consequences. David Elkind argues that postmodern American society has struck teenagers a double blow. It has rendered them more

29. Rowatt, *Pastoral Care with Adolescents in Crisis*, 20.

30. These are the words of Tim Condor, a youth pastor at the Chapel Hill Bible Church in North Carolina. He is quoted in Ford, *Jesus for a New Generation*, 18.

31. Luce, *Battle Cry for a Generation*, 29.

vulnerable to stress while at the same time exposing them to new and more powerful stresses than were ever faced by youth in previous generations.[32] The same could be said for teenagers in most so-called advanced societies around the world.

Adolescence: Invention, Myth, or Stage?

Not all Christian educators and youth ministry experts agree with the above assessment that suggests adolescence is a distinct developmental stage of life characterized by crisis and turbulence. How parents, youth workers, and congregations understand adolescence will have a significant impact on how they treat teenagers and view youth ministry. There are three views of adolescence currently held by Christian workers and ministry specialists. One theory suggests *adolescence is a cultural invention,* and while we may not like it, we must live with it and do our best to treat teenagers as adults in a less than satisfactory situation. A second approach views *adolescence as a myth.* Proponents of this view suggest that the notion of adolescence is unbiblical and to be disregarded entirely, either as a cultural invention or stage of life. The third view, and the one held by the authors of this book, is what sociologists call *developmental contextualization.* This approach recognizes adolescence as a stage of development that is impacted by the environment in its widest sense (especially family, geographical, historical, social, and political settings).[33]

Adolescence Is a Cultural Invention

According to this commonly held belief, adolescence, the transition period between childhood and adulthood, is essentially a cultural invention, more specifically an invention of postindustrial civilization. It suggests that in many cultures past and present, where puberty was or is regarded as a sign of adulthood, adolescence as Western culture understands it simply does not exist.[34] Prior to the industrial revolution, a rapid transformation from childhood to adulthood took place, with no evidence of a stage of life separating the two. Proponents of this view would remind us that teenagers of the Middle Ages, for example, often made history at

32. Elkind, *All Grown Up & No Place to Go,* 22.
33. Coleman and Hendry, *Nature of Adolescence,* 11–12.
34. Elkind, *Sympathetic Understanding of the Child,* 203.

an age when today's adolescents are still going to high school. Edward, the Black Prince, was sixteen when he triumphed at the Battle of Crecy in 1346, and Joan of Arc was seventeen when she captured Orleans from the English in 1429. Ivan the Terrible was also seventeen when he began to make his name as the "Terrible" and had himself crowned czar of Russia in 1547.[35]

With the industrial revolution, however, came increasing urbanization and industrialization. With increasing technology there emerged a growing concern and need for formal education and occupational training, which in turn gave rise to new educational institutions. Furthermore, the fact that children were no longer needed in the labor force, coupled with a more humanitarian attitude towards them, led to a series of child labor laws. By 1914 in the United States, almost every state had laws prohibiting the employment of young people below a certain age. In most cases, this age was fourteen. Individuals who engaged in education and training found themselves in a phase of life that was neither childhood nor adulthood. David White argues that "these developments relegate most youth to institutions in which they have less than full power for longer than any age cohort in the history of the world, leaving them considerably less free to make their distinctive mark on history, and . . . quickly shaping them as passive consumers rather than active agents and shapers of history."[36] This inability to contribute directly to societal development has had a lasting impact on adolescent efforts to gain social status and fulfillment through other means.

Furthermore, advocates of the *cultural invention* theory propose, throughout history men and women married at much earlier ages, generally around the age of puberty. As recently as two hundred years ago in the United States, men could legally marry at age fourteen and women at twelve. However, in the last two centuries, while laws increasing the minimal age for marriage to eighteen were enacted, the age of puberty was dropping significantly. So while the age of puberty was decreasing, the minimal legal age for marrying was increased; emphasis on education grew, and labor laws raised the legal age for working. This was the creation of adolescence it is suggested, an invention of culture.

35. Sebald. *Adolescence,* 12.
36. White, "Social Construction of Adolescence," 4.

Christian psychologist Ronald Koteskey holds to this view and believes that "adolescents are adults, not children, in their thinking."[37] He seems to concede, however, that adolescence is a stage of life, even if it is an invention of our culture. He would like to treat adolescents as adults, but seems to allow for the fact that, through cultural invention or otherwise, they are still adolescents. The title of his book itself, *Understanding Adolescence: Helping your Teenager Navigate the Turbulence of Adolescence,* reinforces this notion (he twice refers to the teen years as "adolescence"). His advice to parents is to treat their teenage children as adults, but he concedes that they may not always act as such. For example he encourages parents to "let them make decisions *as long as they act like responsible adults.*"[38] Elsewhere he writes, "the basic thing you can do is to help your adolescents now is to *treat them as much like adults as possible.*"[39] Simply put, Koteskey admits that adolescence exists as a transition period between childhood and adulthood, but only as culture or society has made it so. We may not be able to change culture, but we can do the best for our teenagers by treating them as adults rather than children and expecting the best responses from them. Koteskey, unlike those in the *adolescence is a myth* camp, would not necessarily disregard age-appropriate ministries to teens such as youth group, student-only activities, or Sunday school classes.[40] He encourages youth ministers to give teens responsibilities such as leading small groups, leading the whole group, doing maintenance on church vehicles, planning and carrying out youth activities, and raising money for some of their activities.[41] The cultural invention theory is currently called into question, as experts propose that adolescence exists in most societies and is almost universal for boys.[42]

Adolescence Is a Myth

Youth experts who hold to this interpretation dismiss adolescence altogether—as either a stage of life or invention of culture. Strongly held

37. Koteskey, *Understanding Adolescence,* 28.
38. Ibid., 32 (italics added).
39. Ibid., 20 (italics added).
40. Ibid., 49, 69.
41. Koteskey, "Adolescence as a Cultural Invention," 56, 66.
42. Schlegel and Barry, *Adolescence,* 42.

by a growing number of churches and advocated by Voddie Baucham[43] and David Black,[44] this approach argues that the notion of adolescence is foreign to the Bible and that in those times children moved directly from childhood into adulthood. Thus Black identifies three stages of life— childhood or preadulthood (ages one to twelve), emerging adulthood (ages twelve to thirty), and senior adulthood (age thirty until death).[45] He goes on to suggest, "at puberty the child is moving out of the pre-adult world and is making a preliminary step into adulthood. The basic developmental tasks of this phase are exploring the possibilities of adult living, imagining oneself as a participant in the adult world, and learning how to make responsible choices in life."[46] Youth ministry (as an age-level program that would cater to adolescent issues and crises) is also dismissed as unbiblical. The biblical alternative, proposes Black, is that "if adults make the church a community to which young people want to belong, they will be helping teenagers move more smoothly into adulthood."[47]

Adolescence is a Stage of Life—Developmental Contextualism

The third and most prevalent view (and the one held by the authors of this book) is what sociologists describe as *developmental contextualism*. It holds that adolescence is a stage of life recognizably distinct from either childhood or adulthood, a brief period between childhood and adulthood during which preparation for adulthood is initiated and intensified. Adolescence is summed up as "including biological and affective reorganization, severance of early emotional ties to parents, and experimentation with social roles."[48] While the beginning is clearly marked by biological development (by the onset of puberty), the end is determined socially (by, say, graduation from high school or reaching the age of majority). In contrast to the two other perspectives, this theory argues that adolescence exists in most societies (not just industrialized ones) and is possibly universal for boys.[49] The *developmental contextualism* version of

43. Baucham, *Family Driven Faith*.
44. Black, *Myth of Adolescence*.
45. Ibid., 7.
46. Ibid., 8.
47. Ibid., 26.
48. Schlegel and Barry, *Adolescence*, 3.
49. Ibid., 42.

adolescence emphasizes the interaction between the growing individual and the multifaceted and ever-changing environment within which the adolescent lives. Several principles define this theory.[50]

There is a context for adolescent development. While the context for development is primarily and most obviously the family, other settings such as the geographical, historical, political, and social settings in which the family and adolescent live have profound effects on the development of teenagers. For example, the parents' place of work, with which the adolescent may have little interaction, will have a significant impact on his or her life conditions (consider salary, work schedule, benefits). Unique contributions of individual societies dictate or influence the shape of the pathway from childhood to adolescence. For instance, as marriage often takes place earlier in life in preindustrial cultures, adolescence tends to be relatively short in those societies.

There is continuity to adolescent development. Originating from the life-span concept of epigenesis, this principle is important for two reasons. First, it conveys to us the notion that development is gradual rather than characterized by sharp or sudden changes. Second, it points to the fact that adolescence is a continuation from childhood (as adulthood is a continuation from adolescence). It is important that youth workers not treat adolescence as unconnected or unrelated to childhood or adulthood. Erik Erikson contends that before an individual can navigate through one stage, he or she must have successfully resolved challenges in previous stages. For example, before young adults can achieve intimacy in their twenties, they must first must succeed in identity achievement in adolescence (or early adulthood).

Adolescents and their families influence each other reciprocally. According to this principle, both the family and adolescent child grow, develop, change, and affect each other at all times. The size, structure, climate, decision-making strategies, harmony, and leisure-time activities of one's family, not to mention parent supervision within the family, all have the potential to influence adolescent development. For example, the extent to which the adolescent is involved in family decision making or encouraged to make his or her own decisions may influence the developmental task of gaining independence.[51]

---

50. Coleman and Hendry, *Nature of Adolescence*, 11–13.

51. Muuss, *Theories of Adolescence,* 340–41.

A multidisciplinary approach helps us best understand adolescence.
Life-span theory has brought together biologists, psychologists, educators, and sociologists to construct a comprehensive theory of *developmental contextualism*. For example, consider recent brain-scan studies
that shed significant light on adolescent development from a biological
perspective. According to the National Institute of Mental Health, studies
of children and adolescents indicate that "the brain does not resemble that
of an adult until the early twenties. The scans also suggest that different
parts of the cortex mature at different rates. Areas involved in more basic
functions mature first: those involved, for example, in the processing of
information from the senses, and in controlling movement. The parts of
the brain responsible for more 'top-down' control, controlling impulses,
and planning ahead—the hallmarks of adult behavior—are among the
last to mature."[52] The report goes on to say that "the capacity for learning
at this age, an expanding social life, and a taste for exploration and limit
testing may all, to some extent, be reflections of age-related biology."[53]
Other chapters will address various elements of adolescent development.

Adolescents are significant shapers of their own development. One of
the key principles of *developmental contextualism* is that the adolescent is
an "'active agent' in shaping or determining his or her own development."[54]
Major decisions to run away, marry early, or to join the army have obvious implications for development. But even day-to-day choices (for example, to study or not study for an exam, to obey or disobey to a parent,
to choose this person or that person as a friend) collectively impact how
a young person progresses through the adolescent years.

Developmental contextualism disaffirms the notion that adolescence
is a myth or invention of culture and proposes that a brief life span exists between childhood and adulthood such that adolescents should be
treated differently and will behave differently from either children or
adults. Various developmental constructs related to physical, cognitive,
moral, social, and faith domains inform youth workers and parents of
characteristics unique to teenagers and offer insights to doing ministry
with teenagers. Furthermore, the *developmental contextualism* approach
to adolescence affirms the importance of age-related programs for youth,

---

52. National Institute of Mental Health, "Teen Brain."

53. Ibid.

54. Coleman and Hendry, *Nature of Adolescence*, 13.

while not ignoring the importance of programming for intergenerational activities.

A GENERATION AT RISK

Teenagers today are part of a troubled generation—a generation at risk. Consider the statistics below, summarized from a 2007 nationwide Youth Risk Behavior Surveillance of youth in the United States in grades nine through twelve.[55]

- 35.5 percent of the students had engaged in a physical fight at least once in the previous twelve months.

- In the previous twelve months before the survey, 9.9 percent of the youth had been physically hurt intentionally by their girlfriend or boyfriend.

- 7.8 percent of the students had been forced to have sexual intercourse when they did not want to. As one might expect, the incidence of rape for girls was significantly higher than for boys (11.3 percent).

- During the previous twelve months of the survey, 7.8 percent of the students had been threatened or injured with a weapon such as a gun, knife, or club; 12.4 percent had been in a physical fight on school property at least once.

- During the previous year, 28.5 percent of the students surveyed had felt so hopeless or sad every day for two or more weeks in a row they stopped doing some normal activities.

- In regard to suicide, 14.5 percent had seriously considered attempting suicide, 11.3 percent made a plan for suicide, 6.9 percent attempted suicide at least once, and 2 percent made an attempt that resulted in injury, overdose, or poisoning that had to be treated.

- 26 percent of the surveyed students engaged in binge drinking (five or more drinks of alcohol in a row within a couple of hours) at least once in the thirty days before the survey.

- 38.1 percent had used marijuana at least once in their life, and 19.7 percent had smoked marijuana at least once in the thirty days prior

55. Centers for Disease Control and Prevention. *Youth Risk Behavior Surveillance—United States, 2007.*

to the survey. Other drugs used (at least once in a lifetime) included cocaine (7.2 percent), inhalants (13.3 percent), hallucinogenics (7.8 percent), heroin (2.3 percent), methamphetamine (4.4 percent), and ecstasy (5.8 percent).

- 47 percent reported to never having sexual intercourse, while 14.9 percent indicated they had had intercourse with four or more individuals during their life.

This alarming index of problems tells us the current generation of youth is indeed in crisis, and there is no indication that things will get better. And we might add to this list a number of less dramatic yet significant issues such as loneliness, depression, hopelessness, boredom, school problems, and family conflict that might be considered normal as one progresses through adolescence.

The phrase *at risk* emerged in literature in the 1980s in a number of fields, such as education, psychology, and medicine. Some experts have used the term to describe many of today's youth. One source uses *at risk* to denote a set of cause-and-effect dynamics that place the individual child or adolescent in danger of negative *future* events. For example, young people who use tobacco are at risk for alcohol use; teenagers who use alcohol are at risk for illicit drug use.[56] Many of our teenagers—including churched youth—are at risk. That is, they are involved in activity or in situations that may lead to more destructive behaviors or activities, and many more have already reached the point where their activities and behaviors are harmful in a number of ways.

Factors Contributing to a Generation at Risk

Today the seriousness of adolescents' problems and critical issues causes us to question why today's teenagers are experiencing such a difficult time coping with life. Some possible factors contributing to the serious problems teens face are the breakdown of the family, a diminishing role for the church and religion, a crumbling public education system, and a growing negative influence from the media.

56. McWhirter et al., *At-Risk Youth*, 6.

Breakdown of the Family

The family in North America has undergone significant and critical changes in the twentieth century, especially in the last three decades. In the first half of the century the extended family—a familial network of parents, children, grandparents, and perhaps an aunt or uncle—was replaced by the nuclear family. The nuclear family normally consisted of one adult of each sex and five or six children. Since the 1960s, however, radical changes have taken place in the family structure. Skyrocketing rates of divorce, separation, remarriage, out-of-wedlock births, and single parenting have all contributed to the restructuring and breakdown of the "traditional" American family. Over four hundred thousand children are in foster care yearly, 1.6 million are homeless yearly, and 2.7 million lived with their grandparents in 2011.[57] Today many teenagers are growing up without the support, nurturance, guidance, and modeling of parents and other relatives. Stephanie Staal, after extensive interviews with children of divorce, asserts that divorce may be the defining mark of this generation.[58] In fact, empirical studies have estimated that the probability that a child will live with only one parent at some time before he or she reaches the age of eighteen is between 40 and 60 percent.[59] The U.S. Census Bureau reports that in 2010 alone 30.6 percent of all youth lived with one or fewer parents.[60] Andrew Root claims that this "break of community in which the child's identity rests . . . is a threat to his or her very being."[61]

The quality or lack of quality in family life today is a key contributor to the critical condition of our current youth generation. Children and adolescents need the discipline, security, and affection exhibited in strong families, and when these characteristics are not present, loneliness, alienation, stress, and frustration are likely to emerge. Indeed virtually every risky or destructive behavior, including suicide, running away, substance abuse, sexual promiscuity, and violence, can be linked to some degree to the dysfunctional or broken home.

57. Children's Defense Fund. *State of America's Children Handbook.*
58. Staal, *Love They Lost*, 3.
59. Ibid., 42.
60. United States Census Bureau, "Families and Living Arrangements."
61. Root, *Children of Divorce*, xvii.

Diminishing Role of Christianity

Paralleling the breakdown of the family is the diminishing role of Christianity and Christian institutions in the lives of North American adolescents. While teenagers still affirm a belief in God and admit that they have spiritual needs, their involvement in churches and other religious organizations has deteriorated. According to a 1993 report by Eugene Roelkepartain and Peter Benson, more and more young people are leaving organized religion, and for those who remain, only a small minority experience a life-transforming faith characterized by a strong relationship with God.[62] According to a 1999 Barna study, there was a minor decline in teenagers who describe their faith affiliation as Christian in that decade.[63] The downturn has continued in a persistent move away from core Christian doctrines and opposition to organized religion. Finally, in the most recent and most ambitious and extensive research efforts ever conducted on the religiosity of American teenagers, Christian Smith reinforced the notion that most U.S. teenagers identify themselves as Christian, but he determined that the majority of these teenagers practice their religious faith sporadically or not at all.[64] Smith found that only 8 percent of American youth can be categorized as highly devoted Christians—teens who believe in God, attend religious services at least weekly, recognize faith as extremely important in their lives, regularly participate in youth group activities, and pray and read the Bible regularly.[65] Kenda Creasy Dean noted that these teenagers also readily talked about their faith in a manner that showed they had clearly thought about it beforehand.[66]

Most young people today are shaping their values and beliefs in the absence of systematic Christian education in formal settings (such as the Christian school) or nonformal settings (such as youth group). Without such instruction or even modeling, they unconsciously embrace attitudes, principles, practices, and ethics that are appealing to self and friends, and those that are proclaimed through music, television, and movies, and modeled by parents or other adults such as teachers. Because Christianity is no longer the central guidance institution for developing

62. Roehlkepartain and Benson, *Youth in Protestant Churches*, 5, 7.

63. Barna, *Third Millennium Teens*, 45–46.

64. Smith, *Soul Searching*, 68.

65. Ibid., 110.

66. Dean, *Almost Christian*, 40.

consciences with convictions, other sources of significantly less positive influence have come to take up that function.

A Crumbling Public Education System

In addition to the family and church, it has fallen to the school to contribute to the development of the young person. Since the 1960s, however, the public education system has come under fire from many who believe that it is in shambles and is in many ways failing our young people. Numerous studies compare the standardized test scores of American students with those of other countries, and the scores consistently favor others. While some might charge that these standardized tests are inaccurate measurements of true learning, many would argue that the education that is taking place in United States schools is far from what it should be. *USA Today* reports that nearly half of America's public schools (over 43,000) did not meet federal achievement standards in 2011.[67]

Crime, violence, and other at-risk behaviors are also prevalent on the campuses of American high schools. The Centers for Disease Control identified the following at-risk behaviors of high school students:

- 5.9 percent carried a weapon on school on property at least once in the month prior to the survey;

- in the previous year, 7.8 percent had been threatened or injured with a weapon;

- 12.4 percent had been in a fight on school property at least once in the previous year; 27 percent had property stolen or intentionally damaged on school property in the previous twelve months;

- 5.5 percent of the students refrained from going to school at least once in the previous month because they felt unsafe;

- 4.1 percent had at least one drink of alcohol on the school campus in the 30 days prior to the survey;

- 4.5 percent had used marijuana on school property at least once in the previous 30 days;

- in the previous year, 22.3 percent of the students surveyed had been offered, sold, or given an illegal drug on campus at least once.[68]

67. Center on Education Policy, "Almost Half of U.S. Schools."
68. Centers for Disease Control and Prevention. *Youth Risk Behavior*

Sad to say, students have come to accept the fact that at-risk activities such as fighting, violence, drug use, and alcohol use are all part of going to school.

Influence of Television and Other Mass Media

It would be inaccurate and unfair to suggest that the institutions of the family, church, and public school system have no positive impact on attitudes, values, thought patterns, and behaviors of teenagers. Nonetheless, it is true that the positive influences of these institutions have in many ways been eroded or offset by the influence of the mass media. In the 1980s sociologist Tony Campolo argued that television dominated the consciousness of young people.[69] In the twenty-first century the Internet has no doubt surpassed television in terms of impacting adolescents and is clearly transforming the way teenagers are growing up in the United States and Canada. While there is still debate as to the effect of visual media on the actions and thoughts of viewers, researchers are finally admitting that viewed violence does indeed have an impact on behavior. For example, evidence demonstrates that depicted violence can lead to a short-term rise in aggressive behavior such as getting into fights and disrupting the play of others.[70]

Campolo suggests that television, and we might add video games and online gaming, has also rendered real life uninteresting. Its ability to create an environment that is much more exciting than reality makes it difficult for parents to involve their children in family activities. Creating family activities that can compete with media techniques often proves to be a monumental task for parents and youth workers alike.[71]

Mass media—television, movies, and music—are designed with the intent of shaping and influencing attitudes, values, thinking, and behavior. Adolescents today are exposed as never before to varieties of ideologies, values, lifestyles, and worldviews—most of which are antithetical to Christian standards. Adolescents who no longer inherit a consistent value system from family, church, and school are cast adrift to make hit-and-miss choices from among a variety of known values and sources.

Surveillance—United States, 2007.

69. Campolo, *Growing Up in America*, 74.

70. Allman, "Science Looks at TV Violence," 64.

71. Campolo, *Growing up in America*, 74.

CONCLUSION

While always considered a difficult time of life, adolescence seems to be an increasingly troublesome age span, as teenagers encounter a more complex, stressful, and confusing world. Sociologists and others who work with adolescents speak of a generation in crisis. Many of today's adolescents are in some way at risk, and there is a growing concern in the United States and many other countries about the future status of today's youth. The institutions that have traditionally contributed to the development and well-being of teenagers—the family, the church, and the school—have in many ways failed in recent decades. On the other hand, mass media, especially television, have played a greater role in shaping the values of children and teenagers. Unfortunately, the ideologies and beliefs that young people are receiving challenge traditional values and the teachings of a Judeo-Christian heritage. The scope and significance of the issues and the opportunities of youth and emerging adults cannot be underestimated. Sundene and Dunn speak about the "spiritual global pandemic" and the importance of the task of tending to the spiritual lives of teens: "This generation . . . has reached an acute level of spiritual crisis. Continued failure to prayerfully and proactively gather local communities of Christ's disciples to invest relationally in the spiritual journeys of young adults will ultimately have catastrophic spiritual consequences."[72] The purpose of this book is to assist youth workers in the difficult tasks of ministering to adolescents in crisis. Each chapter will deal with a specific area of need that contemporary youth encounter.

72. Sundene and Dunn, *Shaping the Journey of Emerging Adults*, 20.

2

Who Am I?
The Adolescent Search for Identity

One of the most urgent yet difficult challenges of adolescence is discovering who one is, the task that psychologists call identity formation. During the formative teenage years young people face the crises of discovering how they fit into society and what roles they will play in life. Identity formation includes the evaluation of the goals, values, and beliefs acquired from one's family, church, school, peers, and other elements of society. It also necessitates the asking of questions such as *Who am I? Where did I come from?* and *Where am I going?* with the goals of achieving self-certainty, coming to terms with sexuality and gender roles, developing a system of beliefs and attitudes, and choosing an occupation. One of the main goals in youth ministry, consequently, is to help adolescents develop a coherent and stable sense of self that can withstand a host of identity problems while allowing them to commit to an "in-process" identity in Christ.

First, this chapter will explore the foundational issues and challenges related to the adolescent task of identity achievement. Second, it will define and describe identity and identity formation. Finally, it will address ways the church can engage youth in healthy identity formation. Subsequent chapters will address the various dimensions related to the achievement of identity such as sexuality, gender roles, vocation, and faith system.

CHALLENGES TO IDENTITY DEVELOPMENT

Achieving a sense of personal identity is no doubt a more formidable task for today's teenagers than it has ever been. Until the nineteenth century technological and societal changes came very slowly, and one's occupation and place in society were often predetermined by class structure or family pursuits. Gender roles were well defined both in business and the home. Men were given the economic responsibilities, while homemaking duties fell to the women. This pattern is no longer characteristic of most American families. Many wives are in the workforce before and after marriage, as well as after the birth of children. The impact of changing gender roles has affected men as well. In many modern families in which both the husband and wife work, men have come to assume a greater role in childcare and other household responsibilities. Thus, societal changes present a huge challenge to the identity formation of adolescents.

Furthermore, adolescents are continually faced with developmentally related questions of meaning, inner conflict, or conflicting assumptions that underlie their personhood. A nonintegrated or compartmentalized position with regard to identity development will potentially cause the adolescent to experience permanent immaturity or, worse yet, a psychological disorder.[1]

Compartmentalized thought provides limited capacity for adaptability, a prerequisite for success in identity achievement and general maturity, including in one's faith. Often various childhood experiences are unevaluated and absorbed into the personal identity, causing individuals to become dysfunctional in adolescence and adulthood.[2] For example, consider Linda, a thirty-year-old woman, a mother whose children have never heard her laugh. This odd behavior is the response to something that happened in her early childhood. At a birthday party, in front of a roomful of other children, one of the boys blurted out that she laughs like a donkey—likely an innocent remark with no real hurt intended. But as a young child, Linda vowed to never laugh again in front of other people. While a reasonable response for a child, an adolescent or adult who habitually reacts to the environment in this way will have difficulties in adapting to the social environment.

---

1. Elkind, *Sympathetic Understanding*, 198; Erikson, *Identity and the Life Cycle*, 97.
2. Mezirow, *Transformative Dimensions*, 138–39.

Identity has a direct impact on motivation, commitment, and action—characteristics that are vital for the healthy development of adolescents. Furthermore, changes in perception of oneself and one's social environment are necessary before changes in ideas, attitudes, and behavior will take place.

A METAPHOR FOR IDENTITY: THE HOUSE

A helpful metaphor for understanding the identity development of the adolescent is the house. Picture first the identity of a child as a series of rooms that revolve around three elements: explanations, behaviors, and solutions. An example of an explanation element is, "Jonah was swallowed by a whale because he disobeyed God." An example of a solution is "2+2=4." A behavioristic element is, for example, "When I do this, such and such always happens." Children furnish these rooms, a kind of house for their identity, with information, processes, and concepts throughout their childhood. The rooms are furnished by significant experiences and especially important figures in their lives such as their parents and teachers. Children are very limited in their ability to sort, monitor, or exclude the contents of the rooms in their metaphorical house; thus, beliefs about self and the world are received with little control or sorting.

The teenage and young-adult house is far more complex. Five new rooms are added to the original three, labeled "*Who am I?*", "*What if?*", "*How will this affect my relationships?*", "*Why?*", and "*How does it fit together?*" Adolescents add on to their house and attempt to make connections with preexisting structures. Often some form of compartmentalization is prevalent throughout the teen years. Compartmentalization is the classification of conflicting values, attitudes, behaviors, commitments, habits, and rituals, and is contingent on the social-cultural context. A pastor relates an illustration of compartmentalization as follows: "As a teenager in our youth group, I was asked to do the senior recognition Sunday sermon at my church on graduation weekend. I prepped the sermon, went to graduation, got drunk with my friends on Saturday night, and preached with a hangover on Sunday morning. I never saw the conflict between what I did Saturday and Sunday until years later." Teens struggle to reconcile childhood explanations, solutions, and behaviors with the increasingly complex, difficult, and fuzzy needs of adulthood and the adult world. There is almost always residual compartmentalization still resident in the lives of teens. Much of what they see as their identity is a set of uncritically accepted ideas or a conditioned group of responses to a set of social cues.

Fidelity is an important element in healthy identity formation.[3] Fidelity, or faithfulness to obligations and relationships that are driven by adherence to an ideology, provides the stability for action in the world. These form the doors or the bridges of meaning that can be built between the rooms. Successful identity formation provides a host of benefits to individuals and their social context, yet a significant number of adults do not achieve identity fidelity. Thus, unresolved issues here may perpetuate immaturity in the adult.

IDENTITY FORMATION—WHAT IS IT?

The concept of identity as used in current developmental literature and research originates in the work of developmental psychologist Erik Erikson, who proposed eight psychosocial stages of humankind.[4] Erikson's theoretical structure is based on the notion that an individual's personality is shaped by a coinfluence of psychological or intrinsic forces (psycho) and societal or extrinsic elements (social), such as parenting and educational opportunities.

Erikson's stages begin with the first contacts after birth that lead to trust or mistrust, and proceed to the final struggles for integrity or the assuming of responsibility for what one's life is and was. The critical stage of adolescence is characterized by the crisis of identity achievement versus identity diffusion, whereby the individual becomes concerned with self-esteem as well as societal roles and responsibilities. Simply put, the adolescent seeks to understand who he or she is in relationship to the surrounding world. The young person seeking an identity does not go around asking the question, *Who am I?* Nor does the person with a secure sense of identity usually stop to think or to brag about the fact that he or she has achieved it and of what it consists. Rather, it is a subtler harmonizing of inner resources, traditional values, and opportunities of action, derived from a fusing of intrinsic personality processes

---

3. Stevens, *Erik Erikson*, 50.

4. Erikson's view of the life cycle is presented in Erikson, *Identity, Youth and Crisis*; Erikson, *Identity and the Life-Cycle*; and Erikson, *Life Cycle Completed*.

and extrinsic environmental forces.[5] *Identity* refers to a clearly defined definition of self, a self-definition composed of beliefs, values, and goals that the adolescent finds personally worthy and to which he or she is unquestionably committed. These commitments are chosen because the goals, values, and beliefs are regarded as worthy and virtuous in providing direction, purpose, and meaning to life.

In the search for identity most adolescents are apt to go through a crisis or some sort of struggle that includes emotional and mental stress, or a point of challenge that includes the possibility of turmoil.[6] Note that the crisis need not be extreme, nor should it meet the popular depiction of a lost teen shedding every value and societal norm. This crisis is most often quiet, internal, and process oriented, and can take several years to complete. Yet crisis is essential if an adolescent is going to arrive at a wholesome and integrated sense of identity. Identity development and faith development are interwoven, thus making "identity formation research helpful in understanding the importance of allowing adolescents space to wrestle with their faith in the midst of a caring community of believers."[7]

FOUR IDENTITY STATUSES

While there have been a considerable number of efforts, the most productive study of personal identity was done by James Marcia, who was able to identify and describe four identity types of adolescents.[8] These types, or *statuses*, as Marcia calls them, are *identity diffused, identity moratorium, identity foreclosed,* and *identity achieved.* Each status describes where an adolescent might possibly be in regard to identity formation. According to Marcia, two criteria are necessary for the achievement of a mature identity in youth: *crisis* and *commitment.* The four identity statuses are defined by their positions on these two conceptual dimensions. Crisis has already been described as the struggle or emotional turmoil one goes through in making choices, while commitment refers to the amount of personal investment an individual exhibits in a choice.

5. Erikson, "Youth and the Life Cycle," 256.

6. See Steele, "Identity Formation Theory and Youth Ministry," 91.

7. Cannister, *Teenagers Matter*, 52–53.

8. For a more complete description of Marcia's identity theory see Muuss, "Marcia's Expansion," 260–70.

Figure 2.1
Identity Statuses

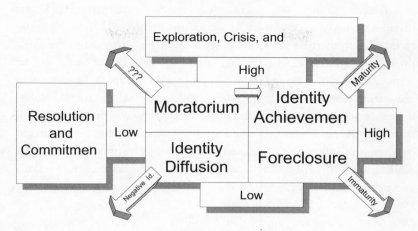

Identity Diffusion: Adolescents enter young adulthood detached and
                        disengaged
                            or
Identity Foreclosure: Uncritically committed to beliefs and
                        emanating from a rather limited range
                        experience

Moratorium: Exposure to alternate views may motivate
                        exploration of alternatives
                            helps develop
Identity Achievement: Formation of critical commitments

Identity-Diffused Youth

In terms of the two criteria crisis and commitment, identity-diffused youth are characterized as not experiencing crises and as making no or few commitments. In other words, these adolescents have not thought seriously about goals, values, or beliefs, nor have they made any decisions in those areas. These teenagers, for example, have not chosen an occupation or career, and are little concerned about it. Simply put, many adolescents and young adults are relatively aimless and uncommitted to any set of goals, values, and beliefs.[9] Identity-diffused youth perceive religiosity or faith as "a belief system that is compartmentalized, exclusionary, utilitarian, and self serving. Participation in religious activities is based

9. Setran and Kiesling, *Spiritual Formation,* 16; Smith and Snell, *Souls in Transition,* 166–68.

on cost versus benefit analysis."[10] Diffusion is common among young or early adolescents, although possible among adults as well.

Identity-diffused adolescents use a variety of psychological defenses to ward off anxiety caused by an undefined identity. They may engage in intense, immediate experiences such as parties, drugs, and thrills to provide a "right-now" sensation and enable them to ignore or put off the responsibilities of making commitments and important decisions. Some move from peer group to peer group trying to establish a sense of belonging, while others engage in extreme fad behavior to escape the anxiety of meaninglessness. Identity-diffused adolescents are further characterized by a sense of inferiority and alienation, as well as by poor self-concepts. These adolescents are generally less mature in the areas of cognitive skills and emotional development.[11]

Ministry with Identity-Diffused Youth

How can youth workers help identity-diffused adolescents? Ministry to these individuals begins by understanding why they tend to be aimless and uncommitted. Identity-diffused youth often come from families that are more rejecting and detached. Often the father is absent through separation or divorce, and the fathers who are at home may not be very encouraging to their teenage children and may show signs of negativity.[12] Consequently, these young people need to be given the opportunity to observe adult youth workers and role models who are, by contrast, accepting, warm, and encouraging.

In looking for ministry procedures that touch teenagers as whole individuals, that shape emotions, perceptions, values, and behaviors in an integrated manner, youth workers must consider the importance of modeling and learning by imitation.[13] Psychologist Albert Bandura notes that "much human learning occurs either designedly or unintentionally from the models in one's immediate environment."[14] However, modeling will be especially effective with identity-diffused youth because they may be averse to formal instruction and are in special need of good role models.

10. Griffith and Griggs, "Religious Identity Status," 16.

11. Gullotta et al., *Adolescent Experience*, 83.

12. Ibid., 251.

13. Richards, *Theology of Christian Education*, 80–82.

14. Bandura, "On the Psychosocial Impact and Mechanisms of Spiritual Modeling," 169.

Spontaneous modeling is not planned; rather, it simply happens. In the context of youth ministry, it is the youth worker living out his or her life before adolescents.[15] It is the youth worker demonstrating to the teenager how he or she might behave or live. It is how the youth worker reacts to having a flat tire, to being abruptly cut off in traffic, or to the displaying of enthusiasm over prayer or personal study of the Bible. In essence, modeling is demonstrating the validity of what it means to be Christian through intimate relationships with God and others. Consequently, it is critical that the youth worker spend time with teens outside the formal instructional setting, in daily life and in their world.[16]

A beneficial summary of effective modeling principles has been compiled by Lawrence Richards.[17] A modification of his seven points provides youth workers with the kind of direction they need in modeling a lifestyle that might positively influence the behavior of identity-diffused youth as well as other adolescents.

- Adolescents need frequent, long-term contact with models.
- Adolescents need to experience warm, loving relationships with models.
- Adolescents need to be exposed to the inner values and emotions of models.
- Models need to be observed in a variety of life situations and settings.
- Models must exhibit clarity and consistency in attitudes, values, and behaviors.
- There must be compatibility between the behavior of the models and the standards and beliefs of the larger community.
- There must be explanations of the life-style of the models, along with accompanying demonstrations of life.[18]

Identity-diffused adolescents need to be given recognition and offered approval for the things they do well. Youth workers should help them to see their strengths in personality, performance, knowledge, skills, and attitudes. There are a number of simple activities that can be

---

15 Issler and Habermas, *How We Learn,* 85.

16. Richards, *Theology of Christian Education,* 85.

17. Ibid., 84–85.

18. Issler and Habermas, *How We Learn,* 85.

effective in affirming and encouraging adolescents who struggle with feelings of rejection and failure. For example, people can encourage one another (not just identity-diffused youth, but all members) by pinning a piece of paper on each person's back. Have group members then circulate and write on the paper one positive attribute or quality they see in each person. Allow time for each person to read his or her list.

Identity-diffused adolescents also need special help focusing on an occupation or career, or on selecting of a college. The student unable to decide what steps to take toward reaching such significant goals will not continue to mature until he or she has learned to plan ahead and set goals. Most likely such an individual will drift in and out of college, shift from one major to another, and achieve less than desirable grades. Youth workers should help these students develop abilities to assess possibilities, evaluate these possibilities, and make valid and meaningful choices based on the values placed on each. Adolescents can be led to understand that their lives matter by addressing immediate practical issues about work as well as the underlying issues of identity and purpose.

Finally, using identity-diffused teenagers as summer camp workers or involving them in work or service projects can help them develop a sense of purpose and direction. Often such ministries and projects can lead young people into a deeper commitment to Jesus Christ, can instill or trigger in them a desire to serve God in a particular capacity, and can challenge them to have an impact on the lives of others. Some ideas for service projects that teenagers can be involved in include working on an orphanage or school, repairing a run-down church, assisting the elderly in home maintenance or upkeep, and helping in food distribution programs.[19]

Identity-Foreclosed Youth

Identity-foreclosed adolescents are characterized by not having experienced crises yet having expressed commitments to goals, values, or beliefs. These teenagers, however, assume a commitment that is handed to them by significant others, most notably their parents, rather than through personal searching and exploring. However, "motivation is still

---

19. Three helpful sources on mission and service projects are Clark and Powell, *Deep Justice in a Broken World*; Campolo, *101 Ways Your Church Can Change the World*; and Livermore and Linhart, *What Can We Do?*

external and self-serving. Adherence to religious beliefs tends to be superficial and compartmentalized due to a lack of rigorous critique and
evaluation. Through religious teachings, social learning, and participation in rituals, a foreclosed religious identity is uncritically adopted."[20]
Identity-foreclosed teenagers can tell you what they want to be but cannot
clearly express why, or they indicate that this is what their parents desire.
In terms of values and faith, identity-foreclosed adolescents accept what
others (such as parents, teachers, and youth workers) tell them to believe,
with little reflection and appropriation. These youth might say something
like, "If it is right for my parents, it must be good enough for me!"

Identity-foreclosed adolescents tend to pursue quiet, orderly, and
industrious lifestyles and endorse authoritarian values such as obedience, strong leadership, and respect for authority.[21] They often come
from child-centered families, where the parents may be possessive and
intrusive with their children.[22] While parents appear to be highly encouraging and supportive, there is some evidence of strong pressure on the
children to conform closely to family attitudes, values, and beliefs. Often
helicopter parenting is present, where parents are overly involved with
their children and provide incessant supervision to the detriment of the
teen's self-confidence and competency.[23]

To parents and youth workers, identity-foreclosed youth usually
demonstrate attractive personalities, and are generally compliant and
easy to work with. However, these adolescents may remain cautious and
overly dependent on others, and are unlikely to provide creative leadership or direction.[24] When parents or church leaders are not present these
individuals lack an individualized value system that can guide decisions.
In terms of faith, they simply believe what significant others have told
them, with little or no serious personal reflection on those faith-related
beliefs, values, and attitudes.[25]

20. Griffith and Griggs, "Religious Identity Status," 17.

21. Gullotta et al., *Adolescent Experience*, 84–85.

22. Ibid., 84.

23. Schiffrin et al., "Helping or Hovering?" 548–57.

24. Gullotta et al., *Adolescent Experience*, 84–85.

25. Steele, "Identity Formation Theory and Youth Ministry," 93.

Ministry With Identity-foreclosed Youth

In moving adolescents beyond the identity-foreclosed status, wise and sensitive youth workers will avoid a preachy, authoritarian type of teaching and strive to create an atmosphere that encourages questioning and exploration. Adolescents should be equipped to discover truth for themselves, be encouraged to ask questions, be given the freedom to doubt, and be taught to do independent and critical thinking. Protecting students from crisis and exploration is counterproductive.[26] Small-group discussions, role-playing activities, moral and faith dilemmas, and discovery learning can facilitate identity-formation for these teenagers. Another strategy is for youth workers to play the devil's advocate and challenge students to search for answers.

Youth ministry pioneers Wayne Rice and Mike Yaconelli have compiled a collection of what they call "tension getters." Tension getters are real-life situations or issues designed to get young people to think through alternatives and consequences before arriving at a moral or ethical decision. They are designed to create tension in the cognitive and affective domains of the adolescent by introducing conflicting or over-lapping values that make a simple, black-and-white answer impossible. Consider, for example the following case study:

Judy is twenty-nine years old and the mother of four children. Very recently she has learned that she is pregnant once again. Her husband does not want another child and is extremely upset. He insists that Judy abort the baby. Judy understands that they cannot afford another child, yet the thought of getting an abortion frightens her and goes against everything she believes. She is torn in several directions: loyalty to her husband whom she loves very much, responsibility for the care of her other children, and her personal belief that abortion is wrong.

- What would you do if you were Judy?
- What would you do if you were Judy and you only had one other child?
- What if preliminary tests showed that the baby would be born with developmental disabilities?
- What if Judy found out that her husband was having an affair?[27]

26. Schiffrin et al., "Helping or Hovering?" 548–57.
27. Adapted from Yacconelli and Lynn, *Tension Getters Two,* 58.

Part of the identity-formation task is helping adolescents sort out values that are personal from those that are fixed and absolute. Values pertaining to clothing, hairstyle, occupation, and music are generally individualistic, and freedom of expression should be encouraged. In contrast, premarital sex, lying, cheating, and disobeying parents are examples of absolute values and are not matters of personal choice. It is important that youth workers model the ability to differentiate between personal values and absolutes. If adults who minister among youth are as judgmental of teenage males wearing earrings as they are of adolescents using drugs, suggests Bonnidell Clouse, these youth workers can hardly expect young people to discriminate between behaviors they have a right to accept or not accept for themselves and behaviors that must be accepted as givens.[28]

Unfortunately, many of our parenting and educational strategies encourage the foreclosure type of identity formation. Parents and youth workers become uncomfortable and defensive if adolescents ask too many difficult questions about their faith and belief system. However, it is by this very process of questioning and intellectual exploration that teenagers internalize values and beliefs, and develop a faith they can call their own.

Identity-moratorium Youth

Like the identity-diffused youth, moratorium adolescents are rather vague about commitments. They are distinguished, however, by the appearance of an active struggle to make commitments. These youth experience crisis and actively searching for alternatives but have not yet made any commitments. This is the teenager who is going to be an astronaut today and a missionary tomorrow. These are not flippant choices or changes, however, but seriously considered options.[29]

These adolescents are the most anxious of the identity types, yet are able to maintain a stable sense of self-esteem. They tend to be extreme in their views, independent, competitive, and unpredictable.[30] The homes of these young people are generally active ones, and autonomy, self-expression, and individual differences in areas such as dress and hairstyle are usually encouraged.

28. Clouse, "Adolescent Moral Development and Sexuality," 193–94.
29. Steele, "Identity Formation Theory and Youth Ministry," 92–93.
30. Clouse, "Adolescent Moral Development and Sexuality," 192.

Identity-moratorium might be considered the most normal approach to achieving identity. In fact, our culture treats the whole decade of adolescence as a moratorium during which the individual gradually assumes more and more adult responsibilities and characteristics, yet without being fully accountable as an adult. Adolescents should be encouraged to involve themselves in honest and active struggles to find answers to unsolved questions and to explore or try out various roles.

Ministry With Identity-Moratorium Youth

The trauma of moratorium may not be a pleasant experience, but adolescents should not cut it off too quickly or before an adequate exploration of alternatives has been accomplished. Adolescents may, for example, hastily marry after high school graduation rather than explore the possibility of singleness. Others may choose a career predetermined by their parents, without searching out viable options. Youth workers can reassure young people that late adolescence does indeed involve a certain amount of anguish and trauma as teens make life choices and form attitudes, values, and ethical opinions. In regard to religious identity, "honest self-reflection, guided by sincere spiritual inquiry, provides the courage to admit to and move beyond self-serving or conformist religiosity. These spiritual seekers are in the process of reformulating and internalizing spiritual beliefs."[31]

Perhaps parents need as much support as the adolescents themselves. Mothers and fathers surely do not enjoy watching their children suffer emotional distress and psychological pain. Parents will often actively discourage a moratorium status because they do not feel comfortable with uncertainties and lack of commitments. As painful as it may be, however, parents should be encouraged to allow and enable their adolescent children to go through the healthy process of exploring and searching for answers and options to life's questions and possibilities. For example, rather than insisting that a teenage son or daughter pursue a particular career, parents might help the child explore valid choices by setting forth both the strengths and drawbacks of each option.

31. Griffith and Griggs, "Religious Identity Status," 18.

Identity-Achieved Youth

Identity-achieved adolescents have not only experienced crisis but are committed to decisions made in regard to critical life issues. This status is the ideal type of identity formation. These individuals have seriously considered, for instance, a number of occupational choices and have come to decisions on their own terms, even though their ultimate decisions may be a variation of their parents' desires.[32] In regard to a faith or belief system, these youth have reevaluated past beliefs and have now achieved a resolution whereby they have internalized and appropriated these beliefs and values. In other words, their faith is their own. It is important to note that there is an interactive relationship between faith development and identity achievement. As teenagers mature in faith, they also develop in identity, and vice versa.[33]

Identity-achieved youth tend also to be more developed in moral reasoning and to have a clearer sense of ethics and empathy.[34] They are more stable and mature, consistent in behavior and attitudes, and effective in social relationships.[35] In general, these adolescents have achieved identity and are ready to assume the roles and responsibilities that adulthood brings to them. It does not appear that identity-achieved youth would be overwhelmed by sudden environmental shifts or unexpected responsibilities.

Ministry With Identity-Achieved Youth.

The achievement of identity is one of the adolescent's most important developmental accomplishments and marks the completion of adolescence and the onset of adulthood.[36] For these reasons it is imperative that youth workers carefully nurture adolescents in such a way that they are moving toward the goal of identity achievement. Teenagers who achieve identity or are well on their way to identity achievement will most likely emerge as key leaders in their youth groups and in school. They should be encouraged to carry out meaningful ministry, not simply to perform menial

32. Muuss, "Marcia's Expansion," 268–69.

33. Steele, "Identity Formation Theory and Youth Ministry," 95. For an extensive description of faith development see Fowler, *Stages of Faith.*

34. Sebald, *Adolescence,* 56.

35. Clouse, "Adolescent Moral Development and Sexuality," 191.

36. Parks, *Critical Years,* 76.

tasks. For example, some of them will be capable of leading small group Bible studies or heading up service projects from an internal source of motivation. Identity-achieved youth should be involved, as much as possible, in the planning and carrying out of the overall youth program and related ministries.

IDENTITY TYPES AS STAGES OF DEVELOPMENT

Some psychologists have described identity as a developmental progression.[37] The basic pattern of development is thought to begin with identity diffusion (a state of noncommitment), moving progressively through foreclosure (making choices and commitments without experiencing crisis), moratorium (experiencing crisis and exploring alternatives), and eventually identity achievement (a period of crisis and development of firm commitments). Identity development may begin as early as age ten, and continue into the college-age years.[38]

In light of developmental research and theory, one would expect those in preadolescence and early teenage years to be in the diffusion stage. At this juncture of their identity development, young people expend little or no effort in making serious commitments concerning critical life issues such as career, higher education, or marriage. This is not to say that identity formation is not taking place at all. During the preadolescent years identity is being shaped by the influence of others, the young person's life experiences, and the value system in which they live. Preadolescents and young teens are trying out new behaviors and roles, attempting to fashion a coherent faith system. Peers become increasingly important in early adolescent life, and preadolescence is the time when the shift from dominant parental influence to peer influence takes place.[39]

As teenagers move into middle adolescence they are forced to make decisions, such as selection of school courses that will affect their future. At this point they will be highly dependent on their parents in the decision-making process, and their faith system will be highly influenced by significant others. This is the foreclosure phase of identity achievement. By the time healthy and developmentally mature individuals reach late

---

37. Steele, "Identity Formation Theory and Youth Ministry," 91–99; Muuss, "Marcia's Expansion," 263.

38. Thornburg, *Development in Adolescence,* 522.

39. Ibid., 523.

adolescence, they should be actively exploring and choosing life alternatives with maximum support and advice from parents but with relatively little interference (the moratorium phase of development). Finally, identity achievement, the securing of independence, establishment of roles, and appropriation of beliefs and values, should normally be completed in late adolescence or perhaps in the early twenties.

Other developmentalists, however, warn against oversimplifying the identity-achievement process by viewing it as an encounter of sequential stages. Mark Cannister, for example, calls into question a prevailing notion within the church that we might call chrysalis. According to this perception, identity development is seen as a process tied to a one-time, final transformation, similar to the way a fuzzy bug becomes a butterfly and therefore reaches the end of the developmental process. Rightly seen, however, identity formation is not completed in a brief and finite period but is more often an ongoing process whereby youth and adults enter and reenter "exploratory exercises of identity development."[40] Seeming regression is simply a normal journey of the lifelong developmental cycle of Moratorium-Achievement-Moratorium-Achievement (MAMA).[41]

IDENTITY AS EXPLAINING BEHAVIORS AND PROCESSES

The identity model that has been presented in this chapter is helpful to youth workers in that it describes a host of behaviors and processes central to the adolescent years. This section will consider three significant areas of behavior and process, noting how identity theory informs them: (1) conversion, (2) compartmentalization, and (3) authority dependence.

Explaining Conversion

Conversion results in a significant perspective transformation, radically impacting one's self-identity.[42] The reverse is also true in that an accurate understanding of identity achievement helps us better elucidate conversion as a process. The average person requires multiple exposures

40. Cannister, *Teenagers Matter*, 57.

41. Marcia, "Identity and Psychosocial Development in Adulthood," 15; Muuss, "Marcia's Expansion," 269.

42. Temple, "Perspective Transformation."

to the gospel before making a commitment to Christ. And while some see conversion only as an immediate crisis experience, others hold to the view that it is characterized by a gradual and nonsudden awakening to faith.[43] The transformation of identity through crisis and commitment explains the possibility of a gradual conversion process without denying the reality of an instantaneous salvation experience. Identity theory does not assume that a single decision or piece of information will likely lead to conversion. Rather, the person has multiple competing frameworks, or senses of self, that need to be addressed and resolved.

Explaining Compartmentalization

It is important to note that natural development will likely leave many childhood assumptions unanalyzed.[44] These assumptions will often be in conflict with other assumptions, leading to compartmentalization within an individual. As we mentioned earlier, teens are quite capable of giving the proper answer on Sunday morning after a good time of partying the night before. Compartmentalization is a protective measure to reduce dissonance and crisis, yet crisis is a prerequisite for successful navigation through the identity statuses.

Valerie Grabove asserts that learning should not be viewed simply as behavior change, acquisition of knowledge, or gaining of skills.[45] Learning of this sort will simply reinforce compartmentalization and enhance the negative aspects that accompany it. Thus, in the metaphor of the house, the inner rooms of explanations, solutions, and behaviors can be contained within a person without being integrated into a coherent sense of self-identity. Each view of self is a separate compartment, and each emerges only when a person enters a given setting. This provides an explanation for hypocrisy, "Sunday-only" Christianity, and nonreflective thinking. Rather, the desire of the church and its youth ministry should be for the formation of healthy adolescents who are functioning as Christians not only in certain explicit circumstances, but increasingly in all parts of their lives. To accomplish this change, the many "compartments" or "furnishings," as well as false assumptions of the youth, must be challenged.

43. Bushnell, *Christian Nurture*, 10; Munro, *Protestant Nurture*.
44. Tennant, "Perspective Transformation," 39.
45. Grabove, "Many Facets," 89–96.

Various teaching techniques or strategies are available to challenge assumptions and help students wrestle with identity achievement.

1. *By opening the doors to the rooms.* In the context of teaching youth or facilitating group discussions, one could challenge seemingly conflicting ideas or doctrines. For example, the teacher could present God's attribute of wrath alongside God's attribute of love, or his sense of justice with his mercy. This technique throws open the doors to different rooms allowing or even forcing students to reconcile assumptions that had not yet been subject to reflection.

2. *By challenging falsity tags.* In this technique the youth teacher takes a belief and challenges it. For a teen who feels unworthy or unloved, a simple question such as "Did you know that God sings over you while you sleep?" (Zeph 3:17) can open new lines of thinking. This in effect is *knocking holes in walls* by calling into question a firmly held belief without labeling it as false.

3. *By creating cognitive dissonance.* To create dissonance the teacher might challenge a secure truth such as the efficacy of prayer, or sing a worship song but change a key word: "I could sing of your wrath forever." This is known as *mud tracking.* Clean and sterile environments tend not to produce growth. Instead of unhinging belief, mud tracking helps develop a firm personal ownership of the idea.

4. *By encouraging critical reflection.* To encourage reflection the teacher takes beliefs and assumptions to their logical end so as to expose fallacies by throwing back to the students their ideas or statements. "So do you really mean to say God is incapable of healing someone?" This is a form of *mirroring* and helps youth see their illogical thinking without bearing any shame or embarrassment.

Explaining Authority Dependence

Often teens do not move beyond the stage of needing the opinions and approval of external authorities: "they are confident, efficient, and satisfied only when others provide outside reinforcement."[46] Even many adults have foreclosed identities, and thus past authoritative opinions have ongoing impact on their behavior and entire life.[47] Healthy identity formation

46. Derr et al., *Cross-Cultural Approaches,* 276.
47. Ibid.

fosters fidelity or loyalty to, but not a dependence on, authority. The goal of identity formation is to see the individual "negotiate his or her own values, meanings, and purposes rather than to uncritically act on those of others."[48]

SCAFFOLDING: THE CHURCH
AS GUIDE IN IDENTITY FORMATION

Those teenagers who are successful in navigating the task of identity formation will display healthier personalities, with a stronger sense of self and their relationship to others. However, the rapidly changing world and society in which they live makes this a difficult task in that it demands that they regularly redefine themselves. Consequently, youth might be typified as fluid, emerging, nonlinear, flexible, and ever in process—characteristics that echo instability and unpredictability.[49] How will the church and youth workers provide the necessary challenge, support, and care to adolescents navigating these tumultuous waters? One answer comes in the form of scaffolding.

Mike relates the following story to help us understand the nature and significance of scaffolding. While he was pastoring in the Midwest, a large company built the largest warehouse of its kind a few miles from his church. The walls were mammoth single-unit constructions put in place through the use of cranes and scaffolding. After one wall segment was in place, the crane and scaffolding would be moved to set the next section. During construction there was an unusually large amount of rain, causing the ground to soften. One night the muddy and shifting foundation gave way to the weight of the wall. Without the support of the scaffolding, which had already been moved to prepare for the next segment, the wall crashed spectacularly to the ground, the vibrations waking people over a mile away. In a similar manner our youth are often without a solid foundation provided by either the social or cultural systems. The constant exercise in fluid identity formation and recurring identity crises create a need for much support. It is up to the church to provide "scaffolding" for the lives of youth by (1) helping them work through the process of identity formation, (2) facilitating their contributions to church and society, and (3) providing consolation during the identity-formation process.

48. Mezirow, "Transformative Learning," 11.

49. Turkle, *Life on the Screen*, 17.

The Church and the Process of Identity Formation

As teens make a fragmented and undefined transition from youth to adulthood, they exhibit an array of immature and irresponsible behaviors on the one hand, and they take on adult activities, attitudes, and obligations on the other hand. This happens for teens especially if they lack fully developed thinking skills and benchmarks that signal the onset of adulthood. A helpful response for the church might be to establish for adolescents a graded system of markers not only promoting a sense of achievement and ability in youth but also providing a structure of support for teens, given the challenges that youth face as they develop. These rites of passage communicate approval as well as expectations appropriate for adolescents, given their social context, their emerging thinking skills, and the physical changes they are undergoing having to do with puberty. Going through these rites of passage certainly involves peers but also engages the larger believing community (including all generations) and the family of individual teens. Thus identity formation is nurtured by the entire church community, invariably tying the youth's internal concept of identity to the external community of faith. As the youth participate in larger congregational communities, this participation gives form to their need to express themselves. Group identity then offers a mooring for teens as they explore identity-related possibilities.

This is an opportune time to address a questionable strategy of many churches—to segregate the youth from the larger congregation, in particular from intergenerational worship services. While we do not advocate doing away with youth programs, we do agree with Mark Senter, who suggests that in segregating youth from congregational experiences we marginalize them and rob them of the full richness of Christian community. In the context of our discussion of the church and its role in adolescent identity formation, we emphasize the fact that if we segregate youth, we also remove the responsibility of the congregation to provide stability, mirroring, and modeling for them. Senter goes on to suggest that by providing an inclusive congregational approach, "You lift a tremendous load off the shoulders of youth ministers and place it squarely where it belongs—on the broad shoulders of the church leadership and entire congregations."[50]

50. Senter, *Four Views*, 31.

The Church as Facilitator of Contribution

Teens must also be made aware of what is expected of them in regard to responsibilities, actions, and behaviors. Identity emerges through the processes of expression and action in, among other contexts, the church community. As teens express their new identity through actions, the church assists by providing feedback, or mirroring the message, "this is who I see you becoming." By "contribution," we mean, first of all, that the church provides opportunity for the use of gifts and labor for the good of the body. Second, it offers the youth an investment or stake in the spiritual, physical, social, and economic health of the body through their behaviors and *meaningful* activities. There is an intentional emphasis on the *meaningful* aspect of this. Too often we have engaged our youth in car washes and the like instead of more purposeful endeavors such as leading small groups, ministering to the homeless, or doing children's ministry. Through such meaningful activities teenagers not only learn ideals such as responsibility, compassion, and trust; they also become aware of the reality that they are needed in the church community. If this were the norm in the daily community life of the church, notes Senter, "There would be no second-class citizens in the faith community. The church would honor the contributions of every child and adolescent, realizing that the congregation is impoverished without what young people bring to the fellowship."[51]

Kenda Dean and Ron Foster elaborate on how congregations might accomplish this:

> Inviting youth to assume significant leadership (rather than being elected to nice-sounding offices) powerfully affirms their gifts. Encouraging and supporting their God-bearing presence with peers at school, co-leading meetings with teenagers integrating youth into the overall leadership of a congregation, entrusting a project to a group of adolescents for completion: All of these measures communicate trust and acceptance and send the message that youth are part of the kingdom of God *now*, not just when they grow up to become "real" Christians.[52]

51. Ibid.

52. Dean and Foster, *Godbearing Life*, 96.

The Church as Provider of Consolation

As teenagers are in the process of asking the life-shaping questions of identity, they are in dire need of the safety provided by the community of faith. The notion behind consolation is the conscious yet spontaneous expression of love and care to the youth. A church's level of consolation is determined by its ability to express love and to provide a support system to its youth. The practical implications of a maintained support structure are immense, especially in times of crisis, which are frequent in both our society and particularly in the adolescent years.

Once again, Dean and Foster help us understand the responsibility of the entire congregation in shaping the lives of teens. In what they call "Godbearing youth ministry," they indicate that it

> means helping the entire congregation recognize its role in rais-
> ing up a child in faith—a vow we make at an infant's baptism
> [or dedication], and one we take rather seriously in the case of
> young children but routinely abandon to "youth leaders" come
> adolescence. Godbearing youth ministry embraces all the for-
> mal (Sunday school, confirmation, worship, youth group) and
> informal (worship, casual mentoring, participation in commu-
> nity rituals) ways of passing on faith.[53]

As adolescents wrestle with identity issues such as vocation, aspirations, goals, values, and beliefs, as well as with negotiating roles in church and society, the entire congregation (church leaders, elders, parents, senior citizens) can provide a safe place (both physically and emotionally) and serve as models, guides, mentors, and teachers.

More specifically, adults can assist teenagers in exploring and com-mitting to the various domains of identity in at least three ways.

1. *By being a source of information.* Since identity achievement requires that the adolescent have relevant information about the area being investigated, Christian adults can serve as sources of knowledge and information For example, a young person may have interest in a career in law. He or she may seek out someone in the church to talk with about the legal profession and how to best go about moving towards that end.

2. *By being role models.* Youth pastors, other pastors, elders, teachers, and other adults in addition to parents may serve as role models for

---

53. Ibid., 99.

adolescents. For example, the teen may point to a variety of adults in the congregation as influencing his or her political viewpoints or party choice. More will be said about modeling in the following chapter.

3. *By pacing with teens.* Rick Dunn reminds us that while adolescents appear to want to be left alone or remain aloof from adults, in reality "in the depths of the adolescent's heart is a God-created longing for the embracing of an adult's understanding, affirmation, and guidance."[54] Dunn suggests a strategy for adults that he calls pacing—coming alongside of them physically, intellectually, emotionally, socially, and spiritually at their developmental rate or tempo. To be effective in this time of youth ministry "demands time, the time it takes to go beyond the surface in a conversation or to enter the social turf of a student."[55] Pacing, he goes on to say, promotes trust, relationship, and life exchanges where the Holy Spirit reaches through the life of an adult caregiver to forever change the life of a student—particularly critical in helping youth shape their identities. Consider the importance of pacing—understanding, listening, affirming, and guiding—in helping adolescents wrestle with and come to a commitment on sensitive identity issues such as gender roles, sexuality, ethnicity, and faith itself.

CONCLUSION

It is clearly evident that the process of achieving a healthy identity is not single-faceted undertaking; rather it is a highly complex and interactive process whereby adolescents and emerging adults establish their personal goals, values, beliefs, and lifestyles. This chapter has taken a panoramic picture of the process of identity formation. It has defined identity formation, described four identity types, made suggestions for doing ministry with adolescents in different statuses, and addressed the responsibility of the church congregation and leadership in assisting them through this process. The following chapter addresses specific dimensions of identity, such as gender roles, sexuality, and vocation. It will also speak to related issues of parent and peer influence on identity achievement, gaining independence as a part of identity formation, and self-esteem and identity.

54. Dunn, *Shaping the Spiritual Life of Students*, 18.
55. Ibid.

3

Dimensions of Identity Formation

The struggle adolescents go through in their search for identity, of finding out who they are, what their roles in society will be, and how they fit into the larger world, is a multifaceted task. As mentioned earlier, much of the task of adolescent identity formation is centered on a variety of critical life issues such as autonomy from parental control, vocation, sexuality, gender roles, faith, and self-esteem. While these issues will now be explored in the context of identity formation, most of them will be addressed more fully in subsequent chapters.

THE INFLUENCE OF PARENTS AND PEERS IN IDENTITY FORMATION

Adolescents live in two worlds—one of parents and the other of peers. As an adolescent grows older, peers and friends become increasingly important, while there is somewhat of a distancing from parents. This shift is critical to the achievement of identity and in the individuation process whereby a teenager becomes a unique and separate individual, with his or her own interests, values, attitudes, and personality. In order for the adolescent to develop a healthy concept of self, the need for acceptance from peers increases with each year. By the time an individual reaches the teenage years, acceptance and approval are all-important.

Empirical research studies indicate that adolescents spend more time with friends than with family or parents. For example, teenagers spent 14.4 hours per week with friends, compared to 9.4 hours with family.[1] Studies also indicate adolescents place friends or friendships at the top, or very close to the top, of the list of what they value in life.[2]

As can be expected then, peers and friends have a profound influence in shaping the lives of young people, although parents maintain more impact than they might realize. The Search Institute found that from the fifth through the ninth grades the influence of peers increased while the influence of parents decreased, although in no grade was peer influence greater than parental influence.[3] Whether parents or peers carry more weight often depends on the situation. On issues related to fashion or dress, school-related problems, social activities, and day-to-day concerns, and when they seek to establish an immediate sense of identity or status, peer influence is stronger. On significant long-range issues such as career, basic values, and beliefs, adolescents lean towards their parents.[4] Contrary to what many might expect, most adolescents are likely to choose peer groups with values and expectations similar to those of their parents. Furthermore, adolescents tend to find friends who are already like them, that is, those who have similar tastes in music, dress, interests, and activities. They then influence each other to become even more alike.[5]

Peer activity helps equip the adolescent with necessary interpersonal skills and prepares the individual for successful adult relationships. In sum, healthy peer relationships provide a foundation upon which social skills necessary for adulthood are developed, as well as mechanisms that help loosen dependencies on parental guidance and support.[6] The creation of an adolescent subculture is essentially an attempt to establish identity. One learns from peers to wear the appropriate clothes and hairstyles, speak the teenage argot or lingo, and listen to the right music. Finally, friends are also a source of enjoyment, self-esteem, intimacy, popularity, and emotional security.

Youth workers can have a major impact on how adolescents respond to parents and peers in their search for identity. Adolescents should first be reminded of the powerful impact that friends and peers can have on

1. Wong, "Effects of Adolescent Activities on Delinquency, 321–33

2. Benson et al., *Quicksilver Years*, 92; Bibby and Posterski, *Emerging Generation*, 17; Barna Research Group, *Today's Teens*, 20.

3. Benson et al., *Quicksilver Years*, 27.

4. Bibby and Posterski, *Emerging Generation*, 103.

5. Prinstein and Dodge, *Understanding Peer Influence*, 19.

6. Kaplan, *Adolescence*, 181.

the shaping of their lives, and that this impact can be either positive or negative. They need to understand the value of peers but know when to go against them. Second, adolescents should be encouraged to choose friends whose values and behaviors are congruent with those of their family and church. Third, teenagers should be taught that as they grow in their independence, they are still called to honor and obey their parents. Fourth, adolescents must be encouraged to value their parents' judgments and insights.

Peer pressure is often blamed for negative teen behaviors. However, "while the concept of peer pressure enables adults to explain youths' troubling behaviors . . . analysis of the participants' accounts of their lives reveals peer pressure to be a myth."[7] Teens use peers first to define themselves. Then they move toward purposefully using peer relations to experiment with multiple identities. Last, teen peers collaborate in creating identities in which they will find acceptance. To sum up the impact of peer influence on identity achievement we quote John Coleman and Leo Hendry:

> It would be wrong to assume that all young people are equally susceptible to peer influence. Most are somewhat susceptible to certain peer influences at certain times, under specific conditions. Additionally, adolescents are more likely to experience subtle pressure to conform to group values and standards ("gentle persuasion") than overt attempts to control or manipulate them. Further, small groups of close friends seem to wield more influence on adolescent behavior than individual friends.[8]

GAINING INDEPENDENCE
FROM PARENTAL CONTROL

In establishing their personal identity, adolescents need to exert their independence.[9] Adolescents must learn to act independently and make decisions for themselves; they must give up the identity of "the Browns' little boy" or the "Clarks' little girl" and establish their own identity. This is not a differentiation or separation from family; rather it is a separation from their role as a child. If this issue is not resolved, the adolescent can-

7. Ungar, "Myth of Peer Pressure," 1.

8. Coleman and Hendry, *Nature of Adolescence,* 144.

9. Ibid., 139.

not be expected to achieve healthy heterosexual or peer relationships, confidently pursue a vocation, or achieve a sense of identity.[10]

This creates tension for both parents and children. Teenage children vacillate between breaking away from parents and being dependent on them; parents are often torn between letting their children go and keeping them dependent. Autonomy, however, need not demand that parental ties be broken entirely. While responsibility for decisions concerning day-to-day activities shifts gradually from parents to children, certain emotional attachments between parents and children can remain constant as behavioral autonomy is slowly achieved.[11] Still, adolescents must give up much childhood dependency, learn self-sufficiency and self-reliance, and come to identify with their parents more as friends and confidants.[12]

While a certain amount of conflict between parents and adolescents can be anticipated, open defiance or rebellion should not be seen as the norm. For example, an empirical research study of early and preadolescents by the Search Institute found that while parent-child conflict increased slightly between each of the fifth through the ninth school grades, only a minority of the respondents reported major conflicts with parents.[13] For the most part clashes between parents and teenagers are not over major issues such as economics, religion, or politics. Rather, most arguments are over mundane matters such as schoolwork, chores, friends, dating, curfews, and personal appearance—issues that can be resolved with less trouble than is often assumed.

How can the achievement of autonomy be made as smooth as possible for both parents and adolescents? First, adolescents and adults must remember that gaining independence from parents is a normal part of the developmental process. Activities such as independent thinking, spending more time with peers, and establishing new behaviors should not necessarily be seen as defiance, rejection, or rebellion. In fact, the teenager cannot become a fully mature adult without having achieved a certain degree of self-reliance or without parents accordingly offering decision-making privileges to the youth.[14]

10. Pasupathi and Hoyt, "Development of Narrative Identity," 558–74.

11. Benson et al., *Quicksilver Years*, 36.

12. Thornburg, *Development in Adolescence*, 171.

13. Benson et al., *Quicksilver Years*, 38.

14. Small et al., "Adolescent Autonomy and Parental Stress," 377–91.

We might liken the process of gaining autonomy to that of driving a car. Teenagers are often restless because their parents are in the driver's seat. Parents, on the other hand, are concerned that their teen's restlessness and questioning of established norms are a sign that the teen is rejecting them and their values. For the most part, adolescent children want nothing more than to get behind the wheel—to gain more control over their life and participate in determining where it is going.

Parents walk a fine line between giving their teenage children appropriate independence yet protecting them from the possibility of making immature or bad decisions. The kind of parenting that seems to provide the best balance has an authoritative style that communicates warmth and acceptance; that asserts rules, norms, and values; but that also signals a willingness to listen, explain, and negotiate.[15] The change from dependence to independence proceeds most smoothly if parents are moderate in their disciplinary practice, not overly restrictive and not extremely permissive.

Youth workers and parents should see this change from dependence to independence as a transformation rather than a radical change. As children move into early adolescence, parents should allow them more and more freedom to make their own decisions. As the adolescent matures, increasing responsibility and autonomy should be given, although involving adolescents in decisions relevant to them does not mean that the parents surrender final authority on important family matters. It is simply recognition of the reality of the teenager's intellectual abilities to understand, contribute, and have opinions.[16]

Timothy Foster suggests a strategy of parenting he calls "freedom within boundaries," an approach that ideally begins with a child at about eighteen months. The child has freedom of choice within boundaries, and if she steps out of the boundaries she is disciplined. When a child is five years old, she may choose what kind of cereal to eat for breakfast, although the child is not likely to be given the option of not having breakfast. By the time the same child is sixteen, she should be given the freedom not to have breakfast if she so chooses.

The difficulty for many parents is realizing that these boundaries move so that by the time the child is seventeen, relatively few rules are left. At that point parents should use the influence they have over really

---

15. Papalia and Olds, *Child's World*, 573.

16. Guerney and Arthur, "Adolescent Social Relationship," 90–91.

significant issues of life. Hair length, argues Foster, hardly qualifies as a significant issue, and it is a way for a child to express his uniqueness. It is unfortunate, Foster goes on to say, that parents trying to exert too much control over their teenagers rather than focusing on preparing them for adulthood ruin so many family nights.[17]

Youth ministry activities can help parents ready adolescents for responsible positions in the church and society by involving them in responsible leadership positions. Many youth programs do a good job of entertaining members and keeping them busy but do relatively little to empowering them to become effective leaders and ministers within the church community. In positions of leadership, adolescents are forced to learn how to make decisions; keep commitments; use their gifts, abilities, and talents; and develop personal confidence and self-esteem. As mentioned elsewhere in this book, teenagers can provide leadership in a number of ways: leading small groups, teaching classes, heading up service projects, or coordinating meetings and activities, to name a few. These activities give form to identity exploration.

VOCATION, OCCUPATION, AND CAREER CHOICE AS PART OF IDENTITY FORMATION

Part of identity formation is becoming a more productive person in society in terms of being a worker and economic provider. The problem of deciding on and preparing for a career represents one of the major developmental tasks for adolescents. Furthermore, vocational identity represents an integral part of their overall sense of who they are.[18]

It is important to make a clear distinction among three words often mistakenly used as synonyms: *vocation, occupation,* and *career.* The term *vocation* and the word *calling* come from the same root and have recently been used synonymously. "Vocation," or *vocare,* is used in a broad sense and literally denotes a calling to someone or something. In the context of one's faith, vocation alludes to a calling from God to himself or herself. Vocation speaks more of what an individual is than what he or she does specifically in terms of work. Frederick Buechner, submits that "the place God calls you to is the place where your deep gladness and the world's

---

17. Foster, *Called To Counsel,* 172.

18. Conger and Petersen, *Adolescence and Youth,* 446–8.

deep hunger meet."[19] One's vocation has to do with the central purpose of one's life, and how one's lifestyle reflects that central purpose. [20]

Occupation refers more specifically to the work or employment in which a person engages—bank teller, waiter, mechanic, or high school teacher. The concept of *career*, on the other hand, denotes the idea that there is a certain consistency over the lifetime in a person's relation to work. For example, a person may have a career in education that includes multiple jobs or occupational changes. The person may have held several teaching positions, spent some time as a principal or vice principal, and retired as a college professor. The term *career* carries with it the notion that an individual progresses through a series of phases associated with upward mobility, achieving greater responsibility, mastery of the occupation, and increasing financial remuneration.

Why is it that one's vocation[21] and related occupation are so closely tied to identity development? The importance of vocation to one's identity formation cannot be overstated. Having a job that society values does much to enhance self-esteem, and assists in the development of a secure and stable sense of identity. On the other hand, if one senses that his or her employment is not meaningful to society, there may be resentment, doubt, a loss of self-esteem, or even a dropping out of the work world. Two important aspects of most people's working lives are that their job or employment ties them into the larger system of society and gives them a sense of purpose in life. Donald Super suggests that people choose occupations that are consistent with their sense of self. If the greater world does not value their strengths, talents, and abilities, their self-perception is denied, as is their ability to contribute to society.[22] Furthermore, what one does for a living is a primary source of information about values, social class, and education.

Choosing an occupation in our rapidly changing culture proves to be much more complicated than it was prior to the industrial revolution, when young men and women began their vocational roles as early as at twelve or thirteen years old. At that time children had little, if any, input into the process, as parents usually dictated what their vocation or

19. Buechner, *Wishful Thinking*, 118

20. Olson, *Job or a Vocation?*, 7.

21. When we use the term "vocation" then, we will usually be referring to one's central purpose and lifestyle, which is then expressed by occupations and the career one chooses.

22. Super, "Life-span, Life-space Approach," 282–98.

occupation would be, and in many cases it simply meant assuming the occupational role of the parent.

Some researchers today suggest that vocational choice in contemporary Western societies is developmental in nature and begins in childhood. Eli Ginsberg and his associates describe the process of choosing a vocation as taking place in three specific stages. Up to about age eleven, children are in the *fantasy period*. During this initial period children assume that they can do anything, but there is no serious or realistic testing of occupational choices. Children are in a play orientation, and choices are made within a child's world, not the actual world in which they will eventually function.

The second stage is the *tentative period*, and occurs between ages eleven and eighteen. During this time young people realize that they will have to make decisions about selecting a vocation or occupation. It is a time when individuals assess their skills, capabilities, and interests, as well as academic and training possibilities.

The *realistic period takes* place in late adolescence and early adulthood. It is a time when possibilities are narrowed and commitment to final choices of vocation and occupation take place. This stage is further broken into an *exploratory* phase, when adolescents acquire information about vocational and job opportunities; a *crystallization* phase, when there is the narrowing down of alternatives; and finally *specification*, at which point decisions are made to pursue particular vocations and job possibilities.[23]

Establishing a vocation in life or choosing an occupation is becoming increasingly difficult as our society grows more complex, more specialized, and more technologically oriented.[24] Only twenty years ago the *Occupational Outlook Handbook* described three hundred occupations—covering 104 million jobs.[25] In 2014, the Bureau of Labor Statistics describes over 819 occupations—including well over 150 million jobs in the United States.[26] It is clear that the number of occupations and the kinds of skills the workplace requires are changing as new technologies are developed.

23. Ingersoll, *Adolescents in School and Society*, 133–35, summarizes the theory.

24. Conger and Petersen, *Adolescence and Youth*, 451.

25. *Occupational Outlook Handbook*.

26. United States Department of Labor. "Employment Projections."

Part-time work is one way that adolescents explore possibilities in life vocation and occupation. However some psychologists disagree on the value that part-time work has on adolescent development and argue that extensive involvement in the workplace may in fact interfere with the development of healthy autonomy and social responsibility of adolescents.[27] These experts suggest that teenagers who work are no more independent in making financial decisions than those who do not, that jobs are largely irrelevant to future careers, and that work is likely to interfere with schooling. The benefits of working include the development of personal responsibility and self-reliance, a better understanding of others and the world of work, access to adult mentors, and increased autonomy.[28]

How do parents affect vocational and occupational plans and ambitions of teenagers? Financial support and encouragement from parents are surely influential in aspiration and achievement of career and higher education.[29] A review of related empirical research studies has found that a father's occupation exerts significant influence on the career choice of sons, though not of daughters. For example, sons of scientists, lawyers and physicians are more likely to enter these professions than are other young men of similar socioeconomic status. Several reasons are given for these tendencies: (1) a greater opportunity to learn about the father's occupation as compared to others, (2) a greater access to the occupation, (3) strong parental motivation (and in some cases pressure), and (4) the communication of values from father to son.[30]

The mother is influential in shaping vocational attitudes as well. For example, female adolescents whose mothers are employed outside the home are also more likely to view work as something they would like to do when they are married and become mothers. Furthermore, the vocational aspirations, attitudes, and accomplishments of girls will be influenced by the mother's attitude toward employment, her degree of accomplishment and satisfaction in her work, and her ability to combine the roles of worker, mother, and wife.[31]

27. Greenberger and Steinberg, *When Teen-agers Work*, 47.

28. Mortimer, "Benefits and Risks of Adolescent Employment." 8–11, http://www.ncbi.nlm.nih.gov/pmc/articles/PMC2936460/#.

29. Papalia and Olds, *Child's World*, 552.

30. Summarized from Conger and Petersen, *Adolescence and Youth*, 463–63.

31. Ibid., 468–69.

Gender and ethnicity also affect vocational and occupational plans of adolescents. Traditionally women have been socialized to find their identity in the role of wife-mother-homemaker. Minorities and women are vastly overrepresented in conventional and social jobs, in clerical fields, in semiskilled jobs, and in service jobs. Today, however, women are making significant inroads into job markets such as law, medicine, and business—once considered exclusively male occupational areas. Nancy Cobb notes that "although the career aspirations of minority youth entering the labor market are as high as those of youth in the dominant culture, they do not face the same career opportunities."[32]

How can a youth program help adolescents achieve identity through vocation and occupation? In regard to vocational development, one must consider the words of Florence Nightingale: "I would have given the church my head, my heart, and my hand. She would not have them . . . She told me to go back to do crochet in my mother's drawing room; or to marry and look well at the head of my husband's table."[33] Christian organizations have the opportunity to engage the whole person in the service of God but often fail to ignite the passions or harness the talent. Many young people and adults believe that doing ministry means choosing a church-based occupation and that a disciple is a special person such as a priest or pastor. The myth is perpetuated that if you choose to use your gifts for God you must become a pastor or missionary, and that if you choose neither of these lines of work, then you serve God by working in a secular occupation and by supporting church-based ministries financially. This myth promotes weak view of both work and the opportunity to be light in nonclergy occupations.

In regard to occupational development, churches and non-profit organizations should see their staff as career counselors. Since the societal opportunities for women and minorities are not the same as for their white male counterparts, these counselors must act as change agents by advocating for students. Students who pursue gendered or stereotyped roles must be challenged to consider other options. Here are two examples of how to engage the problem. First, organizations can sponsor vocational fairs where women and minorities of different vocational and occupational fields come to talk and answer questions. Second, youth workers could organize exploration groups where adults from the church

32. Cobb, *Adolescence*, 298.
33. Quoted in Parker, *Women and Welfare*, 124.

meet with small groups of young people who are interested in their particular vocations.[34] On a volunteer staff, gender, ethnic, and occupational diversity may well significantly influence the occupational aspirations and opportunities of adolescents.

Adolescents should also be aware of the options in higher education. Too often high school graduates have not explored the various possibilities for training after high school and are not aware of the offerings from different types of postsecondary schools. Teens should understand the benefits and drawbacks of attending technical schools, private colleges, community colleges, or large universities, and should learn which would be most beneficial for their particular situation. The anticipation of higher education or further training has significant impact on the grades and spending habits of teens.[35]

Youth workers should be prepared to counsel young people in choosing the appropriate educational route for achieving vocational and occupational goals. They might visit college and university campuses with students and invite representatives of postsecondary schools or colleges to address youth groups.

ADOLESCENT SEXUALITY AND IDENTITY

Among the many developmental changes that characterize puberty and adolescence, none is more dramatic or more closely related to identity formation than is sexuality.[36] Achieving personal sexual identity means coming to terms with one's maleness or femaleness, biological maturation, and the sexual differences that accelerate during puberty.

The most profound and noticeable transformations in the teenager are probably the biological changes. The physical and sexual changes that take place during the early and middle adolescent years occur at a rapid pace; only during infancy does a person undergo a comparable period of extensive and accelerated change.[37]

The term given to this period of significant change is *puberty*, the stage of development in which sexual characteristics and features begin

34. Steele, "Identity Formation Theory and Youth Ministry," 97.

35. Cobb, *Adolescence*, 286

36. Conger and Petersen, *Adolescence and Youth*, 272.

37. See Ingersoll, *Adolescents*, 29; and Thornburg, *Development in Adolescence*, 54 for helpful descriptions of puberty and sexual development.

to show and mature. During puberty a sudden increase in height occurs, and the bodily characteristics of boys and girls become increasingly differentiated. Boys develop broader shoulders and experience an overall gain in muscle development, while girls develop more rounded hips and undergo breast development. Boys begin to grow facial hair and experience a voice change. In both sexes genitals increase in size and pubic hair develops; girls experience their first menstruation and boys their first ejaculation. These physical changes require significant adjustment by teenagers, as a number of other areas are affected, including body image, self-image, relationships with peers and parents, sexual feelings, and moods.[38]

If adolescents mature early or late relative to their peers, they may experience significant psychological or emotional effects. For boys, early physical maturity is associated with a more positive perception by self and others, while being late is associated with a poorer evaluation by self and others. The "on-time" developers fall somewhere in between these two extremes. It appears that maturing early has clear psychological and sociological advantages for boys.[39]

For girls, being early or late in physical maturity is associated with more negative attitudes and feelings than those who are on pace with their peers. Early physical and sexual maturation for a girl may carry explicit sexual meanings and generate unwelcome or inappropriate social responses. Early biological maturers may be tempted to identify with older adolescents who may initiate them into a set of behaviors, choices, and pressures for which they are mentally and emotionally unprepared. Late physical and sexual maturers may experience the ridicule or teasing of friends, or suffer considerable anxiety as sexual development is delayed.[40] Most of these effects are social consequences of expectation and are not caused by actual biology.

It is common for preadolescents and adolescents to have concerns or questions about their body and sexuality. For example, adolescents whose physical and sexual development is not "on time" need comfort and reassurance that they are indeed normal. The feelings, thoughts, and behaviors that accompany puberty are unfamiliar and sometimes confusing. Yet most adolescents lack information about pubertal changes and

38. Ibid.

39. Tobin-Richards et al., "Puberty and Its Psychological and Social Significance," 30–31.

40. Ingersol, *Adolescents,* 38–39.

what puberty involves. However, the better prepared for puberty a child is, the more positive the experience will be. It is important that preadolescents know not only what puberty entails in terms of physical change but also what feelings and emotions are attached to these changes and anticipated changes.[41]

The task of preparing children for puberty belongs primarily to parents, though most are uncomfortable discussing issues related to sex and in many cases ignore this responsibility entirely. Churches could make this task easier by providing seminars, classes, and resources[42] to equip parents are to talk to their preadolescents about such matters. It is imperative that youth workers share with parents the responsibility of helping adolescents work through issues related to sexual identity and development.

The ministry must also ask itself key questions in the area of development and sexuality such as, are we mainstreaming? It is vital that youth do not sense that there is a right look or right person for participation in the program. We must intentionally avoid only putting in front of the group or lauding beautiful, articulate, or achievement-oriented teens. These traits are often more connected to socioeconomic status or early biological development than to actual maturity and Christian identity.

SEXUAL IDENTITY AND HOMOSEXUAL ORIENTATION

Although young children label themselves as being one sex or the other, it is in the adolescent years that one's sexual orientation is usually manifested. An individual will be heterosexual (sexually interested in members of the opposite sex), homosexual (interested in members of the same sex), or bisexual (interested in members of both sexes). A plethora of labels are used: gay, straight, bi-, bicurious, questioning, and so forth. These are public labels and can be adopted or given to an adolescent. While most adolescents are heterosexual, many young people—more boys than girls—have one or more homosexual experiences.[43] Why do

41. Tobin-Richards et al., "Puberty and Its Psychological and Social Significance," 40.

42. One such resource is God's Design for Sex, a four-book series that progressively discusses physical and sexual development in age-appropriate ways.

43. Ingersol, *Adolescents,* 191–92 summarizes some of the empirical findings related to adolescent homosexuality.

some young people become attracted to the same sex? Experts cite a number of possible causes. Some adolescents are not secure in their sex-role identification, while others have had homosexual experiences and convince themselves they are not attracted to the opposite sex. For still others, homosexuality has been learned, or they have been conditioned toward homosexual behavior. Paul Meier and associates recognize the possibility of genetic influence on homosexuality but argue that even if such an influence could be proven, it would be erroneous to blame sinful behavior on "bad genes."[44] Psychologist Gary Collins argues that homosexuality is learned and offers several theories as to how this happens: through certain parent and family relationships, through fear of the opposite sex, and through willful choice of homosexual actions.[45] Many teens will use language describing how they "discovered" their same-sex attraction while others will say that they "always knew."

It is important to realize that most young people use *gay* as an adjective to describe attraction rather than a lifestyle or sexual orientation. Participation in a sex act does not define one's sexual orientation or one's lifestyle, although some teens may believe that their sexual behavior automatically classifies them as heterosexual or homosexual. Teens perceive older Christians as waging a culture war by denigrating the gay community rather than helping them deal with the realities of their sexual identity and experiences. The church must do a better job of providing a Christian view of sexuality.

Much like other areas of identity formation, the shaping of a sexual identity is a developmental process. Mark Yarhouse, the director for the Institute of Sexual Identity, describes the movement towards a gay identity, for example, as follows: first, an initial awareness of attractions; second, same-sex behavior; third, questioning of identity; and finally, self-defining attribution (such as *gay*). Yarhouse's research indicates that this is a three-to-four-year process for females and a five-to-six-year process for males. For males it typically begins around age fifteen and can take as long as fifteen years to resolve. Christian college students will often report that first feelings of same-sex attraction occurred at age thirteen and that confusion set in by age fourteen. The confusion over sexual orientation is generated by a host of factors, not the least of which is a conflict between their sexual and religious identities. While a conversation

44. Meier et al., *Introduction to Psychology and Counseling*, 272.
45. Collins, *Christian Counseling*, 282–85.

about orientation can be limiting or even politically charged, a conversation about sexual identity can "broaden the discussion and widen the dialogue."[46] Yarhouse provides a series of components that help explain sexual identity and can be fruitful points of engaging discussions with adolescents:

- whether you are biologically male or female
- how masculine of feminine you feel
- the amount and kind of sexual attraction you feel (toward the same or opposite sex or both)
- how you intend to act, the kind of person you intend to become
- your beliefs and values about sexual behavior
- your behaviors (based on how you feel, what you intended).[47]

While an orientation or label such as *gay* may prescribe certain behaviors, helping teens state that "I am a person who experiences same-sex attraction" gives an "opportunity to look at other aspects of their identity before labeling themselves based on their sexuality."[48]

Yarhouse encourages the church, youth pastors, and Christian institutions to move toward the following practices:

- Institutional transparency—avoiding branding and cultivating civility
- A caring climate—speaking against fear, denouncing the practice of bullying, and embracing teens with same-sex attraction as our people, not outsiders
- Confessional honesty—confessing that we have made mistakes in pastoral care with our adolescents who experience same-sex attraction
- Humility—admitting that there is much that we do not know about sexuality and same-sex attractions
- Stewardship of sexuality—proclaiming a biblical perception and understanding of sexuality and a theology of restoration that ties in with sanctification.

46 Yarhouse, *Understanding Sexual Identity,* 92.

47. Ibid ., 93.

48. Ibid., 94.

GENDER-ROLE IDENTITY

Closely related to the issue of sexual identity is gender-role identity. This refers to the accepting and assuming of sex roles or behaviors and characteristics considered appropriate and desirable by society for males and females. In North American societies, autonomy, independence, dominance, aggression, and the inhibition of emotion are expected of males, while females are expected to be warm, nurturing, emotionally expressive, dependent, and interpersonally competent.[49] Furthermore, occupational and home roles have historically been classified as masculine or feminine, and these remain surprisingly resistant to change despite actual changes in the home and workplace.[50] Traditionally, occupations requiring administrative responsibility and strength have been seen as masculine, while roles that are passive in nature and involve caring for others have been viewed as feminine.[51]

Considerable debate continues as to whether gender roles and orientations are innate or environmentally conditioned. One cumulative empirical research study found significant differences between school-age boys and girls in three areas—girls have greater verbal ability, while boys excel in visual-spatial tasks and mathematics. The authors attributed differences partially to biological factors but emphasized the role of socialization as well.[52] Other experts agree that biological forces such as sex hormones and brain dissimilarities play a significant role in gender differentiation, although they also argue that these forces interact significantly with the environment. The resultant effects are that there are some tasks males do better than females and vice versa. Many argue that better mathematics skills exhibited by boys should be attributed exclusively to environmental factors such as parental expectations.

Carol Gilligan suggests that women have a special innate nature that is different from men, and that these differences should be seen in a positive light. According to Gilligan, the male moves towards justice, rights, and detachment, while the female is predisposed toward attachment, intimacy, and relationships.[53]

49. Ingersoll, *Adolescents,* 119.

50. Seem and Clark, "Healthy Women, Healthy Men, and Healthy Adults," 247–58.

51. Ingersoll, *Adolescents,* 131–32.

52. Maccoby and Jacklin, *Psychology of Sex Differences,* 1–2.

53. Gilligan, *In a Different Voice,* 5–23.

Perhaps the most helpful approach is a holistic one that sees gender dimorphism or differences as best explained by the coinfluence of biological, psychological, and sociological forces. In other words, differences between males and females are best understood to be the resultant effects of predetermined, innate characteristics combined with external influences such as parental and social expectations. This holistic approach finds opposition from much of the feminist movement, which feels that there is neither biological nor social justification for identifying gender-specific roles or categories. Sociologist Hans Sebald suggests that this feminist view is leading our society toward an abandonment or radical modification of traditional sex roles and an emergence of a nonsexist style of human interaction. He goes on to say that "whatever the future, at this time there is a significant eroding of the traditional stereotypes. Sex-role blueprints have become blurred, and prediction of a person's behavior on the basis of gender is no longer as reliable as it used to be."[54]

Females have felt the bulk of this blurring of gender roles. While the role of the male has remained relatively unchanged, the female role has experienced significant transformation from the 1970s onward. This includes increased premarital sexual activity among women, a more competitive attitude among females, an influx of women into the once male-dominated professions, an increase in the number of women in higher education, and overall delays in childbearing. Some of the effects of gender-role changes are harmful, as females are now exposed to some of the same tensions that males experience. These negative effects include a rise in the suicide rate of females, a general worsening self-image of young women, and an increase of violent crimes performed by women.[55]

Charles Sell suggests the breakdown of traditional roles of husband as leader and provider, and wife as homemaker has created a significant amount of confusion, conflict, and controversy in marriages. First, without the traditional understanding of gender roles (which includes the wife's submission to the husband), a relationship may come to be characterized by a striving for power, and individual home responsibilities may be negotiated one by one in the heat of such a relationship. For some women, getting a job may be a strategy to give them leverage in financial decisions. Second, getting a job outside the home may be a striving for

54. Sebald, *Adolescence*, 47.
55. Ibid., 47–52.

significance. For them, caring for children full time is not as fulfilling or rewarding as it was for women in the past.

Third, for many women the movement from the traditional role of the male as sole provider has resulted in more work for most women. While many women have increased their work outside the home, most men have not increased their share of the domestic tasks. Thus many women have two full-time careers, one outside the home and one inside.

Fourth, by questioning their roles in the home, women have forced men to reconsider their roles. With the traditional notions of manhood under attack, there has been considerable restlessness and questioning on the part of men. Finally, couples are forced to search for new ways to solve conflicts and maintain marital harmony, as they are stripped of customary guidelines to order their relationships.[56]

The overall consequence of these significant changes is that many young women are no longer moving into traditional female roles but are working out a variety of role combinations and possibilities. For some, it is making a choice between carrying out the traditional roles of marriage, motherhood, and homemaking, or completing an education and establishing a career. For others, it is combining motherhood and homemaking with career. For an increasing number of females, it is planning their lives in phases, such as education, work experience, career, marriage, motherhood, reeducation, and reentry into the workforce.

Teenage girls will need help as they face the difficult task of choosing from the multiple options and demands that society has placed on them. The message society gives them is that they can have it all—family, education, career—but the result is often frustration and stress. Adolescent girls must be reminded that they must not overextend themselves and should pursue a path of moderation.

Male adolescents should be prepared for changing roles as well. Men must play, for example, a more significant role in parenting. Fathers need to be jointly involved in the efforts of childrearing. The parenting contribution made by the father must be significant enough that deep emotional bonds with his children are made. It also means that young men must abandon the discriminatory attitude that women are generally inferior to men in important aspects of personality and capability.[57]

---

56. Sell, *Family Ministry,* 43–44.
57. Rekers, *Shaping Your Child's Sexual Identity,* 15.

For both adolescent males and females, changing gender roles mean recognizing the important distinctions between men and women and at the same time encouraging individuals to meet their potentials and goals in life through equal opportunities and responsibilities. Achieving the true ideal of Christian womanhood and manhood will be a difficult and sometimes confusing task for adolescents in today's world. It remains, however, a critical aspect of developing one's identity.

IDENTITY AND SELF-ESTEEM

One of the most important psychological aspects of identity is self-esteem, defined as one's attitude toward self. In fact, William Glasser argues that there are two basic psychological needs of people: love and self-esteem, or self-worth. These, he adds, are the two pathways to the successful achievement of identity.[58] Usually, self-esteem is thought of in evaluative terms. A person may be described as having either a positive or negative self-esteem; either an accepting or a critical view toward self.

An adolescent's self-esteem is shaped by a number of factors including treatment by parents, a perception of his or her own body development and physical attractiveness, evaluation by peers, and a response to the standards portrayed by society. Parents can foster a negative self-esteem by abusing or unduly punishing a child; by berating, rejecting, or criticizing; by comparing a child with others; or by placing unrealistic expectations on a son or daughter.[59]

Some relevant empirical research indicates that during early adolescence, self-esteem tends to become more negative than during childhood or late adolescence. Girls, especially, may look at their bodies and feel unsatisfied with what they see. Weight, in our society, is a particularly important component as to how a girl feels about her body. Society places a strong emphasis on slimness, thus the heavier a girl is, or thinks she is, the more dissatisfied with herself she becomes.[60] The self-starving disorder of anorexia nervosa is often related to self-esteem. Most common among girls and young women of middle and upper classes, anorexics place tremendous pressure on themselves to be slim. This is often a re-

58. Glasser, *Schools Without Failure*, 12–15.

59. Narramore, *You're Someone Special*, 79.

60. Tobin-Richards et al., "Puberty and Its Psychological and Social Significance," 29–30.

sponse to society's decision that being slender equals being beautiful and adored, and fatness equals being ugly and unloved. [61]

An adolescent also perceives him- or herself as attractive, successful, or acceptable because of the responses of others, especially peers.[62] Most people take seriously the opinions of others about them, and these opinions become part of the definition of themselves.[63] Finally, personal competence contributes to one's self-esteem. When an adolescent is successful in sports, academics, music, or whatever, there is a greater likelihood that the individual will feel confident about himself or herself. Likewise, experiences of failures or incompetencies will lead to low self-esteem.[64]

In his extensive study of churchgoing adolescents, Merton Strommen found one cry of teenagers to be the cry of self-hatred, characterized by distress over personal faults, lack of self-confidence, and low self-regard. He concluded that one in five church youth harbors thoughts of severe self-criticism.[65] Other studies indicate that as many as 95 percent of the population (including adults) feel inferior and inadequate.[66] Adolescents with low or poor self-esteem are more susceptible to peer pressure, are more likely to engage in at-risk behaviors such as alcohol and drug abuse, are more suicidal, and are more likely to seek acceptance though sexual activity.[67]

Most youth experience periods of feeling quite worthless, especially when they experience difficulties in their relationships with friends or fail to measure up in school or in activities such as sports and music. Such feelings usually pass, but if they persist and dominate the adolescent, they can become destructive and interfere with many aspects of life such as peer relationships, studies, and spiritual development. These adolescents need special attention.[68] Jerry Aldridge identifies four basic requirements for the development of positive self-esteem in adolescents: a sense of

---

61. Newman and Newman, *Adolescent Development,* 142.

62. Ibid., 277.

63. Ibid., 279.

64. Ibid., 281.

65. Strommen, *Five Cries of Youth,* 18–23.

66. Collins, *Christian Counseling,* 313.

67. Johnson, *Developing Student Leaders,* 21.

68. Strommen, *Five Cries of Youth,* 21.

belonging, a feeling of individuality, the opportunity to choose, and the presence of good models.[69]

Building a Sense of Belonging

Adolescents often feel lonely and isolated from other people, but this is especially so for youth suffering from low self-esteem.[70] A youth ministry to adolescents who feel isolated and poorly about themselves begins by recruiting or hiring adult workers who demonstrate and model the warmth and empathy of a concerned person. Many times the teaching procedures and programs that are offered matter little to the teenager with low self-esteem if the worker-adolescent interaction does not establish a warm relationship. The effective relationship means communicating to youth that they are loved, that they are important, and that they do have potential.[71]

Low-esteem youth also need a community or small group where they can sense they are accepted. For larger youth groups, it may be necessary to systematically break the group into smaller units. These small groups of six to eight might meet once a week in homes or on a regular basis in conjunction with large-group functions. It is important, however, that the small-group membership remain constant for a period of time (perhaps six months or a year) so that a sense of belonging or community can be nurtured.

Finally, avoiding unnecessary competitive activities and comparisons is important in working with youth who have difficulties with low self-esteem and have trouble experiencing a sense of belonging. Competitive activities such as "head-trip" discussions and competitive sports tend to encourage unfavorable comparisons and threaten some youth. While competition cannot be avoided entirely, youth ministries should stress cooperative activities and games that neutralize the superior skills of some of the participants. For example, rather than playing a regular softball game that emphasizes the skills of the athletes while isolating those who cannot catch and hit the ball so well, try modifying the game by using a whiffle ball and plastic bat. Add another dimension to the game by requiring batters and fielders to each get inside a large garbage bag,

---

69. Aldridge, "Preadolescence," 107.

70. Strommen, *Five Cries of Youth*, 24.

71. Ibid., 37–38.

forcing them to hop rather than run to the ball and bases. Or try three-legged soccer. Participants on each team are paired off and instructed to tie their adjacent legs together. Team members are only allowed to kick the ball with the "middle" leg. These modifications bring the athletic and nonathletic participants much closer together in skill levels and add a new dimension of humor and fun to the games.

Developing Individuality or Uniqueness

While adolescents have a strong need to belong, they also have the need to be distinct or unique. However a primary distinctive of adolescents with low self-esteem is that they tend to perceive themselves as having little worth or importance.[72] Furthermore, they often lack self-confidence and live in fear of failing or being humiliated by making a mistake or blunder. Adolescents with low self-esteem may also be convinced that they lack talent or abilities and yet realize their dependence on the praise of others.[73]

A sense of individuality and uniqueness can be enhanced in youth ministry settings by encouraging adolescents to express their own ideas. Parents and youth workers alike should be encouraged to listen to the viewpoints of teenagers even when they differ from one's own.[74] Teenagers should be encouraged to share their talents and abilities. It may be difficult, however, to get low-esteem youth to involve themselves in activities where they might fail. They tend not to try out for the school play or work on important committees or join in a volleyball or softball game.[75] They should know that they are loved and accepted even if they make mistakes or their performance lacks a certain amount of quality.

Getting adolescents involved in the leadership level of youth ministry will provide valuable benefits in the areas of self-esteem and individuality. Involvement in leadership will help young people feel significant and responsible, will enable them to gain competence in certain skills, and will help them develop character.[76] Allow the adolescent leaders a certain amount of freedom so that they can perform their duties with a

72. Strommen, *Five Cries of Youth*, 23.

73. Ibid., 21–22.

74. Aldridge, *Self-Esteem*, 87.

75. Aldridge, "Preadolescence," 108.

76. Johnston, *Developing Student Leaders*, 20–21.

measure of individuality. Teenagers need opportunities to explore and implement their newly discovered thinking and problem-solving skills in order to enhance their sense of competence.[77]

Most important, young people should achieve a sense of uniqueness by recognizing who they are in relationship to God. Adolescents should understand that they are created in God's image (Gen 1:26), that they are the pinnacle and culmination of his creation (Ps 8:4–5), purchased by the blood of Christ (1 Cor. 6:20; 1 Peter 1:18–19), and proclaimed to be of great value by Christ (Matt 6:26). Because we are created in God's image, we possess great significance, worth, and value.[78]

Nurturing the Ability to Make Choices

Aldridge suggests a third essential to healthy self-esteem is the ability to make personal decisions and maintain a certain amount of control over the environment. The ability and privilege to make choices increases as a child grows in age and maturity. Adolescents can be given increasing responsibility to participate in the decision-making processes of the youth group.[79] An essential component of a healthy self-esteem is influence. Holding positions of leadership allows youth to feel that they are making important decisions, thus giving them a sense of influence.

It is important, however, when youth group members are asked to participate in decision-making activities that they be listened to when they contribute worthwhile insights and information. Youth, especially those with low self-esteem, may become annoyed or hurt when adult leaders ask for their input and then fail to respond to what the youth have shared.[80]

Providing Good Role Models

The final requirement for the development of healthy adolescent self-esteem is the presence of good models. For adolescents, models include parents, teachers, church workers, employers, and certain peers. One of the primary roles of the volunteer or full-time youth worker is that of

77. Aldridge, Self-Esteem, 88.

78. See Narramore, You're Someone Special, for a biblical perspective on self-esteem.

79. Aldridge, "Preadolescence," 109.

80. Edwards, Total Youth Ministry, 31.

modeling. Donald Posterski suggests adults ponder the question, *Does my behavior deserve to be duplicated?*[81] He goes on to say that adults who hope to serve the best interests of youth will lead the way with their living; they will model what matters. Adults who have high aspirations for the younger generation will give them something worth watching.

CONCLUSION

This chapter has explored the critical and arduous adolescent task of identity formation. From the material presented in this chapter it is clearly evident that identity achievement is not a single-faceted undertaking; rather, it is a highly complex and interactive process by which the individual establishes his or her personal goals, values, beliefs, and even lifestyle. In an increasingly complex, fast-paced, and stressful world adolescents seek answers to questions such as *Who am I?* and *How do I fit in?* The task of youth workers is to assist adolescents in achieving a sense of identity by focusing on issues related to autonomy, vocation, sexuality, gender roles, and self-esteem.

81. Bibby and Posterski, *Teen Trends,* 320.

4

Adolescent Faith Development

At its core youth ministry is all about outreach (cultivating in teens a saving relationship with Jesus Christ) and nurture (fostering a growing and ongoing relationship with Christ). The outcome we work towards is the spiritual or faith maturity of youth. In reality this is what youth ministry with all its activities, programs, philosophies, and strategies boils down to. Thus one of the most important tasks related to adolescent development is the appropriation or internalization of one's faith. In other words, teenagers must come to the point where they personalize what they believe.

From a theological perspective, "saving faith is trust in Jesus Christ as a living person for forgiveness of sins and for eternal life with God."[1] Fully understood, such faith has three stages—past (justification: *I have been saved* from the penalty of sin), present (sanctification: *I am being saved* from the power of sin), and future (glorification: *I shall be saved* from the penalty of sin). Disciple making of youth is all-encompassing, as it is concerned with salvation (outreach), sanctification (nurture), and security and hope of final redemption—what we call faith development.

While definitions of faith and understandings of faith development abound, surely the most discussed characterization of faith development is that of James Fowler, who sees faith as the way to put meaning into life.[2] While Fowler contributes much to the understanding of faith development, his definition of faith has some shortcomings. Fowler is not

1. Grudem, *Systematic Theology,* 710.
2. Fowler, *Stages of Faith.*

concerned so much with the content or substance of faith as he is with the activity or process of faith making or putting meaning into life. According to Fowler, faith is not necessarily religious in its content or context and to ask serious questions of oneself or of life does not necessarily mean to elicit questions concerning religious beliefs or commitment.[3] While helpful for understanding faith formation, his definition is clearly more psychological than theological in nature, and we must be careful as to the degree we embrace it and how we make use of it.[4]

Once again, from a theological perspective, faith is seen as an activity of the person in response to the redemptive work of the Holy Spirit in one's heart.[5] In understanding faith as a human activity and response to a divine work, it is further defined here as the spiritual aspect of life that includes such dimensions as beliefs and convictions, attitudes and values, and behaviors and lifestyle.[6] In distinctly Christian terms, faith implies not only a general personal allegiance to a transcendent entity, but also a content-specific agreement with stated truths (Scripture) and practices related to belief in the triune God—the Father, Son, and the Holy Spirit.

Perhaps it is helpful to note that while Scripture contains the substance of faith and the Holy Spirit provides the redemptive work, Fowler's psychological theory simply gives us the structure for faith development. We further contend that adolescence provides an important setting for faith since faith formation is strongly related to the achievement of identity and self-autonomy.[7] It is a complex activity that is made up of three interactive domains: the intellectual, the emotional, and the volitional.[8]

---

3. Ibid., 4.

4. While his schema is embraced by many evangelicals, not everyone agrees that Fowler is helpful in our efforts to understand biblical faith, and some might suggest there is too much emphasis on the psychological aspect of faith. Indeed there is even some disagreement with the authors of this book as to the relevance of Fowler's theory to our understanding of faith and faith development. For a helpful critique of the strengths and weaknesses of the theory see Downs, *Teaching for Spiritual Growth*, 118–23.

5. See Steele, *On the Way*, 102; and Downs, "Faith Shaping," 50.

6. Dykstra, "Faith Development and Religious Education," 252–53.

7. Gillespie, *Experience of Faith*, 126.

8. Steele, *On the Way*, 102–4, Downs, "Faith Shaping," 49–60; and Westerhoff, *Will Our Children Have Faith?*, 91, describe faith in accordance to these three categories.

THE INTELLECTUAL DOMAIN

The *intellectual,* or cognitive, domain is concerned with the knowledge of faith. It includes the content, or the beliefs and convictions that form the foundation of one's religion and faith. Perry Downs describes Christianity as a "propositional religion with truth to be known."[9] These truths can be concrete or abstract/supernatural in nature. Understanding these supernatural truths requires higher-level cognitive skills.

Often what is believed and adhered to in the preadolescent and early adolescent years, however, is that which is handed down from parents, teachers, pastors, and youth workers. Preadolescents are what developmental psychologist Jean Piaget calls concrete thinkers. At this stage of development thinking is limited to the here and now, to concrete objects and situations. There is relatively little capacity to do personal critical reflection or independent and abstract thinking. This does not negate faith or the ability to believe but does limit the ability to understand certain concepts related to that belief.

At about age twelve, when children move into early adolescence, they enter what is called the *formal operations* stage. At this point, as Fowler puts it, thought takes wings.[10] The developing cognitive or thinking skills begin to be characterized by the ability to carry out abstract thought and to go beyond the here and now in thinking. Adolescents can hypothesize and suppose situations, which means they can now concern themselves with national and international affairs. They ask questions about meaning and values of human existence; they imagine the ideal—the ideal family, the ideal church, the ideal world. And they can understand, in the words of William Yount, the "un-concrete" world of spiritual matters.[11]

It is here that a number of faith development theorists better help us understand faith shaping, especially as it relates to identity formation. Fowler proposes that in developing a faith system, teenagers first go through a stage he calls the *Synthetic-Conventional* (age twelve years on). It is synthetic in that it is the drawing together of distinct and different elements into a new whole or unity. It is conventional in that the beliefs of the individual conform to or are shaped and pulled together

9. Downs, "Faith Shaping," 50.

10. Fowler, *Stages of Faith,* 71.

11. Yount, *Created to Learn,* 105.

by, significant others: family, peers, clergy, and the like.[12] John Wester-hoff calls this type of faith *affiliative,* characterized by a strong sense of belonging and a need for the interaction of significant people.[13] In other words, faith is not based on self-reflection alone.[14] The greatest danger for teenagers at this stage of development is that their faith may quite likely be secondhand. This is the entrance point of most youth ministry activi-ties. By creating a Christian community of teenagers, the leader is able to utilize interplay of cognitive and social development to teach matters of faith and create a "loyalty" to both the church and the youth group. The danger lies in the next transition where adolescents become willing to break from the group or outgrow the youth group thus possibly becom-ing disconnected.

The next stage of development according to Fowler is characterized as an *Individuative-Reflective* faith and normally emerges at about age seventeen or eighteen. This faith is individuative in the sense that it is a faith that is one's own, and is reflective in the sense that an individual who has moved into this stage has personally examined and critically thought out what he or she believes. The adolescent has begun to take seriously the burden of responsibility for his or her personal beliefs, attitudes, and lifestyle.[15] The emergence of a strong sense of self influences how the teen will view these beliefs and shape his understanding of personal Christian identity. Understanding what it means to be a child of God greatly affects how teens see themselves spiritually.[16] It is this firsthand faith, as youth ministry expert Duffy Robbins puts it, that we want to see our teenagers come to.[17]

With the development of cognitive skills and the resultant ability to internalize one's faith, a number of implications arise for youth workers. To begin with, rather than being frustrated when students ask questions, express doubts, or challenge the teachings of the church, the youth work-er should in fact be doing all he or she can to encourage such activity. The wise youth worker will welcome difficult questions, remind adolescents

12. Fowler, *Stages of Faith,* 151–73.

13. Westerhoff, *Will Our Children Have Faith?,* 94.

14. Yount, *Created to Learn,* 125.

15. Fowler, *Stages of Faith,* 174–83.

16. Anderson and Park, *Stomping Out the Darkness,* 18.

17. Robbins, *Ministry of Nurture,* 63.

that it is not wrong to have doubts about their faith, and encourage youth to grapple with theological and life-related issues.

Adolescents should be taught to do independent and critical thinking, which means youth teachers should avoid spoon-feeding youth or simply filling them with content through the overused lecture method. Too many youth workers tell teens what to think without teaching them how to think, and far too many youth workers are concerned with telling young people what to believe, without enabling them to develop a firsthand faith of their own. The Effective Christian Education Study of mainline churches by the Search Institute found that only 45 percent of the youth say their church encourages them to ask questions, and just 42 percent say their church challenges their thinking.[18]

Youth leaders must be intentional when teaching students to think about matters of faith and belief. While some youth teachers shy away from theology, stating that teenagers are not intellectually ready for those matters, it should be understood that the same adolescents study topics such as biology, physics, and algebra on a daily basis. This indicates that they are capable of understanding appropriate levels of theological teaching. Youth workers must raise the bar and challenge teens with matters of spiritual depth rather than viewing and treating them as large children[19]. Keep in mind that matters of faith are not always tied to cognitive abilities. Indeed a teen can choose to believe a biblical truth that he or she cannot fully comprehend. In fact, there are many truths or concepts in Scripture that Christians are called to believe yet cannot fully understand such as the Trinity, the virgin birth, the problems of suffering and evil, or even salvation itself. As they work through difficult and hard-to-understand theological concepts, however, youth must be reassured that they are not alone in wrestling with these issues and there are answers. This will be addressed later in the chapter.

One way youth teachers can help move adolescents toward higher levels of thinking and can better equip them to wrestle with the tough issues of faith is by employing Benjamin Bloom's taxonomy of cognitive functioning.[20] Bloom and his associates have identified six levels of thinking. In order of complexity from the lower to higher levels they are (1) *remembering* (recalling information), (2) *understanding* (rephrasing

---

18. Roehlkepartain, *Teaching Church*, 206.

19. Reid, *Raising the Bar*, 20.

20. Bloom and colleagues originally developed this taxonomy in 1956. It has since been revised and updated, most recently by Anderson, *Taxonomy for Learning*.

the information, giving a description in one's own words), (3) *applying*
(using previously learned information to solve a problem or determine
a correct answer), (4) *analyzing* (identifying motives, reasons, or causes;
using available information to reach a conclusion), (5) *evaluating* (judg-
ing the merit of an idea or an aesthetic work, based on specific criteria),
and (6) *creating* (producing original communication, making predictions). By asking adolescents questions that go beyond the knowledge
and comprehension levels, the youth teacher enables teenagers to probe,
reflect, and think about their walk with God, their faith, and their beliefs.
Figure 4.2 includes examples of questions or statements at the various
levels of thinking.

Table 4.1
Bloom's Taxonomy of Thinking and Teaching for Adolescents

Level	Type of Skill	Sample Question/Statement
Remembering	Recalling Recognizing	Recite the definition of faith given last week.
Understanding	Comprehending Describing Paraphrasing	Explain faith in your own words. What do you think Jesus means when he says . . . ?
Applying	Implementing Solving	How could you apply Jesus's principle "Love your enemy" to a situation at school?
Analyzing	Identifying Concluding Separating	What was the apostle Paul's purpose for writing the letter to the Galatians?
Evaluating	Judging Appraising	Which is better, option A or option B? Which type of evangelism is the most effective and why?
Creating	Producing Designing Revising	Construct a collage of pictures that represent your ideas, feelings, and values concerning . . . Write an essay on . . .

A natural part of adolescent faith development is doubt or a questioning of one's faith. The newfound cognitive skills that teenagers acquire (Piaget's *formal operations*), along with their need to establish

independence from their parents, will likely result in some form of questioning of the faith system they have developed to this point. This should not be seen as a spiritual problem but rather as a normal phenomenon of adolescent development.[21] Doubt can even be seen in a positive light when one recognizes that adolescents desire to understand more deeply the beliefs that they had previously embraced. Doubt can lead to sincere soul-searching and a quest for answers that the teenager was previously not able to understand.

Downs offers the following suggestions for youth workers who are helping adolescents struggling with doubts or troubled over difficult questions of faith:[22]

1. *Remind adolescents that doubt is not a sin.* The Bible provides examples of followers of God who doubted. The Old Testament book of Jeremiah provides a clear example of the prophet's struggle with doubt (Jeremiah 20:7–8, 14–18). Likewise John the Baptist expressed his doubt when he questioned if Jesus was the Messiah (Matthew 11:1–6). Neither is doubt the same as unbelief. Os Guinness proposes,

   > Doubt is not the opposite of faith, nor is it the same as unbelief. Doubt is a state of mind in suspension between faith and unbelief so that it is neither of them wholly and it is each only partly. This distinction is absolutely vital because it uncovers and deals with the first major misconception of doubt—the idea that in doubting a believer is betraying faith and surrendering to unbelief. No misunderstanding causes more anxiety and brings such bondage to sensitive people in doubt.[23]

2. *Provide a safe context where doubts can be expressed.* If adolescents get the message that it is wrong to doubt, they may go elsewhere with their questions. By accepting their questions, and even encouraging them to doubt, the teacher can provide a safe context in which doubts and questions can be raised.

3. *Provide answers for some of their questions.* This does not mean that the youth pastor or teacher should quickly provide the answer so

---

21. Downs, "Faith Shaping," 50.

22. Ibid., 56–57.

23. Guiness, *In Two Minds,* 27.

the doubt may be quickly resolved. But the youth worker should be familiar with the basic issues of apologetics, the rational defense of Christianity. In some cases the teacher might direct the youth toward sources that might help the questioning person find helpful answers.

4. *Provide the teenager with a real Christian experience.* While it is true that doubt is an intellectual issue, adolescents are also very much experience oriented. If the doubting youth has a place where he or she is accepted and supported, if it is a place where the presence of God is felt, the teenager has a basis for belief that transcends the intellectual.[24]

One youth group has a creative manner of addressing the tough intellectual questions of faith with which adolescents contend. Periodically they have a "Skeptics Night Out," where they submit questions anonymously. These questions are addressed one at a time, either by a panel of individuals or by an appointed person. This could be the youth worker, pastor, or anyone else who has a solid knowledge of the Christian faith and church doctrine, the way adolescents think, and the honest ability to admit he or she does not have all the answers.

Questions might range from *How do we know we can trust the Bible?* to *What about the claims of evolution?* to *Can God forgive any sin?* Youth group members are encouraged to bring their unchurched friends from school so that there is an added measure of authenticity to these sessions.[25]

Gillespie accurately argues that freedom is an essential ingredient in people who want to personalize their faith, and we must at some point allow our adolescents freedom of choice. We cannot make our beliefs theirs.[26] Eugene Roehlkepartain suggests that the thinking climate within a youth ministry program can be evaluated and adjusted by struggling with a series of questions:[27]

- *To what degree are questions encouraged or discouraged?* If a teenager asks a question concerning faith, is he or she affirmed or discounted? Is it safe to ask any kind of question?

24. Downs, "Faith Shaping," 56–57.
25. Robbins, *Ministry of Nurture,* 154.
26. Gillespie, *Experience of Faith,* 130.
27. Roehlkepartain, "Thinking Climate," 61–62.

- *How does the church congregation handle diverse opinions?* It is said that when all think alike, no one thinks much. By stifling diverse thoughts, youth education programs discourage critical thinking.

- *Are youth group members challenged to examine their faith and lifestyles?* Is faith simply an intellectual exercise, or does it challenge teenagers to develop and change? Are youth challenged to think about the implications of faith on school, family relationships, recreation, vocation, dating, and other domains of life?

- *Do youth teachers and other adults model a thinking faith?* When adolescents observe their pastors, youth pastors, parents, and other adults in the church, do they see people who are actively thinking about their faith and faith-related issues?

- *Are adolescents given answers, or are they led to discover answers for themselves?* Are youth given the skills to discern truth, think reflectively about their faith, and come to their own conclusions on critical issues?

THE EMOTIONAL DOMAIN

A second dimension of a personalized faith is the *emotional* or affective. This is that part of one's faith that is related to how he or she feels: the emotions, attitudes, and values. It refers to the conviction or passion one has about that of which he or she has knowledge. While the intellectual or cognitive domain is linked with the head, the emotional or affective domain is linked to the heart.[28] Much of faith development lies in the affective range as God speaks to the individual's heart thus provoking an emotional response. It is the part of faith that embraces and personalizes that which one believes with the head. Westerhoff suggests that perhaps we become too concerned too early with the activities of thinking in Christian education of youth and forget that the affections are just as important as the intellectual.[29]

Youth leaders must be careful to balance the need for emotional and experiential activities while not creating a faith that is totally dependent upon emotional experiences. Duffy Robbins refers to what he calls Tarzan Christianity whereby teenagers swing from one spiritual high or

28. Lee, *Content,* 196.
29. Westerhoff, *Will Our Children Have Faith?,* 94–95.

event to another without ever finding a solid ground upon which to build a personal faith.[30] What kinds of experiences heighten the emotional element of the faith experience? Opportunities for experiencing the awe, wonder, and mystery of God abound in wilderness camping and outdoor activities such as hiking, cross-country skiing, rock climbing, canoeing, and backpacking. Leading students to participate in the spiritual disciplines is another beneficial faith-enhancing experience. Participation in worship and prayer, as well as in the arts such as drama and music, gives adolescents opportunities for enhancing spiritual affections and facilitating the presence of faith. Journaling is a particularly good way to nurture reflection on how the adolescents feel about their faith experiences. Two suggestions for journaling are (1) reading a psalm a day and jotting down thoughts on what was read and (2) writing one's own psalms.[31]

Finally, classroom procedures that promote active learning are key elements in bringing matters of faith to life through personal and group experiences. Role-playing and simulation games help adolescents identify their feelings related to the faith experience. *Role-play* is the process of assigning participants roles of people in hypothetical or real situations. In role-playing, youth explore life-related problems or issues by spontaneously acting them out and then discussing the enactments. Together, participants can explore feelings, values, attitudes, as well as strategies for solving problems.

For example, assign the role of a skeptic or non-Christian to a capable individual—one who might clearly understand and be able to articulate questions in opposition to the Christian faith. Have others take turns trying to convince the skeptic to embrace the Christian faith. Following a role-play such as this, the teenagers can talk about the interaction, look for solutions to problems they encounter, and explore the feelings of the people whose roles they have assumed.[32] Role-play is a beneficial and powerful teaching tool for a number of reasons, some of which are related to the affective domain of faith shaping:[33]

- Role-play affords teenagers an opportunity to experience new, unusual or problem situations in a protected, caring environment.

- Role-play allows youth to experience and articulate their feelings.

30. Robbins, *Building a Youth Ministry*, 15.

31. Robbins, *Ministry of Nurture*, 65–66.

32. LeFever, *Creative Teaching Methods*, 94.

33. Ibid., 94–98.

- Teenagers learn to identify with the feelings and experiences of others.

Simulation games or activities try to reproduce some aspect of reality such as poverty, world hunger, or power struggles, often an event that is out of reach or beyond the adolescent's own life experience because of time, environment, or circumstances. Because simulation activities teach experientially, participants are likely to feel much more intently than if they were merely receiving information. For example, try the popular World Hunger simulation. Upon arriving at a banquet, group members are given a ticket signifying what they will eat. A large percentage will eat crackers and water and represent the millions of people who go to bed hungry each night. Another group might be fed plain rice, representing the multitudes that have enough food to live, but not in overabundance. Another group of teenagers might be given a full meal, obviously representing those who have the luxury of having an abundance of food available to them. Expect some from the "poor" tables to come begging at the "rich" tables. Be prepared too for some anger to be expressed because of the unfairness of the situation. After the meal is eaten, the adolescents can not only discuss their thoughts on world hunger but express their feelings as well, which will surely be influenced and affected by their allotment of food at the banquet.

Following are suggestions for the effective use of simulation activities in teaching adolescents:[34]

- *Place simulation activities within the proper context of the learning experience.* Simulations should never be used simply to fill time. Rather, they should be used as a portion of the whole learning experience.

- *Build in adequate time for debriefing and reflection.* Many simulations are powerful in their impact on the feelings of participants. Consequently, it is important to discuss the experience and to take time for the ventilation of the feelings generated.

- *Schedule in time for developing a plan of action.* If the youth group has just experienced the hunger simulation described above, sending everyone home without discussing a plan of action is achieving only part of the goal. Ideas of what can be done in response to what has been learned should be brainstormed.

34. Rice et al., *Creative Learning Experiences,* 110–12.

- *Provide opportunity for a variety of viewpoints to be shared and digested by each individual.* Learning takes place even when the results are not precisely the same as those anticipated by the facilitator, and results will be different every time the activity is played. Large groups might be broken down into smaller groups of four or five, to optimize the possibility of individual participation in discussion.

- *Play the simulation in an environment conducive to the particular activity chosen.* Often the atmosphere or environment is critical to the effect of the simulation. If the activity is simulating, for example, an underground church in a country where Christian worship is restricted, the impact will be enhanced by creating surroundings that help the participants sense the reality of worshiping in seclusion and in fear of authorities.

- *Choose activities that are respectful of the youth you are working with.* Some simulation activities are more difficult to learn than others; some take more time than others. Make sure the activity respects the ages and learning capacities of the group members.

THE VOLITIONAL DOMAIN

Real faith is more than just knowing or feeling. The "crowning aspect" of faith, as Downs puts it is the *volitional*.[35] It is the choice of the will to live or act out in obedience through one's lifestyle that which is believed (intellectual) and valued (emotional). Jesus refers to this element of faith when he says, "If you love me, you will obey what I command" (John 14:15, NIV).

A critical component of the Christian education of youth is giving the skills and confidence to examine options and make lifestyle choices that are pleasing to God. Unfortunately Scripture does not always give us clear instruction on how to respond in every ethical or moral situation. Consequently churches and parents tend to take away from adolescents the freedom of making their own lifestyle choices. Adults often want to make life painless as possible for teenagers by making choices for them, even to the point of establishing a censoring list of what movies to watch or songs to listen to. Once again, Gillespie points out that freedom is a very important reality in faith shaping. He says, "It is an essential

35. Downs, "Faith Shaping," 50.

ingredient in people who want to personalize faith. We are well aware that freedom always implies some limitations. But for religious people, freedom implies the possibility to make personal choices, or at least perceive that the choices are personal and free."[36]

While age and situation must be taken into consideration, effective youth ministry must include teaching adolescents to make wise and well-thought-out lifestyle choices. In regard to choice of music, for example, rather than censoring certain songs for listening, why not give adolescents some tools or criteria for examining lyrics and music? *Case studies* provide adolescents the opportunity to work through some of the difficult lifestyle decisions and choices in the youth group setting before they have to face them on the streets or in the locker room, where there is considerably less support.[37] Chet Meyers and Thomas Jones describe the case study as a narrative of an actual event that brings learners and teachers together in an attempt to examine, discuss, and suggest solutions to real-life problems and situations. The case study is designed so that adolescents can identify with a particular situation and the individuals described in it. The ideal studies will present a dilemma or difficult situation that youth workers hope will stimulate a variety of responses and suggestions for action from teenagers.[38]

The format for employing the case study follows a clearly defined path: (1) participants receive information about the case and study it for themselves; (2) they then participate in group discussion, together exploring possible solutions or answers to the dilemma; and finally (3) they reflect on the case, summarizing the possible solutions, as well as thoughts on their actions, attitudes, and behaviors.[39] Here is a short case study on dating:

The Sanderson family thought Gary was a fine young boy. Their fifteen-year-old daughter, Mindy, however, was forbidden to date him. Gary was Chinese. The Whites adopted him when he was only a few months old. He grew up in a typical suburban church where most of the members were Caucasian. For the most part, the church had accepted him in spite of his nationality—that is, until he wanted to date Mindy Sanderson.

36. Gillespie, *Experience of Faith,* 130.

37. Robbins, *Ministry of Nurture,* 154.

38. Meyers and Jones, *Promoting Active Learning,* 103–4.

39. Ibid., 106.

Sandersons were prominent church members; Mr. Sanderson served on the church board, and his wife was the church organist. The whole church was talking. The Sandersons considered leaving the church. They were not going to allow their daughter to date someone who was Chinese or who was of any other minority group. It was fine for Gary to participate in the church, and they were glad he was a Christian. However, when it concerned their daughter, it was a totally different matter.[40]

- What should Mindy do? What are her options?
- What are her responsibilities to her mother and father?
- What would you say to her parents?

CONCLUSION

Youth workers must be intentional in approaching faith and faith development from a biblical perspective. Certainly, some youth will make lifestyle and faith-related decisions that may not be pleasing to youth workers or parents, but in the long run they can learn to reason in a mature and biblical manner. Unfortunately well-meaning and loving teachers and workers often short-circuit the faith development of adolescents by placing prohibitions on them rather than nurturing mature decision making and providing good models for living.[41] While spiritual formation is driven primarily by a teen's willingness to allow the Holy Spirit to transform him or her, an understanding of the developmental process that takes place in the adolescent is extremely helpful in the youth worker's role in faith shaping and facilitating opportunities for spiritual growth. This chapter has addressed the spiritual task of faith shaping in the intellectual, volitional, and emotional domains. Chapter 5 addresses adolescent issues related to and impacted by the family.

40. Adapted from Rice and Yaconelli, *Tension Getters*, 49.
41. Gillespie, *Experience of Faith*, 131.

5

Adolescence and the Contemporary Family

Of the numerous groups to which adolescents belong, the family clearly is the most significant in affecting and shaping their lives. Family dynamics penetrate the very personality of an individual, significantly influence the manner in which a teenager weathers the storms of adolescence, and have a profound bearing on how a young person positively emerges into young adulthood. No other social institution or group offers an adolescent what a family does—security, affection, emotional support, and protection against a harsh and sometimes cruel world. Furthermore, empirical research indicates that critical family issues are related to a number of youth crises and destructive patterns, such as suicide, premarital sexual activity, running away from home, substance abuse, and low self-esteem. Thus, it is not only fitting but also imperative that any discussion of contemporary youth issues includes the impact the family has on the adolescent.

THE RAPIDLY CHANGING AMERICAN FAMILY

The traditional concept of family in the United States and Canada as well as much of Western culture finds its roots in Judeo-Christian heritage and has been based on the ideal of families as conjugal units. Historically, the wife was primarily a homemaker, the husband was the chief source of economic income and main source of authority, and children were a source of pride and satisfaction, expected to carry on the cycle of marriage and procreation. Often families included close relatives such as grandparents, uncles, and aunts, which meant there were generally many adults who served as role models and guardians, and shared in the child rearing process.

In the first half of the twentieth century in America the extended family was all but replaced by the nuclear family—normally one adult of each sex and two or three children. However, since the 1960s, the family has seen even more radical changes, to the point that some insist we can no longer speak of a typical family or that the family is no longer a viable unit.[1] The rate of change in living arrangements has declined since 1990,[2] however this does not mean that families are back to "normal" but simply that there are fewer major changes.

The most dramatic change comes in regard to society's view and practice of divorce. In 1885, the rate of divorce per 1,000 people was 0.6. That rate has risen steadily and peaked in 1980 when there were 5.2 divorces per 1,000. In 2014 the rate was 3.2 per 1,000, or 813,862 divorces.[3] Another trend that has considerably altered the shape of the family is the choice to remain single. The marriage rate dropped from 8.2 per 1,000 in 2000 to 6.8 per 1,000 in 2010.[4] The single or unmarried adult population includes those who have never been married as well those who are divorced, separated, widowed, or cohabitating and is the fastest-growing family type in America.

Because of these trends, children are now being reared in a variety of situations. Many, of course, are still a part of a family that includes a biological mother and a biological father, but even in many of these cases both parents work full time. Other families include at least one parent who has been married before; sometimes both have been married several times. A growing number of families are headed by a single parent—either a divorced parent or a "never-been-married" mother. Babies born to single women represent over 40.6 percent of all newborns.[5] While there are also a growing number of homosexual marriages, some of which involve the rearing of children, only 1 percent of families are characterized

1. Thornburg, *Development in Adolescence,* 148.

2. Kreider and Ellis, "Living Arrangements of Children: 2009," 3.

3. Centers for Disease Control and Prevention, *National Marriage and Divorce Rate Trends.*

4. Ibid.

5. Martin et al., "Births: Final Data for 2013."

as homosexual.[6] It is estimated that 40 percent of the youth we work with will experience the divorce of their parents.[7]

While research indicates that instability of the family and breakup of marriages has negative and destructive repercussions, there are those who acclaim and promote the transitions in family structure as described above. As early as 1972, reactionaries, especially feminists, expressed opposition to the traditional heterosexual marriage as the basis for rearing children and establishing family life. One source proposed, "The end of the institution of marriage is a necessary condition for the liberation of women. Therefore, it is important for us to encourage women to leave their husbands and not live individually with men. We must build alternatives to marriage."[8] A decade later, another writer argued that the significant changes the family has been going through should stimulate interest in new family processes and in trying new family structures such as cohabitation, part-time marriages, communes, cooperatives, and post-marital singlehood.[9]

In a 1992 edition focusing on the century to come, *Time* magazine featured an article on the family titled "The Nuclear Family Goes Boom!" The article not only predicted significant changes to come but also portrayed the nuclear family in a cynical and sardonic manner. The very term *nuclear family*, suggested the writer, gives off a musty smell and eventually will not be seen as normal but rather as a fascinating anomaly. In the future, she says, the family will look like this: "The family of the 21st century may have a robot maid, but the chances are good that it will also be interracial or bisexual, divided by divorce, multiplied by remarriage, expanded by new birth technologies—or perhaps all of the above. Single-parents and working moms will become increasingly the norm, as will out-of-wedlock babies, though there will surely be a more modern term for them. The concept of the illegitimate child will vanish because the concept of the patriarchal nuclear family will vanish."[10] Decades later, it appears that many of those predictions are coming true, though the nuclear family is still the norm.

6. Centers for Disease Control and Prevention, "Same-Sex Couple Households."

7. Santrock, *Adolescence,* 300.

8. Lehmann and Sullinger, *Document,* 11–12.

9. Thornburg, *Development in Adolescence,* 148.

10. Wallis, "Nuclear Family Goes Boom!" 42–44.

This grim analysis of where the family is today and where it may be in the years to come is a bleak reminder to the church of the formidable yet indispensable task it has of making sure the family is not rendered obsolete. While the nuclear family will not cease to exist, as many social scientists would like to suggest, we must be cognizant of the fact that many of the children and adolescents we work with will be products of nontraditional families. In addition, these youth will be shaped largely by cultural influences such as postmodernism and moral relativism, philosophies that are antithetical to Judeo-Christian teachings and values.

Much of the effectiveness of youth ministry now and in the future will be contingent on the church's and youth worker's capacity to work with parents and to strengthen the family. Researcher George Barna says the battle and opportunity for the future will be to redefine the family in a sensible manner and to insist that the standards of God's Word become the basis for family policies, systems, and teachings.[11]

THE TRAUMA OF DIVORCE

Divorce is more common today than it ever has been in the past, not only in North America but in other parts of the world as well. It can be predicted with a good degree of certainty that at least two out of every five marriages will end in separation or divorce.[12] Divorce has literally ravaged the American family, and the instability of the institution of marriage is a matter of great concern for the church and those who do ministry with adolescents.

Empirical research studies indicate that divorce has negative effects on both the emotions and behavior of children and adolescents. One of the most significant research endeavors on the impact of divorce on children and teenagers was a ten-year study carried out by Judy Wallerstein and Sandra Blakeslee. As a result of their research on 131 children from sixty families, they concluded that while most men, women, and children appear outwardly to get their life on track after divorce within two and a half to three and a half years, the profound internal changes experienced in the wake of divorce continue to affect people long after this time of resolution is over.[13]

11. Barna, *Future of the American Family*, 38.

12. Sell, *Family Ministry*, 42.

13. Wallerstein and Blakeslee, *Second Chances*, xii.

Children's fundamental attitudes about society and about themselves can be forever changed by divorce and by events experienced in the years afterward. These changes can be incorporated permanently into their developing characters and personalities. The postdivorce family and the remarried family are radically different from the original intact family. Relationships are different. Problems, satisfactions, vulnerabilities, and strengths are different. People may get their lives back on track, but for most the track runs a wholly different course than the one they were on before divorce.[14]

Among the conclusions of this study are the following:

- Children of all ages tend to feel intensely rejected when their parents divorce.

- Children tend to feel intense loneliness as most of the supports fall away.

- Many children tend to feel guilty, and think that it is their duty to bring the marriage back together.

- The severity of a child's reaction at the time of the divorce is not indicative of how a child will fare years later. Some of the most troubled children turned out emotionally healthy a decade later, while some of the least troubled were in much poorer shape ten or fifteen years later.

- Ten years after the divorce, nearly half of the boys (now between nineteen and twenty-nine) were unhappy, lonely, and had few, if any, lasting relationships with women.

- Thirty-seven percent of the children of divorce had severe problems adjusting; 29 percent were coping but not recovered, while another 34 percent adjusted adequately.

Other empirical research studies have made similar discoveries. For example, David Cline and Jack Westman found 52 percent of the families they studied continued to have hostile encounters requiring court intervention after the divorce. Nearly all of these interactions involved the children in some manner.[15]

14. Ibid.

15. Cline and Westman, "Impact of Divorce on the Family," 78–83.

In his impacting study of church youth, Merton Strommen was able to make several generalizations based on comparisons between young people who experienced divorce and those who did not. Youth whose parents are divorced or separated

- are more bothered by lack of family unity and more likely to report family pressures,

- have a lower estimate of self worth,

- have more difficulty in school studies,

- demonstrate a lower interest in religious matters.[16]

Researcher George Barna found that divorced parents are less likely to spend time with their children than married parents, in seven of eight areas:

- watching television

- doing homework or educational activities

- going out for a fun meal together

- driving to a special place that would be of interest to the kids

- playing a sport together

- experiencing a cultural activity together

- going to a movie.[17]

The only item where there was no significant difference was "spending more than thirty minutes at a time talking about life."

Children of divorce will usually encounter a number of negative emotions and feelings as they attempt to cope with the trauma of divorce. Some of the most common reactions are[18]

- guilt (I am the cause of the divorce),

- denial (this is not really happening),

- fear (what will happen to me),

- shame (I am not like other teenagers who have two parents),

- confusion (I do not know who to believe),

16. Strommen, *Five Cries of Youth*, 44.

17. Barna, *Future of the American Family*, 87.

18. Carter and Leavenworth, *Caught in the Middle*, 81.

- sadness (I cannot allow myself to be happy now),
- depression (it is hopeless),
- hurt (someone I love has disappointed me),
- blame (one of my parents is responsible for this), and
- anger (I cannot change anything and it is not fair).

How can the youth worker effectively work with adolescents from divorced homes? It is essential that adolescents verbalize their feelings related to their parents' divorce. While a youth worker can encourage teenagers to talk about their feelings by spending individual time with them, it might be better to have them join support groups where they can talk to other teenagers who have divorced parents. A youth ministry support group is a small group of five to ten individuals who share a common problem or need (in this case the commonality is divorced parents), meet on a regular basis, and covenant to give emotional, spiritual, and even physical support to each other in their struggles and hurts. Support comes by sharing their experiences, learning from one another, offering suggestions to group members, giving encouragement to each other, talking about their problems, and praying for each other. Support groups might also engage in recreational activities such as attending a baseball game together or going bowling.[19]

A critical but often overlooked dimension of youth ministry is working with parents. In the context of divorce, the youth worker might encourage adolescents and their parents to speak openly about the divorce and related issues. For example, parents and teens should talk about the future, including the parents' intentions for remarriage, living arrangements, financial arrangements, and the possibility of moving. These are all major concerns for the teenage children, but unless they are urged to, parents may avoid talking about them.[20]

As mentioned above, what teenagers experiencing divorce need most is a listening ear and someone to say, "I understand how you are feeling." However, there are some words of advice the sensitive youth worker can share with these hurting adolescents.[21]

19. It is important not to confuse a support group with psychotherapy and counseling groups. Counseling and psychotherapy groups usually focus on the alleviation of some type of problem and are professionally led. Support groups are usually led by individuals struggling with the same issues as other group members.

20. Rowatt, *Pastoral Care with Adolescents in Crisis,* 87.

21. Vigeveno and Claire, *Divorce and the Children,* 113—24.

1. *Find someone to talk to.* Besides the youth worker, they might seek out some other teenagers who have endured their parents' divorce.

2. *Do not blame yourself.* Many adolescents identify themselves as a reason for the divorce of their parents. While children may have agitated the situation or caused some family disruption, parents are adults and accountable for their own actions.

3. *Do not take sides or try to retaliate against one or both of your parents.* Retaliation often comes in the form of refusal to communicate with or see a parent.

4. *Resist the temptation to isolate yourself.* While some private time for reflection is important, shutting themselves in a room and pouting or allowing themselves to get depressed is unhealthy for teenagers.

5. *Try not to agitate the situation.* Perhaps the thinking is, if I stir up enough trouble, they will get back together. However, in such family situations there is enough trouble and disharmony already.

6. *Look for help and friendship in the right places.* Church youth groups, Christian friends, Christian camps, and good sports programs can all be effective in providing the teenager with healthy surroundings.

The "divorce panel" is a teaching procedure that Mike Yaconelli and Jim Burns suggest can help all youth group members better understand the effects of divorce. It can be a supportive experience for youth whose parents are already divorced, it can help teenagers currently going through a divorce experience to better understand what is happening, and it can teach other youth group members how to help a friend whose parents are divorced or divorcing.

The first step is to ask several teenagers whose parents are divorced to serve on a panel. Give them a list of possible questions, so that they can make a decision as to whether they can handle the experience. If they decide the activity would be too difficult for them, give them the privilege of declining.

Select an adult to moderate the panel. This person should be sensitive to the pain that most adolescent children of divorce would be experiencing. Make sure the moderator does research and is well prepared to understand the effects of divorce. Here are some sample questions youth members might ask of the panel:

- How did you find out your parents were going to get a divorce?

- Did the way in which you were told of your parents' divorce help or hinder your acceptance of it?

- Did your role in the family change in any way after the divorce? How?

- What kinds of things did friends and peers do or say in response to the divorce? Is there anything you wish they had done or said?[22]

FAMILY CONFLICT AND PROBLEM SITUATIONS

As unfortunate and difficult as divorce is for many adolescents, acute family problems are not confined to children of divorce. For many youth, parent-youth conflicts, father absenteeism, abuse, distrustful parents, or overly authoritative parents characterize home life. Merton Strommen insists that the most poignant cry of adolescents is that of despair or sheer frustration that comes from living in atmospheres of parental hatred and distrust.[23] Such distress sometimes results in teens running away from home, in teen suicide or in attempted suicide, in delinquent behavior, and in low self-esteem.

Strommen's study of church youth found that one in five teenagers could be placed in the category of experiencing a troubled home situation. These "psychological orphans," as he describes them, demonstrate four major characteristics:[24]

- family pressures such as divorce or separation of parents, illness, financial pressures, father absenteeism, unemployment, death, and parent-youth strife;

- distress over parental relationships such as lack of communication and understanding with parents, feelings of being treated as a child, overly strict parents, and parental distrust and rejection;

- family disunity, including a lack of closeness and oneness of family members; and

- lack of concern among members—some troubled youth do not see their parents as caring people.

22. Adapted from Yaconelli and Burns, *High School Ministry*, 193–94.
23. Strommen, *Five Cries of Youth*, 41.
24. Ibid., 44.

Some of these family situations will be explored in this section.

Stressed and Dysfunctional Families

In addition to divorced families, there are a number of other family types that might be considered stressed or dysfunctional in nature. Most stressed and dysfunctional family situations lead to some at-risk behavior from the teenager. Some of the family types that may place all family members—but certainly adolescent children—under moderate to extreme stress are single-parent families, blended families, absentee (latchkey) families, substance-abusing families, families experiencing violence and conflict, and father-absent families.

Single-parent Families

One of the most troublesome and widespread family dysfunctions is the single-parent family. In the United States approximately 29.5 percent of children under eighteen live in a single-parent home, the majority of these living with the mother.[25] The effects of living in a single-parent household can be quite devastating. One study found that children of single mothers were more likely

- to have repeated a grade in school
- to have been expelled from school
- to have been treated for emotional and behavioral problems.[26]

Merton and Irene Strommen compared responses of single parents to responses of parents in intact families (where there has not been separation, divorce, or death) in regard to the well-being of their children. More single parents than parents of intact families,

- rated their child in the direction of being disobedient, rebellious, likely to get in trouble, disrespectful of authority, and not a good student;
- used extreme measures of discipline—either being too lenient or reacting in anger by yelling or hitting the child; and

25. U.S. Bureau of the Census, "Statistical Abstract of the United States: 2009."
26. Dawson, "Family Structure and Children's Health and Well-Being," 573–84.

- were less active in church and community organizations—something that held true for their children as well.[27]

The Search Institute compared at-risk behaviors of children from single-parent families to at-risk behaviors of children living in two-parent families. The researchers concluded that youth in single-parent families are, on the average, clearly more at risk than adolescents from two-parent families. For example, the percentage of adolescents who have experienced sexual intercourse at least twice rises from 35 percent (two-parent families) to 53 percent (one-parent families). The percent of adolescents who have attempted suicide once or more jumps from 12 percent (two parents) to 19 percent (one parent). On twenty at-risk behaviors (other behaviors include illicit drug use, alcohol use, binge drinking, depression, fighting, theft, school absenteeism) this pattern remains consistent. The authors conclude that whether we are looking at males or females, younger or older adolescents, whites or ethnic minorities, teenagers in one-parent families tend to engage in risk-taking behaviors with greater frequency than do adolescents in intact, two-parent families.[28]

An effective way to work with teenagers in single-parent families is to involve them in the larger church community. One strategy is to divide the church into "family pods" where people of different ages and from different family structures are clustered in "family" groups for lessons, socials, and other activities.[29] In these group structures adolescents from single-parent families have the opportunity to be in close proximity to intact families.

A "buddy program" is a good way to provide role models for adolescents in single-parent families. In this program, adults in the church or parish volunteer to periodically spend time with teenagers from single-parent families.[30] If, for example, a male adolescent lives in a home without a father, a man in the church might volunteer to do something with this young person from time to time. They could attend a baseball game, go fishing, work on a car, or play tennis. The activities they engage in, of course, would depend on the interests and abilities of the parties involved.

27. Strommen and Strommen, *Five Cries of Parents*, 25.

28. Benson and Roehlkepartain, *Youth in Single-Parent Families*, 7–8, 17.

29. Pancoast and Bobula, "Building Multigenerational Support Networks," 180.

30. Sell, *Family Ministry*, 330.

Blended Families

Blended families, also known as reconstituted or stepparent families, are those in which one or both of the remarried partners bring children into the new family relationship. As divorce and remarriage become more common, the number of children living in blended families progressively increases. Given the growing rate of divorce and remarriage this trend will likely continue.

Citing a Search Institute study, Merton Strommen reported more adolescents in stepfamilies evidenced deviant behavior, erotic activities, parent-youth conflict, and identity and achievement problems. In addition more of these youth felt they received less parental affection and nurturance, and either more authoritarian or permissive treatment.[31]

Several additional problems may emerge in reconstituted families. First, children may become confused living with a stepmother or stepfather while their biological parent lives elsewhere. In other words, a difficulty may exist in determining the proper relationship between the child and stepparent, and divided loyalties will certainly exist. A second source of difficulty may be an unrealistic expectation on the part of the stepparent, such as the equal sharing in each other's lives. Finally, stepchildren are often more tolerant of the mistakes of their natural parents than those of stepparents. Thus, they may enter a blended family situation with suspicion, overcautiousness, and resentfulness. Stepparents may initially try very hard to be loving and caring, but when they are rebuffed, they tend to retreat to a less active parenting role.[32]

Once again, ministry to youth must include ministry to parents. How parents handle the dynamics of a blended family powerfully impacts the spiritual and emotional development of their adolescent children. Needed for both adolescents and adults of single-parent and blended families are classes on relating to one another, on creating a close family life, on communicating with one another, and most important, on praying and sharing faith with one another.[33]

Parent education has become extremely popular in churches. Many such programs focus on teaching parents attitudes, knowledge, and skills critical to successful adolescent rearing. Parents learn how to listen to their teenage children, how to communicate so that they will be heard,

31. Strommen, *Five Cries of Youth,* 65.

32. Balswick and Balswick, *Family,* 267–69.

33. Strommen, *Five Cries of Youth,* 66.

how to effectively discipline, how to instill responsibility in adolescents, and how to nurture spiritual growth.[34]

One such program is the Parent Effectiveness Training (PET) program developed by Thomas Gordon. Convinced that most parents desire to rear emotionally balanced children but often lack the knowledge and skills to do so, Gordon developed a systematic program of training for the task of parenthood. In these classes parents are taught effective forms of communication such as active listening, empathetic open-ended questioning, and reflecting of feelings. They also learn methods of preventing conflicts between parents and children as well as conflict resolution.[35]

Parents in all types of family structures must see the need for developing and nurturing a supportive network of relationships for themselves and their children. Parent networks are initiated by linking parents with one another so that they can share common problems, questions, concerns, experiences, and activities. The following activities might be included in a supportive parent network:[36]

- Contact and become acquainted with the parents of youe teenage children's friends.

- Talk with other parents about some of your concerns. (What movies are you allowing your children to watch? What guidelines or rules do you have for dating?)

- Meet together to talk over shared concerns (e.g., drugs and alcohol in the school).

- Swap services such as chaperoning activities or transporting children to school or church activities.

- Cooperate to offer alternative activities to those in which parents feel their teenagers should not be involved (such as a party instead of a rock concert).

- Offer each other help in times of crisis (perhaps a meal during sickness).

- Provide nurture and support to the adolescent children of others.

34. Garland, "Developing and Empowering Parent Networks," 92.
35. Gordon, *Parent Effectiveness Training*.
36. Garland, "Developing and Empowering Parent Networks," 91–101.

Absentee (Latchkey) Families

On any given weekday in the United States and Canada, between the hours of 3:00 p.m. and 6:00 p.m., millions of children and young adolescents are left without adult supervision. In the United States, estimates of the number of unsupervised children vary from two to fifteen million, or between 7 and 45 percent of all elementary-school children. However, there are also appreciable numbers of preschool children and adolescents who must provide such self-care, and authorities maintain that the number of latchkey children will continue to increase.[37] Absentee families are those in which the parents are not available to their children before or after school and on school holidays. Unsupervised children often have a house key to let themselves into their homes independently after school. At least three factors contribute to the absentee or latchkey phenomenon. First, the number of mothers in the workforce continues to grow. Second, single-parent families have become a norm. Third, affordable childcare is seldom available. With the increasing number of children and adolescents supervising themselves, professionals interested in the welfare of children have raised concern about the consequences of being in self-care. Frances Dowd summarizes the detrimental impact of the latchkey experience on children and adolescents as follows. They are prone to[38]

- a high incidence of loneliness, fear, stress, and conflict,
- increased use of drugs and alcohol;
- unsupervised television viewing
- increased sexual activity
- risking their safety (research indicates that children are more likely to be seriously injured when they do not have an adult caregiver available)
- difficulties in school.

Many parents, but especially single parents, agonize over the fact that they have many demands on them and do not have adequate time for supporting and exercising proper supervision over their children and teenagers. Given the fact that many parents have no choice in the matter of work and that the number of latchkey children will rise, perhaps

37. Dowd, *Latchkey Children in the Library & Community*, 6–7.
38. Ibid., 13–18.

it is time for churches and youth ministries to consider the possibility of after-school programs. While many organizations and institutions are offering supervision and activities for elementary-age children, there are few programs offered to teenagers.

Youth ministries that desire to take advantage of the opportunity to reach out to adolescents of absentee families might consider the following activities in an after-school program:

- sports and games
- tutoring and homework assistance
- counseling
- music and art
- Bible studies.

Extended Families

The number of children and adolescents living with grandparents continues to rise. An estimated 2.5 percent of children live with their grandparents and without the presence of a biological parent.[39] This does not reflect the growing number of single parent families that reside with grandparents.

Substance-Abusing Families

Children and adolescents from homes of drug- or alcohol-abusing parents are at extreme risk for abuse, neglect, and emotional damage. Empirical studies relate substance abuse by parents to family problems such as physical abuse[40] and denial of clothing, food, and education to children.[41] Children of alcoholic parents may also exhibit antisocial behavior, experience problems with the law, and have difficulties at school.[42]

Two self-help or recovery groups that operate throughout the United States and Canada for family members of alcoholics are Alateen (for teenage children of alcoholics) and Al-Anon (for family and friends of

39. Kreider and Ellis, "Living Arrangements of Children: 2009," 4.

40. Kempe and Kempe, *Child Abuse*, 69.

41. Worick and Warren, *Alcohol, Tobacco and Drugs*, 10.

42. Jesse et al., *Interpersonal Effects of Alcohol Abuse*, 58–61.

alcoholics). In these recovery groups family members of alcoholics meet together much as alcoholics thelseves do in the twelve-step Alcoholics Anonymous.[43] Participants learn about alcoholism, exchange feelings and experiences, are helped to increase their self-esteem, and are taught to rely on a higher power. Through the sharing of common problems, members of alcoholics' families find that they are not alone and that they do have the power and ability to cope with and overcome their difficulties.[44]

Parental Violence and Conflict

Merton P. Strommen insists that by far the most decisive variable in identifying hurting youth and families is whether parents are at odds with each other. Conversely, one of the predictors of greater family unity is the degree of parental accord. Strommen found that only about half the population of church youth reported accord between their parents.[45] According to another study of church youth by the Search Institute, serious conflict and violence are regular occurrences in 5 to 10 percent of the homes, and less frequent in many more.[46]

The degree of violence between spouses correlates directly with the severity of the child's problems, including destruction of the child's self-esteem and confidence, the child's svulnerability to stress disorders, and other psychological disturbances.[47] In the aforementioned Search Institute study, a measure of spousal violence was constructed and compared to other elements of family life. The investigators found that family harmony, high quality of life, and family closeness were unlikely to accompany a family life characterized by violence. On the other hand, abuse of the child, coercive methods of discipline, and child-authority conflict were often present.[48]

---

43. Alcoholics Anonymous is a popular recovery program for alcoholics based on twelve steps developed by Bill Wilson. The twelve-step format has been adapted for a myriad of other dysfunctions and addictions. These support-and-recovery groups are easily put into a Christian context by making it clear that the "Higher Power" they refer to is Jesus Christ.

44. For information concerning Al-Anon and Alateen access http://al-anon.ala-teen.org/for-alateen/.

45. Strommen, *Five Cries of Youth*, 53–54.

46. Benson et al., *Quicksilver Years*, 194.

47. McWhirter et al., *At-Risk Youth*, 52.

48. Benson et al., *Quicksilver Years*, 194–95.

Father Absenteeism

With the diminishing presence of the traditional family, father-absentee-ism is on the increase. In most cases father-absenteeism occurs because of divorce and separation, but even with intact families, father absence has become more frequent (the father who spends little or relatively little time with his family). In fact, Christopher Anderson asserts that almost every adult American alive today has been reared in his or her father's absence.[49] Thus, in many, if not most, homes, parenting is primarily the task of the mother.

When the father's presence is not felt at home, development of traits such as independence and achievement orientation are impeded.[50] Further, there is increased likelihood for youth violence,[51] a deterioration of school performance,[52] dependent and submissive personality features,[53] and retardation in sex-role and masculinity development. Father absence also appears to be a major factor in the development of homosexuality among males.[54] On the other hand, David Blankenhorn concludes that "paternal investment enriches children in four ways. First it provides them with a father's physical protection. Second, it provides them with a father's money and other material resources. Third, and probably most important, it provides them with what might be termed paternal cultural transmission: a father's distinctive capacity to contribute to the identity, character, and competence of his children. Fourth, and most obviously, paternal investment provides children with the day-to-day nurturing—feeding them, playing with them, telling them a story—that they want and need from both of their parents."[55] Clearly the well-being of adolescent children depends pivotally on the high level of fatherly investment. Teenagers who experience father absenteeism in one form or another especially need male youth workers who serve as role models and provide the presence of a father figure.

49. Anderson, *Father, the Figure and the Force,* 37.

50. Sebald, *Adolescence,* 42.

51. Blankenhorn, *Fatherless America,* 26–32.

52. Lamb, "Fathers and Child Development," 28.

53. Sebald, *Adolescence,* 42.

54. Biller, "Father and Sex Role Development," 320–35.

55. Blankenhorn, *Fatherless America,* 25.

Parent-Teen Conflict

It is not uncommon for teenagers to be at odds, at least to some degree, with one or both of their parents. Strommen, for example, found that one in four teenagers reported trouble getting along with the father, and of these nearly half were at odds with the mother.[56] Another study found that only half the teenage population surveyed claimed they were very close to their parents. Furthermore, the strength of the relationship deteriorated as the teenager grew older.[57]

Not everyone agrees that a struggle between parents and their teenage children is inevitable or an accurate characterization of adolescence. In fact, there is more evidence than concerned parents realize indicating that teenagers are often satisfied with their parents as well as with their family situations. For example, the Search Institute found that for young adolescents at least, there is relatively little parent-youth conflict. Although the amount of conflict increases slightly between each of the school years from the fifth grade through the ninth grade, only a minority of young adolescents reported any major conflict. When parents were questioned, similar findings were evident.[58]

Psychologist Albert Bandura argues that the "storm and stress" of adolescence—which includes conflict with parents—is largely exaggerated, and that in most middle-class families both parents and teenagers are relatively satisfied with their relationships with one another. In his study of young boys, Bandura found that (1) the parents tended to be trustful of their children, (2) independence was largely completed before adolescence, and (3) the boys tended to choose friends who shared similar value systems and behavioral norms. His conclusion was that intergenerational conflict was minimal.

Bandura explains some of the difference between his theory and traditional thinking: (1) nonconformity and fad behavior is wrongly characterized as rebellion, (2) the media mistakenly sensationalize the "storm and stress" view of adolescence, (3) generalizations have been made from studies of delinquent adolescents, and (4) if one accepts the premise that youth are rebellious, one stands behind a self-fulfilling prophecy.[59] Bandura would not leave us with the notion that adolescence is free from

56. Strommen, *Five Cries of Youth*, 47.

57. Barna Research Group, *Today's Teens*, 8.

58. Benson et al., *Quicksilver Years*, 38.

59. Bandura, "Stormy Decade," 22.

stress or without conflict; rather, he suggests that much of the conduct of teenagers that is characterized as rebellious is consistent with natural adolescent development and normal social behavior. For example, it is entirely appropriate for adolescents to need space away from the family, to experience mood changes, to spend more time with peers, and to adhere to beliefs different from those of their parents.

Although there may be much truth to the notion that parent-youth conflict is exaggerated, and while serious antagonism may not be the mark of many relationships, most families will experience at least some conflict. In other words, a certain amount of strife between teenagers and their parents is inevitable. The intensity of this conflict will likely be progressive—that is, it will increase with the age of the adolescent.[60] There are several reasons one can anticipate a certain amount of conflict or struggle between parents and teenagers during the adolescent years. These reasons include overprotection, parental distrust, rigid authoritarianism, poor parent-teen communication, and the adolescent struggle for autonomy.

Parental Overprotection

As adolescents grow older, they become increasingly independent, meaning that parental influence wanes. Many parents, however, have a difficult time adjusting to the fact that their teenagers are no longer little children. Thus, from the perspective of most adolescents, much parent-teen conflict exists because parents treat them like little children. Overprotective or helicopter parents offer consistent support, but they do so with many rules and regulations, inappropriate emotional involvement, and high levels of anxiety. These parents might be comparable to a mother or father bear protecting a cub from a hostile environment. While the inclination to protect is a parental instinct, and a certain amount of protection is desirable and admirable, overprotection can be life denying to the adolescent child. It robs the teenager of natural social, spiritual, and intellectual development, and of course is the source of much conflict in the life of the youth.

---

60. Benson, et al., *Quicksilver Years*, 39; and Sebald, *Adolescence*, 134.

Distrustful Parents

Feelings of mistrust by parents of their teenagers are a potent factor in family conflict, says Merton Strommen. In fact, his study found that parental distrust is nineteen times more likely to predict family disunity than divorce. His empirical data also demonstrate a positive correlation between suicide and a youth's feeling of being distrusted. In other words, the percentage of teenagers who consider killing themselves grows in direct relation to a teenager's feeling of not being trusted. Conversely, parental trust—along with open communication and parental accord—is singled out as a strong predictor of family unity.[61] In a survey of professional workers (i.e., counselors), respondents identified "a sense of trust" as fourth in a list of fifty-six characteristics of a healthy family.[62]

What can parents do to nurture or reclaim the trust of their adolescent children? Parents should be encouraged to allow their teens to move toward a healthy independence. They should give them age-appropriate choices yet hold them responsible for the consequences of their choices.[63] In addition, parents should allow teenagers greater involvement in decision making in family matters, although parents should not surrender final authority on such issues.

Rigid Authoritarianism

In an overly strict home, parents and teens don't discuss problems: rather parents simply tell teens what must be done. In an overly strict home, parents nag teens and pry into their lives. In an overly strict home, parents disapprove of their teenager's friends. In an overstrict home a power struggle will likely emerge between parents and teenage children.[64] Overly rigid parents may appear cruel in their interactions with their children, have a large number of rules and regulations, and enforce them in a cold and precise manner. Sometimes these parents appear to enjoy punishing their adolescent children for misbehavior.[65]

---

61. Strommen, *Five Cries of Youth,* 51–54.
62. Curran, *Traits of a Healthy Family,* 99.
63. Bibby and Posterski, *Teen Trends,* 216.
64. Strommen, *Five Cries of Youth,* 48.
65. McWhirter et al., *At-Risk Youth,* 57.

Youth reared in an overly strict, authoritarian home are more likely to reject traditional moral standards, involve themselves in acts of rebellion, and reject a personal faith.[66] These young people may also display fear and rejection of authority figures or adopt highly delinquent behavior.[67] Finally, an authoritarian home life may contribute to running away. Homes of many runaways are characterized by excessively rigid family rules and regulations, and by little or no planning or sharing of family activities and responsibilities.[68]

Some adolescents may perceive that their parents are overly strict when, in fact, this is not the case. Sometimes negative peer influence is the cause of a teenager's notion that his or her parents are overly strict. The youth pastor can play a significant role in helping misguided teenagers to understand the importance of parental authority and guidelines, as well as the need to obey and respect all authority. For example, if a young teenager comes to a youth worker complaining about her curfew time being unfair, the worker can explain to the adolescent why this parental regulation is not only fair but also important. The youth worker might encourage the adolescent in understanding that such parameters exist because of the love her parents have for her, and are designed to protect and nurture her.

Readers must not infer, however, that there should be a lack of parental control in the home. While adolescents in an overly strict home may develop undesirable behaviors, the same is likely when overpermissiveness is the norm. Ideally, parents should strike a balance between exercising consistency, firm rules, and discipline with trust and freedom appropriate to the age, maturity, and responsibility of the teenager. Strommen determined from his study of adolescents that teenagers given authoritative and firm guidelines along with increasing freedom to make personal decisions were more likely to reflect a strong self-esteem, embrace the Christian faith, and become more involved in serving other people.[69]

66. Strommen, *Five Cries of Youth*, 49.

67. McWhirter, et al., *At-Risk Youth*, 59.

68. Burgess, *Youth at Risk*, 10.

69. Strommen, *Five Cries of Youth*, 49.

Poor Communication

In a revealing study of three thousand teenagers and their families conducted by Gordon Sebine, 79 percent of the parents involved reported that they were communicating well with their teenagers. On the other hand, in a complete reversal, 81 percent of the teenagers said that their parents were not communicating with them.[70] This study indicates (1) that there is little common understanding between parents and teenagers as to what good communication is, and (2) that a large percentage of adolescents recognize the need for better communication in the home.[71]

Other empirical studies divulge information that suggests parent-teen communication to be a major source of family trouble. The Barna Research Group found that among teenagers whose fathers are living in the home, the average amount of time the teenager spent with the father discussing things that matter to the teen is less than forty minutes per week. (That amounts to a little over five minutes a day.) With the mother the teen averages fifty-five minutes per week.[72] Fathers have long been know as shirkers of the responsibility of communicating with their children—excusing themselves because of their jobs and because males are supposed to be less intimate and relational than females.

This communication problem is no doubt compounded by the fact that today many mothers are likewise absorbed in the pursuit of careers and higher education. One-third of the church youth in Strommen's study were bothered by their inability to communicate with their mother.[73] Peter Benson, Dorothy Williams, and Arthur Johnson conclude from their empirical research study of early adolescents that both parents and young people want to talk about issues, interests, and problems, but in only a few families does this take place, and then it is not often or long enough.[74]

The results of poor communication between teenagers and their parents may be more severe than either parents or youth workers realize. A study of runaways in Los Angeles County revealed that almost three-quarters of the young people said they ran away because of communication problems with their parents—more than those who identified

---

70. Cited in Dausey, "Communication Killers," 226.

71. Neff, "Communication and Relationships," 162.

72. Barna Research Group, *Today's Teens*, 10.

73. Strommen, *Five Cries of Youth*, 47.

74. Benson et al., *Quicksilver Years*, 212–13.

divorce or separation, physical abuse, or sexual abuse.[75] A similar investigation by Ann Burgess for the National Center for Missing and Exploited Children found that almost all the runaways in her study had engaged in a serious argument with one or both parents.[76]

One of the goals of ministry should be to assist in the improvement of communication between teenagers and their parents. Blake Neff suggests using the following strategies to enable the youth pastor to accomplish this goal:[77]

1. *Model effective communication.* Youth workers will want to begin by modeling effective communication skills to both the adolescents in the youth group and their parents. Reading nonverbal messages, speaking through appropriate touch, making good eye contact, and asking open-ended questions (questions that cannot be answered with a simple yes or no) are some techniques that will aid greatly in teaching communication skills.

2. *Develop a ministry of presence.* Communication and relationships go hand in hand; thus, youth workers must concentrate on simply being available to teenagers or parents. By this ministry of presence, the youth worker says, "I care about you, and I am interested in being a part of your world." Often the most effective time a youth worker can spend with either parents or teenagers will be outside the formal educational setting. Meeting with a youth group member over the lunch hour or in a restaurant after youth meetings are effective ways to develop relationships. The youth worker will do well to realize that parents too have interests outside the church. Finding out what these interests are and finding ways to participate in them help the youth worker earn the right to gain an audience with parents. Special attention should be given to search out and identify the interests of parents who are not a part of the regular church community.

3. *Educate in communication.* Many young people and parents are either unsure of what effective communication is or have never taken the time to learn effective communication skills. An effective church ministry to youth and their parents might include programs that

75. Rothman, *Runaway & Homeless Youth*, 75.

76. Burgess, *Youth at Risk*, 10.

77. Neff, "Communication and Relationships," 174–75.

teach communication skills such as nonverbal communication, listening and attending, and asking questions.[78]

4. *Facilitate communication.* Often church ministries and programs minimize communication between young people and their parents. The effective youth pastor will plan for some intergenerational activities that bring parents and teens together. Fathers and sons might do some outdoor or adventure camping together while mothers and daughters meet for a luncheon. A sport such as a softball or volleyball is a possibility. Another idea might be an open or panel discussion on an issue pertinent to both parents and adolescents such as choice of music or substance use and abuse.

Struggle for Autonomy

In 1952 developmental psychologist Robert Havinghurst drew up a list of developmental tasks appropriate to the various stages of life. He described a developmental task as a task that arises at a certain period in the life of an individual, of which successful achievement leads to happiness and to success with subsequent tasks, while failure leads to unhappiness, disapproval by society, and difficulty with later tasks. Several of the tasks identifiable with adolescence are related to gaining autonomy from parental control. These include achieving emotional independence from parents, achieving assurance of economic independence, selecting and preparing for an occupation, and preparing for marriage and family life.[79]

Unfortunately, while gaining autonomy is a natural part of adolescent development, it is often an origin of conflict between adolescents and their parents, and a source of stress for both. In fact, Anna Freud concluded that it may not be the teenager who experiences the greater stress but rather the "parents who need help and guidance so as to be able to bear with him [because] there are so few situations in life which are more difficult to cope with than an adolescent son or daughter during the attempt to liberate themselves."[80]

Stephen Small and associates discovered that while mothers and fathers experienced an equal amount of stress resulting from adolescent

78. The youth worker who would like to teach communication skills to parents and youth will find helpful insights in Atkinson, *Power of Small Groups*, 223–66.

79. Havinghurst, *Developmental Tasks and Education*, 6–96.

80. Quoted in Small et al., "Adolescent Autonomy and Parental Stress," 378.

autonomy, they experienced stress for two very different reasons. Fathers reported greater stress as a result of teen nonadherence to parental advice and the adolescent's involvement in deviant behaviors. Mothers, on the other hand, were stressed more because of their child's desire and demands for more autonomy.[81]

The task of growing up includes acquiring the skills to act independently, making one's own decisions, and being accountable for one's own actions. For parents, allowing a teen to gain autonomy means letting go absolute control, and for adolescents this means assuming more responsibility. It is a process that begins in preadolescence and gradually gains momentum through the teenage years.

The adolescent or young adult is developmentally successful when autonomy is achieved in three areas—the emotional, the behavioral, and the ideational. In regard to *affective* autonomy, the teenager lessens emotional ties to parents and family, and increases bonds of love, affection, care, and support with nonfamilial individuals. This is not to suggest that all bonds with parents will be severed. Attachments such as care and affection can and should continue to exist between parents and teenagers, but adolescents will become less dependent on parents as a primary or sole source of emotional support.

A second area of autonomy is *behavioral* in nature. The teenager has acquired both the skills and boldness to take part in activities or tasks he or she wants to. For example, the adolescent should now be able to drive the car, hold down a job, go shopping alone, or prepare a meal. Along with the ability to carry out tasks or activities without direct parental supervision comes increased decision-making freedom. Finally, *ideational* autonomy is achieved whereby the adolescent works through and establishes personal convictions and beliefs.[82]

Stress between parents and adolescents may emerge because although self-governance and independent decision-making are expected and normative, there may be disagreement between parent and adolescent as to the speed and circumstance with which these new forms of behavior are assumed.[83] For example, a teenage daughter may feel that upon receiving her driving license she should be able to drive the family car without supervision. Her parents, on the other hand, may insist

81. Ibid.
82. Sebald, *Adolescence,* 133.
83. Small et al., "Adolescent Autonomy and Stress," 379.

that she does not drive the car unsupervised until she turns seventeen. The difficult task for parents is in finding the right balance between freedom and control. If too much control on the parent's part is a source of parent-adolescent conflict, too much or unbridled freedom may result in irresponsibility or abusive behavior on the part of the teenager.

The goal of moving a son or daughter toward healthy autonomy actually starts in the preteen years when parents gradually give children age-appropriate choices. For example, while a mother may dictate what a six-year-old wears to school, a preadolescent twelve-year-old should be given a certain amount of freedom in choice of clothes. As preadolescents move into the teenage years, they should be given more freedom to make their own decisions. Adolescents should be given freedom to make decisions related to eating and sleeping. As long as they are eating nourishing foods, they might be allowed to choose their own diet. Perhaps they could also be included in planning the family menus and cooking the food.[84]

However, teenagers must realize that consequences come with these choices, so rather than nagging teens about completing homework, parent might offer occasional reminders and comments about the consequences of not being diligent with studies. Ultimately, the only way to really learn how to make independent decisions is to actually make them, and then to live with the consequences.[85]

Teenagers can also be given greater involvement in family decision-making. They might be included in planning vacations, choosing a particular place of worship, or making decisions about moving. It should be understood that involving adolescents in making decisions relevant to them does not mean that parents relinquish final authority on family matters. Nor does it mean, as mentioned earlier, that emotional support is altogether withdrawn. It does mean, however, that there is less telling and more empowering and equipping. It is the parents' responsibility to make sure the adolescents have sufficient information related to the issue at hand, and to allow the teenager to make the decision.[86]

---

84. An excellent source of help for moving a teenager towards autonomy is Koteskey, *Understanding Adolescence*.

85. Ibid., 36.

86. Ibid.

Child Abuse

One of the tragedies facing children and adolescents today is abuse. Statistics indicate that the rate of child abuse is on the upswing. It is almost impossible, however, to know whether there is actually an increase in abuse or if other factors simply make it appear to be so. First, it is difficult to determine if rates of reported abuse are rising because of an actual increase of abuse, or because of an increased sensitivity among professionals working with children and adolescents and their families. Second, a continual change in the definition of child abuse along with constant revisions of laws related to abuse tend to broaden the definition of child abuse.

Four major types of abuse have been defined: *sexual, physical, parental neglect,* and *emotional.* Sexual abuse is defined as the exploitation of an adolescent for the sexual gratification of an adult, and includes fondling of the genitals, exhibitionism, incest, and rape.[87] Physical abuse includes harmful actions such as slapping, choking, punching, cutting, or burning. Parental neglect involves the harming of an adolescent through lack of care or supervision. Emotional abuse refers to parental behavior and actions that jeopardize a teenager's patience, ability to set reasonable goals, interpersonal skills, or self-esteem.[88] It includes punishing normal social behaviors and consistently putting the adolescent in negative light.

There are problems with both defining abuse and subsequently accurately estimating or reporting the incidence of abuse. At what point does parental discipline become abusive? Must a parent's behavior result in injury in order to be considered abusive? At what point should a distinction be made between abusive and nonabusive parental behavior? Perhaps more difficult than defining the issue of child abuse is the measuring of occurrence or incidence of abuse. Part of the problem lies in the fact that there appear to be no clear distinctions of what constitutes child abuse and what constitutes neglect. More significant is the problem of underreporting. While all states have passed legislation requiring the reporting of child abuse and neglect, fewer than one-fourth of all cases are actually reported.[89] Nonetheless, in spite of the ambiguity of defining and identifying cases of abuse, there is substantial evidence available suggesting adolescent abuse is a serious problem. In 2013 public social service

87. Burgess and Richardson, "Child Abuse during Adolescence," 127.

88. Ibid., 128.

89. Ibid., 129.

and child protection agencies in the United States reported 679,000 cases of child abuse or neglect, including 1,520 fatalities.[90] A large proportion of these abused children were adolescents.

Sexual Abuse

While it is very difficult to talk about and more difficult for a society to acknowledge, sexual abuse of children and youth is a common occurrence in the United States. Numbers regarding reports of sexual abuse from the Children's Bureau demonstrate over sixty thousand incidents of sexual abuse were reported in 2013.[91] Family members commit the greater proportion of offenses. Of these, father-daughter incest accounts for 75 percent of family-related sexual abuse cases, with mother-son, father-son, mother-daughter, and brother-sister incest accounting for the remaining fourth.[92] Experts estimate that ninety women out of every one thousand have been sexually victimized by a family member, and five to ten women out of every thousand have had an incestuous relationship with their father at some point in their childhood or adolescent years.[93]

The number of reported cases of sexual abuse is only the tip of the iceberg, as many incidences go unreported. Fear of social disapproval, embarrassment and shame, and the fact that no physical harm may have been done discourage many children and adolescents from reporting sexual abuse. They may feel that their parents will blame them, they may be apprehensive about losing their family, they may feel guilty themselves for any pleasure they might have experienced, they may fear repercussions from the perpetrator, or they may experience shame as a result of the abuse. Consequently the incidence of sexual abuse are surely far greater than the statistics indicate and no doubt more widespread than physical abuse.

Incest in the United States seems to be on the increase in recent years, and significant changes in family life and structure might be contributing to this increase. Henry Kempe, an expert on various kinds of child and adolescent abuse, argues that rising divorce rates, birth control,

90. U.S. Department of Health and Human Services, "Child maltreatment 2013," 20.

91. Ibid., 23.

92. Kempe, "Sexual Abuse," 100.

93. Finkelhor, "Psychological, Cultural and Family Factors," 263.

abortion, and increasing tolerance for sexual acts between consenting household members who are blood related likely contribute to the increased rate of sexual abuse.[94]

As one might naturally expect, the effects of sexual abuse in the teenager are devastating. Some of the consequences include[95]

- serious rebellion, especially against the mother
- unforgiveness (girls may eventually forgive their fathers but rarely forgive their mothers, who failed to protect them.)
- serious delinquency
- extremely low-self esteem ("I am a whore.")
- prostitution and running away
- chronic depression, social isolation
- pregnancy, venereal disease, and drug abuse.

Sexual abuse is linked to running away from home. According to an empirical study of runaway youth by Ann Burgess, 70 percent of the female runaways and nearly 40 percent of the male runaways had been sexually abused.[96] Yet another study found that one-fourth reported that they ran away from home because of sexual abuse.[97] The consensus in the past among researchers has been that the majority of incestuous families come from the lower end of the socioeconomic scale. More recent studies indicate, however, that sexual abuse crosses all social strata, and there is a growing awareness of middle-class incest.

The first task of the youth worker is identifying adolescents who have suffered from some form of sexual abuse. Teenagers may make it rather difficult to detect that sexual abuse has taken place. While victims often want to be identified and assisted, the embarrassment of letting others know may cause them to cover it up. Youth workers might use questionnaires to discover high-risk adolescents. Whether the issue is sexual abuse, suicide, or drug abuse, a personal-response sheet that gives adolescents an opportunity to identify their involvement with the issue can be helpful. Information should remain anonymous unless students

---

94. Kempe, "Sexual Abuse," 100.
95. Ibid., 104.
96. Burgess, *Youth at Risk*, 11.
97. Rothman, *Runaway & Homeless Youth*, 75.

choose to fill in their names and indicate that they would like an opportunity to meet with a counselor

Youth workers must understand the legal responsibility to report
sexual abuse. In all states and most countries, sexual abuse is a criminal act, yet youth workers are not required in all states to report abuse.
However, there are states, such as California, where the law requires reporting. Youth workers should contact their local police department or
social service agencies to obtain information and requirements regarding
reporting in their area. Every state has at least one agency mandated to
receive and investigate reports. That agency is usually called the Department of Social Services, the Department of Protective Services, or the
Department of Family and Children Services. Persons who report in
good faith—that is, who have an honest belief that a child is being sexually abused—are immune from civil and criminal court action, even if
the report proves to be in error.

Teaching children and adolescents about their bodies and appropriate sexual behavior may enhance the prevention of sexual abuse. Being
taught how to say no to sexual advances and how to ask for help when
they need it may help many teenagers to defend themselves against incestuous sexual abuse. All children, even the very young, can learn the
following rules:

- You have rights to the privacy of the parts of your body that are
  covered by a bathing suit.

- No person has a right to touch your body in any place that you do
  not want to be touched.

- You are an individual and have the right to say you do not want that
  kind of touch.

Physical Abuse

Research investigations of rates of physical abuse of children and adolescents describe varying degrees of incidence, with some estimations
as high as 1.5 million cases of physical abuse per annum.[98] One study
found that nearly three-fourths of all parents had used violence on their
children at some time. Nearly half reported that they had pushed or
shoved their child, and another fifth admitted hitting their children with

98. Gelles, "Violence toward Children," 36.

an object. Most disturbing was the fact that close to four in one hundred parents had engaged in kicking, biting, punching, beating, or using a knife or gun in the previous year. Over half of the ten- to fourteen-year-olds and a third of the fifteen- to seventeen-year-olds had been abused in some manner.[99] The Search Institute study of students in grades five through nine (approximating the ages ten to fourteen) asked parents if they got angry enough to hurt their children. Approximately one-third of the respondents indicated this was so "once in a while," "sometimes," "often," or "very often."[100] Many children and adolescents most unfortunately learn to accept abuse as the norm and learn to live with it. Often adolescents grow up accepting beating as a part of their parents' rights in child-rearing. Furthermore, abused teenagers adopt a wait-and-see attitude and hope the conflicts will not develop into further violence.

The consequences of child abuse greatly exceed the immediate pain and suffering a young person might experience. One review of pertinent research identified the following characteristics of abused children:[101]

- They are aggressive and full of hatred.

- They are uncontrollable, negativistic, and subject to severe temper tantrums.

- They are lacking in impulse control.

- They are emotionally disturbed, with behavior problems.

- They are withdrawn and inhibited.

- They have cognitive and neurological deficits.

Another tragedy of physical abuse is the runaway. Burgess discovered that a third of the runaways in her study had been physically beaten at home,[102] while Jack Rothman found that over a third ran away because of physical abuse.[103] Finally, the effects of physical abuse go far beyond adolescence, as many abused teenagers grow up to become abusive parents themselves and the cycle of abuse continues.

Many empirical research studies have attempted to identify or discover the relationship between various demographic characteristics

99. Straus et al., *Behind Closed Doors*, 62–64.

100. Benson et al., *Quicksilver Years*, 191.

101. Reidy, "Aggressive Characteristics," 471–77.

102. Burgess, *Youth at Risk*, 11.

103. Rothman, *Runaway & Homeless Youth*, 75.

and abuse. One of the most extensive attempts in the United States was a national study that identified family structure as a significant factor. Over 29 percent of the sample lived in homes without a father or father substitute, while 12 percent were without a mother. Nearly 20 percent of the mothers and 2 percent of the fathers were separated, divorced, deserted, or widowed. This study also found that both the educational level and occupational status of these parents were fairly low. A mere 6 percent of the parents fell into a professional, technical, or managerial occupational status. Only 52.5 percent of the fathers and 30 percent of the mothers were employed throughout the year. The overall conclusion of this revealing study was that child abuse was concentrated among the socioeconomically deprived segments of the population.[104]

While certain studies do indicate a higher incidence of sexual abuse at the lower end of the socioeconomic ladder, some researchers suggest this is not so. Theo Solomon, for example, argues that the problem is common to parents of all economic and educational levels, and that institutions are more likely to intervene in the more visible and vulnerable lower classes than in the affluent.[105] It is probably best concluded that the majority of deprived families do not abuse their children, and some well-to-do parents do.

The youth worker's responsibility in responding to physical abuse is similar to those already identified under the topic of sexual abuse. The youth worker must initially identify the indicators of physical abuse and neglect:[106]

- welts and bruises on the body from being hit
- lagging social development
- poor hygiene (dirty teeth, offensive body odor)
- hunger and thirst, indicating deprivation of nourishment
- failure to attend school regularly
- change in school performance
- lagging physical development
- weight loss

---

104. Gil, *Violence against Children,* 108–11.

105. Solomon, "History and Demography of Child Abuse," 67.

106. Braun, *Someone Heard . . . ,* 9.

- fatigue or listlessness

- fear of family members or caregivers

- stomachaches or abdominal pains that may come from physical injuries but may also be psychological symptoms

- low self-esteem.

Logically, consideration should be given to preventive measures.[107] One of the key factors in abusive parenting is that the parents often lack the appropriate knowledge of childrearing, and that their expectations, attitudes, and parenting techniques set them apart from nonabusing parents. In addition, and as mentioned earlier, many abusers represent dysfunctional families. Churches should encourage family education and require premarital counseling for adolescents and young adults preparing for marriage. While such programs should be geared to strengthening nonabusive, functioning families, they could also serve as a screening device to identify dysfunction in any area of individual and family. [108]

Most abusive parents are themselves emotionally crippled because of circumstances they experienced in their childhood and adolescence, many having been abused themselves. Abusive parents are further described as isolated, lonely, and lacking in support. Support groups can provide these individuals with an immediate support system and an opportunity to reduce their overwhelming sense of aloneness.[109] Parents Anonymous is a national association of support groups patterned after Alcoholics Anonymous and available to help parents who abuse their children.

There is no single format that characterizes support groups. Some gather simply to discuss issues of common interest while others spend large amounts of time in Bible study and prayer. But whatever the process or design of the small group, a common purpose is to offer emotional and spiritual support to the group members. Often the supportive element of these groups is enhanced by interaction and socializing that occurs before and after the formal meeting time and between meetings.

107. A number of organizations are dedicated to the prevention and treatment of child abuse. One such center is the Kempe Foundation for the Prevention and Treatment of Child Abuse and Neglect (http://www.kempe.org/).

108. Gil, *Violence against Children*, 146.

109. Strommen and Strommen, *Five Cries of Parents*, 183–84.

Runaway Youth

Another of the frightening and tragic consequences of family conflict and breakdown is the runaway youth. Although it is difficult to determine exactly how many children and teenagers are runaways, it is evident that this is reaching alarming proportions. One source estimates that there are 700,000 to one million runaway youth between ten and seventeen per year.[110] Another cites a figure in excess of 1,155,000 runaway and homeless youth annually in the United States, but adds that researchers consider this a conservative estimate.[111]

While adolescents offer a number of reasons for running away from home, most run away because of family conflict. In a study of runaways at a shelter in Toronto, the following profile emerged:[112]

- Almost all the runaways had a serious argument with one or both parents.
- Fifty percent reported verbal abuse.
- Only six in ten recalled being happy for more than three days at a time.
- Seven in ten believed they disappointed their families.
- Seventy-three percent had been physically beaten.
- Seven in ten females and four in ten males reported having been sexually abused.

In addition it was found that the runaways in this study did poorly in school, had trouble with authorities, and fought with peers, and that many came from broken homes. Surprising was the fact that most of the runaways in this study came from financially stable homes. Not surprising was the fact that for 60 percent of these youth, religion was of limited or no importance to their families.

A study of Los Angeles County runaways identified the following reasons for leaving home:[113]

- communication difficulties with parents (73 percent)

---

110. Burgess, *Youth at Risk*, 3
111. Rothman, *Runaway & Homeless Youth*, 19.
112. Burgess, *Youth at Risk*, 9–13.
113. Rothman, *Runaway & Homeless Youth*, 75.

- divorce or separation (55 percent)
- physical abuse (39 percent)
- sexual abuse (26 percent)
- desire to be on his or her own (18 percent).

As difficult as the home life may be for many runaways, life on the street is significantly worse. Most turn to crime, drugs, and sex as a means of coping with their situation. Most have some sexually transmitted disease, and many of today's runaways test positive for the AIDS virus.

Adolescents who engage in severe conflict with their parents are strong runaway candidates, and youth workers should endeavor to identify these teenagers. In addition to arguing and fighting with parents, signs to look for are unhappiness, depression, insecurity, impulsiveness, and wrestling with problems that seem unmanageable.

Some churches and youth ministry organizations may be in a position to work with runaway teenagers. One such operation is Helping Hands, an arm of Catholic Charities. Helping Hands has field offices near bus terminals and train stations, and sends out two-people teams (a male and a female) to try to identify new runaways. Their goal is to take young people off the streets and steer them back home or put them into a program or shelter. They are not a treatment center or shelter; rather they provide an intermediate step in helping young runaways get their lives back together. This kind of outreach to teenagers is not for every parish or youth ministry program. However, for certain churches that are in the proximity of metropolitan streets, that have the financial sources to support such a youth-related ministry, and that have a passion and vision to reach the inner city, this type of ministry could prove extremely effective.[114]

INFLUENCE OF PARENTS ON ADOLESCENT BEHAVIOR

While some parents seriously question the impact they really do have on their teenage children, adolescents are, in fact, highly dependent on parents as role models in many areas: in acquiring norms and values, in developing their personality, in making major life decisions, and in less

114. For more details on this outreach ministry, see Rothman, *Runaway & Homeless Youth*, 21–23.

significant matters such as dating and dress. While parents receive, as one might expect, stiff competition from peers, studies consistently demonstrate that youth credit parents as a primary source of influence. For example, the 1985 study by Reginald Bibby and Donald Posterski asked Canadian high school students to what extent they thought other people or forces influenced their life. Parents were ranked as the most influential, as 85 percent of the respondents credited the way they were brought up, while only 73 percent acknowledged the impact of their friends.[115] A decade and a half later the numbers hadn't changed significantly, with a large majority (91 percent) still acknowledging that they were influenced by how they were brought up.[116]

According to the Search Institute study of early adolescents, respondents viewed parents as the most likely source of help; about half would turn to parents on every problem mentioned. Peers were the second choice as a source of help. A noteworthy observation, however, is that there was a steady decline in parental influence as age increased, coinciding with a corresponding increase of peers as a source of help.[117]

When the Barna Research Group asked teenagers who has "a lot of influence" on their thoughts and actions, 70 percent credited their mothers. Sixty percent said their fathers significantly influenced the way they thought and acted, while only 52 percent credited friends with a similar type of influence. However, when teenagers were asked whom they often sought out for help or encouragement, mothers ranked a distant second (54 percent) to friends (72 percent). Only 38 percent said they often went to their father for help. Thus, according to this empirical study, while teenagers may tend to seek out friends over parents for help and encouragement, they admit that parents ultimately have a greater impact over their lives in terms of influencing their thought and behavior patterns.[118]

In the national study of Canadian youth by Bibby and Posterski, teenagers rated parents high as a source of counsel when it came to items such as spending money, what's right and wrong, school concerns, and career decisions. Parents scored much lower on relationships, sex, having

---

115. Bibby and Posterski, *Emerging Generation*, 101–2. This was a national study of Canadian high school students; it was not limited to church attenders.

116. Bibby, *Canada's Teens*, 55–56.

117. Benson et al., *Quicksilver Years*, 200–202. Respondents in this study were members of thirteen youth agencies, most of which were church related.

118. Barna Research Group, *Today's Teens*, 23–24.

fun, and major problems.[119] Another empirical study by Hans Sebald found peers to have more influence over decisions related to social activities, but in regard to major issues such as career or finances, parents had more of an impact in the decisions teenagers made.[120]

When comparing mothers and fathers, it appears that mothers tend to have more influence than fathers in most areas of the lives of their teenage children. Bibby and Posterski discovered that teenagers not only perceived the mother as a greater source of influence in making choices and decisions than the father, but also tended to turn to mother more often than to father when facing problems and looking for moral guidance.[121]

This was found to be true by the Barna Research Group as well.[122] Fathers may be seen as the primary breadwinners and the one in charge, but they are still perceived as distant to their teenage children and considerably less influential in the parenting role. One area in which fathers may have a greater impact than mothers in shaping the lives of their teenagers is in religion and religiosity. While different conclusions have been reached, extensive reviews of studies by Dean Hoge and Gregory Petrillo[123] and Kenneth Hyde[124] noted that fathers were more influential than mothers in areas related to adolescent religiousness such as participation in church-related activities or faith development.

Several parenting principles and procedures emerge from these studies. First, when it comes to being involved in the life of their teenagers, parents should enter at the points of least resistance or at those junctures where adolescent children will be most likely to invite or receive parental participation. Once they have entered, they may move into areas normally reserved for friends and peers. For many parents, fathers especially, sports are a natural entry into their teenagers' lives. Bowling, tennis, fishing, hunting, biking, backpacking, and softball offer some ways to spend time together. For families whose children are involved in activities such as organized sports, music, or drama, efforts should be

119. Bibby and Posterski, *Teen Trends,* 205.

120. Sebald, "Adolescent's Shifting Orientation towards Parents and Peers," 5–13.

121. Bibby and Posterski, *Teen Trends,* 208; Bibby, *Canada's Teens,* 56.

122. Barna Research Group, *Today's Teens,* 24.

123. Hoge and Petrillo, "Youth and the Church"; Hoge and Petrillo, "Determinants of Church Participation."

124. Hyde, *Religion in Childhood and Adolescence,* 233–35.

made by both mothers and fathers to attend performances and games as much as possible.

Second, parents should not expect to be the only source of influence in the lives of their teenagers. Wise parents will recognize that adolescents are moving from dependence to independence and, whether they like it or not, will be influenced by friends and other adults. Parents might be more comfortable with the new influences in their sons' or daughters' lives if they know a little bit about them. Parents should make an honest effort to get to know their teenagers' close friends, perhaps to the point of having an open-home policy.

Third, parents, especially fathers, must make greater efforts to be involved in the lives of their teenage children. This means more and deeper meaningful interaction in all dimensions of life, including the physical, emotional, and spiritual. Many families today are accomplishing aspects of this by returning to meaningful supper or dinner hours when all members are encouraged to be present. With the television turned off, they talk about their day's events, read a chapter of a book, or discuss the world news.[125] It is important that teenagers get focused, one-to-one attention. This might come in the form of a father-daughter outing, a father-son backpacking trip, or a mother-daughter luncheon.

Fourth, parents should be reminded that the positive influence they have on their teenagers comes as much or more through consistent modeling as it does through verbal efforts to advise or instruct. For example, Hoge and Petrillo found that the very strong influence parents have on their teenagers' participation in church-related activities comes mostly through their own behavior rather than through a conscious effort to socialize their children into the church.[126]

Finally, youth workers should attack the myth of "quality time"—the ill-conceived notion that suggests that a little bit of meaningful time is sufficient for a healthy parent-child relationship. While it is important that the time parents spend with their adolescents is quality in nature, it takes time, effort, and sacrifice of other desires and pleasures to develop strong parent-adolescent relationships. Strong families do things together, whether it is working, playing, or sharing meals.

---

125. Arp and Arp, *60 One-minute Family Builders*, 18.

126. Hoge and Petrillo, "Determinants of Church Participation."

FAMILY MINISTRY—A NEW WAY OF DOING YOUTH WORK

Toward the end of the twentieth century there emerged a renewed interest in doing youth ministry in the context of the family. In the twenty-first century this trend gained momentum to the point that a new generation of churches has embraced a way of doing ministry to teenagers that is noticeably different from the traditional age-based programmatic models. Advocates of family models have determined that sufficient evidence indicates serious weaknesses in the ways we have been doing youth ministry. First, churches are losing a significant number of youth before and after they leave high school.[127] Regarding this concerning trend Steve Wright challenges youth workers and churches with the pointed question "With all the time, money, and energy poured into teens, why are we not getting a better return for our investment?"[128] Second, traditional youth ministry, by and large, separates teenagers from the full life and influence of the congregation, which includes, of course, parents. Third, traditional youth ministry is not doing a good enough job in bringing youth into spiritual maturity. One of the primary proponents of family-based youth ministry, Mark DeVries, insists that "the crisis in youth ministry is, simply put, that the ways we have been doing youth ministry have not been effective in leading our young people to mature Christian adulthood."[129] Finally, and most important in the context of this chapter, parents have generally abdicated the role of spiritual nurture to the professional youth pastors and volunteer youth workers.

Thus in an attempt to better address the needs of adolescents and their families, many churches have rethought and ultimately restructured how they do youth ministry. Three identifiable family ministry models have emerged: *family-integrated*, *family-based*, and *family-equipping*. While the advocates of the individual models may disagree on some of the specifics, the models are not mutually exclusive, as each variation seeks to engage and support the family unit in at least three respects. First there is a conviction that a strong family, whether traditional or otherwise, is germane to the healthy development and spiritual growth of adolescents. Second, the models agree that involvement in the full life

---

127. For summaries of the research addressing alarming retention rates of adolescents see Wright, *ReThink*, 18–20; and DeVries, *Family-Based Youth Ministry*, 25–26.

128. Wright, *ReThink*, 22.

129. DeVries, *Family-Based Youth Ministry*, 26.

of the congregation is imperative to healthy spiritual formation and faith development of teens. Third, they insist "that parents are acknowledged, trained and held accountable as persons primarily responsible for the discipleship of their children."[130]

Family-Integrated Model

The Family-Integrated Model promoted by Voddie Baucham[131] advocates a complete break from the traditional age-segregated programmatic format, asserting that making disciples in this manner is unbiblical. In a family-integrated church nearly all age-related programs are eliminated, including youth groups and Sunday schools. Rather, small group studies and home groups bring entire families together, including single adults, single-parent households, and children of unbelieving parents.[132] The family-integrated model approaches the concept of youth ministry in light of David Black's book *The Myth of Adolescence*,[133] which does away with the commonly held concept of adolescence. Consequently this model also eliminates many of the typical church education staff members, including youth pastors. The intent and ultimate purpose of this model is to promote family unity by having families worship, grow spiritually, and learn together. A major focus of this approach is to equip and unleash parents to lead their families in spiritual matters and to be the primary shapers of the spiritual formation for their teenage children.

Like any ministry model the Family-Integrated Model has both strengths and weakness. The obvious strengths are two. First, youth "are not just *partly* the congregation's responsibility, they are wholly so."[134] Second, the responsibility of bringing youth into spiritual maturity is returned to the parents. One limitation of this approach is that it ignores the developmental psychology of Erikson, Marcia, and Elkind, which reminds us that teenagers are in the normal process of gaining independence from parents and parental control. A second drawback is that parents often need the help and support of other adults. Well-trained youth pastors who understand youth culture and adolescent development can

130. Jones and Stinson, "Family Ministry Models," 173.

131. Baucham, *Family Driven Faith*.

132. Jones and Stinson, "Family Ministry Models," 175.

133. Black, *Myth of Adolescence*.

134. Nel, "Inclusive Approach," 4.

be significant supports to parents who are experiencing, along with their teens, the various and sundry crises youth go through. Similarly, adolescents often need and want someone to talk to besides their parents. While many adults in the church can and should help fulfill the roles of counselor, model, and mentor to teens, youth ministry leaders (staff or lay volunteers) are another source of support for teens who feel the need for counseling. Finally, while it is important for youth to spend time with their parents and other adults, much socialization takes place in the context of their peers. It is neither inappropriate nor necessarily dangerous for youth to spend time with others in their age group.

Family-Based Model

Championed by Mark DeVries, the Family-Based Model[135] resembles a typical age-organized approach to ministry with an emphasis on flexibility to accommodate different family structures.[136] Accordingly, the task or responsibility of the youth pastor and church is to, "find ways to build on a foundation of parents providing intentional Christian nurture for their children and students connecting to an extended Christian family of faith-full adults."[137] The ultimate goal is to lead teenagers into "mature Christian adulthood," something, argues DeVries, the traditional ways of doing youth ministry have not been effective in doing.[138] Churches utilizing this approach will blend typical structures with intergenerational and family focused events in each ministry area.

A major strength of this approach is its positive view of the role of parents in youth ministry. At the same time there appears to be a lack of emphasis on intentional training of parents to be disciple makers of their own teens and children. A second strength of the family-based model is that a church need not dismantle its current model or strategy of youth ministry. Rather, a church could undergird its current model "with the kind of family-based connections that will offer the structures for the long-term faith formation in your youth."[139] Third, and like all the family models, it attempts to engage youth in the full life of the congregation.

135. See DeVries, *Family-Based Youth Ministry.*

136. Ibid., 174–82.

137. Ibid., 176.

138. Ibid., 26.

139. Ibid., 176.

Family-Equipping Model

The Family-Equipping Model is a middle approach to the family-based and family-integrated ways of doing youth ministry.[140] This approach arose, in part, as a response to the trend of parents in the church abdicating the responsibility for the discipleship of their children and teens to church leaders. Steve Wright, a key proponent of this model, rightly faults many churches and parents alike for viewing youth ministry as a "spiritual drop-off service best left to the professionals."[141] Unlike the family-based model, which develops intergenerational activities within existing programs, "family-equipping churches redevelop the congregation's structure to cultivate a renewed culture wherein parents are acknowledged, trained, and held accountable as the primary faith trainers in their children's lives."[142] Age-based ministry still exists in this model, and many family-integrating churches retain youth pastors on their staff.[143] A major challenge to the Family Equipping Model is simply getting parents to take seriously their role as disciple makers and to prioritize time to teach and guide their children in spiritual matters. This model also requires that all church staff members embrace the same basic philosophies in order to have a seamless process of parent training in the spiritual growth of children and teens.[144]

CONCLUSION

The purpose of this chapter has been to identify critical family issues and the effects they have on adolescents and adolescent development. It must be remembered, however, that not every family in America is in turmoil and conflict, and not every teenager is at odds with one or both of the parents. If, according to Strommen, one youth in five is from a troubled home, then four in five are from at least reasonably healthy family situations (this is not to say that there may not be some arguments, conflicts, or disagreements—47 percent admit there are some differences).[145] More

140. Nelson and Jones, "Introduction," 13.

141. Wright, *ReThink*, 47.

142. Nelson and Jones, "Introduction," 27.

143. Ibid.

144. A good source of ideas for working with parents is Burns and DeVries, *Partnering with Parents in Youth Ministry*.

145. Strommen, *Five Cries of Youth*, 62, 54.

than four decades ago, Roy Zuck and Gene Getz found that seven out of ten young people who attended church stated that the relationships between themselves and their parents were adequate. They also cited a 1966 *Newsweek* article that reported that a heavy majority of teenagers got along just fine with their parents.[146]

In 1991 the Barna Research Group found that this attitude had changed only slightly, as six out of ten teenagers said they were very satisfied with their current family situation.[147] In the Search Institute study of pre- and early adolescents, nearly three-quarters of the respondents said, "There is a lot of love in my family."[148] Unfortunately, many parents feel ill-equipped to do an effective job of parenting. When 10,467 parents in an adolescent-parent study were asked to rank the importance of sixteen values, one that received top attention was "to be a good parent." Yet four out of five parents said that "to be a good parent is one of the hardest things in life I do."[149] While raising children is one of the most important and difficult tasks parents will face, it is one of the few responsibilities of this magnitude that does not require formal training or equipping.

146. Zuck and Getz, *Christian Youth, an In-Depth Study*.

147. Barna Research Group, *Today's Teens*, 9.

148. Benson et al., *Quicksilver Years*, 103.

149. Strommen and Strommen, *Five Cries of Parents*, 12.

6

The Adolescent World
of Social Relationships

Adolescents live in an ever-expanding world of relationships, membership groups, and social environments. As young people move from childhood through puberty and into adolescence, their web of social and interpersonal relationships broadens. In addition to the family, teenagers find themselves increasingly involved with friends and peers, schoolmates, and dating relationships. The adolescent interests in new social relationships and involvement in expanding membership groups are natural, though they are often a source of consternation to parents and teenagers alike, but for different reasons. Parents sense a gradual loss in the influence and control they have on their adolescent children. For teenagers, friendships, dating relationships, and acceptance by peers become overriding concerns and are often cause for much anxiety as well as the sources of rejection, hurt, and frustration. This chapter investigates the various types of social relationships and membership groups that help make up the burgeoning world of adolescence. In addition the chapter will address many of the issues that emerge in the lives of teenagers as they explore new dimensions of life.

THE SIGNIFICANCE OF FRIENDS AND PEERS

While teenagers are sometimes reticent to admit it, they are greatly influenced by their family. But in the adolescent years there emerges a natural desire to distance themselves from parents and siblings while affiliating more with nonfamily peers and friends. While parents continue to have a significant impact on their teenage children, peers are by far the greatest presence in the lives of adolescents.[1] This shift of significant others can be a source of conflict between youth and parents. Parents generally place a higher value on family relationships and activities, while teenagers more often than not choose friends over parents. Furthermore, there is the concern of adults that teenagers left to themselves will be "up to no good," and that peer relations are disruptive to healthy personal development and to the best interest of society.[2]

While there is some evidence that peer relationships may contribute to deviant behaviors such as drug use or delinquency, friendship and peer associations serve a number of important functions in the socialization of adolescents.[3] First, they operate as a mechanism whereby dependence on parental support and guidance is gradually loosened. Second, the adolescent period is seen as one in which interpersonal skills necessary in adulthood are learned through peer relationships. Third, peer groups offer emotional support at a time when young people are often unsure of themselves, questioning how they fit into the scheme of things. Friends provide an opportunity to discuss pertinent issues and events such as dating, parents, and school. In short, peer groups and friends serve as a training ground for the development of social and personality skills that will be necessary to function in the world of adulthood toward which they are moving.

THE FRIENDSHIP FACTOR

One of the major findings of Reginald Bibby and Donald Posterski through Project Teen Canada was the high value Canadian teenagers placed on friendships. The researchers were so struck with their discovery that they were able to conclude that friendship is the glue that holds Canada's youth culture together.[4] They reaffirmed this in their follow-up study seven years later.[5]

---

1. Csikzentmihalyi and Larson, *Being Adolescent,* 71; Barna Research Group, *Today's Teens,* 11.

2. Csiszentmihalyi and Larson, *Being Adolescent,* 157.

3. Ibid., 156–57.

4. Posterski, *Friendship,* 7; Bibby and Posterski, *Emerging Generation,* 98.

5. Bibby and Posterski, *Teen Trends,* 199.

Why were Bibby and Posterski compelled to make such an assertion? When asked "How much enjoyment do you receive from the friendship?" more than seven in ten responding adolescents said they experienced "a great deal" of enjoyment from friendships. Not surprisingly, socializing is typically accompanied by very positive emotions.[6] In fact Jeffrey Arnett, a foremost adolescent sociologist suggests, "Friends become the source of adolescents' happiest experiences, the people with whom they feel most comfortable, the persons they feel they can talk to most openly."[7] When ranked with other factors, Bibby and Posterski found friendship to be the greatest source of enjoyment, with music the only other factor that was close. In comparison, fewer than half the respondents claimed a high level of enjoyment from parents, with mothers faring slightly better than fathers.[8] "Studies in other European countries confirm that adolescents tend to be happiest when with their friends and that they tend to turn to their friends for advice and information on social relationships and leisure, although they come to parents for advice about education and career plans."[9]

Teens spend their time in a variety of ways. Gender, ethnicity, socioeconomics, and even gaming can affect time spent in each category. Nonetheless, both peer and family relationships stay most significant across all groups.

Table 6.1
How Teenagers Spend Their Time In an Average Weekday[10]

Time with friends	80 minutes
Time with parents	125 minutes
Sports and leisure activities	37 minutes
Studying or doing homework	38–56 minutes

While teens tend to spend more time with family, this pattern changes, as they grow older. Arnett notes that, "the most notable change in family relationships that occurs from middle childhood to adolescence

6. Csikszentmihalyi and Hunter, "Happiness in Everyday Life," 185.

7. Arnett, *Human Development*, 375.

8. Bibby and Posterski, *Emerging Generation*, 32.

9. Arnett, *Human Development*, 375.

10. Cummings and Vandewater, "Relation of Adolescent Video Game Play," Table 1. The large difference in the item "Studying or doing homework" exists because it compares video gamers and nongamers.

in American society is the decline in the amount of time spent with family members."[11] Most of this time with peers involves socializing—talking, joking, or simply "hanging out." Much of what they do is spontaneous, unrelated to the external requirements of adults and adult institutions. In most cases experiences with friends are more positive than negative, and time with friends is the best part of adolescents' daily lives.[12] "When children enter into adolescence, their perceived support from friends passes the perceived support from parents."[13] Adolescents may indeed spend a greater amount of time with their family, but time with friends is considered the best part of their daily lives.

If friendship is, as Donald Posterski suggests, the centerpiece of the teenager's life, how should adult volunteer youth workers and youth pastors proceed to do youth ministry? First, they must work hard at building friendships and nurturing relationships with youth. Second, youth workers must place a high priority on building group community. Third, a relationally warm climate must be created at all youth ministry events. Finally, the physical environment in which youth ministry takes place must appear attractive and friendly.

Building Relationships with Youth

Three hundred youth workers, parents, and pastors from all over the city had gathered to learn about the culture of teenagers and how to reach them with the gospel. The church where we were gathered sat right across the street from the local high school.

I was the moderator, so I sat in the front of the church, along with four teenagers from the community, who each took fifteen minutes to tell his or her story to the crowd. When the teens finished, I invited members of the audience to ask questions of them.

The youth pastor from the host church asked the last question: "I have a question for the young man on the right." The young man, Brian, had openly declared his disinterest in Christianity.

"Every day for the past two years, I have arrived here early in the morning," began the youth pastor. "I park my car and walk around the building to the front entrance. Because the high school is a smoke-free

11. Arnett, *Human Development*, 371.

12. Csikszentmihalyi and Larson, *Being Adolescent*, 158–61.

13. Bokhorst et al., "Social Support from Parents, Friends, Classmates, and Teachers."

zone, you and many of your friends congregate on our church sidewalk to smoke before the school day begins. I walk through and around you on the sidewalk and on the steps to the front door. Every morning when I sit down at my desk, I look out my window at you and your peers and ask God what I can do to reach you. It's so frustrating."

Then, he looked at Brian and asked: "What can I do to connect with you?"

Brian didn't have to think about his answer at all. First, he chuckled loudly as if to say, "You've got to be kidding! How can you not know the answer to that one?" Then he looked at the youth pastor and answered him.

"That's easy!" said Brian. "Get out of your office and come out onto the sidewalk with us!"

Walt Mueller[14]

The promotion of friends in the personal lives of teenagers often means the demotion of adults—including grandparents, teachers, ministers, and youth workers—as sources of influence and relationships. While inter-generational relationships have always been strained, the degree of distance may be increasing. Sociologists Mihalyi Csikszentmihalyi and Reed Larson observe that while adolescents spend a significant amount of time in locations structured or supervised by adults, they spend relatively less time actually involved in adult-oriented activities. They add that adults as a whole invest relatively little time in being with young people.[15]

Effective ministry with youth, however, begins when an adult leader finds a comfortable way of entering into the life and world of an adolescent. If we observe closely the ministry of Jesus, we see that personal relationships were at the core of his strategy. Whether he was confronting the Samaritan woman at the well on a hot afternoon (John 4), talking with the Pharisee Nicodemus at night (John 3), or praying with his closest followers (John 17), Jesus modeled a loving, relational style of ministry.

If youth workers are going to impact teenagers with the gospel of Christ, they must work hard at entering their world and building personal relationships or friendships with them. Part of this aspect of youth ministry is what is called *contacting*—making connections with teenagers

14. "Mueller, "Culture Watch."

15. Csikszentmihalyi and Larson, *Being Adolescent,* 70–75.

on their turf. There are some basic principles that will help the youth worker to more effectively establish relationships with teenagers.

First, building friendships with youth does not involve stripping one-self of his or her adulthood and taking on the appearance of an adoles-cent. Young people do not expect adults to try to dress, talk, or act like teenagers. What they do desire is for adults to feel comfortable around teenagers acting like teenagers. They also need adults who understand adolescents—their ways of thinking, their struggles, and their needs.

Second, there is no one correct way to enter into a teenager's world. The most comfortable way for an adult to earn the right to be heard by an adolescent will differ from individual to individual and situation to situation. The best way to facilitate relationships with teenagers and get to know them better is by doing something with them. Find out what an individual likes to do and do it with him or her. Here is a list of sugges-tions that might trigger some additional ideas as to how a youth leader can spend time with a teenager:[16]

- Have lunch together.
- Go bowling or skating.
- Go hiking or rock climbing.
- Play tennis.
- Attend a school event.
- Attend a professional or college sporting event.
- Go to a concert.
- Go to the mall.
- Shoot baskets.
- Go fishing.
- Tutor a teenager in a subject he or she is struggling with.
- Go to a movie.

Third, relational ministry will not occur unless an adult youth worker earns the right to be heard by a teenager. Many young people are simply looking for someone to love and accept them and to be available to them. Earning the right to be heard usually comes simply with exercising basic interpersonal skills. Relational people are sensitive to others' feelings and

16. Robbins, *Ministry of Nurture*, 186–87.

demonstrate a willingness to listen and talk to others. Relational people also reflect a caring attitude by implementing a few basic communication skills. Maintaining good eye contact is one way to show real interest in what another person is saying. Responding with nods and verbal interjections lets people know you are listening, and using appropriate touch such as a pat on the back or a shoulder hug demonstrates warmth and care. Ultimately it is an intentional posture that finds ways to communicate care that can be received by adolescents.

Community Building

Posterski concludes that in the North American culture at large, people are increasingly more interested in relationships than in ideas and beliefs.[17] This is probably as true or truer of the youth subculture as than with any other group of people. Teenagers today look for a place to belong, find friends, and build relationships first, and then to learn and grow. With this being the case, it is imperative that the youth worker places a priority on building community in the group. To build community is to foster a sense of belonging and to nurture meaningful and genuine interpersonal relationships.

Functions of the Group

In any organization of people the group performs four functions.[18] The four functions provide answers to key developmental questions that teens are asking, making the group a significant force is the life the of the teen.

- *Identity and role: Who am I? Who am I supposed to be in the group, and what is my role?* Chapter 2 talks extensively about identity. In the context of group functions and identity we would add trust as a significant factor. Before young people can rely on one another, they must be assured that the relationships are mutually valued. To trust means to be confident in the loyalty of another person in the youth community.

- *Power and influence (contribution): Where do I fit in or make a difference? Will my need for influence and impact be met?* The gifts and

17. Posterski, *Friendship*, 16.
18. Schein, *Organizational Culture and Leadership*, 149.

abilities adolescents possess as individuals often have to be recognized and drawn out by adult leaders and peers who care for them.
In this way, the community enables its members to actualize their
potential to impact their world. Kenda Creasy Dean states that we
offer car washes and lock-ins instead of a comprehensive vision to
"enlist young people in the mission of God."[19] Steven Garber notes
that young people are interested in framing a coherent vision of
the world that propels them into their calling. To this end, they are
searching for teachers who embody their chosen worldview and for
a community to which they belong and can actively contribute.[20]

- *Acceptance and intimacy (consolation): Am I loved? Is there a group
  of people who love and respect me? How close will our relationships
  be?* Community members have the responsibility and privilege to
  confirm one another's self-worth, as well as to acknowledge the
  gifts and abilities of each group member. When teenagers hear their
  peers and friends saying positive things about them they enjoy their
  participation in the group to a much greater degree and are more
  likely to share their deep feelings.

- *Needs and goals: Will the group's goals allow me to meet my own
  needs?* While it is easy for adolescents to be consumed with individual needs, the nature of community members is both to have
  needs and to be needed. The keys to healthy interdependence are
  mutual support, interaction, and reliance on one another.

Community Building through Small Groups

One of the most effective community-building models for youth ministry is the small group. A small group can be the setting where a lonely
or hurting teenager connects with someone else—another adolescent or
perhaps a caring adult worker. One of the most helpful small-group strategies that works toward the goal of community building is that developed
by Lyman Coleman, the founder of the modern-day small group movement. Coleman describes a process of small-group sharing that begins
at a simple, nonthreatening level and moves toward a *koinonia* or depth
Christianity. He likens this strategy to a baseball diamond. First base is

19. Dean, *Practicing Passion*, 21.
20. Garber, *Fabric of Faithfulness*, 111.

history giving, where group members are asked to tell their spiritual story to one another. It is a time of getting acquainted through the sharing of where they have come from (the past), where they are in their spiritual journey (the present), and where they want to be (the future).

At second base small-group members need a sense of affirmation. The goal at this point is to give each group member some positive feedback and encouragement through statements such as "Thanks for sharing," "I appreciate what you shared," or "Your story is a gift to me because . . . ." Once affirmed, says Coleman, small-group members are ready to move on to third base, where interaction at a deeper level takes place. Youth begin to trust each other with sharing about needs, hurts, aspirations, joys, frustrations, and doubts. Group members are asked to respond to questions like "What is God saying to you concerning . . . ?" or "What is keeping you from . . . ?" Finally, small-group members reach home plate, or that depth of Christian community called *koinonia*. When this level of interaction is reached, group members serve and respect each other and experience a sense of belonging and bonding. Community has been achieved.[21]

Leading a small group, however, is not a task that comes easily to everyone, and effective leadership comes only with practice and experience. The principles identified below will help the small-group leader in the critical task of nurturing interpersonal relationships and deeper community in the youth group.[22]

- *Choose a setting that is comfortable and conducive to sharing.* Physical environment is very important for a small group. Ideally a small group should meet in a warm, comfortable setting. Try to avoid large, cold rooms like church basements and settings that provide too many distractions, such as restaurants. Homes provide the environment that is best suited to small groups.

- *Set up in an appropriate fashion.* Make sure your group sets up in a circular or U-shaped manner. It is important that the leader and each member can make eye contact with every other member. Try to avoid the use of sofas or easy chairs, as they sometimes allow members to get too relaxed or become too distant from the group.

21. Coleman, *Serendipity Small Group Training Manual,* 15–16.
22. Atkinson, *Power of Small Groups,* 267–303.

- *Develop a relationship with each of the group members.* It is important for the leader to get to know each of the group members. Always arrive early, so you can get to know any new attendees. Make sure they are properly introduced to the group.

- *Ask open-ended questions.* One of the keys—if not the key—to effective group interaction and sharing is being able to ask the right kinds of questions. Closed-ended questions should generally be avoided: those that can be answered with a yes or a no, have one-word answers, or have a single correct answer. Open-ended questions generally have more than one correct answer, demand personal reflection, and will result in dialogue. Usually the best open-ended questions begin with *how* or *why,* and sometimes *what.*

- *Show interest in the speaker by using good listening skills.* A good small-group leader is a sensitive listener. Adolescents want more than physical presence in communication; they want the other person's psychological and emotional presence as well. Effective listening includes hearing what the speaker is saying, making good eye contact, and demonstrating interest in the speaker through the use of nonverbal responses such as nods or smiles.

- *Learn to read nonverbal messages.* Often people will say more with nonverbal expressions than they will with verbal. For example, a raise of the eyebrows or a particular head movement may indicate a group member wants to say something. It is important for a leader to be sensitive to these subtle signals.

- *Try to get balanced participation.* It is important that every member has an opportunity to contribute to the dialogue. To integrate those youth who are quiet and tend not to participate, the leader has several options. First, look for nonverbal sparks of interest. Then when it looks like a quiet individual would like to contribute, offer a nonthreatening response like "John, were you going to say something?" A second approach would be to occasionally make a comment to the group like "You know, we would like to hear from everybody!" or "Every person's input is valued in this group!" Try to avoid putting individuals on the spot by asking them to answer a particular question. This can cause great anxiety for some young people, and such an experience may cause them to quit coming to the small group.

- *Discourage domination by individual group members.* For the dominating group member, your first tactic might be to avoid eye contact with this person, while at the same time offering other members an opportunity to contribute. Second, politely suggest to the whole group that you are looking for *everyone* to participate, hoping the dominating member will get the hint. If one individual continues to try to control the discussion, talk to this person outside the group, thanking him or her for contributing to the discussion but reminding the individual that such dominance is discouraging others from participating.

- *Resist the temptation to answer questions yourself.* When a question is raised or asked by group members, many leaders feel constrained to pontificate or answer the question themselves. Often a response by the facilitator will squelch group interaction. This is an ideal opportunity to nurture further group dialogue by throwing the question back to the group and encouraging members to interact with each other.

- *Do not be afraid of silence.* Often group members will greet a question with silence. This often unnerves small-group leaders, and they feel constrained to say something. Do not be afraid of a little silence. It is possible the small-group participants are thinking and that they need a little time before responding. Give them time to ponder the question, and then if nothing is said, rephrase the query.

Building Community in Large-Group Activities

According to youth ministry research, every group has its own personality made of three elements: connection, purpose, and safety.[23] Connection focuses on the relationships within the group and is best exemplified by expressions of love for one another (cf. John 13:35). Purpose provides a sense of why a group exists and where they are going, as well as movement and vitality. Finally, safety addresses issues of expectations and security from threats of embarrassment or physical and emotional harm. Trust is central if teens are to engage in the relationships and mission of the group. Large-group activities and programs must be opportunities

---

23. Patty, *Impact*, 169.

for building these elements leading to making friends and nurturing relationships with both adults and other teens.

Steve Patty identifies a list of strategies that support social relational
health and "good group glue:"[24]

- Act as if there is group glue—your expectations have a way of affecting the climate and behavior of students. Assume it.

- Teach about love within the body of Christ.

- Affirm students yourself and give them opportunity to practice affirmation of one another.

- Provide activities that force people to touch one another (appropri-
ately, of course and not before the group gels).

- Pass on positive comments you have overheard said of students by
students (positive gossip goes a long way).

- Publicly remember common experiences together.

- Celebrate individuals by showing pictures and telling stories about
people.

- Talk about the group as a "family" and "body."

- Pray aggressively and specifically that the group will bond together.

- Make group use of slideshows, graphics, tee-shirts, and pictures

- Pay attention to things that affirm the value of people and relationships (cards, birthdays, care packages, encouraging notes).

- Regularly give students a vision for reaching out to one another, loving one another, and building friendships.

- Above all, worship together. Nothing brings together a group better
than a corporate focus on God.

Instead of playing team sports that stress competition and winning,
such as volleyball or softball, try engaging the youth group in cooperative recreational activities that focus more on working together and the
attainment of a group goal. Such activities sponsor purpose, connection
and safety. One such noncompetitive activity is the "Platform Game," the
object of which is to see how many people can fit on a platform at one
time. Materials needed are

24. Ibid., 173.

- a sturdy piece of plywood approximately 3 feet by 3 feet depending on the number of people in the group

- four bricks, one under each corner of the plywood

- a rope that is long enough to surround the platform with a 2 1/2-foot gap between the rope and the platform.

The space between the rope and the platform symbolizes a deep shaft. If someone steps in the shaft or falls back into this area, he or she must try again to get on the platform. See how many people can pile onto the platform without falling into the shaft.

Another activity that can illustrate the importance of community and relationships is the often-used "Yarn Circle." Youth group members are asked to form a circle, with their elbows touching. The person beginning the activity thinks of a person in the group, holds the end of the yarn, and without mentioning the name of the person she is thinking of, states a quality or attribute the person has that contributes to the unity of the group. She then tosses the ball of yarn to another person who does the same. This process continues, with each person holding onto the yarn and throwing the ball to another person until each member is included in the yarn pattern. Note the beauty of the pattern that has been created. Then ask two or three of the youth to let go of the circle and step out. Notice how ugly the pattern becomes when some of the group members are missing. Tighten the yarn by moving back slowly and then ask two or more youth to drop out. Continue this process and ask the youth to observe what is happening to the pattern as more and more people remove themselves from the circle. Read Phil 2:1-8 and ask youth group members to pick out qualities and actions that contribute to group community. Talk about the scriptural teachings that could help your group attain unity and closeness. Close the session by thanking God for the contributions each member brings to the community of the youth group.

Creating a Relationally Warm Climate

To reemphasize, programmed events must be seen as more than opportunities for teaching. They must be occasions for making friends and nurturing relationships. A positive attitude toward church youth programs is almost synonymous with the friendliness and affirmation received from other youth group participants. Regular youth group attendees should be encouraged to develop relationships with adolescents beyond their immediate circle of friends and to reach out to newcomers and visitors. Sometimes, however, teenagers need to be taught how to communicate effectively with others and build interpersonal relationships. If you have ever tried to shake hands with a junior higher, you know that interpersonal skills are often awkwardly lacking but can be easily taught. The following skills will help adolescents take the initiative in befriending and reaching out relationally to other adolescents.[25]

Remembering Names

One of the most effective ways of demonstrating interest in other people is by remembering and using their names. To help youth group members become more conscious of the importance of names, spend some time talking about their own names by doing the following exercise. Have each member state his or her first, middle, and last name. Then talk about these names by answering questions such as these: How do you feel about the name you were given? Why were you given the name? Do you have any nicknames? What embarrassing or funny experiences have you had because of your name? Do you know the origin of your name? What is the significance of any one of your names?[26] Choose the first person to begin, then have that individual choose the next person. Conclude the session by explaining the significance of names in Scripture. For example, Saul changed his name to Paul after his conversion (Acts 13:9). Jesus changed Simon's name to Peter, which means "Rock" (John 1:35–42).

Listening

In order to practice care, concern, and understanding for others, we must learn how to be effective listeners. Listening is the communication tool that allows us to enter into another person's private world and helps us better understand what someone else is feeling or experiencing. While listening is the most fundamental and basic language or communication skill that we develop, it is one of the most neglected skills at all educational

---

25. Summarized from Varenhorst, *Training Teenagers*.

26. A baby-name book or appropriate website will give meanings and origins of names.

levels. Therefore, young people, as well as the rest of us, need to be taught how to listen more effectively to others.

To help group members become better listeners and learn the important communication techniques of attending, asking for clarification, and paraphrasing try the following listening exercise. Divide the youth group into pairs and ask one partner to begin by describing in detail, an important person (a parent, relative, coach, teacher, minister, or friend, for example) in his or her life. Encourage the listeners to *attend* or listen carefully to the speakers by facing them squarely, maintaining good eye contact, and leaning toward them slightly.[27]

The listeners should be encouraged to ask questions for *clarification,* especially for vague phrases or words the speaker may have used. Good clarification questions are I am not sure what you meant by that? and Could you restate that and tell me a little bit more? When the speakers finish the account, the listeners should *paraphrase,* or feed back to the speakers in their own words the message they heard. The objective is not to repeat a detailed account but rather to feed back the heart of the message, particularly the feeling level of what was initially shared.

Conclude the learning experience with a debriefing time, giving the participants an opportunity to respond to and discuss their encounter. Ask questions such as the following:

- In what ways did your listener show he or she was listening to you?

- Did the listener demonstrate a lack of interest or in any way make it difficult for you as the speaker?

- What suggestions could you give your listener that would make her a better listener?

- How would you rate yourself as a listener?

Asking Questions

Sometimes adolescents find it difficult to initiate or carry on a conversation because they do not know how to find a bridge that connects to another individual. Use the following activity to teach them how to use questions that will help them carry out warm conversations. The acronym L-I-F-E will help some participants generate appropriate questions:

27. Note that these actions are considered aggressive and even hostile in some urban environments and in other cultures.

- Likes: ask questions such as, What are some of your favorite foods? or Where would you like to go on vacation?

- Interests: share enjoyments in hobbies, sports, movies, books, music, and so forth.

- Family: discuss siblings, pets, family holidays or vacation traditions.

- Education: ask questions like What is your favorite subject? What is your worst school lunch item? What are your vocational interests?

Explain the acronym and then ask group members to think of an interest they have such as a hobby, recreational activity, or subject that gives them enjoyment and pleasure. Inform them that they may be asked to share their interest with the whole group. After they have had time to think, go in a circle, asking each person to identify his or her interest. After everyone has shared, choose the person with the most unusual or unique interest. Have the group members brainstorm questions they might ask this person about his or her interest, without the person answering at this time. Write the questions on the board precisely as they have been asked. When the group has run out of questions, ask the selected person to indicate only the questions he or she would prefer to answer. Now ask the members if they see any difference between the preferred questions and the others. The group will probably discover that the individual chose questions about personal feelings or achievements. Have the person answer the top-ranked questions, and then see if the group wants to ask any more questions based on that answer.

Follow up by describing four types of questions often used in conversations:

- *Closed-ended questions*—questions that require a one-word answer—so a question such as, do you like baseball?

- *Open-ended questions*—For instance, what is it you like about baseball?

- *Informational questions*—questions that ask for factual information such as, where did you live as a child?

- *Feeling-level questions*—For instance, How do you feel about living in California rather than Texas? How do you like attending your new school?

Inform participants that most people prefer to respond to open-ended and feeling-level questions rather than closed-ended or informational questions. By asking open-ended and feeling-level questions, the questioner gives others the opportunity to provide more information and develop meaningful conversation rather than short, specific answers.

Welcoming Strangers to the Group

A difficult task for many adolescents (as well as for some adults) is reaching out to strangers or people they do not know. Yet it is imperative that a youth group opens its arms to new people. To help regular attendees realize the importance of accepting outsiders or strangers, let them experience firsthand what it is like to try to get into a group that will not accept them or how it feels to keep someone out. Choose one teen to stand outside of the group while other members stand in a circle and lock arms. Give the outsider about thirty seconds to try to get in while those in the circle do everything they can (without doing bodily harm) to keep the intruder from getting into the circle. The outsider may overpower the group and get in, but usually he cannot penetrate the circle and gives up. Have two or three people attempt to break into the circle.

Try to get the participants to apply the simulation activity to real life, to a time when a stranger or visitor is trying to get involved in their youth group. Follow the circle activity by asking the participants some questions. To those outside who tried to get into the circle ask the following questions:

- If you failed to get into the group, how did you feel? Why did you give up?
- If you did get into the circle, what strategy did you use? Was it worth the effort? Did you feel accepted?

Ask the insiders questions such as these:

- How did you feel as you kept the people from getting in?
- Were you concerned about the outsider's feelings in any way?

Ask the whole group questions like the following:

- How do you think a newcomer feels when she visits a group and members do not make her feel welcome?

- Why is it sometimes difficult to reach out to strangers?
- What can you do to help a visitor feel more comfortable or welcome?

Breaking the Ice

Youth workers who want to encourage youth group attendees to interact with one another should give careful attention to the use of icebreakers or crowdbreakers. These are games designed to open meetings and help group attendees get to know each other. Icebreakers help defuse any uneasiness or tension at the beginning of a session and are also an ideal way to get visitors and first-time attendees to mix with regular attendees in a nonthreatening manner.[28]

For example, an often-used icebreaker is the "Name Tag" game. Create name tags using biblical, historical, or contemporary celebrity names. As youth group members arrive for the group activity attach a tag to the back of each individual's shirt. Each individual is to try to find out his identity by asking questions that can be answered with a simple yes or no. Each participant is limited to three questions per person. When a person discovers her or his identity, he or she is to take a seat. This continues until all have finished.[29]

Another good icebreaker is the "Match Mixer." Give each individual three notecards or slips of paper. Have the participants write something about themselves on each card. Suggest topics such as these:

- My most embarrassing experience is . . .
- My ambition is to . . .
- The person I admire the most is . . .
- My favorite recreational activity is . . .
- If I had a million dollars, I would . . .

Collect the cards and redistribute three to each person. (Make sure no one has his or her own card). At a given signal each participant tries to match the three cards with the correct people by asking questions of participants. Whoever first matches the three cards is the winner. Allow

---

28. Many great websites with icebreakers can be found on the Internet. A helpful book for icebreakers and other games is Christie, *Best-Ever Games for Youth*.

29. Bushman, "Breaking the Ice at the Beginning," 13–14.

all the youth to finish matching their cards and, if time allows, let each member share his or her findings with the whole group.[3031]

Creating a Warm Environment

The environmental conditions of the settings where youth ministry takes place are critical in creating a relationally warm setting. James Michael Lee insists that the extent of an individual's learning depends on the power and nature of the environment, including on the design and arrangement of the room in which the group activity is carried on.[32] Elements such as the size of the room, the decor, the floor coverings, and even the appearance of the building can influence the emotional climate and the process of relationship building. Church basements with cold concrete floors, drab walls with little or no wall ornamentation, exposed electrical wiring and ductwork, and hard metal folding chairs arranged in straight rows should be avoided.

Rooms used for youth ministry should be as warm, attractive, inviting, and comfortable as possible. What is communicated when one enters a meeting room? Does it feel warm and friendly or cold and rejecting? Is it a place for lectures and impersonal meetings, or is it a setting where friends gather for warm fellowship and meaningful interaction? Often large homes with recreation rooms are ideal for youth group activities and meetings. Homes usually communicate automatically a sense of warmth and friendliness.

PEER INFLUENCE

Since adolescents spend a significant amount of time with each other, it follows that peers exert significant influence in the shaping of conduct and value systems of teenagers. Empirical studies related to adolescent development identify several patterns in regard to peer influence.

First, as mentioned earlier, the strength of peer versus parental influence depends on the nature of the issue involved. A number of empirical

30. Taken from Rice and Yaconelli, *Play It,* 152.

31. Following is a set of small books that include ideas for conversation starters: Aitkins, *Tough Topics;* Christie, *What If . . .?;* Christie, *Have You Ever . . .?;* Christie, *450 Tantalizing Unfinished Sentences;* Edwards et al., *Name Your Favorite . . .*

32. Lee, *Flow of Religious Education,* 65, 71.

research studies have found that when choices or issues pertain to long-term and future aspirations such as school, moral and ethical issues, the choice of a part time job, and religious convictions, youth tend to seek out parental influence and advice. For status and short-term social values regarding length of hair, style of dress, or dating, adolescents tend to follow peers.[33] Thus, it appears that personal identity (*Who am I?*) is largely influenced by peers, while future identity (*Who am I to be?*) is influenced more by parents.

Second, parents and peers will generally have more similarity than dissimilarity in moral orientation. Contrary to what adults may think, most adolescents choose friends who have values and expectations similar to those of their parents. Thus disagreements, as already noted, will tend to be over minor issues such as music or dress.[34]

Third, the relationship of the adolescent to his or her parents affects the impact of peer influence. Peer-oriented adolescents are more likely to exhibit antisocial behavior than those who have strong relationships with their parents.[35] Furthermore, it appears that the tendency to conform to peer-group norms occurs only in the absence of monitoring by parents and teachers. In other words, the threat of exposure to adults has the effect of diminishing pressure to conform to the standards of peers.[36] The presence of parents and other adults in the lives of teenagers is critical if young people are going to be equipped to withstand the negative pressures of their friends and peers. Again, it is normal for youth to spend more time with their peers than with their parents. But, as Walt Mueller argues, parents who choose to become overinvolved in work, recreation, and other activities are making the choice to spend less time with their family. They are, as a result, opening the door for their teenagers to spend more time with members of their peer group.[37]

Fourth, the influence of peers plays a greater role during the adolescent years than in either childhood or young adulthood. It is in the adolescent years that peer pressure reaches its greatest intensity. In their empirical study of preadolescents and early adolescents, Benson, Williams, and

33. Bibby and Posterski, *Teen Trends,* 205; Brittain, "Adolescent Choices," 230; Sebald, "Adolescent's Shifting Orientation towards Parents and Peers"; Sebald, *Adolescence,* 230.

34 Guerney and Arthur, "Adolescent Social Relationships," 96.

35. Ibid.

36. Bronfenbrenner, "Response to Pressure from Peers, 438.

37. Mueller, *Understanding Today's Youth Culture,* 184.

Johnson found the influence of peers to increase with each succeeding age.[38]

Philip Costanzo and Marvin Shaw extended their study into late adolescence and young adulthood and found a curvilinear pattern whereby peer influence peaked in early adolescence and declined in the later teenage years. This decline continued into the early adulthood years, at which point individuals no doubt learned that there are some situations that call for conformity while others call for individual action.[39]

This shifting in loyalty from family to peers appears to be a necessary phase in the process of *individuation,* or in the manner in which an adolescent becomes a separate, unique individual, with his or her own interests, identity, values, and personality. The need for peer acceptance increases with age so that by adolescence this need is most acute. During adolescence peer approval becomes central to a positive concept of self.[40] In early and midadolescence, teens seek affiliation with others rather than trying to distinguish themselves, because of the heightened need for connection, affiliation, and belonging.[41]

Finally, peer influence can be either positive or negative. Peter Benson and his colleagues found that by and large preadolescents and early adolescents did not experience a great deal of peer pressure toward negative behavior. They did find, however, that at each age boys reported higher levels of negative peer pressure than girls[42] while girls were more likely to conform to negative pressure from peers.[43] Empirical research studies indicate that the influence of friends and peers indisputably contributes to deviant behaviors such as drug and alcohol use,[44] difficulties with teachers and school,[45] and delinquency.[46]

Negative peer pressure is of great concern to parents and youth workers alike. Adults often point to the negative effects of peer influence such as substance abuse, delinquent behavior, or rudeness. But adolescents can also influence each other in positive ways: to be compassionate,

38. Benson et al., *Quicksilver Years,* 27.

39. Costanzo and Shaw, "Parent and Peer Group Influences on Adolescents."

40. Guerney and Arthur, "Adolescent Social Relationships," 91.

41. Newman and Newman, "Group Identity and Alienation," 516.

42. Benson et al., *Quicksilver Years,* 30.

43. Pearl et al., "Resisting or Acquiescing to Peer Pressure," 44.

44. Lutes, *What Teenagers are Saying,* 24, 50.

45. Simons, et al., "Effect of Social Skills, Values, Peers, and Depression," 466–81.

46. Sebald, *Adolescence,* 170.

to share their faith, to pray and study the Word, to help those in need, to be friends to others, and to reach out to the lonely and hurting.

Many youth workers are recognizing the powerful impact adolescents can have on one another and are training their young people for what is called "peer ministry." Ministry to teenagers is often best done by other teenagers, not adults, and youth ministries grow only as young people are equipped, encouraged, and released to do the work of ministry to their peers. Merton Strommen concludes that adolescents, when properly trained, can become an important and effective resource for reaching lonely and alienated youth. He bases his assumptions on the results of a Search Institute study that tested the effectiveness of programs that trained high-school youth to reach out to the friendless.[47]

It then becomes the task of adult leaders to equip young people to carry out ministry to their friends and peers. This is the challenge Paul gave to Timothy when he said, "And the things you have heard me say in the presence of many witnesses entrust to reliable men who will also be qualified to teach others" (2 Tim. 2:2, NIV). It is also the strategy modeled by Christ, who spent the majority of his time and efforts in the choosing of his disciples, instructing them in the techniques of ministry, and sending them out to do ministry.

Mike Yaconelli and Jim Burns offer the following suggestions for a healthy peer ministry:

- Teenagers should not just *go* to the youth group. They should *do* the youth group. They should be given opportunities to use their gifts and abilities in youth ministry programs, rather than passively occupy seats and watch.

- Youth ministry should provide plenty of small-group activities, the primary source of peer ministry opportunities.

- Youth should be encouraged to write letters, cards, and notes of encouragement to their peers.

- Youth ministry should involve adolescents in service projects such as feeding the hungry, tutoring immigrants, or visiting shut-ins.[48]

Yaconelli and Burns conclude that adolescents are the best programming resource an adult leader has and can participate in almost

47. Strommen, *Five Cries of Youth,* 90–91.
48. Yaconelli and Burns, *High School Ministry,* 107.

any aspect of ministry. This chapter, as well as other parts of the book, includes many suggestions for preparing and involving adolescents in peer ministry.

POPULARITY

Over the decades researchers have noted that popularity is one of the most emphasized values among teenagers. For example, James Coleman, in a well-known survey of high school students in the early 1960s, found a strong desire to be popular, a desire that was more intense for females than for males.[49] In a longitudinal study of suburban high school students done between 1976 and 1982, Hans Sebald and Karen Krauss discovered the importance attached to being popular in high school. The 1976 responses to the question "How important is it to be liked and accepted by other teenagers?" showed that 47 percent felt it to be of "very great importance," 37 percent of "great importance," 14 percent of "some importance," and only 2 percent of "no importance." The 1982 study revealed a distribution of 17 percent ("very great importance"), 37 percent ("great importance"), 41 percent ("some importance"), and 4 percent ("no importance") on the same question. The 1982 study reported a sharp decrease in the "very great importance" category and a marked increase in the "some importance" category. However, when all categories reporting "importance" were combined, there was only an insignificant decrease from 98 to 95 percent from 1976 to 1982.[50]

In the 1987 study of early adolescents by Search Institute, "to be popular at school" was seen as important by a little less than half of respondents; however, this response ranked near the bottom of twenty-four items. The desire for popularity did increase slightly, though, as the respondents got older.[51]

Interestingly, not all research studies support the notion that popularity is highly valued by teenagers. According to a 1992 study by Bibby and Posterski, only 22 percent of Canadian youth viewed "being popular" as very important. Compare this response to freedom (86 percent) and friendship (84 percent), the items that ranked first and second as valued

---

49. Coleman, *Adolescent Society*, 30.

50. Reported in Sebald, *Adolescence*, 228.

51. Benson et al., *Quicksilver Years*, 92–93.

goals in life by Canadian youth.[52] The responses did not differ significantly from a 1984 study that asked the same question.[53] A 2002 study by
Bibby, however, indicated that only 16 percent of Canadian youth viewed
popularity as very important, marking a significant drop in that value.[54]

Teenagers seem to make a clear distinction between personal relationships or friendship, and being popular. Popularity may be seen more
as pleasing or leading the crowd, whereas friendship is identified with intimacy and meaningful acceptance. This may very well represent a recent
and positive trend, as earlier researchers noted popularity as one of the
most emphasized values among teenagers. It may be that contemporary
adolescents are not concerned with being popular as much as they are
with fitting in and being accepted.

Nonetheless, adolescents want to feel accepted by their peers, and
often this is displayed through a seeking to be popular. However, one
of the main prices of popularity is conformity. This is especially true of
younger adolescents up to age thirteen. When Sebald and Krauss asked
respondents "What is expected of a teenager by his or her friends in order to be popular with them?" they ranked the conformity principle first
(that is, doing, speaking, thinking, dressing, and so forth, "our way"). The
second criterion was a "good personality"; the third was "being yourself";
fourth was taking an interest in others and helping them; fifth was being
honest and trustworthy.[55]

Rather than overindulging in conforming to harmful or questionable activities in attempts to gain popularity, adolescents should be encouraged to build meaningful friendships within and outside the youth
group. The youth worker can assist group members to establish deepening friendships by encouraging them to apply five relation-building
steps:[56]

- *Place a high priority on relationships.* Deep friendships require much
  time and effort and should not be taken for granted.

- *Cultivate transparency.* Learn to be open and honest with others;
  talk about what is on your heart.

52. Bibby and Posterski, *Teen Trends,* 15.

53. Bibby and Posterski, *Emerging Generation,* 17.

54. Bibby, *Canada's Teens,* 13–14.

55. Sebald, *Adolescence,* 228.

56. McGinnis, *Friendship Factor,* 20–58; Rice, *Up Close & Personal,* 128.

- *Share your affections.* Tell your friends how you feel about them; that you like them and care for them.

- *Learn and offer the gestures of love.* Do things regularly for others that affirm the friendships. Giving a gift or taking a friend out for supper are examples of gestures of love.

- *Create space in your friendship.* Do not try to control, manipulate, or smother the other person. Strong relationships allow for both closeness and freedom.

Many teenagers go to great lengths to be accepted and affirmed by large groups of peers. They get a strong sense of security through an active social life and large groups of people. However, getting close to a few friends is even more important than receiving 100 "likes" on a social-media post.

LONELINESS

Fifteen-year-old Trevor woke up with a dull, empty feeling in his stomach. It was time to get ready for another day at school, but it was the last thing in the world that he wanted to do. Trevor always had a difficult time making friends and developing relationships. But two months ago his dad was transferred to a new city, and the whole family, of course, was forced to move. This meant leaving the few friends he had, his school where he had begun to feel somewhat comfortable, and his youth group—the only place besides his home where he felt any measure of belonging and acceptance. Now Trevor was convinced that he did not have a friend in the world and felt an intense loneliness he was sure could never go away.

Loneliness has been called "the world's most common mental health problem," "one of the most universal sources of human suffering," an "almost permanent condition for millions of people,"[57] and an "emotional epidemic."[58] One might think that teenagers, with all the activities they are involved in and the people they are constantly with, are immune to the trauma of loneliness. However, several research studies indicate that between 25 and 45 percent of American teenagers experience serious

---

57. Collins, *Christian Counseling,* 92.
58. Ellison, *Loneliness,* 17.

loneliness at some point during their adolescent years.[59] Bibby discovered similar numbers for Canadian youth. Thirty percent of these teens indicated that they were bothered "a great deal" or "quite a bit" by loneliness. Interestingly, this was a drop of about 5 percent from his 1984 study. Females in both studies expressed more of a concern over loneliness than did males.[60]

Samuel Natale suggests that adolescents are at a stage of life when they are extremely vulnerable to feelings of loneliness. Adolescence is normally seen as a time during which friendships and relationships become more valued, peers become increasingly significant, and the need for social acceptance is at its peak. For some teenagers, unfortunately, the adolescent years are spent in rejection, alienation, and loneliness.[61] Youth pastors and volunteer workers must enable youth to effectively deal with feelings of loneliness and help them understand their source. Furthermore, it is of utmost importance that youth ministry programs be designed and implemented so as to minimize the possibility of loneliness being perpetuated in the youth group setting.

Causes of Loneliness

Loneliness is an emotional state that involves a conscious lack of warmth, contact, and friendship. It involves feelings of inner emptiness, isolation, and intense longings to be accepted by other human beings. Loneliness is not necessarily a matter of aloneness, for even people who are surrounded by others often feel alienated, left out, rejected, or unwanted. On the other hand, individuals can be by themselves and have no sense of loneliness whatsoever. Adolescent loneliness can have a variety of causes, most of which can be grouped into the following categories: (1) developmental, (2) psychological, (3) cultural, (4) social, and (5) spiritual.

Developmental Causes

Because adolescence is a period of profound physical, affective, and cognitive change and maturation, new capacities for intimacy and identity emerge. If the developmental needs for the intimacy and identity are not

59. Ibid, 18.

60. Bibby, *Canada's Teens,* 36, 180.

61. Natale, *Loneliness and Spiritual Growth,* 94.

fulfilled, loneliness is often the result. Intimacy includes the ability to be committed to close and lasting relationships, as well as the willingness to sacrifice and compromise as those relationships require. One alternative to intimacy is isolation and loneliness. Francine Klagsbrun, in her book on youth and suicide, says that youth who have received little love from their earliest days have, in a sense, lost love before they have even found it. As adolescents, they may retreat into a fantasy world and isolate themselves from others. They are incapable of giving or receiving love, and in the most severe cases they often become seriously depressed and suicidal, refusing to allow anybody to intrude on their lonely world.[62]

The issue of loneliness is not so much not having friends as not having the ability to commit oneself to others. To know the trust of deep attachments young people must entrust themselves to others, and the inability to do so robs them of the affections they need so desperately. When they are unable to open their lives to others in caring and loving ways, they do not experience the love and affection of others and consequently suffer through the experiences of loneliness.[63] An ideal way for adolescents to learn to entrust and open themselves up to others is by engaging in the ongoing life of a small group. A small group provides an opportunity to develop close relationships and offers a safe context for promoting and nurturing care and self-disclosure among members.

Identity achievement is another of the major tasks of adolescent development. This is the process, as described in chapter 2, whereby the individual is faced with the crises of answering the questions *Who am I? Where have I been?* and *Where am I going?* In the adolescent years the young person experiences the need and desire to be weaned from his or her parents while simultaneously feeling a linkage with them. No longer a child and not yet an adult, the adolescent agonizes over his or her identity in terms of a variety of roles and responsibilities. With struggle and a certain amount of emotional pain, the adolescent seeks identity in relation to sexuality, the opposite sex, peers, career, and self-worth. Because the teenager often feels separated or somewhat disconnected from the security of what has been, and at the same time is seeking new relationships and identity, adolescence can be a time of severe loneliness and frustration.

62. Klagsbrun, *Too Young to Die*, 46.
63. Strommen, *Five Cries of Youth*, 25.

Youth workers and the group itself can provide that sense of security that lonely, identity-diffused teenagers are searching for. Adult workers are advised to make special efforts to identify and spend time with lonely adolescents. While not allowing their time to be consumed with these individuals, youth workers must make sure these teenagers receive a certain amount of special attention and acceptance. This might include making sure lonely adolescents have opportunities to serve and to be involved, doing one-on-one activities with them, giving them a phone call from time to time, sending them a text message, or simply talking to them during a youth activity. Youth workers must resist the temptation to focus only on the attractive, successful, or identity-achieved teenagers.

Furthermore, the identity-seeking questions that teenagers are asking in the formative years of adolescence are best answered in the community or context of their friends and peers. The peer group contributes in many positive ways to the growth toward identity. During this period of alienation from parents and family, the peer group, in this case made up of youth group members, offers teenagers a forum in which they can communicate with people of their own age. There is a sense of security in sharing problems and tough questions with friends and peers they know well and feel they can trust. In a healthy community, adolescents can also experience the feeling that they are needed, a feeling that is critical for a healthy self-concept.

Finally, and most important, the youth group can reinforce the norms and values that have been taught by parents in the family context. In this sense, youth group members provide a social environment in which adolescents' identities are shaped, and they decide what kind of persons they will become.

Psychological Causes

In some cases certain psychological predispositions lead adolescents toward loneliness. Loneliness tends to appear more in adolescents who have low self-esteem, who lack self-confidence, who are shy and fearful, and who demonstrate an inability to care for others. Low self-esteem or perceiving oneself as a person of low regard is generally associated with high degrees of loneliness or social alienation.[64] The adolescent who feels worthless, unattractive, unpopular, or stupid, may have difficulty initi-

---

64. Ibid., 24.

ating as well as maintaining relationships. In contrast, high self-esteem assists in forming close personal relationships, which, in turn, reinforces that self-esteem, with the end result being a decrease in loneliness.[65]

Related to low self-esteem is a lack of self-confidence. Young people lacking self-confidence tend to screen out activities where they might fail. They generally will not try out for the school play, work on an important committee, or join in a spontaneous game of volleyball or softball because of a fear of failure. Adolescents who suffer from self-contempt may retreat into the world of imagination where they dream of themselves as worthy, or they may put up a false front to convince others that they are worthy. Both responses tend to separate the teenager from others.[66]

One way to be sensitive to youth who lack healthy self-esteem and confidence is to make sure recreational activities are noncompetitive and cooperative in nature. In cooperative games, youth play with one another rather than against each other; consequently, these games help eliminate fear and feelings of rejection. Activities that stress cooperation, acceptance, and success present more opportunities for teens to develop healthy self-concepts and self-confidence than do games and activities that guarantee failure and rejection for many. Some cooperative recreational activities were described earlier in this chapter.

Shyness and fear of social risk-taking can also hinder the initiation and development of relationships. In addition to the insecurity of reaching out to others, shy teenagers often erect barriers to keep others out because of fear of intimacy, fear of being known, fear of rejection, or fear of being hurt.[67] These youth need to be taught how to build and maintain friendships, nurture relationships, and effectively communicate with others. Skills that will assist the teenager in relating and communicating include listening and attending, conversation, and self-disclosure, all of which were described earlier in the chapter.

Teenagers who show an inability to care, or even demonstrate hostility toward others, may also find they are restricted in the initiation, maintenance, and development of social and intimate relationships. Selfishness and lack of interest in other people have also been found to be characteristics of lonely adolescents.[68] Involving youth in inner city

---

65. Collins, *Christian Counseling*, 96.

66. Ibid., 22–23.

67. Collins, *Christian Counseling*, 97.

68. Brennan, "Adolescent Loneliness," 202.

or Third World ministry is one way to develop a heart or compassion for other people. A mission trip to a country such as Haiti, the poorest nation in the Western Hemisphere, can be effective in creating a sense of compassion and concern in an otherwise uncaring youth.[69]

Cultural Causes

Some commentators suggest our contemporary society itself may very well be a significant contributor to loneliness. Rapid social changes in recent history have isolated people from close meaningful contact with each other and have made loneliness increasingly widespread. With the great migration from rural communities to the city that has taken place in the twentieth century, we can sense the dislocation and loneliness that has come with it. In 1900 over 70 percent of all persons in United States lived on farms and in rural communities. By 1975 it was just the reverse.[70] Psychologists suggest that although cities crowd people together physically, several factors about large urban configurations seem to create isolation, anxiety, and loneliness.[71] As people have moved closer together, there has been a tendency to withdraw from others. A fear of strangers or crime often leads to suspicion and avoidance, while crowding appears to increase feelings of stress, anxiety, and hostility toward others.

The technological-urban society of the contemporary world has a number of characteristics conducive to loneliness. Natale suggests that rapid technological and scientific changes have left young people deprived of a sense of belonging and community.[72] Psychologist Craig Ellison cites television as a technological advancement that promotes loneliness in at least two ways. First, television programs often depict aggressiveness and violence, traits that hardly promote intimacy and relationships. Second, the addictive nature of television tends to break down communication and interaction among family members, as each member is locked into a fantasy world. When television rules the household, there tend to be fewer family walks and discussions, and less playing together. Even

---

69. Two nondenominational organizations that are successful in engaging teenagers in cross-cultural ministry opportunities are Teen Missions International (www.teenmissions.org/) and Group Workcamps (www.groupworkcamps.com/).

70. Jackson, *Understanding Loneliness*, 24.

71. For example see Ellison, *Loneliness*, 81 and Collins, *Christian Counseling*, 95.

72. Natale, *Loneliness and Spiritual Growth*, 78.

when family members watch television together, there is relatively little discussion of the programs.[73]

The online expansion of social networks has not necessarily expanded the number of friends in the adolescent's social circles. Late adolescents have six to seven close Facebook friends, which matches their four to six close friends in real life.[74] What social media has satisfied is a deep need to present a best version of oneself to an omnipresent audience. Several studies have showed ties between the use of social media and narcissism and depression, given that social media feeds the infatuation with one's own self-projected image and isolation from real-life interactions.[75]

Inextricably related to technology is mobility, in that better transportation, the development of large corporations, and opportunities for advancement have required increased movement. Families today move so much that adolescents have little chance to form meaningful and long-lasting friendships and relationships with those of their own age. Consequently, argues Natale, for many youth, adolescence consists of a series of relationships that have been broken or never secured.[76]

In this impersonal, technologically heightened world where people communicate through computers and snapchats, text messaging, wi-fi, and cellular phones, teenagers need an emotionally warm environment where they can receive love, friendship, understanding, care, and touch. A scene from the popular 1980s comedy *Cheers* helps illustrate this. An overweight gentleman in a rumpled overcoat enters the bar to a welcome chorus of "Norm!" He walks to his seat at the end of the bar where he is at home with his friends who accept and know him. The theme song of the show says, "Sometimes you want to go where everybody knows your name. And they're always glad you came. . . ." Youth workers who want to meet the emotional, psychological, and spiritual needs of today's lonely and disenfranchised adolescents are encouraged to build a strong youth ministry program that promotes Christian community. Today's teenagers, as much as anybody else, want a place they can go where everybody knows their name.

---

73. Ellison, *Loneliness*, 68–73.

74. Landau, *Obesity* discusses the research from Christakis and Fowler, *Connected*.

75. Primack, et al. "Association between Media Use in Adolescence and Depression," 181–88.

76. Natale, *Loneliness and Spiritual Growth*, 81.

Social Causes

We stressed earlier that one of the significant changes taking place during the adolescent years is the distancing from parents and the movement toward peers and friends as significant others. The development of this peer and friendship network is an essential part of healthy development as peer groups provide emotional security, empathy, and friendship. Strommen found that a significant issue for lonely youth is having or not having friends. Most lonely adolescents in his study (87 percent) said that outside of their families they really belonged to no particular group and were bothered by the lack of friends at school.[77]

Clearly one of the deepest needs of human beings is the need to belong and be accepted. Rejection by peers has a terrible impact on an adolescent's sense of loneliness. One of the reasons adolescents are rejected is that they are not skilled in the activities that count in the eyes of their peers, such as athletics or music. Another reason is appearance. Those who are less beautiful or handsome, or have some sort of physical "defect" may have difficulty being accepted. Other adolescents may be rejected because their value system differs from that of the majority.

Wayne Rice, in his book on community building, tells the story of Dolores, a teenage girl. As a sophomore in high school, Dolores was short, was overweight, and wore clothes that were not in style. For these reasons she had few friends and endured life as a loner. For a short time, Dolores tried attending a church youth group but quit because the youth group rejected her for the same reasons she was rejected at school. She found that there was no difference for her between the youth group environment and the school environment.[78] The church youth group must be a place where teenagers who, like Dolores, normally feel lonely, isolated, and rejected can experience inclusion and acceptance—a place where scholastic abilities, appearance, or athletic prowess do not matter. This is what Christian community is all about!

Spiritual Causes

Even if a teenager's interpersonal relationships are secure and generally satisfactory, that individual may still experience a sense of loneliness or

---

77. Strommen, *Five Cries of Youth*, 24.

78. Rice, *Up Close & Personal*, 11–12.

alienation. Centuries ago the great church father Augustine wrote, "You have made us for yourself, O Lord, and our hearts can never rest until they rest in you." In the twentieth century, existential writers like Jean-Paul Sartre and Albert Camus have written poignantly concerning the anxiety, anguish, alienation, and loneliness that characterize a life without God.

There is a loneliness or sense of isolation that is spiritual in nature and comes to the individual who is separated from God or senses that life has no meaning or purpose. Life without God, Ellison reminds us, is impersonal and irrational, with no lasting intimacy. Ultimate intimacy, he goes on to say, depends upon finding, knowing, and sharing God.[79] Lloyd Ogilvie, in his collection of devotional reflections says, "We shall be lonely, in spite of the people around us, until we experience friendship with God."[80] This *existential* loneliness often comes because sin has alienated an individual not only from God but also from others. When God is ignored and sin is unconfessed, loneliness is likely to persist. There is a sense of despair and alienation among youth who lack a faith.

Perhaps no recent generation of youth is more alienated from God or senses a more profound despair than today's young people. Gallup polls find that while 95 percent of adolescents in United States believe in God, less than one-third have ever personally experienced the presence of God.[81] In one large denomination it was reported that 63 percent of the youth felt some degree of apartness from God and man; half of this group gave evidence that it was an acute issue.[82] In the ecumenical sample used by Strommen for *Five Cries of Youth,* 43 percent of the responding youth strongly wished they could find a deep faith in God, and the same proportion said they were "much bothered" because they did not feel close enough to Christ.[83]

Today's teenagers are part of the generation tagged as millenials—adolescents and young adults born before 2000. Sociologists and religious leaders characterize this generation as being distinctly different from preceding generations in many areas of life. Some of the most significant areas of difference from previous generations include a need to

79. Ellison, *Loneliness,* 212.

80. Ogilvie, *God's Best for My Life,* n.p.

81. Gallup and Bezilla, *Religious Life of Young Americans,* 23–28.

82. Strommen, *Five Cries of Youth,* 145–46.

83. Ibid.

achieve, high personal and social standards, and parents who see them as part of their own identity and purpose in life.[84] Nowhere is this difference more evident than in the area of religious faith and practice. Christian Smith observes that while many contemporary youth still believe in one all-powerful God, there is a general shift "away from certainty about God . . . and definite belief in other traditional, 'biblical' teachings."[85]

David Setran and Chris Kiesling describe many of the young people of the 2010s as ambivalent toward religion, not rejecting it as much as neglecting it.[86] This has played out into what is described as a practical atheism or therapeutic deism, a god who is most concerned with my happiness but is distant. Christian Smith and Patricia Snell found significant declines in the number of teens agreeing that faith was "very important" in daily life.[87] Teenagers who are seeking religion as an answer to this existential loneliness and life's tough questions are looking for a practical kind of faith that will make a difference in their everyday lives and communities. They tend not to be concerned about denominational affiliation, participation in formal liturgies and traditions, or traditional Christian practices such as evangelism and Scripture reading. Scholars across the board agree that these practices decline significantly across adolescence and into emerging adulthood.[88]

Ministry to Lonely Adolescents

How do youth workers assist increasingly alienated and ambivalent adolescents in establishing an intimate relationship with God through Jesus Christ? Reaching today's youth with the gospel message of hope and reconciliation means abandoning, for the most part, a preachy, confrontive approach that may have worked in the past. This strategy needs to be replaced with a personal, process-oriented approach. It is what Kevin Ford calls, "incarnational evangelism" and means becoming incarnate or being figuratively born into a teenager's world. He describes a five-step process in this approach to evangelism.[89]

84. DeBard, "Millennials Coming to College."
85. Smith and Snell, *Souls in Transition*, 125.
86. Setran and Kiesling, *Spiritual Formation in Emerging Adulthood*, 12.
87. Smith and Snell, *Souls in Transition*, 112.
88. Setran and Kiesling, *Spiritual Formation in Emerging Adulthood*, 15.
89. Ford, *Jesus for a New Generation*, 200–202.

First, do what adolescents do. Rather than inviting unchurched youth to a Bible study, worship meeting, or conference build relationships with them by taking part in activities that they enjoy doing, such as going to the beach, skiing, watching a movie, or attending a sporting event.

Second, enjoy and accept them as they are. The youth worker will be most effective in sharing the hope of the gospel with teenagers when the presentation is natural and unprogrammed. Adolescents tend to be suspicious, perhaps cynical, of adults who want to get close to them. However, when teenagers sense that a youth worker is genuinely accepting and caring, they generally respond.

Third, affirm that which is good in their interests and values. There are many points where the values and interests of the youth worker can intersect with those of an alienated yet seeking teenager. It is usually easy to find common interest in areas such as sports, hobbies, or music. However, the youth worker might also establish philosophical commonality such as an acceptance of the existence of the supernatural or an emphasis on responsible care and management of the environment.

Fourth, share the gospel message of hope and reconciliation in their terms. Jesus was a master at contextualizing, or telling his story in terms that the listener could best relate to. For example, when conversing with the Samaritan woman who came to get water from the well, Jesus told her about "living water" (John 4:1-26). When an adolescent refers to getting high on drugs or alcohol, the youth worker might talk about a "better high" one can receive through a relationship with Jesus Christ.

Fifth, invite teens to establish a relationship with God. This is no time, as Merton Strommen suggests, for a hard sell of the gospel. Rather, it is an occasion for enabling alienated teenagers to reflect on their relationship with God, their lonesomeness for God, and even their desire to flee from him. They need the freedom to discuss their rebellion and proneness to go it alone; they also need to be encouraged to remain open to God's voice and to take advantage of times when they can be heard. Finally, says Strommen, youth need to understand that Christianity is a relationship with a personal and caring God, and when that relationship is secured, the emptiness of a lonely life disappears.[90] It is imperative to remember that relationships are not be used as a tool to some other end, such as evangelization or program participation, but in order to live out Christian community and hospitality.

90. Strommen, *Five Cries of Youth*, 155.

DATING RELATIONSHIPS

One day, the 1920s story goes, a young man asked a city girl if he might call on her. We know nothing else about the man or the girl—only that, when he arrived, she had her hat on. Not much of a story to us, but any American born before 1910 would have gotten the punch line. 'She had her hat on': those five words were rich in meaning to early twentieth-century Americans. The hat signaled that she expected to leave the house. He came on a 'call', expecting to be received in her family's parlor, to talk, to meet her mother, perhaps to have some refreshments or to listen to her play the piano. She expected a 'date', to be taken 'out' somewhere and entertained. He ended up spending four weeks' savings fulfilling her expectations.

Beth L. Bailey, *From Front Porch to Back Seat*[91]

In the early twentieth century, a style of courtship that we today call *dating* was introduced to the American culture. What was to eventually become an institution of the youth subculture in United States began to supplant the old courting system of *calling*. According to the calling system, a gentleman would pay a visit to the home of a young lady where he might be served something to eat and drink, and the couple would engage in polite conversation.

Dating moved the courting patterns from the parlor to the streets and public forum. The urban setting with its restaurants, theaters, and sporting events provided young people with opportunities for new kinds of freedom to engage in close opposite-sex companionship without adult supervision. Furthermore, there was a reversal in gender roles as to who was the initiator in the courting experience. Whereas in the old style of courting the girl or young lady (or perhaps the mother) invited the gentleman to call, an invitation to go on a date came from the young man.[92]

By 1925 dating had become a universal custom in the United States and has been described as an American invention. In most societies or cultures throughout history, mate selection was a decision made solely by parents. In a few societies the parents still decide whom the children will marry while the children are yet infants, or even before they are born. In these situations the bride and groom often meet for the first time at

---

91. Bailey, *From Front Porch to Back Seat*, 13.
92. Ibid., 13–21.

the wedding; thus, there is no need for dating as a part of the mate selection process. In Canada and the United States, however, dating is firmly
entrenched in the youth subculture as an institution. Many teenagers,
though not all, begin this activity in early adolescence.

What is dating? A simple definition suggests simply that when a
boy and a girl plan to meet alone or in a group at a specified place and
time, a date has been arranged. Another definition describes dating as
activity that allows opposite sexes to interact socially with nonfamily
age-mates.[93] Romantic relationships are a central aspect of the adolescent social world, contributing to the development of both intimacy and
identity.[94]

Dating in Early, Mid-, and Late Adolescence

With the onset of puberty, adolescents begin to think about and interact
more with the opposite sex. Typically dating activity moves from mixed
groups or group dates to one-on-one romantic relationships that involve
a sense of passion and fidelity. The intensity and exclusiveness of dating
relationships become more intense across adolescence. In early adolescent dating relationships, adolescents tend to be concerned with how the
relationship will affect their status in their peer group. Early or casual
dating provides entertainment and opportunity for acquaintance but
little in the way of nurture, attachments, or support. Sexual activity is not
central to dating in early adolescence. Conversation about sexuality tends
to center on how to engage in sexual activity and on which activities to
engage in. Couples are relatively uninvolved emotionally, and conversation for the most part is superficial.

In midadolescence, many young people have developed at least
one exclusive partner relationship lasting several months to a year. Girls,
as an extension of their intimacy in same-sex friendships, experience
greater ease in romantic relationships than boys do. Having an exclusive partner or "going steady" still may mean different things to different
people. For some teenagers the relationship may be very serious, perhaps
approaching marriage; for others it simply means an exclusive arrangement between the two.

93. Guerney and Arthur, "Adolescent Social Relationships," 97.
94. Papalia et al., Child's World, 496.

By middle adolescence, or age sixteen, "adolescents interact and think about romantic partners more than about peers, friends or siblings."[95] This does not mean that these relationships can serve the gamut of emotional and intimacy needs typically only achieved through long-term young adult relationships. The end of a romantic relationship in a breakup is a strong predictor of depression and suicide.[96]

Functions of Dating

Dating serves a number of purposes in the youth subculture including social activity, status achievement, socialization, and marriage mate selection.

Social Activity

In many instances adolescent social dating is nothing more than an outlet for social enjoyment, recreation, and entertainment. Teenagers often go out on dates simply to have fun and to have companionship at social functions. Youth group social activities are ideal opportunities for teenagers to experience the enjoyment of dating without the pressures of getting physical or serious. This low-key atmosphere presents a healthy alternative to the tight dating patterns found in other adolescent circles such as at school, where one's lack of dating experience may lead to reduced acceptance from peers. The community aspect of the youth group should be broad enough to include those involved in various kinds of dating relationships and those who are not.

Socialization

Dating serves as a form of socialization. In this sense dating gives adolescents an opportunity to better understand themselves as well as members of the opposite sex. It gives a young person an opportunity to try out and learn about his or her own feelings and personality while discovering the personalities of members of the opposite sex. It allows young people to discover emotions such as anger, jealousy, love, and patience.

95. Ibid, 497.
96. Bouchey and Furman, "Dating and Romantic Experiences in Adolescence."

Status Achievement

Dating also may be a means of status achievement. Being seen with a popular or attractive boy or girl, a star football player,or a cheerleader, may bring prestige to an individual and raise his or her status within the peer group. Although status achievement is often at the center of early adolescent dating, Christian young people should be encouraged not to date for status or to allow physical appearance to be the center of a relationship.

Mate Selection

Finally, dating plays a significant role in the mate-selection process. Dating is often viewed as a form of courtship, with marriage as the ultimate goal. Teenagers find out what kind of person they get along with or do not get along with, what kinds of relationships are satisfying and what kinds are not. Dating is also seen as preparation for future marital and family roles.

Dating and Violence

Unhealthy dating relationships can lead to abuse and violence. According to the Youth Risk Behavior Surveillance report published in 2013, among students nationwide who dated or went out with someone in the previous twelve months, 10.3 percent had been hit or injured with an object or weapon on purpose by someone they were dating during that period of time,[97] and 7.3 percent of the students had been forced to have sexual intercourse.[98] According to another survey, one in eight high school girls reports rape during her high school years.[99]

There are three common types of dating violence: (1) physical—when a partner is hit, pinched, shoved, or kicked; (2) emotional—when a partner is threatened or verbally abused; and (3) sexual—when a partner is forced to engage in a sex act. Those who have experienced dating violence are more likely to face depression, eating disorders, and suicide.

97. Centers for Disease Control and Prevention, *Youth Risk Behavior Surveillance—United States, 2013*, 10.

98. Ibid.

99. Young et al., "Adolescents' Experiences of Sexual Assault by Peers."

They are also at greater risk for lower school performance, alcohol and drug use, and other risky behaviors. While we tend to think of girls as being at greater risk of abuse, studies indicate that there is mutual aggression. Peggy Giordano and her colleagues reached the following conclusions based on her studies of middle school and high school students:

> More than half of the girls in physically aggressive relationships said both they and their dating partner committed aggressive acts during the relationship. About a third of the girls said they were the sole perpetrators, and 13 percent reported that they were the sole victims. Almost half of the boys in physically aggressive relationships reported mutual aggression, nearly half reported they were the sole victim, and 6 percent reported that they were the sole perpetrator.[100]

If dating violence is as prevalent as the research indicates, then it is imperative to recognize the risk factors as well as to have policies in place to act on victimization. Teens at risk for dating violence tend to have been involved in substance abuse, to experience depression or anxiety, to participate in high-risk sexual activities, and to have had previous involvement in abusive relationships.[101] Those who perpetrate the violence also share a set of common characteristics:[102]

- high levels of anger towards women
- a need to dominate and be in control of women
- hypermasculinity
- a lack of empathy
- evidence of psychopathic and antisocial behaviors.

We urge conversations in schools, churches, and colleges regarding the inherent dignity of people, which rests in the image of God. Youth workers should describe how common relationship violence is and encourage conversations about dating and violence. Questions such as, how do you know someone you are interested in wants to kiss you? can be asked in small groups. Running scenarios can be a healthy training in assertiveness and values. John Foubert recommends asking teenagers this question: "If you are visiting some high school friends and find yourself

100. Mulford and Giordano. "Teen Dating Violence," 261.

101. Cutter-Wilson and Richmond, "Understanding Teen Dating Violence."

102. Lisak and Miller, "Repeat Rape and Multiple Offending," 73.

in a situation where you see a drunk girl going off with a guy to his room, do you think you have any responsibility to do something?"[103]

Me Rah Koh, herself a rape victim, identifies thirteen characteristics of date or acquaintance rapists that young girls should pay close attention to:[104]

1. Displays anger or aggression, either physically or verbally (the anger need not be directed toward you, but may be displayed during conversations by general negative references to women, vulgarity, curtness toward others, and the like. Women are often viewed as adversaries).

2. Displays a short temper; slaps and/or twists arms.

3. Acts excessively jealous and/or possessive (be especially suspicious of this behavior if you have recently met the person or are on a first or second date).

4. Ignores your space boundaries by coming too close or placing his hand on your thigh, etc. (be particularly cognizant of this behavior when it is displayed in public).

5. Ignores your wishes.

6. Attempts to make you feel guilty or accuses you of being uptight.

7. Becomes hostile and/or increasingly more aggressive when you say no.

8. Acts particularly friendly at a party or bar and tries to separate you from your friends.

9. Insists on being alone with you on a first date.

10. Demands your attention or compliance at inappropriate times, such as during class.

11. Acts immaturely; shows little empathy or feeling for others, and displays little social conscience.

12. Asks personal questions and is interested in knowing more about you than you want to tell him.

13. Subscribes excessively to traditional male and female stereotypes.

---

103. Foubert, "Supporting a Campus Culture," slide 63.

104. Koh, "13 Characteristics of a Date Rapist." See also Koh, *Beauty Restored*, 116.

If an adolescent, male or female, experiences rape, it is imperative to take them to the hospital, listen well, believe the adolescent by taking seriously their claims, do not ask a lot of questions, and engage with a professional counselor.

Dating and Sexual Activity

While not necessarily in conflict with the norms and values of most parents, adolescent dating does bring with it some parental concern. Parents may be concerned that their adolescent children not begin dating at too early an age—and for good reason. Many studies find a clear correlation between the age at which a girl's first date occurs and the likelihood of sexual intercourse before high school graduation. In other words, the younger a girl began dating, the more likely she was to have had sex before graduating.[105] Given the liberal view of sexuality in contemporary culture, one might expect sexual activity to be an accepted and integral part of adolescent dating. This is indeed the case. The Project Teen Canada discovered 11 percent of the teenage population to have engaged in sexual relations on the first date. Another 42 percent agreed that intercourse is appropriate after a few dates.[106] Since early dating appears to lead too soon to an inappropriate intimacy, there is good reason, as Bonnidell Clouse suggests, for keeping teenagers in groups and providing chaperones as much as possible.[107]

Readiness for Dating

When is a good time to allow adolescents to date? This is a question parents frequently ask. There is no right age, although midadolescence, around sixteen, seems to be an acceptable age for permitting either a daughter or son to begin normal dating—that is, to go to an activity or event without a chaperone. Before the teenager's sixteenth birthday, parents might allow him or her to go on occasional dates such as homecoming. Younger adolescents may occasionally be permitted to go on group or double dates. Another consideration is the maturity and responsibility level of the individual. Rather than setting an arbitrary age limit at

105. Miller et al., "Dating Age and Stage."
106. Bibby and Posterski, *Emerging Generation*, 75–77.
107. Clouse, "Adolescent Moral Development and Sexuality," 204.

which dating can begin, parents might work out a plan with each son or daughter.

CONCLUSION

This chapter has explored the expansive world of adolescent social relationships. The social-role changes that occur in adolescence have a profound impact on the teenager as well as his or her parents. Adolescence inevitably introduces significant change and upheaval in the typical family. Parents must learn how to relinquish power and autonomy to the teenager. In turn, the adolescent must learn how to cope with and function in an ever-expanding world of relationships. While this period of social transition may create a certain amount of emotional pain and anxiety for most teenagers, parents and youth alike can be assured that in most instances the struggle to achieve maturity in social relationships is followed by a state of relative quietness and stability.

7

Adolescents and the Institutions of School, Work, and Church

To understand the lives of adolescents and what it means to be a teenager, one must know where and how they spend their time. Sociologists suggest the paths of teenagers pass through three main domains—home, school, and public life. The home is the most pervasive context of adolescents' lives, claiming over 40 percent of their time. However, school can also be seen as a setting where significant socializing takes place, as youth are constantly exposed to the pervasive influence of peer relationships. For a number of teenagers, work consumes a significant portion of their day, and for many more the church and church-related activities constitute a vital dimension of their lives. This chapter addresses the adolescent worlds of school, work, and the church.

ADOLESCENTS AND SCHOOL

School is a way of life for most teenagers today. The various dimensions of the educational setting consume almost a third of the weekday schedules of teenagers—formal classrooms, the cafeteria, halls, and extracurricular activities. While in 1900 only one out of ten fourteen- to seventeen-year-olds were in school, today nine of ten in this age bracket attend,[1] and slightly over 85 percent of Americans earn a high school diploma.[2] For many teenagers, however, the experience is not always pleasurable. For

1. Busch-Rossnagel, "Adolescence and Education," 283.
2. Statistics Brain Research Institute, "High School Dropout Statistics."

a great number of adolescents school is faced with little enthusiasm or
enjoyment and is a source of strain and drudgery, especially as they grow
older. Nonetheless, most adolescents recognize school as a crucial part of
their lives, illustrated in part by the high percentage of adolescents who
actually remain in school. Reginald Bibby and Donald Posterski asked
Canadian secondary students how the government should arrange pri-
orities, and found education to rank in the number-one position.[3]

The education and school experience for American and Canadian
teenagers is a good-news / bad-news situation. In the United States, elementary, secondary, and higher schooling is considered a basic right for
every American citizen. In Canada the attitude is much the same, and
over the years both countries have prided themselves in their efforts to
make a quality education available for every individual. The bad news
is that the public school systems are under considerable strain and are
plagued by a plethora of problems. As early as 1983 the National Commission on Excellence in Education reported to the United States public
on the status of public or government-sponsored schooling in this country. The publication, called *A Nation at Risk,* included some dire warn-
ings for the future: "We report to the American people that while we can
take justifiable pride in what our schools and colleges have historically
accomplished and contributed to the United States and the well being of
its people, the educational foundations of our society are presently being
eroded by a rising tide of mediocrity that threatens our very future as a
nation and a people."[4]

Furthermore, secondary students have new forces to contend with,
as violence and victimization are a growing part of public schools every-
where. The discipline problems public school teachers are faced with in
the new millennium bear no resemblance to the issues they had to deal
with four decades ago. In the first half of the twentieth century concerns
were limited to what we would call minor or almost ignorable infrac-
tions—chewing gum, talking out of turn, making noise, running in the
halls, cutting in line, littering, and violating dress-codes. Today we would
list drug use, pregnancy, suicide, rape, theft, bullying, and shootings as
critical school issues.

3. Bibby and Posterski, *Teen Trends,* 224.
4. National Commission on Educational Excellence, *Nation at Risk,* 5.

Mediocre Grades and Low Achievement Test Scores

One of the major concerns of many people is that the academic performance of American students has been gradually declining. The National Commission on Educational Excellence asserted, "If an unfriendly foreign power had attempted to impose on America the mediocre educational performance that exists today, we might well have viewed it as an act of war . . . . Moreover, we have dismantled essential support systems, which helped make those gains possible. We have, in effect, been committing an act of unthinking, unilateral educational disarmament."[5]

Following are some indicators that conditions in American public education are declining:

- In a Program for International Student Assessment of math for fifteen-year-olds, the United States ranked twenty-fourth out of twenty-nine countries. The number-one-ranked country was Finland; Canada ranked fifth.[6]

- Fourteen percent or 32,000,000 Americans cannot read, or they read below a basic level.[7]

- About 19 percent of all high school graduates in the United States cannot read.[8]

- "Many 17-year-olds do not possess the 'higher order' intellectual skills we should expect of them. Nearly 40 percent cannot draw inferences from written material; only one-fifth can write a persuasive essay; and only one-third can solve a mathematics problem requiring several steps."[9]

By the 2000s, in spite of attempts to reform the public educational system, test scores for American students remain low and do not compare favorably with those of other industrialized countries. Parents and experts alike continue to be frustrated with the products of our public high schools. Obviously, the problem has not occurred overnight but rather has been transpiring for decades.

5. Ibid.

6. American Psychological Association, "Math Test Scores across 29 Nations."

7. Statistic Brain Research Institute, "Illiteracy Statistics."

8. National Commission on Educational Excellence, *Nation at Risk,* 9.

9. Ibid., 9.

High School Dropouts

The term *dropout* refers to anyone who leaves high school without a diploma. Dropouts are generally thought of as unable or unwilling to learn.[10] Compared to the 1920s and 1930s, when most students left school after the eighth grade, the percentage of students who graduate from high school is high.[11] Furthermore high school dropout rates in the United States continue to decline. As of 2013 the percentage of high school dropouts was 7 percent, down from 12 percent in 1990.[12] In Canada the rates are very similar—the rate plummeting to 7.8 percent in 2012 from 17 percent in 1990.[13] These lower dropout rates are an encouraging trend in education, although the number of students who quit school prematurely is still cause for concern.

There are a number of characteristics of dropouts, most of which probably overlap various socioeconomic and minority groups:[14]

- Their marks tend to be well below average.
- They have failed at least one school grade.
- They tend to display behavior problems that require discipline.
- They tend to change schools frequently.
- They seldom participate in extracurricular activities.
- Parents often have lower levels of education and occupation.
- Families tend to be characterized by lack of communication, by a lack of personal satisfaction with each other's company, by a low level of happiness in the home, and by nonacceptance of one another as total persons.
- They tend to have low self-esteem.

Not all dropouts exhibit lower academic ability. Some average or above-average students drop out of school because they feel the requirements of high school are stifling or not challenging enough. They may sense that school and the available curriculum are not effectively

---

10. Sebald, *Adolescence*, 164.

11. Busch-Rossnagel, "Adolescence and Education," 300.

12. National Center for Education Statistics, "Status Dropout Rates."

13. Employment and Social Development Canada, "Learning—School Dropouts."

14. Summarized from Busch-Rossnagel, "Adolescence and Education," 301–2.

equipping them for life in the real world.[15] Furthermore, the public school system is geared to a large degree to young people who are going on to college or university. Many high schools provide relatively little in the way of preparation for adolescents who are not considering higher education. David Elkind calls this group of teenagers the *forgotten half,* because there is so little provided for them in the way of alternative training.[16] For these teenagers, there is a lack of relevance between the school's curriculum and the circumstances of their lives. The option of dropping out of school and getting a job may appear somewhat more attractive than staying in school and studying courses in which they are not interested. Other variables related to school dropout include poverty, broken homes, abuse at the hands of family members, negative influence from peers, learning disabilities, and lack of interest in schoolwork.[17]

The consequences of dropping out of high school are debilitating. It is likely that the dropout will have low lifetime earnings and a greater possibility of being unemployed. Furthermore, research studies indicate that lower schooling attainment is related to poverty, divorce, and early death.[18]

Here is an opportunity for the youth worker to do informal counseling with the intent of helping the potential dropout realize the necessity of completing high school. It may also mean helping the dropout explore the alternatives to getting a diploma. A regular return to high school may not always be possible because of age differences between the potential dropout and other students or because of a time lapse since the dropout last took courses. Other means to graduation include attending night courses, taking correspondence courses, or attending special schools designed for school returnees.

Violence in Schools

There was a time schools were relatively immune from the violence and crime that has spread throughout American society. This is no longer the situation on most public secondary school campuses. Though the school should be a haven of security like the home, public schools and

15. Ibid., 301.

16. Elkind, *Sympathetic Understanding of the Child,* 206.

17. Sebald, *Adolescence,* 166–75.

18. Busch-Rossnagel, "Adolescence and Education," 303.

schoolyards now often resemble battlegrounds. Gun violence is on the rise in schools all over America—in big cities, small towns, inner cities, suburbs, and rural areas. Inner-city schools have added "drive-by-shooting drills" to traditional fire drills. Some campuses are fenced in, are equipped with metal detectors, have locker searches and student shakedowns, or employ uniformed security officers.

The following striking statistics from the Youth Risk Surveillance Survey (2013) underscore the violence perpetrated in public schools in the United States.[19]

- Slightly more than 5 percent of students carried a weapon such as a gun, knife, or club on school property on at least one day in the month prior to the survey.

- Almost 7 percent of students had been threatened or injured with a weapon on school property one or more times during the twelve months prior to the survey.

- During the twelve months prior to the survey, 3.1 percent of the students nationwide had been in a physical fight at least once in which they were injured to the degree they had to be treated by medical personnel.

- During the twelve months prior to the survey, 8.1 percent of the students had been in a physical fight on school property at least once.

- During the thirty days before the survey, 7.1 percent of the students had not gone to school on at least one day because of safety concerns either at school or on their way to school.

- Close to 15 percent of students had been bullied electronically (through e-mail, chat rooms, instant messaging, websites, or texting) during the 12 months before the survey.

- During the twelve months prior to the survey 19.6 percent of students had been bullied on school property.

In Canada, violence in the public school environment is increasing as well. Fifty percent teenagers feel that violence is a "very serious" problem in their schools. Furthermore, 32 percent have said they knew

---

19. Centers for Disease Control and Prevention, *Youth Risk Behavior Surveillance United States, 2013*," 7–10.

someone who had been physically attacked at school, and 22 percent indicated that they did not feel safe at school.[20]

On April 20, 1999, at Columbine High School in Littleton, Colorado, a teacher and twelve students were killed by senior students Eric Harris and Dylan Klebold. The students also injured twenty-one other students before committing suicide. While shootings have plagued schools since the late 1700s, Columbine marked the beginning of a new wave of violent acts on high school campuses in both the United States and Canada. In the decade following the Columbine tragedy there were 147 school-related deaths, a decline from 162 in the decade of the nineties.[21] Bibby summarizes the violent acts that occurred in Canada in a brief period after the Columbine High tragedy. He notes that the Littleton shooting was[22]

> followed on April 28 by the shooting of two students, one fatally, in Taber, Alberta. Ever since, threats of violence in schools across Canada have been abounding. A knife attack on the one-year anniversary of Columbine April 2000 resulted in the wounding of four students and one staff member at Cairine Wilson High School in the Ottawa suburb of Orleans. In November 2000 a Toronto teen admitted he had shown classmates a list of fourteen students he planned to kill and had attempted to buy an assault rifle over the Internet to carry out his plan. The same month a student was stabbed to death at Calgary's Lester B. Pearson High School.

School violence has obvious detrimental effects on adolescents. With students literally fearing for their lives, learning is next to impossible in some of the most dangerous schools. The ever-present threat of fights, stabbings, or shootings leaves many students more concerned with mere survival than with science or history. Mental health experts are concerned about the psychological impact that all the real-life violence in schools may have on adolescents. One researcher suggests the possibility of an epidemic of posttraumatic stress syndrome, which will significantly hinder normal development.[23] Furthermore, school violence is numbing

20. Bibby and Posterski, *Teen Trends,* 228.

21. K12 Academics, "History of School Shootings in the United States." The number of incidents include elementary schools as well; however the large majority of shootings occur in middle and high schools.

22. Bibby, *Canada's Teens,* 79.

23. Morganthau, "It's Not Just New York . . ."

in that it signals to teenagers that violence is normal. In addition, violence increases the fear of becoming victims, which in turn makes adolescents likely to interpret the intentions of others as threatening, perhaps causing them to resort to violence themselves.[24] The overall result is a shocking increase in juvenile violence and crime, and the loss of human lives.

To what can this new and frightening code of school conduct be attributed? Sociologists point to several sources. Some authorities suggest it is the result of the hopelessness of poverty. While it may be true that poverty, often intensified by discrimination, contributes to violence, it must be recognized that the rise in school violence is seen in all socioeconomic classes. Other specialists agree that the breakdown of the American family is a major contributor. One source says that 70 percent of juvenile court cases involve children from single-parent families.[25]

Many young people are surrounded by violence. Real-life shootings are a way of life for a number of youth, and for nearly all children and teenagers, television brings murders and violent acts into the living room. This exposure to so much violence has a deadening effect on young people and unambiguously communicates that violence is normal. The ready availability of guns has escalated conflict into a deadly affair. According to one survey, 35 percent of inner-city youths carry guns, and 70 percent said family members own guns. In one suburban school, 18 percent of the students owned handguns.[26]

THE ADOLESCENT AND THE WORKPLACE

The nature of adolescence and the adolescent lifestyle has undergone dramatic transformation since the 1950s, and one area of significant change has been the workplace. In growing numbers, adolescents have entered the world of work, holding down jobs that consume a significant portion of their time and energy after school, on school nights, and on weekends. The large adolescent part-time labor force that helps staff fast-food restaurants, all-night corner stores and gas stations, retail stores, factories, and motels has become a familiar part of the North American social landscape.

24. Toch, "Violence in Schools."
25. Ibid.
26. Ibid.

This pattern of full-time students engaged in part-time work exists in distinct contrast to patterns in other parts of the world. In some European countries, for example, young adolescents enter into a work apprentice program in conjunction with their school education. In many other countries of the Western world, it is uncommon for adolescents to participate vigorously in the workforce while attending school. In the United States, adolescents have been a part of the labor force in the past. However, young people who work today have motivations for employment that are very different from the motivations of the youth of earlier years, and the work they perform differs significantly in nature and kind.

Historical Patterns of Adolescent Employment in the United States

Historically, the practice and pattern of working youth in the United States have gone through three stages or phases: up to the twentieth century, the early twentieth century, and 1945 to the present.

Phase 1: Up to the Twentieth Century

Until the beginning of the twentieth century, it was common for almost all youth and, indeed, many children to enter the labor force in a full-time capacity. Until then, less than 10 percent of the nation's fourteen- to seventeen-year-olds attended school.[27]

Several factors contributed to this pattern of youth employment. First, society expected that children would work, and labor was seen as an integral part of the socialization process. Second, it was often necessary for young people to work. The money they earned or the services they provided—for example, on the family farm—was often essential to the survival of the family. A third reason for child and youth labor was to prepare them for their future occupation. This would take place in two ways. Often children followed their parents in the choice of occupation; thus, working with their parents served as on-the-job training. Youth also trained as apprentices, boys often beginning their training as early as twelve years of age. Fourth, child and youth labor was predominant because formal school was optional and often considered unnecessary for most occupations. Finally, there was a sufficient number of

27. Vondracek and Schulenberg, "Adolescence and Careers," 331.

job opportunities available for young people, making it an easy choice to enter into the workforce.[28]

Phase 2: Early Twentieth Century

A second phase spanned the first part of the twentieth century to about 1940–1945. During this period, opportunities for full-time employment for adolescents gradually declined so that the United States Census identified only 9 percent of the fourteen-to seventeen-year-olds as employed.[29] Rarely were school and work combined. In 1940 only 5 percent of the males and 2 percent of the females in the sixteen- and seventeen-year age bracket worked and went to school.[30]

One contributing factor to the major change in the youth employment situation was the steady rise in secondary education—the high school. Secondary education essentially released young people from employment. A second reason was the recognition of adolescence as a distinct stage of life. With the emergence of adolescence came the attitude that young people were not adults and that healthy emotional and psychological development required a period of time to prepare for adulthood roles and responsibilities, including work.[31]

A third contributor to the decline of youth in the workforce was the Great Depression of the 1930s, which left most adolescents jobless. This was followed by improved technology and automation, especially after World War II, which decreased the need for cheap labor and simultaneously increased the number of jobs requiring high school and college diplomas. Thus, a new pattern emerged—school instead of work.[32]

Phase 3: 1945 to the Present

Between 1945 and the end of the twentieth century, a third phase of youth employment emerged. If the first phase found young people almost exclusively in the workforce, and the second saw youth almost exclusively in school, the most recent trend sees adolescents combining

28. Ibid., 330–31.

29. Greenberger and Steinberg, *When Teenagers Work*, 14.

30. Vondracek and Schulenberg, "Adolescence and Careers," 332.

31. Ibid.

32. Greenberger and Steinberg, *When Teenagers Work*, 13.

school and part-time work.[33] According to the United States Department of Labor, 34 percent of sixteen-to nineteen-year-olds were employed during 2014.[34] As we view employment among in-school adolescents, it is important to realize that the above statistics may not clearly depict the student employment situation. It is estimated that as many as 80 percent of in-school adolescents will receive formal work experience before they graduate from high school.[35]

Given the high rate of part-time work among students, it is important to consider some of the factors contributing to this pattern. First, there is the cultural assumption that part-time working experience is helpful in making the transition into the full-time labor force. Thus, teenagers are often strongly encouraged by parents and other adults to seek out part-time employment.

A second factor concerns the surge of interest in youth employment issues in the 1960s and 1970s. Government legislation and education practices took aim at improving opportunities for youth employment, and encouraged the combination of schooling and part-time work experience. Laws such as the 1964 Economic Opportunity Act and the Youth Employment Act of 1977 provided billions of dollars for the development of a variety of youth employment programs. From the perspective of education, panels such as the Work-Education Consortium (1978) stressed the importance of combining school and work experience.[36]

Another major factor contributing to the rise of adolescent part-time employment has been the increase of the low-paying service sector of the economy (for example fast-food restaurants, clothing stores, convenience stores, and gas stations). These types of jobs are usually characterized by low wages, part-time hours, irregular shifts, minimal fringe benefits, nighttime and weekend hours, and little opportunity for promotion. While these are generally considered poor jobs for adults, they are good, or at least acceptable, for adolescents who also attend school.

Finally, it is argued that lower expectations in the school system make it possible for students to work at a job with minimal consequences to grades. Greenberger and Steinberg suggest that students have been allowed to shape academic programs for themselves that are

33. Ibid., 14.
34. United States Department of Labor, "Labor Force Statistics."
35. Vondracek and Schulenberg, "Adolescence and Careers," 333.
36. Ibid., 333–34.

unchallenging, and schools have become so undemanding that teenagers are able to invest considerable hours in the workplace without hindering their performance at school.[37]

Why Do Teenagers Work?

Adolescents seek employment for a variety of reasons. One influencing factor is related to simple economics. The expense of being a teenager has risen steeply in recent years. While the cost of adolescent "essentials" such as gasoline, movies, food, and music has gone up, the money available from parents (allowances) has not increased accordingly.

Coupled with increasing costs of adolescent staples is the unfortunate fact that teenagers have become more materialistic. Or put another way, they have developed over time an inflated desire for the acquisition of luxury goods. Expensive designer clothes, brand-name sports shoes, nice cars, cell phones, and electronic equipment are just a few items teenagers deem necessary. With a limit to what parents can afford or are willing to buy for their adolescent children, teenagers are forced to earn their own spending money.

Of course not all teenagers work for immediate gratification or selfish gain. Some seek employment to gain experience in the occupational field they find attractive, or simply because they are bored. In some cases teenagers are forced to work to help supplement the family income.

Arguments in Favor of Youth Employment

Adolescent employment is often extolled as an ideal opportunity for young people to develop and mature in various aspects of life. One of the strongest arguments in favor of youth employment is that it promotes personal responsibility. Greenberger and Steinberg found evidence for change in adolescents' level of responsibility in three spheres. First, girls who work gain a greater sense of self-reliance than those who do not (in contrast, working may produce the opposite effect on boys). Second, working enhances teenagers' view of themselves in terms of having good work habits. Finally, and most significantly, working leads to increased financial autonomy.[38]

37. Greenberger and Steinberg, *When Teenagers Work*, 191.
38. Ibid., 105.

A second argument in favor of student employment is that it can enable the adolescent to become better acquainted with the world of work and other practical matters, such as the handling of money. This argument, however, does not take into consideration the fact that work available to teenagers is usually menial and is often undertaken with little genuine commitment and motivation.[39] Furthermore, it is argued that most teenagers learn relatively little about the responsibility handling of money. The majority of adolescents save none or very little of the money they earn through working and spend it largely on themselves.[40]

A third argument for student employment is that work uses the adolescent's time and energy in a productive manner, for which the individual is financially compensated. Furthermore, employment can help the teenager in the process of attaining autonomy and self-identity. Finally, for some adolescents part-time work provides an opportunity to gain experience in the occupational field that they desires to pursue. While some teens successfully seek and find jobs that will provide them with firsthand experience in their anticipated occupation, experts counter this argument with the suggestion that most adolescents do not seek employment to gain experience in a chosen vocational field. Furthermore, the majority of the part-time jobs available to teenagers are menial and routine, and contribute relatively little to the shaping of one's future vocation.[41]

Drawbacks to Youth Employment

While there are identifiable arguments in favor of engaging adolescents in the labor force, there may be extensive costs incurred. Moving young people into employment situations can have negative, stressful consequences for the working student. One study found that working a great deal during the school year related to higher rates of drug and alcohol use, higher delinquency rates, poorer grades, and absence from school.[42]

Second, most part-time jobs involve highly repetitive and routine activities with few opportunities for creativity and decision making.

39. Csikszentmihalyi and Larson, *Being Adolescent,* 92.

40. Greenberger and Steinberg, *When Teenagers Work,* 106.

41. Csikszentmihalyi and Larson, *Being Adolescent,* 93; and Vondracek and Schulenberg, "Adolescence and Careers," 343.

42. Steinberg et al., "Negative Impact of Part-Time Work," 470–71.

Thus, they may nurture boredom and cynicism toward gainful employment rather than fostering a positive attitude.

A third argument against student employment is that there is decreased time with family and family activities, as well as less time available for friends and church activities. For the youth worker this can create some serious difficulties. Some youth ministries struggle because a majority of the potential youth-group attendees are consumed with school and work. This leaves them little time for involvement in youth activities. Furthermore, work schedules of different youth vary, making it difficult, if not impossible, to find a slot of time satisfactory for everyone.

Youth workers must be flexible and creative if they are going to have a significant impact on teenagers who work. One tactic the youth worker can take is visiting teens at their places of employment, perhaps over the lunch hour or coffee break. While this may be a cumbersome and time-consuming approach to youth ministry, it is personal. For a generation of youth who highly value friendships and relationships, this could prove to be a fruitful endeavor.

A second approach might be to replace or complement weekly large-group activities with a variety of small groups that meet at different times and on different days. It is easier to gather groups of four or five teens at a time than it is to convene a larger number of adolescents.

Helping Adolescents Make a Decision about Employment

Should adolescents be encouraged to work while in school? Essentially two alternative points of view must be considered. One view suggests that work is good and profitable for a teenager, while another argues that work interferes with healthy adolescent development and may in fact be detrimental to personal growth. The fact is that to hold exclusively to one view or the other is probably unwise. Whether an adolescent should engage in part-time employment or not depends on the situation and the nature of the individual. In helping young people to make the decision to work or not, the following questions should be considered:

- Will the job build and enhance commitment to work and promote responsibility and competence?
- To what degree will the employment interfere with school?

- Will the job interfere with family and peer relationships, church and youth group involvement, or personal well-being?

- Will the job contribute, even minimally, to future career goals? For example, a young person aspiring to be a mechanic might get a job at a garage so as to receive mechanical experience.

- Is the student capable of handling money through savings and responsible spending, or will he or she spend earnings selfishly or foolishly?

THE CHURCH AND RELIGIOUS LIFE OF TEENAGERS

The church is another institution that has traditionally played an important role in the lives of young people in the United States and Canada. There is considerable concern however, that adolescent interest in the church and religion[43] is rapidly declining. The evidence suggests that the church is failing to interest and retain the adolescent segment of the population.

The Role of the Church in the Lives of Teenagers

For at least three decades studies indicate that in the United States and Canada religion and the church play a moderate and diminishing role. According to a 1991 Barna Research study, just one-third of the adolescent population (34 percent) claimed that religion was an important dimension of their everyday activities, while 44 percent felt it was somewhat important. This is compared to 53 percent of the adults who felt religion was important to them.[44]

George Gallup and Robert Bezilla of the Gallup Institute identified similar results. They determined that less than half of America's adolescents (43 percent) believed it was very important to have a deep religious faith. On a list of nine personal values, religious faith ranked only eighth.

43. Typically evangelical Christians are reticent to use the terms religion or religiosity when referring to church activities or Christian formation. However when studying church activity from a sociological perspective the language is fitting. Since this section will be citing a number of sociological studies, we will use the terms religion or religiosity where appropriate.

44. Barna Research Group, *Today's Teens*, 34.

According to the study, teenagers gave greater importance to having personal peace and happiness, being well educated, helping people in the community, getting married, and having children.[45]

Regular attendance at a church or synagogue, suggests Kenneth Hyde, is a strong indicator of personal religious commitment.[46] If this is the case, how religiously committed are young people in the United States? According to Gallup and Bezilla, 48 percent of the teenagers surveyed said they had attended a religious service the previous week, down from a high of 57 percent in 1989.[47] Forty-one percent of the youth interviewed attended Sunday school or Bible study classes, while 36 percent were active in a church youth group.[48] The Barna report found that 47 percent of the teenagers researched attended church services every week. Another 22 percent went two or three times a month. Thirty-three percent attended church once a month or not at all.[49] In a 2005 study of Protestant teenagers Phil Schwadel and Christian Smith found that 45 percent of the teens attended church at least once a week, 47 percent indicated they were currently in a church youth group, and 55 percent reported attending Sunday school at least a few times in the past year.[50]

Studies of Canadian youth indicate that they are even less interested in religion and church involvement than their American counterparts. In 1984 only 23 percent of Canadian teenagers said they "very often" attended religious services.[51] By 1991, just 18 percent of the fifteen- to nineteen-year-olds indicated they were attending religious services—a decrease of 5 percent in just seven years.[52] In 2001, 22 percent indicated they attended a religious activity weekly or more often.[53]

The diminishing role of church and religion in the lives of contemporary youth is measured in other ways as well. The following findings from empirical research underscore this tendency:

45. Gallup and Bezilla, Religious Life of Young Americans, 11.

46. Hyde, "Adolescents and Religion," 120.

47. Gallup and Bezilla, Religious Life of Young Americans, 38.

48. Ibid., 32–33.

49. Barna Research Group, Today's Teens, 34.

50. Schwadel and Smith, Portraits of Protestant Teens, 15–17.

51. Bibby and Posterski, Emerging Generation, 121.

52. Bibby and Posterski, Teen Trends, 50.

53. Bibby, Canada's Teens, 118.

- When seeking help or encouragement, only 6 percent of adolescents surveyed would go to ministers or priests. Clergy ranked far below friends (72 percent), mothers (54 percent), fathers (38 percent), and teachers and school counselors (13 percent) as a source of help. More positively, 29 percent of the respondents indicated clergy have a lot of influence on them.[54]

- Friends, home, school, music, and television are rated ahead of religion as factors that adolescents believe have the greatest influence on their generation. Only 13 percent of the teenagers interviewed felt that religion holds a great deal of influence in their lives.[55]

- Only one youth in four expressed a high degree of confidence in organized religion—a lower ratio than within the adult population.[56]

- When asked if religion can answer specific problems, teenagers were usually evenly divided on whether religion could or could not. The problems and percentage of adolescents who felt religion could answer were as follows: drugs and alcohol (58 percent), sexual issues (55 percent), marriage and divorce (54 percent), government morality (45 percent), and world problems (45 percent).[57]

- In 1991, only 5 percent of Canadian youth indicated they received "a great deal" or "quite a bit" of enjoyment from religious groups, down from 24 percent in 1984.[58] In 2001, 21 percent indicated they received a "high level of enjoyment from" religious activities.[59]

- Only 1 percent of Canadian teenagers indicated they would turn to religious leaders for counsel on the subject of sex, and only 2 percent would turn to a minister or priest about what's right or wrong.[60]

Hyde reminds us that regular church attendance, as a mark of commitment, is even more powerful when it is accompanied by the habit of private personal prayer.[61] Most teenagers pray but not necessarily on

54. Barna Research Group, *Today's Teens*, 22.

55. Gallup and Bezilla, *Religious Life of Young Americans*, 11.

56. Ibid.

57. Ibid., 62.

58. Bibby and Posterski, *Teen Trends*, 51.

59. Bibby, *Canada's Teens*, 118.

60. Ibid., 248.

61. Hyde, "Adolescents and Religion," 120.

a consistent basis. According to Gallup and Bezilla, 42 percent of the
teenagers surveyed said they prayed frequently. For 49 percent, however,
it is only an occasional or rare practice, and 8 percent never pray.[62] In the
study of Protestant youth, 60 percent reported praying alone at least a few
times a week.[63]

The statistics having to do with church-related activities raise concerns in both Canada and the United States. Authors of the Barna report
of young people in the United States ask the telling question "Are we witnessing the emergence of a new generation that is decidedly turning its
back on religion as an important force in their lives?"[64] Gallup and Bezilla
conclude that churches and organized religion turn off many youth, and
that churches are failing to play a central role in the religious lives of
many youth.[65]

Canadian sociologist Reginald Bibby concludes, "Organized religion is in serious trouble with young people."[66] Fellow Canadian and
coauthor Donald Posterski sums up the situation in Canada by saying,
"The majority of young people in Canada are sending a sobering message
to those who value organized religion. Attendance continues to decline
and participation in youth groups is low. Relatively few teenagers place
much value on religious involvement. In the minds of the vast majority of
young people, religion is something marginal to everyday life."[67]

George Barna is not so pessimistic. Perhaps it is a matter of seeing
the glass half empty, as the aforementioned analysts do, or half full. Barna
argues that many teenagers are spiritually inclined and are open to giving
the local church or parish with which they are involved an opportunity
to prove its worth. He goes on to suggest that the attendance and participation figures of adolescents indicate amazingly high levels of religious
activity. The bad news, however, is that having given the church a fair
chance at persuading them to stay, large numbers of youth choose to end
their interaction with the church once they have the freedom to do so.[68]

62. Gallup and Bezilla, *Religious Life of Young Americans,* 38.

63. Schwadel and Smith, *Portraits of Protestant Teens,* 32.

64. Barna Research Group, *Today's Teens,* 34.

65. Gallup and Bezilla, *Religious Life of Young Americans,* 11.

66. Bibby and Posterski, *Teen Trends,* 50.

67. Ibid., 247.

68. Barna, *Generation Next,* 85–87.

Factors Related to Youth Involvement in Church-related Activities

What types of teenagers are most likely to be involved in church-related activities such as a worship service, a Sunday school class, a catechism class, a youth group, or a Bible study? Several factors characterize the participants of church-related activities.

Family Configuration

One important determinant of who participates in religious programs is family configuration. Youth who have both parents living at home are more likely to be involved in church activities than teenagers from single-parent families.[69] One reason adolescents from single-parent homes are less active in church-related activities is that the single parent is consumed with surviving in a less than ideal family situation. Emotional problems associated with separation or divorce may override other concerns the parent may have. Consequently, single parents often have relatively little time or energy left to make sure their adolescents are attending religious activities.

How can the youth worker encourage greater participation of teenagers from single-parent homes? One strategy is to take special care in ensuring that adolescents from these homes are informed of youth ministry activities. A special phone call or personal reminder from an adult worker or member of the youth group would be helpful. Furthermore, youth workers can take some pressure off single parents by providing transportation for their teenagers to youth group functions and other church-related activities.

Parents' Attendance

Parental religious practice is another major predictor of adolescent religiousness and attendance at church-related activities. In their study of Catholic adolescents, Antanas Suziedelis and Raymond Potvin found parental modeling to have a pronounced effect on the church attendance and religiousness of adolescent children—more so for girls than for

---

69. Barna Research Group, *Today's Teens,* 41.

boys.[70] Fern Willits and Donald Crider's study of Protestant and Catholic youth indicated that the parents' attendance correlated substantially with church attendance of both sons and daughters.[71] Dean Hoge and Gregory Petrillo interviewed Roman Catholic, Southern Baptist, and United Methodist youth and likewise found that parents have a strong influence on their children's church attendance and youth program participation.[72]

The research clearly indicates that commitment to participation in church and other religious activities is sometimes better caught than taught. It must be entrenched deeply in the minds of parents that they serve as significant role models for their teenagers' own religious practices.

Size of Church

Teenagers who are affiliated with large or moderate-sized congregations are more likely to engage in religious activities than those involved in smaller congregations.[73] Why are smaller churches and parishes failing to interest and attract teenagers to their activities and programs? Perhaps it is because the programs in smaller churches have so few members that the programs are limited in quality and resources and consequently are not appealing to youth. It is also possible that the lay volunteers are not truly qualified to be working with today's adolescents.[74] What can smaller congregations do upon realizing they are not reaching the teenagers around them or attracting new teens?

- Several small churches could band together, using their combined numbers and resources to develop a more exciting and impacting youth ministry.

- The church might invite a faith-based organization such as Youth for Christ or Young Life to cooperate in working with their teenagers.[75]

70. Suziedelis and Potvin, "Sex Differences."

71. Willits and Crider, "Church Attendance."

72. Hoge and Petrillo, "Youth and the Church."

73. Roehlkepartain and Benson, *Youth in Protestant Churches*, 72–73; Barna Research Group, *Today's Teens*, 41.

74. Barna Research Group, *Today's Teens*, 54.

75. Young Life is an independent organization that forms clubs of high school students; their website address is https://www.younglife.org/. Youth for Christ is a nondenominational organization that also works with junior/middle and senior high

- The church should be committed to making youth ministry a priority by sending adult volunteer workers to one or more of the numerous national and regional training seminars or conferences available in the United States and Canada.[76]

Academic Standing

Adolescents who are among the best students academically seem to be most likely to engage in religious activity.[77] The challenge goes out to youth workers to reach the below-average students, a group that sometimes feels rejected or ignored by the church. How can youth programs help integrate them into the full life of the church? One way to impact youth who are below average academically is by offering a tutoring program. Tutoring will not only assist these teenagers in their education but will also help them attain personal confidence and a stronger self-image.

Age

One of the most important predictors of participation in church and church programs is age. Older teenagers are less likely to take part in church-related activities than younger adolescents. Eugene Roehlkepartain and Peter Benson of Search Institute report an 11-percent drop in attendance to religious programs after the seventh and eighth school years.[78] The Barna report found that the oldest teenagers are consistently less likely than younger adolescents to take part in religious activities.[79] A dramatic downward curve of church participation was found among Canadian teenagers. Teenage church attendance among those who go "very often" drops by nearly 50 percent between ages fifteen and nineteen. Thirty percent of the fifteen-year-olds attend church regularly, 25 percent

school students. Their website is found at http://www.yfc.net/.

76. For example, Youth Specialties is a nondenominational organization that offers youth ministry seminars across Canada and the United States. Their website address is http://youthspecialties.com/. Group is a ministry organization that also offers training opportunities for youth workers. Their address is https://www.group.com/.

77. Barna Research Group, *Today's Teens*, 41; Gallup and Bezilla, *Religious Life of Young Americans*, 11.

78. Roehlkepartain and Benson, *Youth in Protestant Churches*, 72.

79. Barna Research Group, *Today's Teens*, 41.

of the seventeen-year-olds are regular attendees, but only 16 percent of the nineteen-year-olds continue to participate in organized church life.[80]

This dip in participation that comes with an increase in age is a matter of concern for youth ministries. Why do many youth drop out of the church and youth ministry activities as they increase in age? One could simply argue that disinterest in church and faith is a predictable dimension of growing up, part of going through the turbulent adolescent years. Barna argues that teenagers have always had a penchant for rejecting activities that adults revere or deem important.[81]

One analyst, however, insists that the inflexibility of some churches on theological and lifestyle issues causes many older adolescents to depart from the church. Many teenagers contend that they are given insufficient latitude to subject their faith to intense and deep scrutiny. Sensing they have been given a "take it or leave it" ultimatum, many youth choose to move in different directions, seeking different spiritual dimensions to examine or rejecting religion altogether.[82] By providing a safe context for youth to ask questions and explore answers to difficult questions, the wise and sensitive youth worker will reduce the possibility that adolescents under his or her spiritual care will leave the church.

Gender

Most research studies on gender differences indicate that females are at least slightly more active in religious activities than males at every age.[83] In their study of teenagers who are a part of mainline denominations in the United States, Roehlkepartain and Benson discovered this to be true. They found a greater percentage of girls (74 percent) than boys (67 percent) attended worship services at least once a week; more girls (43 percent) than boys (25 percent) volunteered for three or more hours of work in the church in the past month; a greater percentage of girls (35 percent) than boys (29 percent) participated in nonchurch religious programs for three or more hours in the past month; and 71 percent of

---

80. Posterski, *Friendship*, 28.

81. Barna, *Generation Next*, 86.

82. Ibid., 93–94.

83. Argyle and Beit-Hallahmi, *Social Psychology of Religion*, 71–79; Nelson and Potvin, "Gender and Regional Differences"; Suziedelis and Potvin, "Sex Differences"; Hyde, "Adolescents and Religion," 121.

the girls compared to 66 percent of the boys were involved for three or more hours in church programs other than the worship service in the last month.[84]

A study of Southern Baptist youth also revealed that females were more likely to participate in religious activities than their male counterparts.[85] On the other hand, a national Gallup poll of American teenagers found little difference between males and females in their church and youth ministry attendance patterns.[86]

While the research literature identifies females as generally more religious than males, much less empirical work has been done to explain these differences. Suziedelis and Potvin, however, posit one possible explanation. Based on their exploration of Catholic adolescents, they determined that certain aspects of the stereotypical male role such as aggressiveness, strength, and toughness are not compatible with particular dimensions of religiousness.[87] Thus adolescent males tend to be less attracted to religious activities than are adolescent females.

The youth ministry program of a church might be made more attractive to boys by including male-oriented activities. Outdoor and wilderness activities such as camping, backpacking, whitewater rafting, or rappelling can challenge the male psyche and competitive spirit. Competitive sports such as basketball, tennis, ultimate Frisbee, or soccer will also be appealing to many (though not all) teenage males.[88]

Are Our Youth Dropping Out of Church?

Late adolescence and early adulthood has always been a time of life when young people have dropped out of church. Recent research, however, indicates that they are disengaging in larger numbers and they are less likely than ever before to return to the church. David Kinnaman reports that almost 60 percent of young people with a Christian background and

84. Roehlkepartain and Benson, *Youth in Protestant Churches,* 73.

85. Nelson and Potvin, "Gender and Regional Differences."

86. Gallup and Bezilla, *Religious Life of Young Americans,* 33, 41.

87. Suziedelis and Potvin, "Sex Differences."

88. It is important to note that while guys tend to be drawn to competitive and more aggressive activities, not all boys enjoy them. Many male youth who are more oriented towards the arts, computers and technology, academics, and other less aggressive pursuits will feel alienated if youth ministries are dominated by sports and adventure-based activities.

who were regular church attenders in high school leave the church. He notes that they are not necessarily losing their faith—just the church. In fact he suggests, most of these young Christians "are struggling less with their faith in Christ than with their experience of church."[89] Kinnaman offers six reasons for the exodus of twentysomethings, along with some suggestions as to how youth workers might respond while they still have input into the lives of adolescents. While Kinnaman's insightful book *You Lost Me* speaks to the church disengagement of young adults, it is important to note that the answer to how we stem the tide of this disconnection really begins in ministries to children, families, and youth. With that said, we summarize the findings of Kinnaman, including some implications and suggestions for youth ministry. Young adults find the church to be

1. *Overprotective:* We are all familiar with "helicopter parents." Likewise, insists Kinnaman, youth find the church overprotective. For example, they feel that (1) the church demonizes everything outside the church, (2) Christians are afraid of pop culture (such as music and movies), (3) Christians create a false dichotomy between the sacred and the secular, and (4) the church does not want to deal with the complexities of the world. In response to this, youth workers might encourage their teens toward creative self-expression and risk-taking in areas such as music and the fine arts, or youth workers might help teens recognize that there is no difference in the kingdom between the sacred toil of ministry and work within secular professions.

2. *Shallow:* For many young people church is boring, is irrelevant to their career, does not prepare them for life, does not help them find purpose, and does not teach the Bible clearly. Consequently, many young people have a shallow understanding of their faith and are unable to connect their faith with their gifts, passions, and abilities. Youth ministries must be designed to bring teens into a mature and holistic relationship with God, to make disciples by "showing (not just telling) them how to trust Jesus, live for God, and participate in the Spirit's work."[90]

3. *Antiscience:* Many young Christians, because of the teachings of their churches, have concluded that faith and science cannot be

89. Kinnaman, *You Lost Me*, 27.
90. Ibid., 127.

reconciled. Yet these same young people have grown up in a world where science and scientific discoveries have shaped their reality through digital technology, medical research, environmental studies, brain studies, genetics, and discoveries about the universe. Today's teens have been more profoundly impacted by science than any other generation. And while over 50 percent of youth group teens aspire to science-related careers, only 1 percent of youth pastors addressed scientific issues in the past year.[91] Youth pastors "must do a better job challenging and training all young Christians—not just the science geeks—to think clearly, honestly, and comprehensively about matters of science."[92]

4. *Repressive:* Young people often feel that the church is too stifling with its rules—especially related to sexuality. Christian youth are torn between two contrasting views of sex and sexuality. The traditional view, which is repressive and controlling, and the individualistic view, which values all expressions of sexual freedom. Interestingly, young Christians hold more conservative beliefs than the culture at large about sexuality (the traditional view) but are generally just as liberal in their behavior as non-Christians (who hold the individualistic view). Generally Christian parents have frowned upon the practice of discussing sex and sexuality in youth group settings. In response to that position, Kinnaman argues that "we need a new mind to cultivate a deeper, more holistic, more Christ-filled ethic of sex."[93] Youth workers must start talking (and listening) about sex. Some topics to consider are marriage, gender and gender roles, and sexual orientation, as well as birth control and reproduction.

5. *Exclusive:* This generation of young Christians has been shaped by a culture that highly regards tolerance, open-mindedness, and acceptance. Consequently they have a difficult time accepting the Christian claim to exclusivity (John 14:6). This in turn causes the current generation of young Christians to be less likely to share their faith with others than previous generations have. Kinnaman teaches that the Christian story rejects both exclusion and tolerance: "The Creator was not content to exclude those who had rejected him, but

---

91. Kinneman, *You Lost Me*, cites two Barna Group polls from 2009—one of youth, and one of youth leaders.

92. Ibid., 142.

93. Ibid., 160.

neither was he prepared to tolerate our hatefulness and sin. So what did he do? He became one of us, one of the 'other,' identifying with us to embrace us in solidarity, empathy, and selfless agape love—all the way to the cross."[94]

6. *Doubtless:* Young Christians claim that the church and youth group are not settings where they can feel free to express their doubts. So we remind youth workers that the youth group must be a safe place to doubt, a place where teens can belong even though their faith might be wavering. In terms of how we create this safe environment, we affirm Kinnaman, who reminds us that "our posture toward students and young adults should be more Socratic, more process-oriented, more willing to live with their questions and seek answers together."[95]

CONCLUSION

The life of a teenager is multifaceted. The contexts in which adolescents experience life are divided primarily between the home and family (see chapter 5), school, work, and church. After the home, school takes up the largest block of time in the life of a teenager. Unfortunately while youth readily admit that school is a critical dimension of preparing for adulthood, teens often face it with little enthusiasm or enjoyment.

For as many as 80 percent of in-school adolescents, the work experience, whether part- or full-time will be a part of their preparation for young adulthood. For some teenagers, work will provide an opportunity to gain valuable experience in the occupational field of pursuit. Yet many of the jobs secondary students hold will be menial and routine, contributing relatively little to the shaping of their future vocations.

The church continues to play a significant though diminishing role in the lives of teenagers. There is considerable concern that in the United States and Canada that traditional religious institutions are failing to interest and retain the adolescent segment of the population. Many youth will depart from church for a period of time, and fewer and fewer of these dropouts will renew their relationship with the church in their middle or late twenties, as they did in the past.

94. Ibid., 180.
95. Ibid., 194.

8

The Maze of Teenage Sexuality

One of the central issues facing adolescents is sexuality, something that consumes their thoughts as they worry about their behavior and anticipate their sexual development. We live in a society that is characterized by an openness towards sex, led by the various strands of media and entertainment—television programs, various forms of advertising, movies, the Internet, stand-up comedy, and music. Sexuality is clearly a predominant thread of the adolescent developmental experience, with the biological maturation beginning at the onset of puberty and continuing for three or four years. Sexuality is on the mind of both adults (especially parents) and teens alike but for different and sometimes contrasting reasons. Parents and other adults responsible for the care and education of adolescents are rightly worried about teen sexual behaviors while teenagers themselves are consumed with thoughts about sex, which often bringing on a sense of anxiety. The words of a seventeen-year-old female from Canada may very well sum up the attitudes of many teenagers when she says, "Sex is like an everyday thing for teens now."[1] This chapter will explore the many facts and issues related to teenage sexuality, including sexual behaviors and attitudes, teenage pregnancy, abortion, homosexuality, masturbation, and sexual abuse.

1. Bibby, *Canada's Teens*, 89.

SEXUAL BEHAVIORS AND ATTITUDES

Some of the most alarming statistics concerning adolescents are related to their sexual habits, values, and attitudes. Permissive sexual activity among youth is clearly commonplace, even with churched teens. However, while sexual permissiveness reached its peak in the '60s, more recently adolescents have shown greater restraint and more conservative attitude towards sex and sexuality.[2] It is probably safe to say that the more conservative approach to sexuality is not due primarily to an increase in moral or ethical standards. Rather, the fear of life-impacting results of premarital sex such as infection from sexually transmitted diseases (STDs) or an unwanted pregnancy likely cause some teens to change their sexual practices.

The consequences for engaging in sex before marriage can be devastating—and not just for physical reasons. Most teenagers are not psychologically mature enough to engage in sexual activity without suffering painful emotional results from their experiences. While adolescents are physically capable of bearing children, they are generally neither emotionally nor economically capable of raising them. Of course, one of the most potentially harmful consequences of premarital sexual activity is acquiring an STD. Because sexuality presents so many dilemmas and harmful effects to adolescents, youth workers and parents alike are greatly concerned about the moral behavior of the teenagers they are involved with.

Premarital Sexual Intercourse

Contemporary adolescents live in a world where sexual intercourse is no longer seen as a moral issue or as an activity reserved for marriage only. The pervasive attitude of young people seems to be that sex is a personal right or choice and is associated more with a standard of permissiveness. An eighteen-year-old from Washington DC says, "In high school, everyone assumes you've already done it. The emphasis moves from 'Are you doing it?' to 'How are you doing it?'"[3] A fifteen-year-old from New York says, "Nobody cares anymore whether or not you're a virgin."[4] "For me, as

2. Coleman and Hendry, *Nature of Adolescence,* 98.
3. Painter, "Fewer Kids Save Sex for Adulthood."
4. Williams, "U.S. Teens Increasingly."

long as it's in a caring relationship, as long as you're making love and not just having sex, it's OK," says a seventeen-year-old from the Atlanta area.[5]

With regard to sexual intercourse, however, there has been a significant decline in its occurrence among teenagers in the last decade or so. The Centers for Disease Control and Prevention has gathered data from teens who report (1) having sexual intercourse in the past year and (2) never having had sexual intercourse. Comparing data from 1988 with data from 2002 researchers have seen a significant decline of teenagers (ages fifteen to nineteen) who had sexual intercourse at least once in the last year (51.1 percent in 1988 to 45.7 percent in 2002).[6] Since 2002 there has been only a slight decline in this type of sexual activity.[7] When asked the question in the form of ever having sex, they found the following results:

> During 1991–2013, a significant linear decrease occurred over-
> all in the prevalence of having ever had sexual intercourse (54.1
> percent–46.8 percent) . . . The prevalence of having ever had sex-
> ual intercourse decreased from 1991–2001 (54.1 percent–45.6
> percent) and then did not change significantly from 2001–2013
> (45.6 percent–46.8 percent). The prevalence of having ever had
> sexual intercourse did not change significantly from 2011 (47.4
> percent) to 2013 (46.8 percent).[8]

Adolescents in America are engaging in sexual intercourse at younger and younger ages as well. Nationwide, 5.6 percent of students had their initial experience with sexual intercourse before the age of thirteen years. The prevalence was higher among males (8.3 percent) than females (3.1 percent).[9]

Adolescents have always been troubled by sexual temptations and preoccupied with sexual thoughts and concerns. But the behavior of adolescents has changed dramatically in the last half of the twentieth century and into the twenty-first, and the sexual revolution among American youth is overwhelming to say the least. Why the drastic change in teenage

5. Pendered, "Sex: Teens More Open, Active."

6. Centers for Disease Control and Prevention, *Teenagers in the United States: Sexual Activity, Contraceptive Use, and Childbearing, 2002,* 16.

7. Centers for Disease Control and Prevention, *Teenagers in the United States: Sexual Activity, Contraceptive Use, and Childbearing, 2006–2010,* 5.

8. Centers for Disease Control and Prevention, *Youth Risk Behavior Surveillance— United States 2013,* 24.

9. Ibid.

sexual behaviors? Perhaps young people are simply finishing what was started by the sexual revolution in the 1960s. They are reflecting or adhering to the overpermissive sex norms of society at large, including those of their parents. Multiple factors are in play in influencing the premarital sexual behavior of teenagers, including parental modeling, parent-teen relationships, family structures, peers, religion or church involvement, and media.

The Effect of Parental Modeling

As indicated above, one of the variables in the relationship between family configuration and adolescent sexual activity is the effect of behaviors and attitudes modeled by parents, especially mothers. While most parents would not likely want their young unmarried child to be sexually active, many find themselves in personal conflict as they often endorse and model ideas such as individual choice and freedom to select one's lifestyle. Thus many teenagers feel they have evidence of adult hypocrisy, such as the Virginia high school student who rightly argues, "When my mother has a date Friday night and he is in the kitchen eating breakfast Saturday morning, how can she preach about premarital sex?"[10]

Adolescents simply follow the lead set by adults. When adults did not engage in extramarital or premarital sex, neither did adolescents. Since so many adults view premarital sex as socially acceptable, so do teenagers.[11] Empirical studies consistently support this notion. Results of one research study indicated that the mothers' dating behavior was positively related with their sons' early sexual behaviors (heavy petting and sexual intercourse).[12] Another empirical study of parental influences on adolescent sexual behavior revealed that if adolescents believed the mother had experienced sexual intercourse before marriage, then these adolescents were likely to engage in sexual activity. The researchers concluded that the mother's premarital experience might have served as a model to be imitated.[13] Susan Newcomer and Richard Udry discovered that the more sexually active the mother was before marriage, the more likely the adolescent child was to engage in premarital sexual intercourse.

10. Cited in Williams, "U.S. Teens Increasingly."
11. Elkind, *Sympathetic Understanding of the Child,* 194.
12. Whitbeck et al., "Effects of Divorced Mothers' Dating Behaviors."
13. Hovell et al., "Family Influences on Latino and Anglo Adolescents."

However, this relationship was weaker for sons than for daughters.[14] Finally, a national study of fifteen- and sixteen-year-olds revealed that those adolescent females whose parents expressed and modeled traditional attitudes about marriage and family life were only half as likely to report having sex as those with less conservative parents (9 percent as compared to 20 percent).[15]

The old adage *some lessons are better caught than taught* certainly rings true when it comes to teaching lifestyle practices and behaviors to adolescents. The onus is on parents to model a lifestyle that evidences purity and wholeness in the realm of sexual behavior. Single mothers or fathers who may be going out with someone themselves must be especially careful in their dating relationships. Teenagers are more likely to imitate the dating and sexual practices of a mother or father, than to follow rules and guidelines set forth by the parents.

The Effect of Parent-Adolescent Relationships and Communication

The effect of parent-youth relationships on the sexual behavior of adolescents has been well documented. The *Teen Sex Survey* of Josh McDowell Ministries revealed that sexual contact (fondling breasts, fondling genitals, and/or having sexual intercourse) was much less likely among teenagers who had a close relationship with their father. The researchers also found that youth who perceived that their parents spent a lot of time with them were less likely than others to report having engaged in sexual contact. They concluded, however, that spending time in conversation with their adolescent children was not enough to persuade teenagers against engaging in premature sexual activity. While building relationships is important, even more critical is taking advantage of that forum to lead adolescents into knowing how to resist sexual pressure.[16]

In a national study of fifteen- and sixteen-year-olds, the researchers divided the subjects into two subgroups: (1) those whose parents expressed traditional values about marriage and family life, and (2) those

14. Newcomer and Udry, "Mothers' Influence on the Sexual Behavior," 477–85.

15. Moore et al., "Parental Attitudes," 777–82.

16. *Teen Sex Survey in the Evangelical Church,* 5–8. The participating denominations were the Church of the Nazarene, the Evangelical Covenant Church, the Church of God–Cleveland, the Free Methodist Church, the Lutheran Church–Missouri Synod, the Grace Brethren Church, the Wesleyan Church, and the Salvation Army.

who transmitted more permissive values. Among daughters of traditional parents, a mere 3 percent of those who discussed sex with either parent reported being sexually active, compared with 20 percent of the daughters who did not discuss sex with either parent. Interestingly, among daughters whose parents expressed more liberal attitudes, discussion of sex with parents was unrelated to behavior. Discussing sex with sons had no positive impact on sexual behavior of subjects in either group.[17]

In another study of factors associated with sexual risk-taking behaviors among adolescents, Tom Luster and Stephen Small measured the influence of family characteristics on three groups: *high-risk, low-risk,* and *abstainers.* High-risk adolescents were those who had more than one sexual partner and rarely or never used contraception. Low-risk teenagers were those who had only one partner and always used contraception. Abstainers were those adolescents who practiced sexual abstinence. When the three groups were compared, the results indicated (1) that abstainers were more closely monitored by their parents (for example parents knew the whereabouts of their teenage children), and (2) that abstainers received more support from parents (parents were there when adolescents needed them) than either high-risk or low-risk males and females.[18]

The research underscores the significance of healthy relationships between parents and youth, as well as the importance of communication concerning sexual matters. Unfortunately, studies also indicate that too little communication between adolescents and their parents is devoted to sexuality.[19] How can the youth ministry program assist parents in talking to their teenagers about sexual matters? One possibility is to offer a seminar or class on "Talking to Your Teenager about Sexuality." If the youth worker does not feel comfortable with addressing or adequate to discussing this topic to parents, he or she might have an expert (for example, a medical doctor, nurse, pastor, or counselor) teach the class or seminar. The church or youth ministry program should also make available books or curriculum that parents would find helpful in discussing sexual issues with their adolescent children.

---

17. Moore et al., "Parental Attitudes."

18. Luster and Small, "Factors Associated with Sexual Risk-Taking Behaviors."

19. *Teen Sex Survey in the Evangelical Church,* 5; Moore et al., "Parental Attitudes."

The Effect of Family Structure

Clearly the structure or configuration of the family has a strong effect on the premarital sexual behavior of adolescents, daughters in particular. Keri Kinnaird and Meg Gerrard found that daughters from divorced or reconstituted families were more likely not only to engage in premarital sexual activity but also to have begun sexual intercourse at younger ages than daughters from intact, two-parent families. While only 53 percent of the subjects from intact families reported that they had engaged in premarital sexual activity, 70 percent of the divorced group and 80 percent of the reconstituted group reported that they were sexually experienced. In addition, among the daughters from divorced families, 57.1 percent of the sexually experienced teenage girls had their first intercourse by age sixteen. In contrast, 33.3 percent of the girls from reconstituted families and only 18.8 percent of those from intact families had their first intercourse by the age of sixteen.[20]

Newcomer and Udry reported that the state of being in a mother-only household predicted subsequent sexual activity of daughters, though not of sons.[21] Likewise, Brent Miller and Raymond Bingham found daughters from single-parent families more likely to have engaged in sexual intercourse than those from intact families.[22] A Search Institute study of both boys and girls revealed that 52.9 percent of the youth ages fourteen to seventeen from single-parent homes had sexual intercourse two times or more; this compared to only 34.5 percent of those from two-parent families who indicated having sex twice or more.[23]

What reasons can be given for more permissive attitudes and sexual behavior patterns of teenagers, especially daughters, from single-parent divorced households? There are a number of plausible explanations:

- Father-absent girls are deprived of the father's important teaching related to sexual behavior.

- Families with inferior interpersonal relationships, poor communication, and weak problem-solving skills, characteristics often found in broken or single-parent households, may inadvertently cause young people to look to peers for nurturing relationships and love.

20. Kinnaird and Gerrard, "Premarital Sexual Behavior and Attitudes," 757–65.
21. Newcomer and Udry, "Parental Marital Status Effects."
22. Miller and Bingham, "Family Configuration," 499–506.
23. Benson and Roehlkepartain, *Youth in Single-Parent Families*, 17.

- A single parent is unable to monitor or supervise teenage activities as effectively as two parents are. Single mothers are more likely to work full time than are mothers in two-parent households.

- Divorced mothers are less religious and have more sexually permissive attitudes than do continuously married mothers.

- Single mothers may be dating and may also be sexually active, thus modeling habits that overwhelm their attempts to control their children's sexual behavior.

- Single parents are beset by and preoccupied with problems and burdens that interfere with the supervision and teaching of their teenage children. Experiencing divorce represents a set of circumstances that is characterized by emotional turmoil, preoccupation with the marital problem, removal of one parent from the home, financial problems, and shifting responsibilities. In general, family life is in disarray. In such adverse conditions parents may lose control of their adolescent children's behavior.

Chapter 5 addressed the importance of building strong intact families. The need for functional two-parent homes is underscored once again in terms of the effect family structure has on adolescent sexual behavior. At every level or in virtually every domain of church ministry, efforts must be made to strengthen the family. Unfortunately, in contemporary society many teenagers come from homes in which marriages are no longer intact.

The responsibility for building strong marriages and healthy families primarily lies outside of the domain of youth ministry (and in the domains of premarital and marital counseling or marriage enrichment). However, there are some strategies youth programs can engage in to assist single parents and their adolescent children in handling the stress and pressures of life that contribute to inappropriate sexual behavior. For example, a support group might be formed for single parents of teenagers. In such a group, parents could be encouraged to talk about issues such as dating habits or pressures they experience in dating relationships. Support groups would also give single parents who are dating an opportunity to be accountable to others for their behaviors and practices.

While every adolescent needs contact from caring and responsive adults, the need is acute for teenagers from single-parent homes. Mark DeVries reminds us that more than anything else, these youth need roots into an extended Christian family that will be there for them. Doing several things can create this caring community:[24]

- Keep an accurate list of these adolescents' names, addresses, and phone numbers, so that they do not "fall through the cracks" of a traditional youth program, as so many teenagers from broken homes do.

- Create a strategy whereby these youth are contacted on a regular basis. Since youth from single-parent homes may not have the support and help that teenagers from intact families have to be involved in youth activities, it may take much more effort on the part of the youth workers to reach them.

- Have youth leaders sit with teens during worship services.

- Invite a teenager to an all-church fellowship event, such as a dinner or concert.

- Have adult youth workers invite teenagers from single-parent households to serve with them in local or out-of-town service or mission projects.

- Design publicity for programs and youth events in such a way that adolescents from single-parent families get a personal invitation or reminder about the activity.

The Influence of Peers

Peer influence can affect adolescent behaviors, as has been documented in previous chapters. Without strong family support and healthy parent-child interaction, teenagers are especially susceptible to peer influence. Consequently other teenagers become a primary factor in the decision whether to engage in sexual activity or not. This assumption reinforced by numerous studies, two of which are noted below.

Robert Sorenson, for example, found peers to have a significant influence on the sexual activity of adolescents. Sixty-two percent of the adolescents in his study agreed with the statement "When it comes to sex, a lot of young people these days do the things they do because everyone else is doing it." This response seems to indicate that many teenagers use sex in order to gain acceptance in the eyes of others. However,

24. DeVries, *Family-Based Youth Ministry,* 111–12.

when specifically asked whether others influence their sexual behavior, 72 percent of the boys and 79 percent of the girls agreed that "so far as sex is concerned, what other young people do doesn't have any influence on what I myself do." Age variance among boys makes a significant difference in the tendency to conform. Younger boys have a much greater tendency to conform to their peers in areas of sexual behavior than do older boys and most girls.[25] Sorenson suggests that strong pressure to conform is usually exercised by the boy in an attempt to persuade the girl to have sex. Otherwise, in most instances the influence to conform is exerted by example rather than by enticement or argument.[26]

According to a French study on the influence of peers on sexual behavior,

> the sexual permissiveness of peers is associated with a higher risk of being sexually active. The belief that one's peers approve of one-night stands is linked to an initiation into sexual relations and with multiple sexual partners, especially for boys, as was shown previously. The belief that one's peers approve of one-night stands is also linked to pressure felt by adolescent virgins to have sexual relations, and by a three times higher incidence of short-lived sexual relationships.[27]

The Effect of Church Involvement

What influence does involvement in church-related activities have on the sexual behavior of adolescents? There is no lack of studies assessing the relationship between church involvement and adolescent sexual activity, and while most empirical research indicates that church activity does have some positive influence on the sexual behavior and attitudes of teenagers, it does not have the enormous impact that concerned Christian parents and youth pastors would hope for or expect. For instance a study of teenagers in major denominations by Phil Schwadel and Christian Smith found that almost 20 percent of Protestant teenagers report engaging in sexual intercourse in the previous year.[28] The

25. Sorenson, *Adolescent Sexuality in Contemporary America*, 53.

26. Ibid.

27. Potard et al., "Influence of Peers," 268–69.

28. Schwadel and Smith, *Portraits of Protestant Teens*, 55. The participating denominations were the Assemblies of God, the Disciples of Christ, the Episcopal Church in

Teen Sex Survey in the Evangelical Church reported that 43 percent of the responding church youth said they had experienced sexual intercourse by their eighteenth birthday; 35 percent of the seventeen-year-olds, and 26 percent of the sixteen-year-olds admitted to having premarital sex.[29] Eugene Roehlkepartain and Peter Benson of the Search Institute studied adolescents who were members of six Protestant denominations and found that 31 percent of the subjects had intercourse by eleventh and twelfth grades (approximately ages sixteen and seventeen).[30] By comparison, according to the earlier-mentioned Centers for Disease Control and Prevention national study of sixteen to eighteen-year-olds in the United States, 48.6 percent have had sexual intercourse.[31]

In an empirical study of church participation and adolescent behavior, Arland Thornton and Donald Camburn determined that adolescents who attend church frequently and who value faith in their lives are less experienced sexually and have less permissive attitudes toward sex. In other words, the acceptance of sexual intercourse is lower among those with high involvement in churches. However, when they broke the respondents into religious-affiliation categories (Catholic, fundamentalist Protestants and Baptists, nonfundamentalist Protestants, Jews, and those with no religious preference), they found little difference in sexual behaviors and attitudes. The researchers concluded that religious participation is more important in determining sexual behavior and attitudes than is religious affiliation.[32]

Roehlkepartain and Benson found a difference in the incidence of sexual behavior between teenagers of selected Protestant churches who were *highly active* in the church and those who were *inactive*.[33] While 32

---

the USA, the Evangelical Lutheran Church in America, the Lutheran Church–Missouri Synod, the Presbyterian Church (USA), the Southern Baptist Convention, the United Methodist Church, and the Church of God in Christ.

29. *Teen Sex Survey in the Evangelical Church*, 3.

30. Roehlkepartain and Benson, *Youth in Protestant Churches*, 102–3. The participating denominations were Christian Church, Evangelical Lutheran Church in America, Presbyterian Church (USA), Southern Baptist Convention, United Church of Christ, and United Methodist Church.

31. Centers for Disease Control and Prevention, *Youth Risk Behavior Surveillance—United States, 2013*, 24.

32. Thorton and Camburn, "Religious Participation."

33. *Highly active* adolescents were classified as those who said they attended worship services once a week or more or spent six or more hours in programs and events in the past month and six or more hours doing volunteer work in the church in the

percent of the inactive youth admitted to having had sexual intercourse at least once, only 12 percent of the active youth reported ever having had sex.[34] In other words its not simply enough for teenagers to have affiliation or membership to be impacted in regard to their sexual behaviors—they must be involved and engaged.

While empirical research clearly indicates that participation in church-related activities has some positive influence on sexual behavior and attitudes of teenagers, it is naive for Christian parents and youth workers to think that many of their youth are not engaging in some form of premarital sexual activity. In fact it can be determined that the sexual patterns of churched teenagers are not excessively different from those of the American and Canadian youth population at large. It can be concluded, however, that the more active teenagers are in church-related activities, the less likely the possibility that they will engage in premarital sexual intercourse.

The Influence of the Media

Through mass media young people are exposed to a variety of ideologies, lifestyles, and value systems that promote a freewheeling and overpermissive approach to sex. While parents and peers primarily influence basic values and norms of teenagers, there is a legitimate concern about adolescents' exposure to sexual content through television and other electronic media and its effects on their sexual attitudes, convictions, and behaviors. For instance, Carol Pardun and associates studied early adolescents and concluded that they "live in a sexual media world, and that the more sexual media a teen sees, the more likely he or she is to be sexually active and to anticipate future sexual activity."[35]

Take television for example. The average American teenager watches about 20 hours of television per week, or three hours a day.[36] With content that includes significant measures of sexual material ranging from touching, kissing, joking, and innuendos to conversations about sex and sexual activity and depictions of intercourse. Sex is often portrayed as a

---

last month. *Inactive* youth were on membership rolls but attended services only a few times a year or not at all.

34. Roehlkepartain and Benson, *Youth in Protestant Churches,* 102–3.

35. Pardun et al., "Linking Exposure to Outcomes," 88.

36. Teen Health and the Media, "Fast Facts."

casual activity with little risk or few consequences. Conventional wisdom holds that the messages young viewers absorb from television promote sexual activity in this group. Two recent studies led by behavioral scientist Rebecca Collins examined the impact of television on teenagers' sexual beliefs and behaviors. The results reinforced the commonly held notion that television promotes sexual activity and shapes values of teenagers. The studies determined that (1) watching television programs with sexual contact accelerates the initiation of sexual activity, and (2) sexual talk has the same impact on teenagers as actual depictions of sex.[37] Neil Postman observes that "in its quest for new and sensational ventures to hold its audience, TV must tap every existing taboo in the culture: homosexuality, incest, divorce, promiscuity, corruption, adultery, and terrible displays of violence and sadism. As a consequence, these former taboos have become as familiar to the young as they are to adults."[38]

Advertising, whether in magazines, on billboards, or on television, uses sex as a primary ingredient for selling. Women are often portrayed in swimsuits, underwear, or see-through clothing in a state of semiundress or with considerable body exposure. Contemporary advertising uses sex to sell everything from soda to jeans to cars to deodorant, to one of the biggest markets in the United States—the twenty-six million-plus teenagers who spend money or have money spent on them amounting to $259 billion dollars.[39] Sexual content appears infrequently in prime-time television advertising, occurring in about 1.2 percent of the ads, down from 21 percent a decade earlier. In magazines, sexual content in advertising varies from magazine to magazine, and ads are far more racy than those in television, with over 50 percent of ads in popular magazines presenting women as sex objects. In magazines directed specifically towards teens, six out of ten ads objectify women.[40]

For decades rock and pop music has been synonymous with sex, and it continues in the new millennium. In much of contemporary pop

37. Collins et al. "Does Watching Sex on Television Influence Teens' Sexual Activity?"

38. Neil Postman made the comments in an interview for *U.S. News and World Report* in 1981. While the statement was made in the 1980s, it holds just as true for today as it did then. The interview was reproduced in Rissover and Birch, *Mass Media and the Popular Arts*, 278.

39. Statistic Brain Research Institute. "Teenager Consumer Spending Statistics." http://www.statisticbrain.com/teenage-consumer-spending-statistics/.

40. Kirsh, *Media and Youth*.

and rock sex is imaged as a means for immediate gratification, women are portrayed as mere objects of desire, and relationships are depicted as temporary, little-consequence affairs. In comparison to other media, music and music videos contain by far the greatest percentage of sexual content. Pardun and associates, for example, noted that 40 percent of the lyrics young teens listened to included sexual content. By way of contrast other forms lagged far behind in sexual references—movies (12 percent), television (11 percent), and magazines (8 percent).[41]

Encouraging Abstinence

While research studies demonstrate that a significant number of teenagers are sexually active, as mentioned earlier there are indications that a growing number of adolescents are choosing abstinence and chastity over engaging in premarital sexual intercourse. According to the study by Reginald Bibby, about half of Canadian teens are not currently sexually involved, and 41 percent say they have never been involved sexually.[42] Sixty-three percent of Protestant teenagers believe that they should wait until they are married before having sex.[43] In both the United States and Canada, teenagers are hearing the message of abstinence from church, community, and school leaders. For many adolescents, seeing how premarital sex has ruined the lives of others by STDs or pregnancies has caused them to either pledge virginity until marriage or at least drastically change their behaviors. Other teenagers are committing to sexual abstinence because of religious beliefs and values that teach that God made sex for marriage.

Many churches and faith-based organizations are following the lead of the Southern Baptist Convention and their True Love Waits program. Concerned that teenagers who practiced abstinence were feeling that they were a small minority and that even many adults fully expected them to be sexually active, leaders developed a national campaign involving local churches and ministries. According to the program, teenagers and college students, after hearing Bible studies, messages, or talks on sexual purity, are encouraged to sign covenant or pledge cards saying they will abstain from sex until they are married. Those who are currently sexually

41. Pardun et al. "Linking Exposure to Outcomes," 84.

42. Bibby, Canada's Teens, 94–95.

43. Schwadel and Smith, Portraits of Protestant Teens, 54.

active are encouraged to make a new beginning and sign a covenant to future abstinence as well.[44] The immensity of True Love Waits was first evidenced in the summer of 1994 when some two hundred thousand adolescents had their pledge cards displayed on a three-block stretch of the National Mall in Washington DC. A Christian rock concert and prayer vigil followed the public display of commitment to abstinence.[45] Since then over 2.4 million youth have signed the pledge card.[46]

While discussions or talks on sexual purity are important in relaying important information to teenagers, such instruction is not usually adequate. The message of sexual purity must be fortified by additional teaching techniques. For example, one youth service featured a couple in a skit portraying the consequences of sexual sin. The actors took turns role-playing a person's conscience, future mates, children, boyfriend/girlfriend, family, and God. Following the role-playing, the teenagers in the audience, with their parents standing alongside, placed signed covenant cards on the altar to signify their vow of chastity to God.[47]

Some additional ways to teach abstinence to teens are

- Use the object lesson whereby you have in your hands two roses, a white one and a pink one. Give the pink rose to the adolescents, each of whom picks off a petal. After twelve adolescents have picked off all the petals, the rose is bare. Remind them that teenagers who engage in premarital sexual experiences are like the pink rose. Just like the rose lost its beauty when its petals were picked off, so the adolescent has sacrificed wholeness and purity when he or she has engaged in premarital sex. Contrast this to the still-intact white rose, which signifies the purity of abstinence.

- Pair teenagers up with adults or other mature youth who will hold them responsible for their sexual behavior by meeting regularly and establishing a relationship of prayer, encouragement, and accountability.

- Use panel discussions to introduce and address issues of sexuality and sexual behavior. Allow the teenagers to hear from married

44. For further information about True Love Waits and its curriculum visit http://www.lifeway.com/n/Product-Family/True-Love-Waits/.

45. Morton, "Assessing True Love Waits," 54–60.

46. http://www.lovematters.com/truelovewaits.htm/.

47. Bolen, "Abstinence Plan Grows among Youth," 57.

couples, doctors or nurses, church staff, an unwed mother, and/or
an individual with AIDS.

- Show a video clip to introduce the topic of sexual purity or use statistics from newspaper or magazine articles to illustrate a point such as the rates of teenage pregnancy or sexual activity, or the incidence of STDs among adolescents.

Teenagers are getting mixed messages from society concerning premarital sexual behavior. Parents and youth workers may be telling unwed teenagers to say no to sex, but almost everything adolescents see and hear is saying, "go for it!" Teenagers need to understand the wrongness of premarital sexual activity and the dangers and consequences of promiscuous behavior. Premarital sexual activity may bring physical consequences such as pregnancy and disease as well as emotional pains of guilt, loneliness, and depression.

Are highly visible programs such as True Love Waits having a significant impact on behavior? Certainly, signing covenants does not indicate whether or not youth will actually keep their pledges. In other words, there is no guarantee behavior will match attitudes. Nonetheless one study indicates that teenagers who pledge to abstain from sex until married are 34 percent less likely to have sex than those who do not take a pledge.[48]

Other evidence shows, however, that programs encouraging abstinence are less effective with teenagers who are already sexually active.[49] If abstinence-only programs are going to be effective in changing the behavior of adolescents, they should incorporate the following components:

- skills to resist social and peer pressure
- the support of fellow teenagers
- the support and teaching of older teenagers and adults
- education about sexuality.[50]

---

48. Brückner and Bearman. "After the Promise," 271–78.

49. Tom Morton discusses the success of Postponing Sexual Involvement, a program developed by Grady Memorial Hospital in Atlanta, in Morton, "Assessing True Love Waits." See also, Clouse, "Adolescent Moral Development and Sexuality," 205–6.

50. Clouse, "Adolescent Moral Development and Sexuality," 205–6.

Masturbation

Randy was a senior in high school. He did not have a steady girlfriend, though he dated once in a while. Randy was deeply troubled by his sexual fantasizing and thoughts, and one day he gathered up the courage to talk about this to his youth pastor, in whom he placed much trust and confidence. After a series of sessions, however, Randy admitted that his real struggle was with masturbation. Once he got an erotic thought in his mind, he had trouble getting rid of it until he relieved the tension through masturbation. Sometimes he could go a few days without masturbating; then there were days when he would masturbate two or three times. Randy experienced tremendous guilt and frustration over this compelling habit.

Clearly, the most frequently practiced sexual activity among adolescents is masturbation, the stimulation of one's own genitals to the point of orgasm without the participation of another person. Most young people masturbate during their adolescent years, although it is more popular among young boys than girls. Robert Sorensen found that 58 percent of all adolescent boys and 39 percent of all adolescent girls have masturbated at least once.[51] According to a study done by Indiana University sexual health researchers 62 percent of male and 40 percent of female fourteen- and fifteen-year-olds had masturbated in the last year; this increased to 81 percent of the males and 60 percent of females in the eighteen- and nineteen-year-old category.[52]

Masturbation is also one of the most widely discussed and controverted issues related to human sexuality. A hundred years ago masturbation was generally condemned, not only by Christians but also by those in secular society as well. It was blamed for a number of physical and mental illnesses including loss of hair, heart stress, insanity, mental retardation, syphilis, and interference with the normal functioning of sexual intercourse. However, there appears to be no medical or scientific evidence that masturbation is physically harmful in any such ways. On the other hand, for the teenager, masturbation is often accompanied by feelings of guilt, frustration, self-condemnation, and anger over its compulsiveness, although these disorders are not attributable to the practice

51. Sorensen, *Adolescent Sexuality in Contemporary America,* 129.

52. Center for Sexual Health Promotion, "National Survey of Sexual Health and Behavior."

alone. These feelings may exist partially as a result of the forbidding and condemning attitudes of society and various religions, even though these postures today are very different from those in years past.

While masturbation is widely practiced and hotly debated, the Bible is silent on the subject; this silence makes it difficult for some Christians to speak to the issue.[53] And where there is lack of clarity about an issue or practice, there is usually a variety of positions or views. Christians specializing in sex education and ethics generally hold to one of three positions, none of which is completely satisfactory.

The Restrictive View

The more restrictive position suggests that masturbation under any condition is sin. Jay Adams holds to this view and bases his position on four principles: (1) it is adultery of the heart, (2) the Bible does not present it as an option, (3) it is a perversion of the sexual act, and (4) we must not be mastered by anything.[54] The Roman Catholic Church has much to say on the subject of masturbation. Historically, the Church's hierarchical magisterium has taught that masturbation is a moral evil and forbids its practice. The Church prohibits masturbation because it is a deviation from the creation of new life through intercourse and thus violates the will of God.[55]

The Permissive View

The permissive position holds that masturbation is healthy and morally permissible in all or most circumstances. Charlie Shedd, for example, calls masturbation "a gift of God," the wise provision of a wise God. To teenagers he says, "So long as masturbation is not humiliating; so long as it helps you to keep on the good side of sociable; so long as you can accept

---

53. While the Bible does not speak directly to the issue of masturbation, there are those who attempt to present a biblical basis for their views on the subject. For example, Johnson, "Toward a Biblical Approach to Masturbation" suggests that biblical principles limit the practice of masturbation but do not preclude it. Penner, "Reaction to Johnson's Biblical Approach to Masturbation," however, argues that Johnson's conclusions are founded on his *interpretations* of the text rather than on the text itself.

54. Adams, *Christian Counselor's Manual*, 399–401.

55. Place, "Masturbation," 841.

it as a natural part of growing up; then you thank God for it and use it as a blessing!"[56]

The Moderate View

Perhaps the most helpful and reasonable approach is the middle position, which argues that masturbation can be a healthy way of releasing sexual tension and frustration but has the potential to be morally unhealthy and inappropriate as well. This is the view of Herbert Miles, who, in his book, has sections titled "When Is Masturbation Sinful?" and "When Is Masturbation Not Sinful?" In answer to the first question, he suggests it is sinful when (1) one's sole motive is sheer biological pleasure unrelated to anything else, (2) when it becomes a controlling, compulsive habit, (3) when the habit results in feelings of inferiority and guilt, and (4) when the individual accompanies the activity with viewing pornography or sensual pictures, and fantasizes having sex relations with the woman depicted. In this case the boy is involved in lust and is guilty of adultery of the heart (Matt 5:28).[57]

When, then, is it not sinful? He says, "When masturbation is practiced on a limited basis for the sole purpose of self-control, when it is guided by basic Christian principles, and has no evil results, it is an acceptable act. It is not lust. It should not be followed by guilt feelings."[58] This middle position will not be a satisfactory response to many people; on the other hand, any view taken will draw a certain amount of criticism.

The following observations will be helpful to share in small, same-sex youth groups:[59]

- Masturbation is very common.

- It is of no harm physically and is not the cause of any mental illnesses.

- It can be harmful if it becomes compulsive, excessive, or accompanied by lust. It can produce guilt, self-centeredness, and low self-esteem.

56. Shedd, *Stork is Dead,* 73.

57. Miles, *Sexual Understanding,* 145–46.

58. Ibid., 147.

59. Summarized from Collins, *Christian Counseling,* 261–62.

- Masturbation is never mentioned in the Bible, and we should be careful not to make strong arguments from silence. God does not affirm or condemn it in Scripture.

- Masturbation can be helpful in relieving tensions, and is a substitute for sexual intercourse apart from marriage.

- Masturbation is rarely stopped simply by a determination to quit.

- Masturbation can be reduced by prayer, by allowing the Holy Spirit to control one's thoughts, by being accountable to another person, by avoiding sexually arousing materials (certain movies, television shows, magazines, or novels), by resisting the urge to dwell on sexual fantasies, and simply by keeping busy.

Adolescent Homosexuality

With the onset of puberty, Rob began to realize some differences between himself and the other guys. While other males his age began to develop fascinations for girls, he was preoccupied with other guys. Even in his earlier childhood, he recalls, he was different—always on the fringe, never one of the gang. In early adolescence Rob realized he was looking at boys because he was gay, and his romantic dream was to save himself for marriage to another man.[60]

For a very small percentage of adolescents, the sexual experience includes homosexual acts or feelings. Homosexuality is defined as a condition whereby an individual prefers sexual involvement with members of the same sex. When referring specifically to a female who has same-sex preference, the term "lesbian" is used; "gay" is a word often used to describe a male homosexual.

Homosexuals cannot be stereotyped. They come from all socioeconomic backgrounds and all age groups, and they possess a variety of interests. All effeminate males are not homosexual, and some masculine, athletic types engage in sexual activity with members of the same sex. Parents and youth workers should be cognizant of the fact that homosexuals are found in churches and youth groups as well as in the unchurched community.[61]

60. Adapted from Hurst, *Overcoming Homosexuality,* 7–8.

61. Ibid., 14–15.

It is difficult to determine precisely how many adolescent homosexuals currently exist or if that number is growing. Some teenagers have engaged in at least one homosexual experience. Nonetheless, since the adolescent years are a time of identity seeking and exploration, most of these teenagers have had no subsequent homosexual relationships. While gays and lesbians are very vocal, Robert Sorensen found that only 9 percent of all adolescents in his survey reported ever having one or more homosexual experiences.[62] Studies vary slightly but indicate the percentage of teenagers who identify themselves as gay, lesbian, or bisexual ranges from 2 to 5 percent.[63] While youth workers may feel ill at ease and inadequate in addressing this thorny problem, it is highly probable that some of the adolescents in their groups are struggling with gay, lesbian, or bisexual behavior, or are wrestling with the rightness or wrongness of homosexuality.

Important Distinctions

The current debate on homosexuality demands that some critical distinctions be made, notably the differences between homosexual behavior, homosexual orientation, and the practice of homosexuality as a lifestyle. *Homosexual behavior* simply refers to engaging in sexual activity with a member of the same sex. In some cases these actions are forced upon an individual; in other situations they may be a unique, one-time occurrence, or experimentation. Thus, homosexual behavior does not necessarily indicate that an individual is a homosexual person.

Some individuals may be described as having a *homosexual orientation* or *disposition*. These persons may feel a sexual attraction toward members of the same sex but for one reason or another choose not to engage in homosexual behavior. It must be noted that nowhere in Scripture is an individual condemned simply for having homosexual tendencies

---

62. Sorensen, *Adolescent Sexuality in Contemporary America*, 285.

63. The Body. "Fact Sheet: Lesbian, Gay, Bisexual, and Transgender Youth Issues," and "Adolescent Sexual Orientation," 619.

or feelings.[64] However, when one dwells on homosexual thoughts and engages in fantasy, then thoughts become lust, and lust is sin.[65]

A *practicing homosexual* is one who engages in homosexual activity at least periodically over a long period of time. This willful practice or way of life is unambiguously condemned and forbidden by scripture (Lev 18:22, 20:13; Rom. 1:26–27; 1 Cor. 6:9–11).

The Ethic of Love

In effectively working with the adolescent who either struggles with homosexual thoughts or is practicing homosexuality, it is the responsibility of the youth pastor or volunteer worker to first check his or her own attitude concerning homosexuals. If the youth worker retains a revulsion about them, jokes about them, condemns them, uncritically stereotypes them, or is unfamiliar with the complexity of homosexuality, then in all probability he or she will be ineffective in ministering to them. Jesus loved sinners and those who were tempted to sin. Youth workers who follow in his footsteps should do the same. If adults who work with teenagers sense no inner compassion for overt homosexuals or for people with homosexual tendencies, then they must ask God to give them the compassion they lack.[66]

Loneliness and Acceptance

For the homosexual teenager the world can be an extremely lonely place. When young people discover that they have homosexual tendencies or feelings, they often experience a measure of terror and anxiety. Afraid to let other youth, teachers, or even their families know of their sexual tendencies, many homosexual adolescents live in fear of being exposed

---

64. Hughes, *Christian Ethics in Secular Society,* 175, argues that to be strongly tempted or disposed to engage in homosexual activity is not itself sin. The sin is in doing it, not in the temptation to do it. All Christians do not hold this view. For example, Bahnsen, *Homosexuality,* 63–84 argues that no distinction should be made between the outward homosexual act and the inward homosexual condition. He argues that homosexuality is immoral in any context, whether it be outward acts, desire, or inclination.

65. Collins, *Christian Counseling,* 282.

66. Ibid., 287.

and exist in a world of social alienation. One man describes what it was like for him to grow up gay:

> The only goal left to me in life was to hide anything that could identify me as gay . . . I thought that anything I did might somehow reveal my homosexuality, and my morale sank even deeper. The more I tried to safeguard myself from the outside world, the more vulnerable I felt. I withdrew from everyone and slowly formed a shell around myself. Everyone could be a potential threat to me. I resembled a crustacean with no claws; I had my shell for protection, yet I would never do anything to hurt someone else. Sitting on a rock under thousands of pounds of pressure, surrounded by enemies, the most I could hope for was that no one would cause me more harm than my shell could endure.[67]

One might think or hope that the church or youth program would be one place a teenager struggling with homosexuality might find relief from his or her loneliness and sense of alienation. In reality, the church has been one of the least accepting institutions toward homosexuals. However, the watchword for churches, suggests David Field, should be acceptance. This does not imply an uncritical recognition of homosexual behavior as acceptable; it does mean that Christians should accept those with homosexual conditions as fellow sinners and love them as fellow sinners.[68]

The youth ministry program should provide an environment where young people with homosexual tendencies can talk about their problem and be treated in the same manner as any other individual who commits a sin. It is unfortunate that so many Christians react to homosexuals with condemnation and horror. Growing up in such an environment, adolescents learn to fear homosexuals and to suppress any gay tendencies within themselves. Instead of admitting and dealing with one's same-sex preferences, the struggling teenager keeps them hidden deep inside.[69]

When the struggling homosexual cannot get help and understanding from the church, youth group, or youth pastor, he or she may drift toward homosexual groups who *are* understanding, accepting, and loving. By its condemning and its attitude of nonacceptance, therefore, the

---

67. Taken from Sadker and Sadker, *Teachers, Schools, and Society,* 463.

68. Field, *Homosexual Way,* 41.

69. Collins, *Christian Counseling,* 287.

church sometimes inadvertently pushes people into situations in which overt homosexual behavior is encouraged.[70]

To the Homosexual Teenager

To the homosexual teenager it must be absolutely clear that homosexual behavior is wrong. In the case of sexual practice, the homosexual is in the same position as a straight person whose situation demands abstinence. Sexual self-control is important regardless of one's sexual orientation and can be nurtured through prayer and meditation, avoidance of sexually arousing situations or people, deliberate decisions to avoid sexual activity, and accountability to a friend or youth worker.

TEENAGE PREGNANCY AND CHILDBEARING

It's not a pretty picture. It's not a TV soap opera either. The reality of pregnancy outside of marriage is scary and lonely. To have premarital sex was my choice one hot June night, forcing many decisions I thought I would never have to make. Those decisions radically changed my life.[71]

Issues related to teenage sexual activity are complex and wide-ranging. One of the most critical issues of adolescent sexual development and activity, however, is that of teenage pregnancy or "babies having babies." As one source indicates, the United States is in the midst of a teenage pregnancy epidemic that is unrivaled by any other industrialized nation.[72] In 2006 750,000 young girls under the age of twenty became pregnant. The pregnancy rate was 71.5 pregnancies per 1,000 women aged fifteen to nineteen, meaning pregnancies occurred among 7 percent of this age group.[73]

As of 2013, the birth rate for girls in this age group in the United States was 26.5 per 1,000.[74] While a historic low for the U.S., the rate was higher than in other developed countries. In Canada, for example the

---

70. Ibid.

71. Quoted from McDowell and Day, *Why Wait?*, 16.

72. Sadker and Sadker, *Teachers, Schools, and Society,* 450.

73. Guttmacher Institute, "U.S. Teenage Pregnancies, Births and Abortions."

74. U. S. Department of Health and Human Services. "Trends in Teen Pregnancy and Childbearing.

birth rate for the same age group was 12.6 per 1,000 in 2011.[75] Nonetheless, the U.S. teen birth rate in 2013 was considerably lower than the peak rate in 1991 of 61.8 per 1000.

The rising incidence in teenage pregnancies is due largely to the increased sexual activity of American youth. It was mentioned earlier in this chapter that teenagers in the United States are engaging in sexual intercourse at younger and younger ages. Moreover, for those youth who are sexually active, a percentage of them use no form of birth control. According to the 2013 Youth Risk Behavior Surveillance survey of high school students, approximately 13.7 percent of currently sexually active students reported that neither they nor their partner used any method to prevent pregnancy.[76] As noted earlier, the pregnancy rate among American youth is much higher than the rate in most Western countries, yet sexual activity in these nations is comparable to levels in the United States. The reason for the high pregnancy rates among American teenagers appears to be that U.S. youth are reluctant to adopt contraception.[77]

The increase in teenage sexual activity and subsequent high number of pregnancies might be traced to several additional factors: (1) a decline in the number of teenage marriages and an increased willingness to have a child out of wedlock, (2) an increasingly early onset of puberty coupled with a rising mean age of marriage, which makes the time gap between physical maturity and marriage much greater, (3) society's increasing acceptance and tolerance of premarital sex as well as of pregnancy for unwed mothers, and (4) easy access to abortion.

Health, community, and public school officials who see teenage pregnancy and birthrates climb despite so-called progressive programs and strategies are frustrated, perplexed, and groping for explanations. For example, a Colorado high school that became the first in the state to introduce a teenage parenting program, including an on-campus nursery and the handing out of condoms, found the birthrate soaring to 31 percent above the national average.[78]

Once a teenage girl becomes pregnant, she faces several options: (1) she could raise the child by herself, (2) she could marry the father, (3)

---

75. Statistics Canada. "Crude Birth Rate."

76. Centers for Disease Control and Prevention, *Youth Risk Behavior Surveillance—United States, 2013*, 28.

77. We note this as a reality, not that as Christians we promote contraception as an option for the youth in our churches.

78. Mazanec, "Birth Rate Soars at Colorado School," 3A.

she could get an abortion, (4) she could have the child raised or infor-
mally "adopted" by a family member, or (5) she could give the child up
for adoption.

Single Parenthood

The choice to keep the child may appear to be an attractive option to
the pregnant teenager. In fact 90 percent of white teens and 97 percent
of African American teenagers who carry their pregnancy to term keep
their babies rather than give them up for adoption.[79] However, adolescent
girls usually lack adequate financial and physical resources to care for
their children and frequently do not have the financial, physical, or emotional support of the child's father. In some cases, they may be rejected
or shunned by their own family. Additional drawbacks may include
an inability to effectively nurture an infant, the loss of a normal social
life, and the inability to complete secondary education. Many times the
children of teenage pregnancies become parents themselves in twelve to
sixteen years, thus repeating the cycle. Consequently it is not uncommon
for a young woman to become a grandmother before reaching the age of
thirty. Furthermore, teenage girls often choose to keep or even intentionally have a child for the wrong reasons: to keep a boyfriend, to force a
marriage, to gain attention, to have someone they can love and hold, or
even to spite a parent.[80]

Marriage

Marriage may appear to be the socially correct thing to do, but parenthood for teenage couples also brings with it acute problems. Adolescent
married mothers still experience many of the struggles and difficulties
unwed mothers do. They experience the loss of normal adolescent social life, lost educational opportunities, and financial difficulties. Many
teenage mothers lack parenting skills. Empirical research data indicate
that adolescent parents are significantly more at risk for child abuse and
neglect, and infants of teenage parents have disproportionately high

79. McWhirter et al., *At-Risk Youth*, 139.

80. For more extensive descriptions of the consequences for unmarried teenaged
girls who keep their babies see McWhirter et al., *At-Risk Youth*, 143–45, and various
chapters in Maynard, *Kids Having Kids*.

numbers of developmental problems.[81] Furthermore, the divorce rate for teenage marriages (most of which are associated with pregnancy) is extremely high.[82] Only 20 percent of teen pregnancies result in marriage.[83]

Abortion

Many unmarried adolescent girls who find themselves in the unfortunate situation of expecting a baby opt for abortion, the external intervention into the reproduction process with the intent of terminating pregnancy.[84] The teen abortion rate has declined a whopping 66 percent, from a peak in 1988 of 43.5 abortions per 1,000 to 14.7 per 1,000 in 2010.[85] In Canada the rate of abortion is similar with 14.2 per 1,000, a decline of 35.7 percent from 1996 to 2006.[86]

While in some nations abortion is an accepted practice with little controversy, in countries such as the United States and Canada few ethical or social issues incite more public or personal debate and discord. While the issue is complex and the arguments are numerous, essentially two predominant views exist: pro-choice and pro-life. *Pro-choice* advocates, including many theologically liberal Christians, argue that it is a woman's paramount privilege to choose or control what to do with her body, including the abortion of fetuses. *Pro-life* or anti-abortion proponents, including most conservative Protestants and many Roman Catholics, oppose the practice of destroying a fetus.[87]

Central to the abortion debate are the questions of the beginning of life and personhood. Pro-choice supporters argue that while the fetus is *a* form of life, it is not yet a "person." For those who advocate choice, birth is the critical developmental mark for conferring full human standing.[88]

---

81. Guerney and Arthur, "Adolescent Social Relationships," 105.

82. Ibid., 104.

83. McWhirter et al., *At-Risk Youth*, 145.

84. This definition of *abortion* is from Feinberg and Feinberg, *Ethics for a Brave New World*, 50.

85. Guttmacher Institute, "U.S. Teen Pregnancy, Birth and Abortion Rates."

86. Sexuality and U.ca, "Statistics on Canadian Teen Pregnancies."

87. Most pro-life advocates allow for abortion in special situations such as 1) to save a mother's life, and 2) in the case of rape or incest. For example, see Feinberg and Feinberg, *Ethics for a Brave New World*, 73–79, and Geisler, *Ethics*, 220–26.

88. Harrison, *Our Right to Choose*, 217–19. Mary Anne Warren is quoted by Harrison as proposing the following criteria for personhood: (1) consciousness, (2)

On the other hand, most individuals who hold to a pro-life position believe the fetus becomes a human life at conception.[89]

The debate over abortion is extremely sensitive, and emotions run high on both sides of the issue. Advocates in each camp accuse members of the other camp of being uncaring or insensitive. The reality is that there are caring and sensitive people in each group. Pro-choice people are interested in protecting the right to a girl's choice over what she does with her body and concerned about bringing an unloved or unwanted child into the world. On the other hand pro-life or anti-abortion supporters affirm the unborn babies' right to life. If it is wrong to unjustly kill a person after birth, is it not just as wrong to take a life before birth?

It is our position that except in rare situations in which the baby must be sacrificed to save the mother's life, abortion is wrong. What about pregnancy resulting from the horrifying crimes of rape or incest? Christians who oppose abortion are divided on whether or not abortion should be permissible under such circumstances. Norman Geisler, for example, argues that in the instances of rape and incest there is no moral obligation placed upon a young woman to carry through with her pregnancy.[90] John and Paul Feinberg, while genuinely sensitive and compassionate toward the victims of such crimes, offer several arguments against abortion even in cases of rape and incest: (1) it is never right to do evil to achieve good; (2) while rape and incest are acts of violence, so is abortion; (3) it is never right to commit murder to alleviate suffering; (4) both physical and psychological harm or pain may come to the mother who aborts.[91]

What about bringing any child into this world who is unwanted or will be unloved because of the situation in which it was conceived? Because a child is unwanted by its birth mother does not mean a child is altogether unwanted. Today there are a large number of couples who are

---

reasoning, (3) self-motivated activity, (4) the capacity to communicate, and (5) the presence of self-concepts and self-awareness. Harrison goes on to suggest that a fetus possesses none of these criteria of a normal "person."

89. Feinberg and Feinberg, *Ethics for a Brave New World*, 73–79. Brody, *Abortion and the Sanctity of Human Life*, 80, identifies six alternatives as to when the fetus becomes life: the moment of conception, the time at which segmentation takes place, the time at which fetal brain activity commences, the time at which the mother feels movement of the fetus, the time at which the fetus has a reasonable chance of surviving if born, and the moment of birth.

90. Geisler, *Ethics*, 222–23.

91. Feinberg and Feinberg, *Ethics for a Brave New World*, 77–79.

unable to have children themselves and desperately wish to adopt. The youth worker, when working with a pregnant teenager, should encourage the girl to carry the baby to term and then make the baby available for a couple who very much want a child of their own.

How does the youth worker respond to the teenage girl in the youth group who has undergone an abortion? At this point the goal is not to condemn or instill guilt. Instead, the sensitive and compassionate youth worker should try to help the girl experience God's forgiveness and assist her in working through the grief process that may follow an abortion.

Some girls may suffer what is called postabortion syndrome (PAS), some form of negative psychological reaction to her abortion. In a collection of interviews by Linda Francke of women who had experienced abortion, approximately 70 percent expressed some type of negative feeling such as guilt, shame, anxiety, anger, and grief.[92]

According to another survey of women who had at least one abortion, 94 percent of the respondents reported they had experienced negative psychological effects attributable to their abortions. Approximately 20 percent said that they actually made at least one suicide attempt, and many others reported that they were unable to put the abortion out of their minds.[93] Most communities and cities have a pro-life crisis counseling center that provide support groups and counseling for girls who may be suffering from some form of postabortion syndrome. The youth worker should be familiar with the assistance available in his or her area so that referral can be made when the need arises.

Adoption

Clearly the preferred response to teenage pregnancy by Christian adults of all persuasions is adoption. Interestingly though, releasing a child for adoption is the least popular choice for teenagers. Contemporary teenagers are far less likely to relinquish their baby to formal adoption than they were in the past. Less than 10 percent of the unwed pregnant girls who carry their child to term plan for adoption.

92. Francke, *Ambivalence of Abortion*, 3, 61, 74, 81, 84, 91, 99, 104.

93. The empirical study was done by an organization called Women Exploited by Abortion (WEBA) and reported in Reardon, *Aborted Women*. 22–23. WEBA is an organization made up solely of women who have had an abortion.

One reason a teenage girl might hesitate to choose an adoption plan for her baby is the misconception that a loving person would not allow her child to be given away. Perhaps she thinks others will view her as cold or uncaring. The youth worker can remind this girl that in some situations adoption can be a very caring, loving, and responsible decision.

Adoption can be a traumatic experience for a young girl. Releasing a baby for adoption marks the end of one of life's most intimate relationships. After carrying a child for nine months and giving birth, relinquishing the child to strangers will most likely be extremely difficult. It is then that the girl may experience postpartum depression. The challenge to the youth worker during these vulnerable times is to be available to the girl, especially during the hospital stay and in the weeks following her discharge. Visits, flowers, cards, or anything else that lets the teenager know the youth worker is thinking of her will be helpful.[94]

Some adolescent mothers, particularly those younger girls, for whom abstract and hypothetical reasoning are not fully developed, will benefit from structured individual or small-group contact with peers who have chosen to release their babies through adoption, with those who have kept their children, or with adoptees. Often young adolescents have a difficult time perceiving the reality of the difficulty of rearing a child. They consider only the innocent-looking, helpless infant and cannot fathom relinquishing the child. They have difficulty imagining the times they may have ahead should they choose to keep their infant. Group experiences with other teenagers who have relinquished or parented a baby can help girls see the reality of parenting beyond infancy. These experiences can also give them the opportunity to talk to adoptees about their perceptions of being adopted and the feelings they have about their birth mothers.[95]

Finally, the youth worker can assist the girl in the adoption process by putting her in touch with a credible adoption agency. In the United States each state licenses public or private agencies to serve as adoption agencies. Public agencies are usually subsidiaries of the state and may be called the state welfare program or child welfare department. Private adoption agencies are typically nonprofit organizations, often operated by churches or denominations. The agency serves as an intermediary between the mother and the adopting parents. In private and public agencies the procedure is essentially the same. The birth mother signs legal documents relinquishing

94. For additional insights in assisting an unwed teenage mother through adoption, see the manual by Brandsen: *Case for Adoption*.

95. Brandsen, *Case for Adoption*, 39.

the rights to her child to the agency. The agency then places the child with the parents who have been selected for the adoption.[96]

ADOLESCENT SEX OFFENDERS

The sexual revolution begun in the 1960s has wrought more disturbing trends than were previously imagined. One trend that has been identified by experts is the sexual abuse of children by other children and adolescents. A few years back the *Atlanta Journal-Constitution,* one of the leading newspapers in the United States, ran a startling report titled "New Sex Abuse Trend: Kids Attacking Kids." In the article the following hideous crimes were described:[97]

- "A 6-year-old Atlanta girl was at home playing video games when she was dragged into a bedroom and raped. Her alleged assailant: a thirteen-year-old neighborhood boy.

- In a middle-class suburb of northeast Atlanta, a fourteen-year-old girl was asleep in her bed recently when she was attacked, beaten and raped. The rapist was her seventeen-year-old brother.

- An Atlanta woman learned that her four-year-old son had gonorrhea, a sexually transmitted disease. Police eventually identified the boy's molester as his baby-sitter's grandson—a 12-year-old boy who admitted he had both anal and oral sex with the child."

One expert in juvenile crime says, "We always look at the kids being the victims. Now we're looking at kids victimizing other kids." The following national U.S. statistics bear this out:[98]

- More than 50 percent of young boys and as many as 20 percent of girls who are sexually abused are molested by teenagers.

- Sixty to 80 percent of adult sexual offenders say they committed their first sex offense as teenagers.

- The average age for the first offense by all adult sexual offenders is about thirteen years old.

---

96. Bethany Christian Services is a national Christian organization that serves as an adopting agency. Their website is https://www.bethany.org/.

97. Hansen and McIntosh, "New Sex Abuse Trend."

98. Ibid.

- The rate of juveniles arrested for rape doubled from 20 per 100,000 to 40 per 100,000 in the past decade.

The most common trait among adolescent sexual abusers is that they themselves were the victims of similar abuse. Somewhere between 80 and 90 percent of those teenagers who have completed treatment for sex abuse crimes say they themselves were abused as children. Offenders come from a variety of socioeconomic backgrounds and cut across all religious, races, and class lines. There are, as one expert put it, just as many sons of senators who get into trouble for sexual crimes as there are sons of fathers in any other profession or occupation.[99]

It is crucial that adolescent sexual offenders are identified and dealt with so the cycle of child abuse and molestation is broken. It is naive for parents or youth workers to believe that if left alone, an adolescent will grow out of his or her deviant behavior. There is no such thing as a one-time child molester or rapist. Adolescent sex offenders average seven victims; adult offenders who committed their first sex offense as teenagers average 380 victims.[100] If a youth worker discovers that someone in the youth group is guilty of child abuse, molestation, or rape, this should be reported to the appropriate child protection agency in the community. While some states tend to lock up offenders, there are counseling centers nationwide designed to intensively treat adolescent sex abusers.

CONCLUSION

There are no simple answers to the immense problems related to adolescent sexual activity. Empirical research indicates that the number of teenagers engaging in premarital intercourse will not decline significantly. Furthermore, adolescents will become sexually active at younger and younger ages. But as long as youth continue to engage in illicit sexual activity, they will risk the painful consequences from their experiences such as unwanted pregnancies or STDs. Nevertheless, the situation is not hopeless. Studies suggest that participation in church-related activities has some positive influence on sexual behavior and attitudes of teenagers. Furthermore, there are indications that a growing number of youth are choosing abstinence and chastity over engaging in illicit sexual activity.

99. Ibid.
100. Ibid.

9

Risky Adolescent Behaviors and Health Issues

In contemporary society addictive and abusive health-related behaviors occur in epidemic proportions and are a hazard to the well-being of people of all ages and backgrounds. In the United States and Canada millions of people, including teenagers, abuse or are addicted to any number of behaviors or substances, including drugs, alcohol, tobacco, and sex. While there are many factors that contribute to the health risks of teenagers (such as poverty, abuse, violence, and genetics), in this chapter we will focus on the personal behaviors of adolescents that contribute to ill health or even mortality. More specifically we will address the particular issues of eating disorders, the use and abuse of alcohol, the use of illicit drugs, self-injury, sexually transmitted diseases (STDs), and acquired immunodeficiency syndrome, more commonly known as AIDS.

THE EATING DISORDERS OF ANOREXIA NERVOSA AND BULIMIA NERVOSA

On February 4, 1983, at the age of thirty-two, pop singer Karen Carpenter suddenly died of heart failure. Further investigation revealed that she had been struggling with an eating disorder called anorexia nervosa for twelve years, and medical experts concluded that this had contributed to her untimely death. Ms. Carpenter represents thousands of young people, especially females, who struggle with an eating disorder, as well as a small percentage whose compulsion tragically ends in death. At one time considered rare, eating disorders and disordered eating behaviors have become more common. The diagnosed incidences of the eating disorders anorexia nervosa and bulimia nervosa are increasing at a staggering rate. Jane Rees describes the prevalence of eating disorders among adolescents as follows:

> The number of adolescents with diagnosed anorexia nervosa or bulimia nervosa is growing and many adolescents with various eating disorders and disordered eating behaviors remain undiagnosed and untreated. Uncounted teenagers preparing to be models, entertainers, dancers, gymnasts, jockeys, and other athletes who manipulate their weight also suffer from long-term effects of chronic malnutrition, whether they do or do not meet the criteria for anorexia nervosa or bulimia nervosa."[1]

As many as 25 percent of today's teenagers in the United States and Canada, mostly girls, are affected by anorexia nervosa, bulimia, or other less known disorders.

Anorexia Nervosa

While anorexia nervosa, which literally means "nervous loss of appetite," is the better known of the two eating disorders, it is not as common. About 2 percent of the total population suffers from anorexia nervosa; about 90-95 percent of those are adolescent females.[2] While the condition was first described in a medical journal in 1689, anorexia only became well known as a disorder in the 1970s and 1980s. The incidence of anorexic behavior is increasing among teenage populations.[3]

Anorexia is essentially a self-inflicted starvation, whereby the individual compulsively refrains from eating in order to attain thinness. The victim continues to see herself as overweight when in reality she is often abnormally thin. The following are characteristics of anorexia:[4]

- refusal to maintain minimal normal body weight for age and height

1. Rees, "Eating Disorders during Adolescence."

2. Grant and Fodor, "Adolescent Attitudes," 269–82.

3. American Psychiatric Association, *Diagnostic and Statistical Manual of Mental Disorders*, 543.

4. The characteristics of anorexia nervosa are summarized from ibid., 544–45.

- intense fear of becoming overweight or obese, which does not diminish with progression of weight loss

- disturbance in the way one's body weight or shape is experienced, such as feeling fat even when distinctly underweight

- for postmenarcheal females, the loss of menstruation.

In addition, the anorexic adolescent generally suffers from physical side effects such as intolerance to cold, excessive skin dryness, low blood pressure, chemical deficiencies, and heart problems. She may also manifest depressive symptoms such as depressed mood, social withdrawal, insomnia, and irritability.[5] Extreme cases of anorexia may result in death, about half of which are caused by suicide.[6]

Bulimia Nervosa

Closely related to anorexia is bulimia nervosa, which literally means, "ox-hunger." This eating disorder is characterized by binge eating followed immediately by purging through self-induced vomiting, laxative abuse, excessive exercise, or fasting. Although bulimia has only come to medical attention in recent years, it is the more common of the two eating disorders. Approximately 20 percent of female adolescents engage in bulimic behaviors.[7] The following are some primary criteria for the assessment of bulimia:[8]

- recurring episodes of binge eating. An episode of binge eating is characterized as (1) a rapid consumption of a large amount of food in a short period of time (e.g., within a two-hour period), (2) a sense of lack of control over eating during this period (e.g., a feeling that one cannot stop eating or control what and how much one is eating).

- the practice of inducing vomiting, using laxatives, fasting, or vigorous exercising to prevent weight gain

- an average of at least two binge episodes a week for at least three months

5. Ibid., 541.

6. Agras, *Eating Disorders*, 15.

7. Rees, "Eating Disorders during Adolescence."

8. Adapted from American Psychiatric Association, *Diagnostic and Statistical Manual of Mental Disorders*, 549.

- a persistent concern about weight and body shape

Additional complications as a result of bulimia nervosa may include menstrual problems, dental problems,[9] and depression. Compared to anorexics, however, many bulimics enjoy reasonably good health and are generally within the normal weight range. Bulimics are typically ashamed of their eating disorder and prefer to binge on food when they are alone, or as inconspicuously as possible. There is, however, a social element involved in that purging techniques are often learned from friends and through the media.

Who Is Vulnerable to Eating Disorders?

Eating disorders are complex in nature, and it is difficult for most people to understand or appreciate why certain individuals are addicted to such behaviors. The body has built-in mechanisms that generally tell us when it is time to eat, and regular feeding is a normal and routine function. Nonetheless, many adolescents struggle with and suffer through eating disorders, often experiencing physical consequences as severe as death. The causes and factors related to eating disorders are complicated, and no one influence leads to these illnesses. Rather, anorexia and bulimia are the result of the complex interaction of a number of cultural and psychological forces.

Gender

An overwhelming majority of adolescents suffering from these compulsive behaviors are females—about 90 percent of all anorexics and bulimics.[10] What makes young girls so much more vulnerable to eating disorders? Contemporary Western society places significantly greater emphasis on dieting and slimness for girls and women than it does for boys and men. Beginning as early as the elementary school years, girls are more likely than boys to consider themselves in need of dieting or to

9. Bulimics often experience dental problems because of the acids in the vomit. Dental problems may also occur because of the high sugar content in bringing foods such as ice cream and cake.

10. Andersen, "Distributions of Eating Disorders"; Anderson-Fye and Becker, "Sociocultural Aspects of Eating Disorders," 579.

see themselves as being overweight.[11] In fact, many males are more concerned with putting on bulk and muscle than they are with losing weight
and dieting. However, the importance of being attractive and feminine
is conveyed to girls from an early age. Thinness is inextricably related to
femininity and beauty; to achieve thinness girls engage in dieting and
weight control, which, in turn, contributes to the development of eating
disorders.[12]

For males, self-worth and masculinity are defined more by power,
intelligence, and occupational accomplishments than by body shape or
weight. Males who may be more susceptible to eating disorders are those
who participate in activities that require them to keep their weight down
to a minimum. Wrestlers, for example, will do whatever it takes to make
weight, and then after matches engage in binge eating. Male ballet danc-
ers, long-distance runners, and models may also resort to starvation to
keep their weight down.

Age

The age of onset for both anorexia and bulimia is usually between twelve
and eighteen years, and the disorders occur predominantly among adolescent girls and young women.[13] The incidence of eating disorders in
young children is rare.[14] Peer pressure to be slender, accompanied by the
desire to look like the models in teenage glamour magazines, no doubt
encourages many adolescent girls to go on slimming diets, a few of which
develop into anorexia or bulimia.

Social Class

Another major factor contributing to eating disorders is social class.
Interestingly, anorexia and bulimia are much less common in pre-indus-
trialized, non-Western societies than in Western countries. The disorders
are most common in the industrialized countries such as the United
States, Canada, Australia, Japan, New Zealand, South Africa, and the

11. Andersen, "Distributions of Eating Disorders," 177; Kalodner, *Too Fat or Too
Thin?*, 3.

12. Kalodner, *Too Fat or Too Thin?*, 142–44.

13. Siegel et al., *Surviving an Eating Disorder*, 15, 24.

14. Garvin and Striegel-Moore, "Health Services Research," 137.

European nations.[15] Furthermore, eating-disordered adolescents come almost exclusively from the middle and upper socioeconomic classes. It is possible that this is due, at least in part, to underreporting, especially in Third World countries. However, it is probable that eating disorders are indeed more prevalent in affluent societies where the economy is thriving. A number of factors contribute to a Western view of the importance of thinness, including a, "desire to emulate the higher social classes, a desire for control over the body, and changing role expectations for women."[16]

How Eating Disorders Begin

A teenage girl does not start a diet with the intention of becoming emaciated; she does not initially decide to control her weight by vomiting, using a laxative, or purging in any other manner. However, for the adolescent who is to become controlled by an eating disorder, dieting and weight loss subtly take on a function that is both unplanned and unanticipated. What begins as an attempt to control one's appearance and weight ultimately becomes a behavior that is out of control. A number of factors precipitate the onset of an eating disorder in teenage girls.

Perfectionism

One common characteristic of anorexic adolescents is their propensity toward perfectionism. They are nearly always hardworking, conscientious, and dependable. They are often model children, usually above average in their school performance yet highly demanding and critical of themselves. They are continually trying to prove their competence.[17]

Low Self-Esteem

Bulimics and anorexics alike tend to be adolescents who do not feel secure about their self-worth. They tend not to have developed sufficient

---

15. American Psychiatric Association, *Diagnostic and Statistical Manual of Mental Disorders*, 542, 548; Anderson-Fye and Becker, "Sociocultural Aspects of Eating Disorders," 566–67.

16. Kalodner, *Too Fat or Too Thin?*, 138.

17. Siegel et al., *Surviving an Eating Disorder*, 15.

means of feeling worthy, competent, or effective.[18] The eating-disordered teenager struggles to be perfect yet feels she must strive to prove her competence to others as well as to herself.

Identity Issues

Adolescence is a period of great vulnerability to a variety of identity struggles. Some psychologists theorize that anorexia is a rejection of female sexuality and an attempt to remain a "little girl."[19] One hypothesis is that anorexic girls avoid many of the social consequences of adolescence by reducing their weight, expunging secondary sexual characteristics such as breast development, and reverting to a prepubertal role.[20] For some adolescents an eating disorder is the only way to assert the autonomy every teenager longs for: "I am an individual and I have control of my life." Being in control of their diet and eating habits, controlling what they do to their bodies, and what they weigh, may be a way of exercising and expressing their individuality.[21] "With the passage of time," add Jim Kirkpatrick and Paul Caldwell, "an individual's very identity may become incorporated into the eating disorder. The eating disorder is all-pervasive and all-consuming, and the person no longer maintains his or her own identity, but takes on the identity of the disorder, becoming 'someone with anorexia nervosa.'"[22]

Family Pressures

The children of parents who espouse the notion that weight and physical appearance are critical to self-worth may be predisposed toward eating disorders.[23] And if parents model excessive dieting and judge themselves harshly in terms of weight or shape, the children are even more likely to apply these same standards to themselves. When parental approval is connected to appearance, the risk of incurring an eating disorder is

18. Ibid., 15, 24.
19. Parrott, *Helping the Struggling Adolescent,* 143.
20. Agras, *Eating Disorders,* 11.
21. Collins, *Christian Counseling,* 512–13.
22. Kirkpatrick and Caldwell, *Eating Disorders,* 107.
23. Hoffman, "ABCs of Eating Disorders," 37.

increased.[24] Eating-disordered teenagers often come from homes where standards are high, achievement is prized, attractiveness and slimness are seen as important, and dieting is praised.

Social Influences

Clearly the greatest barrage of messages teenage girls receive concerning body image, appearance, and the importance of slimness come from society at large. The media and advertising agents target females, telling them to change their bodies or please others through their physical attractiveness.[25] As young girls grow up, they are unfortunately sold on an ideal that few can realistically reach. However, this does not keep adolescent girls from trying, and a small percentage of them will inadvertently develop eating disorders. For some teenagers the words of counselor Les Parrott unfortunately ring true: "A thin body is more important than a healthy one."[26]

Seeking Help for the Eating-Disordered Adolescent

Youth workers can assist adolescents to overcome eating disorders in two ways: by referring them to medical or psychological professionals or both, and by involving these teens in support groups.

Referral

The eating disorders of anorexia and bulimia represent psychological problems that are beyond the expertise of most youth pastors or volunteer workers. In most cases the intervention of medical or psychological professionals is necessary in order to significantly facilitate recovery and to ease the burden that youth workers may be feeling to help the individual get well. The various types of treatment that might be necessary for the eating-disordered adolescent include psychotherapy and medical and nutritional help. In severe cases where an individual is in a life-endangering condition, hospitalization may be necessary.

24. Smolak and Murnen, "Gender and Eating Problems," 97.
25. Kalodner, *Too Fat or Too Thin?*, 141–42.
26. Parrott, *Helping the Struggling Adolescent*, 144.

Support Groups

Involvement in a psychotherapy, a support group, or a self-help group can be invaluable in helping an anorexic or bulimic teenager address the problem of an eating disorder and feel less isolated. A support group differs from a psychotherapy group in that a therapist does not lead a support group. Usually the leader or facilitator of a support group is an individual who has herself recovered from an eating disorder and is in the position of helping and inspiring others through her own experience. Support groups can be structured in a variety of ways. In some groups a specific topic is addressed at each meeting, while in others there is no particular agenda. In some groups the session begins with a speaker, and then participants break into smaller discussion groups to explore their feelings about the topic. Examples of topics that support groups might discuss are how relationships are affected by eating disorders and what to do if you are hungry.

ALCOHOL USE AND ABUSE

Many people are not aware of how pervasive the problem of alcohol is for adolescents since other illicit drugs often get much of the public attention. But while in the United States the consumption of alcohol is illegal for the large majority of adolescents, experience with alcohol is almost universal among them. It is clearly the drug of choice for teenagers in the United States and Canada, and one of the most common contributors to injury, criminal behavior, and death among adolescents.[27] A national survey of American secondary students in grades nine to twelve, the Youth Risk Behavior Surveillance survey, indicates that 66.2 percent of these youth had consumed alcohol at some point in their life. As one might expect, the prevalence of alcohol use increased as students progressed from ninth grade (55.6 percent) to twelfth grade (75.6 percent). Most disturbing, perhaps, is the widespread occurrence of binge drinking. According to the same study, 20.8 percent of the students had consumed five or more drinks of alcohol in a row (within a couple of hours) at least once in the previous thirty days. As one might also expect, boys engage in binge drinking at significantly higher rates than girls.[28]

27. Stewart, "Preventing Underage Alcohol Access," 8–11.

28. Centers for Disease Control and Prevention, *Youth Risk Behavior*

Such statistics are alarming and identify teenage alcohol consumption as a national concern, though the most recent youth behavior surveillance in the United States indicates that most drinking patterns follow a downward trend.[29] Nonetheless children are using alcohol at younger ages than ever before, and they are becoming problem drinkers sooner. In the 1940s and 1950s, teenagers took their first drink at ages thirteen or fourteen; today they are starting at age ten or younger, and nationwide almost 19 percent had drunk alcohol before the onset of the teenage years.[30] Clearly the number-one burden for today's youth is created by the consumption and abuse of alcohol. Based on a limited number of local community studies, it is estimated that between 3 and 32 percent of teenagers meet the criteria for having an alcohol disorder.[31] Approximately 47 percent of Canadian youth acknowledge that they have a close friend who has a severe alcohol (or drug) problem.[32]

Studies indicate that alcohol consumption is a problem for church youth as well. According to a cross-denominational study by the Search Institute, 50 percent of the teenagers questioned had consumed alcohol at least once in the past year, while 25 percent had used alcohol six or more times in the past year. More disconcerting is the fact that 28 percent had been on a drinking binge in the last year, and 17 percent had engaged in binge drinking at least three times in the past year. In spite of the popular image that boys are more likely to drink, rates of alcohol consumption between males and females did not significantly differ.[33] According to a report on Protestant teens (who attend church activities) in the United States, Phil Schwadel and Christian Smith discovered that 11 percent reported drinking alcohol a few times a month or more.[34] These statistics should give Christian parents, youth workers, and other church leaders great cause for concern, as teenagers in churches and youth groups are not immune from the use, abuse, and resultant consequences of engaging in alcohol consumption. If there is a silver lining or word of encouragement for churches and youth workers, it is that studies clearly indicate

---

Surveillance—United States, 2013, 17.

29. Ibid., 17–18.

30. Ibid., 18.

31. Windle, "Alcohol Use among Adolescents," 3.

32. Bibby, *Canada's Teens,* 95.

33. Roelkepartain and Benson, *Youth in Protestant Churches,* 100–101.

34. Schwadel and Smith, *Portraits of Protestant Teens,* 58.

church activity has a positive impact on teens and drinking, in the sense that those who are more involved in religious services or church activity are less likely to have used alcohol or to engage in drinking.[35]

Consequences of Alcohol Consumption

While many adolescents view alcohol as a relatively harmless substance, and some parents are relatively pleased that their teenage son or daughter "merely drinks and is not addicted to drugs," experts do not dispute the potentially dangerous effects of alcohol. Indeed, alcohol consumption is not without its perils and often-deadly consequences. Alcohol consumption at an early age is often an indicator of future drug or alcohol problems. One of the greatest risks in teenage alcohol drinking or the experimentation with alcohol is the possibility of becoming addicted to the drug. It is estimated that there could be over four million Americans under the age of eighteen who are alcoholics or are addicted to the consumption of alcohol—and the experimentation age continues to get younger.[36] Furthermore, alcohol is considered to be a gateway drug and often precedes the use of other illicit drugs.

Michael Windle of the Center for the Advancement of Youth Health at the University of Alabama summarizes the detrimental effects of alcohol use among adolescents as follows:

> Alcohol use among teens has been associated with the three most common forms of adolescent mortality: accidental deaths (such as fatal automobile or boat crashes), homicides, and suicides. On average, eight adolescents a day in the U.S. die in alcohol-related automobile crashes, and nine out of ten teenage automobile accidents involve the use of alcohol. With a national school sample, suicide attempts were 3 to 4 times more likely among heavy drinking adolescents relative to abstainers.
>
> In addition, alcohol use among adolescents is significantly associated with a range of other health-compromising behaviors. Higher levels of alcohol use are associated with more frequent, often unprotected, sexual activity among adolescents, which poses increased risk for teen pregnancy and sexually

---

35. Roelkepartain and Benson, *Youth in Protestant Churches*, 100–101; National Center on Addiction and Substance Abuse, *National Survey of American Attitudes*, 26; Mason and Windle, "Family, Religious, School, and Peer Influences," 6–7.

36. Parrott, *Helping the Struggling Adolescent*, 124.

transmitted diseases, including potentially life-threatening diseases such as HIV. An earlier onset of alcohol use and higher
levels of use among adolescents have also been associated
with poorer academic functioning and higher rates of school
dropout.[37]

Why Do Adolescents Drink?

As young people move through the often difficult adolescent years to
young adulthood, they encounter significant physical, emotional, lifestyle, and cognitive changes. Dynamic developmental transitions and
life-related issues such as puberty, increasing independence from parents, and family problems have been associated with alcohol consumption. So one might surmise that simply being a teenager may be a risk
factor not only for the onset of drinking but also for drinking to excess.
But more specifically, adolescents offer a variety of responses when asked
this question. On an online discussion forum, some of the reasons they
gave include the following:

- "I think that most of all teens that drink start by peer pressure."

- "Not only is it peer pressure but the beer commercials, they make it
  look cool to drink, but really it's harmful and deadly."

- "Teens drink to try to be more mature. They see their parents drinking, or their role models, and they assume that to be more like them,
  they should imitate their behavior."

- "I tried drinking for the first time because I was desperate to find a
  way out of reality."

- "I drink to relieve stress and to just get away from it all."

- "I just like to drink. I like the taste, and the feeling."

- "I do it just for the fun of it."

In reality, identifying the motives for adolescent drinking is complex,
and studies indicate that the reasons are different for moderate drinkers,
heavy drinkers, and those with severe drinking problems. Nonetheless,
we can generalize about some of the major categories of motives.

---

37. Windle, "Alcohol Use among Adolescents," 1.

Peer Pressure

Many sources indicate that social pressure from friends and peers has a powerful effect on one's use of alcohol.[38] However, according to interview and statistical studies by Chris Lutes, some teenagers indicate that they drink because they want to, and that blaming peer pressure is simply a feeble excuse. Nonetheless, 71 percent of the respondents admitted they would engage in drinking alcohol if their friends asked them.[39] Perhaps related to peer pressure is the absence or at least erosion of what psychologist David Elkind calls "markers," external signs of progress along the stages of life. Markers might be as simple as pencil lines on the wall marking a child's growth from year to year or as elaborate as a bar mitzvah[40] Building on Elkind's observations, Dean Borgman proposes that adolescents "are searching out replacements for vanishing markers on their road to maturity. Losing one's virginity or getting blasted are touted by media and assumed by friends as ways to prove one's adulthood If this is the subculture's rite of passage, then there will be pressure to conform."[41]

Pleasure, Fun, and Escape

Apart from peer pressure, the most common reason teenagers give for drinking is pleasure or fun.[42] A sixteen-year-old girl from Washington says, "Teenagers drink because it is fun and very social."[43] Teenagers look forward to weekends so they can drink, party, and spend time with their friends. Others drink to escape—to escape from pressures they are faced with, to escape from boredom, and to escape from depression.[44] An eighteen-year-old female from Texas says, "Drinking helps you forget the problems and pressures of the world for a little while."[45]

38. Mason and Windle, "Family, Religious, School, and Peer Influences," 6–7; Kuntsche et al., "Why Do Young People Drink?", 849; Biglan et al., *Helping Adolescents at Risk*, 85.

39. Lutes, *What Teenagers Are Saying*, 49–51.

40. Elkind, *All Grown Up and No Place to Go*, 111.

41. Borgman, *Hear My Story*, 316.

42. Lutes, *What Teenagers Are Saying*, 50; National Center on Addiction and Substance Abuse, "National Survey of American Attitudes," 30.

43. Lutes, *What Teenagers Are Saying*, 48.

44. National Center on Addiction and Substance Abuse, "National Survey of American Attitudes," 30.

45. Lutes, *What Teenagers Are Saying*, 48.

The Influence of Media

While seldom given as a reason for drinking, the pressure of the advertising media must be considered an influence, as there is clear evidence to link alcohol advertising with teenage drinking.[46] The advertising media target those in their late adolescence and early twenties. They not only portray drinking as a socially acceptable activity, but they glorify it by making it especially attractive to these young people. Beer advertisements depict handsome young men and beautiful women who appear to be living "the good life" with no serious life-related problems. Teenagers subtly connect athleticism, material success, physical beauty, fun, and a multitude of good friends with the consumption of their product. Rarely, if ever, do advertisers portray the negative consequences of excessive drinking—tragic traffic accidents, loss of jobs, sickness, family conflict, or crime, to name a few.

Family Factors

It is an understatement to say that the family plays a primary role in the socialization of adolescents. There is no shortage of literature citing the impact parent-child relationships have on teenage alcohol use and abuse. For example, Alex Mason and Michael Windle determined, as a result of their study on family, religion, school, and peer influences, that family social support reduced the risk for alcohol use among teenagers.[47] The National Survey of American Attitudes on Substance Abuse determined that "parental expectations, particularly expressing strong disapproval of substance abuse, can be a decisive factor in their teens' behavior."[48] Teens in the study who said their parents would be extremely upset to find out their child drank were less likely to drink or to say that it's okay for teens their age to get drunk. By comparison, adolescents who indicated their parents would not be extremely upset if they found out their child drinks were ten times likelier to say it's okay for teens their age to get drunk (22 percent vs. 2 percent).[49]

46. Biglan et al., *Helping Adolescents at Risk*, 18; Anderson et al., "Impact of Alcohol Advertising," 229.

47. Mason and Windle, "Family, Religious, School, and Peer Influences," 6–7.

48. National Center on Addiction and Substance Abuse, "National Survey of American Attitudes," ix.

49. Ibid.

Recognizing Alcohol Abuse

It is important that the youth worker is competent in recognizing when adolescents are abusing alcohol. It is also necessary to remember, however, that the presence of one or two of the signs commonly associated with alcohol abuse does not necessarily indicate the teenager has problems with alcohol. On the other hand, if a teenager exhibits several of the following warning signs, it is possible he or she is using excessive amounts of alcohol. The signs may also indicate drug abuse.[50]

- *Social withdrawal:* spends significant amounts of time alone, avoids times of family interaction and fun

- *Deterioration in school performance:* experiences a decline in school grades and consistently skips classes

- *Resistance to authority:* becomes rebellious toward parents, schoolteachers, police, and others

- *Behavior problems:* exhibits behavioral problems such as stealing or shoplifting, lying, or vandalism

- *Sexual promiscuity:* engages in illicit sexual behaviors

- *Physical complaints:* experiences unusual occurrences of illnesses such as colds, flu, headaches, and vomiting

- *Changes in relationships:* forms a new circle of friends

- *Changes in appetite:* experiences an increase or decrease in appetite, accompanied by significant weight gain or loss

- *Additional observable signs:* exhibits obvious signs of being under the influence of alcohol such as slurred speech, staggering, and alcohol on the breath

It is also important to distinguish between those adolescents who are perhaps just experimenting with the consumption of alcohol, regular users, and those who are addicted to or are abusing alcohol. Rich Van Pelt lists five stages in the adolescent's progression toward addiction:[51]

50. Summarized from Parrott, *Helping the Struggling Adolescent,* 125; and Van Pelt, *Intensive Care,* 190–91.

51. Adapted from Van Pelt, *Intensive Care,* 191. Van Pelt credits these stages to Larry Silver, former acting director of the National Institute of Mental Health.

Stage 1. Learning about the mood swing. Adolescents learn how easy it is to feel good with few, if any, consequences.

Stage 2. Seeking out the mood swing. Rather than using alcohol as an accompaniment to social events, the adolescent decides to get drunk as a goal and arranges to have his or her own supply of alcohol.

Stage 3. Being preoccupied with the mood swing. Getting drunk is the main goal of life. Students who drink daily may plan their days around trips to euphoria.

Stage 4. Feeling satisfied. The euphoria derived from alcohol consumption becomes harder to achieve; larger amounts are needed.

ILLICIT DRUG USE

As a high school student in Vermont, Patti was drinking every now and then with her friends. At seventeen she went to a university to study medicine, and by that time she was a weekend alcoholic. By the time she was eighteen, she was addicted to marijuana, and over the next two years she experimented with cocaine. Eventually she completely immersed herself in the drug scene. Patti was not a child of poverty or an abused child from a broken home. She was from a good Christian home. Her father was an elder in the church; she was an honor student in high school, president of the student council, and president of the youth group in the church she attended regularly. If there were signs of drug use, her parents did not see them, because they could not imagine their daughter in that situation.

Wendy is a blond-haired, blue-eyed two-year-old whose every breath is a struggle to live. She is underweight, cannot walk, talk or hold up her head. She is also blind and lives with cerebral palsy; doctors say she is the product of a cocaine habit. Before Wendy was born, her seventeen-year-old mother lived a life of cocaine, parties, and jail. The teenage mother already had one miscarriage due to her drug habit. Instead of turning away from drugs, she continued to use cocaine and a variety of pills, and got pregnant again—this time with Wendy.

While alcohol is the most widely used drug among teenagers, other illicit drugs continue to destroy young lives at an alarming rate. Since the social upheaval of the 1960s, illegal drug use has been spreading at epidemic

proportions among teenagers. During the 1980s there was a sharp decline in the adolescent use of marijuana, cocaine, and other illegal drugs
in the United States. But lest there be any doubt that there is a serious
drug problem among teenagers, even without any major resurgence of
drug use among the youngest cohorts, the following national statistics of
America's students in grades nine to twelve should be noted. Nationwide,
these youth had use the following drugs at least once in their life:

- marijuana (38.1 percent)

- cocaine (7.2 percent)

- inhalants (13.3 percent)

- steroid pills or shots without prescription (3.9 percent)

- hallucinogenic drugs such as LSD (7.8 percent)

- heroine (2.3 percent)

- methamphetamine (4.4 percent)

- ecstasy (5.8 percent).[52]

How do the habits of church youth compare with adolescents in
the general population? One research study indicates that there is not
a significant difference. For example, according to the Search Institute
study of church youth as reported in *Youth in Protestant Churches*, one
out of five (20 percent) sixteen- and seventeen-year-olds admitted to using marijuana in the past year. This rate is only slightly lower than the
national rate of 22 percent. Three percent of the sixteen-and seventeen-
year-olds had tried cocaine in the past year, a percentage identical to the
national rate. In their study of Protestant youth, Schwadel and Smith
found that 10 percent of the teens reported that they used marijuana occasionally or on a regular basis.[53]

The Search Institute study of church youth, however, did make
an important distinction between teenagers who were highly active in
church-related programs and those who were inactive. Inactive youth
were four times more likely to use marijuana or cocaine than active
youth.[54] The positive impact of church involvement found by the Search

52. Centers for Disease Control and Prevention. *Youth Risk Behavior
Surveillance–United States, 2007*, 15–18.

53. Schwadel and Smith, *Portraits of Protestant Teens*, 60.

54. Roelkepartain and Benson, *Youth in Protestant Churches*, 102–3.

Institute is reinforced by the National Survey of American Attitudes on Substance Abuse, which found that "teens who attend religious services at least four times a month are less likely to have used marijuana."[55]

Types of Addictive Drugs

Most addictive drugs, whether legal or illegal, fall into one of seven categories: narcotics, barbiturates, tranquilizers, stimulants, hallucinogens, inhalants, and cannabis. Along with alcohol, they form the nucleus of the drug abuse problem.[56]

- Narcotics depress the central nervous system causing stupor and insensibility. The most widely used narcotics are opium, morphine, codeine, and heroin. Addiction to these drugs, especially heroin, occurs over an abbreviated period of time.

- Barbiturates, also called "downers," depress the central nervous system but when abused are even more dangerous than heroin. They severely distort judgment, which can lead to an overdose.

- Tranquilizers are similar in effect to barbiturates in that they are depressants, and when abused can create a barbiturate-like dependence. Some commonly abused tranquilizers include Valium, Librium, and Methaqualone.

- Amphetamines, also called "uppers," stimulate the central nervous system. The psychological effects of their use include hyperactivity, paranoia, and hallucinations. The most commonly abused amphetamine is methamphetamine, also known as ecstasy (in tablet form) or Molly (in crystalline powder form).

- Cocaine is a dangerous and highly addictive stimulant that creates an intense, though brief, state of euphoria when first taken, followed by severe depression. Addiction to cocaine occurs rapidly, and increased doses become necessary to achieve the high. Cocaine has caused heart attacks in people as young as nineteen, as well as life-threatening damage to the heart, arteries, and brain. Sometimes

55. National Center on Addiction and Substance Abuse, *National Survey of American Attitudes,* 26.

56. Modified from a pamphlet, *Freedom from Addiction,* by the Medical Association of Georgia, Atlanta, Georgia.

cocaine hydrochloride is converted into a smokable form (free base). Cocaine can also be converted to a "rock" form known as crack.

- Hallucinogens have the ability to create vivid distortions of reality, and to create wild and sometimes terrifying experiences for the user. They induce a trancelike state, frequently with visual hallucinations. The most commonly abused hallucinogen is LSD, commonly called acid.

- Inhalants can directly cause death or structural damage to the brain, spinal cord, and liver. They include airplane glue, gasoline, lighter fluid, and aerosol products.

- Cannabis, considered to be the least powerful drug, temporarily alters the user's mood and perception and produces a sense of well-being. Long-term use may cause mental confusion, damage to lung tissue, and psychological dependence. Examples of cannabis are marijuana (also know as pot, grass, or Acapulco gold) and hashish.

Consequences of Illicit Drug Use

The perils of illegal drug use are well documented, and in the United States drug abuse has become a national health crisis. Clearly, the deadliest consequence of a number of drug users is the contraction of AIDS. Worldwide (with the exception of in sub-Saharan Africa), approximately 30 percent of AIDS/HIV cases are associated with drug injection.[57] The transfer of HIV-infected or contaminated blood occurs through the sharing of needles and syringes that are used for injecting drugs intravenously. The use of noninjected drugs such as crack cocaine can also place an individual at risk for HIV transmission in light of the fact that these substances reduce inhibitions and lessen one's reluctance to engage in unsafe sex.

There are additional physiological consequences related to drug use and abuse. Most disturbing is the fact that drug overdoses take the lives of a number of teenagers each year. Drugs such as cocaine and heroin used over a long period of time can cause severe impairment of internal organs and the nervous system. The use of illicit drugs greatly increases the risk of early sexual activity for adolescent males and females. The younger the

57. Avert, "People Who Inject Drugs (PWID) and HIV/AIDS."

reported age at first consumption of drugs, the greater the risk for early sexual activity.[58]

PREVENTION OF SUBSTANCE ABUSE

There are three levels of intervention efforts available to youth workers in dealing with the prevention of substance use and abuse: primary, secondary, and tertiary. Each level involves activity at a different point in the consumption sequence.

Table 9.1
Levels of Intervention

Prevention Type	Sequence	Types of Activities
Primary	before use or abuse	information and youth ministry alternatives
Secondary	the early stages of use or abuse	crisis intervention, diagnosis, and referral
Tertiary	later, more frequent, and higher quantity of use and abuse	detoxification and treatment programs

Primary Prevention

The level of prevention that affects the greatest number of adolescents is primary in nature because many adolescents (especially younger youth) have not yet experimented with alcohol or drugs. Primary prevention strategies include information giving, Christian education that encourages spiritual growth and faith development, and experiences and activities that provide an alternative to alcohol and drug consumption.

Joy Dryfoos suggests that most primary alcohol and drug prevention strategies and programs fall into one of five categories: (1) knowledge-oriented strategies, (2) affective strategies, (3) knowledge and affective strategies, (4) social influence and life skills, and (5) alternative strategies.[59]

---

58. Rosenblaum and Kandel, "Early Onset of Adolescent Sex and Drug Use."
59. Modified from Dryfoos, *Adolescents at Risk,* 153.

Knowledge Strategies

Knowledge only or information-based intervention strategies or techniques are based on the assumption that educating teenagers about alcohol and drugs will change attitudes that will, in turn, reduce consumption. However, according to the research done by Dryfoos, strategies that present only information demonstrate practically no effect on knowledge of substances, attitudes toward substances, skills in saying no to substance consumption, or behavioral change in regard to substance use.[60]

Affective Strategies

Affective strategies are based on the assumption that psychological factors such as low self-esteem or inability to cope with stress put certain adolescents at greater risk for substance abuse. These strategies focus on the psychological issue (e.g., self esteem) with little or no mention of drugs or alcohol. Affective strategies used alone have only minimal effect on lowering substance use.

Knowledge and Affective Strategies Integrated

A number of strategies assume that behavior change will follow knowledge, attitude, and value change. Some techniques that combine information giving and affective content include the following:

- Take members of the youth group to an open meeting of a nearby rehabilitation program to listen to the stories of alcohol and drug addicts in treatment. Some clinics have evenings where the meeting is open to nonresidents.

- Use articles or media reports about lives of individuals negatively affected by drugs or alcohol to stimulate discussion about substance abuse.

- Have a recovering drug addict or alcoholic speak to the youth group about the negative consequences of substance use and abuse. Provide opportunity for members of the youth group to direct questions toward the guest speaker.

60. Ibid.

Social Influence and Life Skills Strategies

These strategies assume that peer pressure is the major factor in substance abuse, that focus on the peer group may be the most effective means to combat substance use, and that peer-taught programs appear to be more successful than adult-taught ones. A combination of approaches that include refusal skills and social or life skills are employed to prevent alcohol and drug consumption. These strategies include components such as

- interpersonal resistance skills
- abilities to cope with social pressures
- problem solving and decision making skills
- the ability to say no to drugs or alcohol
- social skills for resisting peer pressure.

Of the five models, Dryfoos found this one to have the greatest effect in the intervention of teenage substance use and abuse.

Alternative Strategies

Another intervention approach that has proven to be somewhat effective is the creating and providing of alternatives to substance use. By their very nature, healthy youth group functions provide positive options to negative behaviors. However, an effort to include activities that encourage creativity will enable adolescents to realize a degree of accomplishment, pride in work, and a measure of personal satisfaction. Creative experiences include painting, drawing, molding pottery, singing, acting, playing a musical instrument, and writing.

Secondary Intervention

Despite the efforts and successes of primary prevention, there are many adolescents who become involved with substance abuse. Secondary efforts focus on reducing or intervening in this dysfunction. Churches and youth pastors can offer a variety of services and ministries to accomplish that goal. Crisis hotlines, support groups, or drop-in centers are ways some churches and youth ministries assist adolescents who want to talk about drug-related problems.

Since adolescents often respond positively to peer influence and group contexts, youth workers should encourage participation in recovery groups such as Alcoholics Anonymous (AA). Alcoholics Anonymous is a public organization that has benefited thousands of people, adolescents included. The goal of AA is to get individuals to recognize that alcoholism is a personal problem that each alcoholic must own up to and take responsibility for. Some churches have support or recovery programs that adapt the AA steps to recovery to fit their doctrine and religious beliefs.

Support groups for parents of alcoholic teenagers are also available in the community through local churches, schools, and workplaces. One such group that is active throughout the United States (as well as Canada, South Africa, and New Zealand) is ToughLove. ToughLove is a support group for parents of adolescents who are addicted, abusive, uncontrollable, or in some way in trouble with the law or at school. This organization, with headquarters in Doylestown, Pennsylvania, holds workshops, publishes a newsletter and brochures, provides referrals to professionals, and offers ideas for helping adolescents cease their self-destructive behavior.[61]

Tertiary Prevention

The need for treatment for drug or alcohol abuse that extends beyond the skill of the youth pastor or volunteer worker is sometimes necessary for a smaller percentage of teenagers. Detoxification conducted under medical supervision is often the first step in treating a substance abuse problem. Usually detoxification takes place in a special hospital facility and is intended to stop a physiological dependence on a particular drug by eliminating it entirely from the individual's system. Rehabilitation counseling should accompany the detoxification process in enabling the adolescent to develop a positive, drug-free life-style.

A number of residential programs in the United States and other countries exist for the purpose of rehabilitating substance-abusing adolescents. Usually these in-house recovery programs endeavor to help teenagers gain an understanding of their alcohol-related problems and assist them in long-term recovery. The time spent in such a program gives the adolescent an opportunity to develop personal recovery goals, to prepare for reentry into the community, to learn skills necessary for the prevention of a relapse, and to practice an abstinent lifestyle. One such

61. http://www.toughlove.org/.

organization is Teen Challenge, a Christian-oriented program that serves adolescents and young adults with alcohol- and drug-related problems. Teen Challenge has facilities in the United States as well as in a number of other countries.[62]

For teenagers in treatment, the youth worker can be involved in the following ways:[63]

- Continue to support the adolescent and the family through any rehabilitation or detoxification period. Visiting the teenager at the treatment facility is one way to demonstrate ongoing care and concern.

- Maintain support and contact with the adolescent after the period of rehabilitation. Relapses are a common occurrence, and emotional support is needed for ongoing progress. Visit the youth at his or her home, make a telephone call, drop a note of encouragement, invite the teenager into your home, or spend some time with the individual over a cup of coffee in a local restaurant.

- Involve the adolescent in activities that may lessen the attraction to drugs: go hiking, play tennis or racquetball, go fishing, attend a concert or sporting event together.

- Do not give up on a teenager who is recovering from a substance abuse problem. Be prepared to offer continued support in case of a relapse, and do not take a failure personally.

SELF-INJURY BEHAVIORS

Priya, a sixteen-year-old girl, ritualistically burned her arms and legs with a cigarette every few months. She never allowed anyone to see her uncovered skin, which she kept hidden beneath long black skirts and long-sleeved black sweaters or shirts. Sheila was fourteen when she began regularly cutting herself with a razor blade. When her wounds began to heal she often rewounded herself by picking at the scabs until they bled. Mark, a seventeen-year-old, admitted to throwing himself down a flight of stairs in the hope of breaking an arm or leg. When this failed, he resorted to breaking his finger with a hammer.[64]

62. http://teenchallengeusa.com/.

63. Rowley, *Equipped to Care*, 133.

64. Hardy and Laszloffy, *Teens Who Hurt*, 15.

Statistics on self-injury behavior present a very disturbing phenomenon that exists in developed countries such as the United States, Canada, and western Europe. Psychologist Michael Hollender writes that "nothing causes parents as much anguish as kids who deliberately cut, scratch, burn, or hurt themselves in some other fashion. Parents find their children's self-injury to be one of the most painful experiences they have ever had, and one of the most confusing."[65] While cutting is the better known of self-harm behaviors there are a number of additional injurious actions teenagers engage in, including

- burning (for example, with a cigarette butt)
- interfering with the healing of wounds by picking or reopening them
- punching or hitting oneself
- inserting objects into the skin
- intentionally bruising or breaking one's bones
- hair pulling.

Samantha Gluck summarizes the following self-injury statistics:[66]

- One in five females and one in seven males engages in some form of self-injury behavior.
- Ninety percent of the individuals who engage in self-injury begin in their teen or preteen years.
- Almost 50 percent of teens who engage in self-injury activities have been sexually abused.
- Females make up 60 percent of teenagers who engage in self-harm.
- Around half of the adolescents who engage in self-harm behaviors begin around age fourteen.
- Many of those who self-injure indicate they learn the behavior from friends or (pro) self-injury websites.

What would cause teenagers to hurt themselves in a manner that is so contrary to the common thinking of most people? Often teens will respond with something like "I hate myself" or "I deserve to hurt." But

65. Hollender, *Helping Teens Who Cut*, 1.
66. Gluck, "Self-Injury, Self Harm Statistics and Facts."

self-injury behavior is probably one of the most mystifying and complex behaviors adolescents engage in. Often it is related to other mental health conditions such as depression, anxiety, substance abuse, and eating disorders. However, Hollander suggests that sometimes we spend too much time looking beneath the surface for some hidden or unresolved need that is causing the behavior, thereby overlooking a key concept: teens hurt themselves because it makes them feel better momentarily and in some specific way.[67] Nonetheless, Hollander proposes two of the most common reasons as to why teens do it: "1) to control the extremely painful and frightening experience of overwhelming emotions, and/or 2) to escape from an awful feeling of being numb and empty."[68] Jan Sutton adds, it is "fundamentally a coping mechanism, frequently born out of trauma or a deep-rooted sense of powerlessness . . . best described as a 'pain exchange' in that overwhelming, invisible, emotional pain is converted into visible, physical wounds which individuals who use the practice find easier to deal with."[69] She goes on to say that following self-injury, individuals usually feel "calmer, more in control, safe from suicide, and more able to cope and function."[70]

As it is with eating disorders, mental health issues, substance abuse, and other severe issues, the youth pastor is likely ill-equipped to deal with the complexities of self-injury. The rule of thumb for any workers who feel they are in over their heads is referral. For self-abusers there are several options:

- inpatient facilities, best for teens who believe they cannot stop self-abuse without direct supervision
- outpatient treatment programs, which requires greater individual responsibility with less direct oversight
- group therapy or individual counseling
- family counseling.

Beyond referral, Chap Clark indicates the only qualification a youth worker (or any adult) needs for working with hurting teens such as those engaging in self-abuse is the willingness and desire to exhibit genuine

67. Hollander, *Helping Teens Who Cut*, 24.

68. Ibid., 7.

69. Sutton, *Healing the Hurt Within*, 6.

70. Ibid.

care for teens. With this foundation laid, the youth worker can focus on three specific needs:[71]

1. nurturing ministries and programs

2. a stable, secure, and loving presence

3. authentic and intimate relationships with adults.

SEXUALLY TRANSMITTED DISEASES

One of the most permanent and destructive consequences of premarital sexual activity for teenagers is the contracting of one or more sexually transmitted diseases (STDs)—and the statistics are alarming. The Centers for Disease Control estimates that American teenagers and young adults aged fifteen to twenty-four acquire half of the 20 million newly acquired STDs per year, and that one in four sexually active adolescent females has an STD such as chlamydia or human papillomavirus.[72]

How many types of STDs are there? The responses to this question vary wildly from approximately twenty upwards towards sixty, though the more accurate number is probably closer to twenty. However, there may be multiple strains for some of the diseases. Infections can be broken down into three different types: *bacterial* (including chlamydia, gonorrhea, and syphilis), *viral* (including genital herpes, genital warts, and hepatitis B), and *parasitic* (trichonomas). For each of these diseases there are physical and often emotional consequences. The physical consequences of sexually transmitted diseases vary, but most are irreversible. Some sexual diseases can be cured, and in some cases the severity of symptoms can be reduced, but other diseases such as genital herpes are incurable. The symptoms of genital herpes for both sexes include blisters and open sores in the area of sexual organs. Males with gonorrhea experience a pus-like discharge; for females, untreated gonorrhea can cause irreversible infertility. Chlamydia causes a penis discharge in males, while in females it brings about vaginal itching, abdominal pain, and bleeding. In addition there are debilitating, and frankly quite frightening, long-lasting effects of many STDs, as summarized by the Centers for Disease Control:

71. Clark, *Hurt 2.0*, 191.

72. Centers for Disease Control and Prevention, "STDs in Adolescents and Young Adults."

- Untreated gonorrhea and chlamydia can silently steal a young woman's chance to have her own children later in life. Each year, untreated STDs cause at least 24,000 women in the U.S. to become infertile.

- Untreated syphilis can lead to serious long-term complications, including brain, cardiovascular, and organ damage. Syphilis in pregnant women can also result in congenital syphilis (syphilis among infants), which can cause stillbirth, death soon after birth, and physical deformity and neurological complications in children who survive. Untreated syphilis in pregnant women results in infant death in up to 40 percent of cases.

- Studies suggest that people with gonorrhea, chlamydia, or syphilis are at increased risk for HIV.[73]

The suffering and pain that comes with STDs is not limited to the physical. A teenager who has contracted a sexually transmitted disease is likely to experience emotional trauma as well, including depression, embarrassment, and guilt. In some instances the diseased youth will suffer social isolation and loneliness. It might be helpful to summarize several critical points about sexually transmitted diseases. No discussion of premarital sex with adolescents would be complete without emphasizing these important facts:[74]

- Unless there is a sudden and significant change in society's permissive attitude toward sexuality, casual and premarital sex are likely to continue.

- One of the very real dangers of casual sex is that members of both genders may acquire a sexually transmitted disease.

- STDs are infectious diseases spread by sexual intercourse and should be treated by a physician like any other infectious disease.

- Any male or female who develops a pus like discharge from the penis or vagina, or blisters or open sores in the area of sexual organs, should visit a physician and undergo tests.

73. Ibid.

74. Llewellyn-Jones, *Herpes, AIDS and Other Sexually Transmitted Diseases,* 17–18.

- Any teenager who has sexual intercourse with multiple partners should be examined by a medical doctor at regular intervals so that infectious sexual diseases may be detected and treated.

Upon discovering that an adolescent has acquired an STD or may have been exposed to an STD, the youth worker should refer that person to a physician immediately. As was mentioned earlier, serious danger results from failure to medically treat STDs. Teenagers who test positive must also tell anyone with whom they have had sexual intercourse.

THE PLIGHT OF AIDS[75]

> Everybody knows that pestilence has a way of recurring in the world, yet somehow we find it hard to believe that one can crash down on our heads from a blue sky. There have been as many plagues as there have been wars in history, yet always these plagues and these wars take us by surprise. A pestilence isn't a thing made to man's measure, therefore, we tell ourselves that these pestilences are nothing but a bogey of the mind, a bad dream that will pass away. But, it doesn't pass away, and from one bad dream to another, it is the men who pass away. (Albert Camus, *The Plague*)

Since ancient times humankind has been ravaged by plagues or communicable diseases as devastating and destructive as war itself. In the 1980s an epidemic began to spread throughout the world that has the potential to become as deadly as the bubonic plague or Black Death that marked the end of the Middle Ages—*acquired immunodeficiency syndrome,* commonly known as AIDS. In fact, AIDS has already taken more American lives than did the Vietnam War. The first cases of AIDS were reported in the United States in 1981; by 1993 more than three hundred thousand individuals had developed AIDS, and over two hundred thousand had died from the disease.[76] There is some good news, however: "Annual HIV diagnoses in the United States fell by 19 percent from 2005 to 2014, driven by dramatic and continuing declines over the decade among sev-

75. While acquired immunodeficiency syndrome, commonly known as AIDS, is a sexually transmitted disease, it will be treated separately for two reasons. First, it is also a disease that can be contracted from contaminated drug needles; and second, AIDS is a deadly disease that demands special attention.

76. Novella, *Surgeon General's Report,* 1.

eral populations including heterosexuals, people who inject drugs, and African Americans—with the steepest declines among black women."[77]

AIDS is actually caused by the *human immunodeficiency virus* (HIV), which enters the blood and infects certain cells. Once these cells begin to die, flulike symptoms appear. As the disease progresses, the conditions get more severe. In the final stage, the patient is diagnosed with full-blown AIDS and by this time is suffering from extreme tiredness, loss of weight, diarrhea, high temperatures, and sight loss. Thus, an individual could test HIV positive yet not have AIDS. The great majority of those who have HIV, however, will contract AIDS. Full-blown AIDS can take nearly ten years to develop from the initial contraction of HIV.[78] AIDS destroys the immune system, making the body easily susceptible to a large number of fatal diseases such as pneumonia, tuberculosis, or cancers, which it normally would be able to ward off.

AIDS has made alarming inroads into the adolescent population as the following statistics indicate, though the numbers are decreasing:[79]

- One in four new infections occurs in youth between thirteen and twenty-four years old.

- About twelve thousand youth were infected with HIV in 2010.

- About 60 percent of youth with HIV are not aware that they are infected, are not receiving treatment, and can unknowingly pass the virus on to others.

AIDS and HIV awareness among teenagers does not appear to be an issue, as most recently 85.3 percent of adolescents reported having being taught about the infectious disease in school.[80] It appears that the increased AIDS awareness in schools and elsewhere is having a positive effect on teens. The estimated number of HIV-infected teenagers ages thirteen to nineteen decreased from 2,014 in 2010 to 1,863 in 2014.[81] Nonetheless young people may still tend to have the attitude that HIV infection or

77. Centers for Disease Control and Prevention, "NHPC Press Release: HIV Diagnosis."

78. McWhirter et al., *At-Risk Youth*, 145–46; and Ankerberg and Weldon, *Myth of Safe Sex*, 66–67.

79. Centers for Disease Control and Prevention, "HIV among Youth in the US."

80. Centers for Disease Control and Prevention, *Youth Risk Behavior Surveillance— United States, 2013*.

81. Centers for Disease Control and Prevention, *Diagnoses of HIV Infection in the United States and Dependent Areas*, 18.

the AIDS disease could never happen to them, that they are somehow invulnerable to something as catastrophic and devastating as this disease. To some degree this may be because they rarely see people their age who have AIDS. Because of the possible ten-year lag time between contracting the HIV virus and acquiring full-blown AIDS, patients may not show symptoms until they are in their twenties.

The chance of the youth pastor or volunteer worker encountering a teenager with full-blown AIDS will be quite slim. However, the youth worker can help adolescents assess their risk for contracting AIDS. If teenagers answer yes to any of the following blunt questions, they could have the HIV infection.

1. Have you ever had unprotected anal, vaginal, or oral sex with a male or female who

   - you know was infected with AIDS?

   - injects or has injected drugs?

   - shared needles with an HIV-infected person?

   - had sex with someone who shared needles?

   - had multiple sex partners?

2. Have you ever used syringes or needles that were used by anyone before you?

3. Have you ever given or received sex for money or drugs?

4. Have you had sex with someone who had a blood transfusion or received clotting factors between 1978 and 1985?

If adolescents answer yes to any of the above questions, they should be referred to a doctor or health clinic where they can talk about the situation, get more information, and decide if testing for HIV needs to be done. Another option for teenagers who are looking for counseling and testing for HIV is the community health center or public clinic. Some sites will do a test free of charge; others will charge a fee.[82] Youth workers must do all they can to make adolescents aware of AIDS and its deadly consequences. Teenagers must be presented with the data related to these diseases, and warned of the dangers and irreversible consequences that may accompany sexual activity. They must be persuaded that the only

82. The U.S. Department of Health and Human Services provides a list of AIDS/HIV hotlines state by state at http://hab.hrsa.gov/gethelp/statehotlines.html.

truly effective means of preventing HIV infection is refraining from sexual intercourse until marriage, and then limiting sexual activity to a monogamous husband-wife relationship.

"What about safe sex?" some teenagers may argue. The only genuinely safe sex is abstinence before marriage and monogamy within marriage. John Ankerberg and John Weldon rightly remind us that the only solution to STDs such as AIDS is a radical change in sexual attitudes and behavior. To risk infertility, lifelong pain and suffering, cancer, and other diseases, or even death, is absurd. To teach our own youth and children that safe sex is the solution seems almost criminal.[83] Even the Centers for Disease Control teaches teenagers that, "The most reliable way to avoid infection [from an STD] is to not have sex (i.e., anal, vaginal or oral)."[84]

Adolescents should be taught certain facts about AIDS. For example, it is important for them to know how this infectious disease is transmitted and how it is not. AIDS is transmitted through the exchange of body fluids, usually by sexual contact or needle sharing, and not through casual social contact. They should know that condoms are only about 90 percent effective in preventing the contracting of HIV.

Some effective ways to teach adolescents about the crisis of AIDS and its deadly consequences include the following:

- Have someone with AIDS come and talk with the youth group about the tragic consequences of this disease. Be sure this person endorses sexual abstinence before marriage as the only truly form of safe sex.

- Have someone from the medical profession talk with the youth group about AIDS. Be sure opportunity is given for a time of questions and answers.

- Have a panel discussion on AIDS. Possibilities for panel members include a pastor, a medical doctor, an AIDS patient, and/or a parent or sibling of someone with AIDS.

- Use current statistics or a video clip as a starter for a discussion on AIDS.

- Have youth group members visit an AIDS patient in his or her home or in the hospital. Encourage the youth to consider this visit as an opportunity to minister and reach out to someone who is suffering

83. Ankerberg and Weldon, *Myth of Safe Sex*, 63.

84. Centers for Disease Control and Prevention, "15–24-Year-Olds Account for Half of All New STD Infections."

a slow and agonizing death. Following the visit, spend some time debriefing.

- Talk about topics such as the physical and emotional consequences of AIDS, the importance of abstinence from premarital sex, and the response Christians should have to AIDS and those suffering from the disease.

CONCLUSION

Several areas of risky adolescent behavior that may have unhealthy or dangerous consequences have been addressed in this chapter: the eating disorders of anorexia and bulimia, the use and abuse of alcohol, the use of illicit drugs, self-injury behaviors, STDs, and HIV and AIDS. The eating disorders of anorexia nervosa and bulimia nervosa affect a small percentage of adolescents, mostly girls. Adolescents who struggle with either anorexia or bulimia may suffer serious physical and emotional consequences. No doubt the most pervasive problem among adolescents is substance use and abuse. While the consumption of alcohol is illegal for the large majority of teenagers, it is clearly the drug of choice for American youth. As noted earlier, two-thirds of American secondary students (grades nine through twelve) have consumed alcohol at some point in their life. While there has been a decline in illicit drug use from the 1970s and 1980s peak levels, American teenagers demonstrate a level of illicit drug involvement that is greater than in any other industrialized country. The nonalcohol drug of choice for both American and Canadian youth is marijuana.

10

The Tragedy of Teenage Suicide

"I'm tired of it," shrieked distraught fifteen-year-old Brian Head just before he put a pistol to his head and pulled the trigger. Brian, an only child, was a smart teenager who worked as drama club stagehand. But he was shy, overweight, and the object of a considerable amount of cruel adolescent humor, taunting, and physical abuse. For several years Brian had put up with the teasing and tormenting from classmates, but the point came when he could take it no more, and in front of his fellow students, he violently took his own life.[1]

One of the tragedies of contemporary youth culture and adolescent behavior is the widespread incidence of suicide. At an alarming rate teenagers are opting to take their own lives in response to the overwhelming pressures and struggles of daily living. In the latter decades of the twentieth century medical experts and sociological analysts were troubled by the sharp increase in the rate of adolescent suicide, noting that in the 1980s more than doubled the rate of 1960, and tripled the teenage suicide rate of the 1950s.[2] Francine Klagsbrun, in her classic treatment of youth and suicide, described teenage suicide as an epidemic that cannot be ignored or minimized.[3] Most youth pastors and volunteers who work with teens will encounter suicidal adolescents. In fact clinical psychiatrists and

1. Adapted from Hendrick, "Youth's Suicide Highlights Its No. 3 Rank as Killer of Teens."
2. Klagsbrun, *Too Young to Die*, 9.
3. Ibid.

suicide experts Cheryl King, Cynthia Foster, and Kelly Rogalski suggest, "A concern about suicide risk—whether due to a suicide attempt, a text message or diary entry indicating suicidal intent, or an expression of suicidal thoughts—is the most common mental health emergency in this age group."[4]

THE SCOPE OF ADOLESCENT SUICIDE

In the 1950s teenage suicide was given little attention. While adolescents occasionally took their own lives, these occurrences were generally seen as aberrations. By the time the 1990s came around, suicide was recognized as the third-leading cause of death for teenagers in America.[5] In 2012 suicide was the second-leading cause of death for persons aged ten to twenty-four and accounted for 5,178 deaths in this age group.[6] Since many suicides are disguised or reported as accidents, it may in fact be the number-one killer of adolescents and young adults. The problem of adolescent suicide takes on even greater proportions when suicide thoughts or unsuccessful suicide attempts are considered.

Age

In the United States suicide rates increase with age throughout childhood and adolescence. Suicide is rare before the age of nine and increases slightly between ages ten and fourteen (1.17 deaths per 100,000), making it the third-leading cause of death for that age group. The numbers spike in the fifteen-to-nineteen-year-old age group (7.47 deaths per 100,000), becoming the second-leading cause of death for fourteen- to seventeen-year-olds.[7]

Gender

Empirical research on adolescent suicide and suicide thought consistently demonstrates marked differences between males and females. Teenage

4. King et al., *Teen Suicide Risk*, 1.
5. Kachur et al., *Suicide in the United States 1980–1992*, 6.
6. Sullivan et al., "Suicide Trends."
7. King et al., *Teen Suicide Risk*, 17.

girls are far more likely to think seriously of suicide, make a plan for suicide, or attempt suicide than their male peers. Yet males are more likely to die from suicide, as the rate of suicide for boys is five times that of girls by age nineteen.[8] Why are teenage girls more prone to suicidal ideation and suicide attempts, yet males more successful in actually killing themselves? One possible explanation for this pattern is that females respond hastily to an immediate crisis, and because the efforts are so poorly planned the attempts are less likely to succeed.[9] Another suggestion is that females seem to prefer a more passive approach to attempted suicide such as drug overdose, while males tend to employ more violent and unfailing forms such as shooting or hanging themselves.[10]

Ethnicity and Race

Rates of suicide across race and ethnicity are varied. The most noticeable finding is that of suicide rates for American Indians and Alaskan Natives. The chance of these teens taking their lives is 2.3 times that of non-Hispanic Caucasians (20.7 vs. 8.9 per 100,000). Rates for other ethnic or racial groups per thousand are, 5.9 for Asian and Pacific Islanders, 6.3 for Hispanic Caucasians, and 4.4 for Blacks.[11]

SUICIDE IDEATION

Suicide *ideation* refers to fantasizing or thinking about killing oneself. While a relatively small number of adolescents actually commit suicide, a large number of teenagers entertain thoughts of taking their own lives. And a large percentage of teenagers who kill themselves begin by thinking about it, threatening it, or attempting to do it. The suicide ideation of yesterday may very well become the suicide attempt of today or the completed suicide of tomorrow.

The United States Department of Health and Human Services examined the prevalence of suicidal ideation and behaviors of students in grades nine to twelve through the administration of the *Youth Risk Behavior Surveillance*. The research results revealed that for the twelve

---

8. Ibid., 15.

9. Newman and Newman, *Adolescent Development*, 298.

10. Bingham et al., "Analysis of Age, Gender and Racial Differences."

11. King et al., *Teen Suicide Risk*, 17–18.

months preceding the survey 15.8 percent of all the students surveyed (almost one in seven) had seriously considered attempting suicide. Fewer adolescents (12.8 percent) indicated that they had made specific plans for taking their own lives, and fewer still (7.8 percent) actually attempted suicide. However, only 2.4 percent had injured themselves enough to require medical attention.[12]

The Warning Signs of Suicide Ideation

The critical task of any adult who does youth ministry is to learn to recognize the warning signs of suicide or suicide ideation. Among the signs that an adolescent might be contemplating taking his or her own life are the following:[13]

- a depressed mood

- changes in sleep patterns

- changes in appetite patterns

- a decline in school performance

- increased withdrawal

- a loss of interest and pleasure in previously enjoyable activities

- changes in appearance (for example, no longer caring about one's clothing or hair)

- a preoccupation with themes of death (for example, the youth may begin to read books with themes of death and dying)

- increased irritability and behavior problems

- giving away important possessions

- the abuse of drugs and alcohol

- a history of previous attempts

- a history of abuse and neglect

- a history of learning disabilities and a sense of failure

- frequent somatic complaints

12. Centers for Disease Control and Prevention, *Youth Risk Behavior Surveillance—United States, 2011.*

13. Adapted from Papolos and Papolos, *Overcoming Depression,* 126.

- verbal expression about self-death (for instance, a teenager who actually says, "I wish I were dead")
- no longer being concerned about making plans for the future.

Intervention and Referral

Should a youth worker suspect an adolescent is contemplating suicide or should an adolescent threaten suicide, the matter should be dealt with immediately. The following actions should be taken.

Assess the situation. The first step is to discuss the issue of suicide with the teenager and assess the seriousness of the ideation or the lethality of the threat. Often people avoid introducing the subject of suicide because they fear it will plant ideas in the mind of an already fragile or troubled youth. On the contrary, asking a teenager about self-destructive ideas can help him or her feel better understood and less trapped. Does the individual have a plan? How lethal is the chosen method? How available is the method?

Contact the parents or legal guardians. The next step is to notify parents of the imminent danger of suicide. Although this contact breaks confidentiality between the youth worker and the teenager, it is a legally and ethically appropriate response to an adolescent's suicide threat or contemplation.

Develop a written contract. Experts have found that developing a contract with the suicidal youth is helpful in deterring a potential suicide. The contract establishes an agreement that the teenager will call and talk to the youth worker before attempting to take his or her life. Most youth will comply with a contract because it ties the troubled individual with a person who really cares.[14]

Refer to a professional counselor. When it becomes clear that an adolescent is at risk of suicide, it imperative that he or she be referred to a psychologist or psychiatrist for clinical and legal reasons. The professional counselor can then assess the risk of suicide and decide whether hospitalization is necessary, what kind of psychotherapy will be suitable, and whether or not medication is needed.

Maintain contact with the suicidal teenager. Once referral is made to a psychologist or psychiatrist, it is important for the youth pastor or volunteer worker to continue a warm, supportive, and caring relationship

14. Van Pelt, *Intensive Care*, 131.

with the teenager. Continued supportive contact with the teenager is important so that the individual does not feel abandoned by the youth worker or that the referral was made out of disinterest.

RISK FACTORS RELATED TO SUICIDE AND SUICIDE IDEATION

Why are teenagers terminating their lives at such an alarming rate? Why do so many adolescents view life and living as so hopeless that suicide appears to be the only realistic alternative? Suicide is a complex subject steeped in myth, erroneous thinking, and misunderstandings. Unless a suicidal adolescent leaves a note of explanation or clearly communicates his or her intention in some other manner, the full circumstances behind the death are not easily understood.

No single cause can adequately explain the dramatic increase in adolescent suicide. The sources of the problem are as complex as human behavior and contemporary society themselves are. Experts identify five major factors as influencing suicide attempts among adolescents:[15]

- family problems, including broken families, severe marital conflict, lack of closeness and understanding between fathers and sons, and families where the mother is cold, punitive, and detached

- personal loss, including the loss of a loved one or the loss of an important person's love

- social isolation, especially feeling alienated from family and peers, being socially withdrawn and self-conscious, and having few or no meaningful relationships

- depression, including feelings of worthlessness

- substance use and abuse.

Dysfunctional Family Life

One of the key factors related to adolescent suicidal behavior, and one of the most studied variables, is the family and the familial context in which suicide occurs. Suicidal adolescents often come from dysfunctional or disintegrated families where violence, abuse, conflict, and arguments

15. Modified from Newman and Newman, *Adolescent Development,* 298.

are the norm. The breakup of the traditional family through divorce and separation, the rise of single-parent households, and the lack of skills in parenting, discipline, and communication all combine to augment the risk of teenage suicide.[16]

Mohammed Shafii and colleagues, for example, found that 55 percent of adolescents who committed suicide experienced physical and emotional abusiveness in the home, compared to 29 percent of a controlled group of nonsuicidal peers.[17] In a Los Angeles Suicide Prevention Center sample of adolescents who committed suicide, nearly two-thirds of them had reported that they were not on good terms with their parents, while 90 percent felt their family did not understand them. Many of the suicidal youth reported physical fights with family members as well as physical and assaultive behavior among family members.[18] According to a Gallup survey on teenage suicide, of those adolescents who attempted suicide or came close to killing themselves, almost one-half (47 percent) cited family problems or problems at home as a factor.[19] A study of Latino adolescents who committed suicide revealed that most did not get along with their parents or were not living with both biological parents. The victims had experienced significantly more family stressors than the nonsuicidal teenagers in the control group.[20] Alan Berman and David Jobes note that compared to nonsuicidal adolescents, those who are suicidal have poorer family relationships, receive less affection, enjoy time with their families less, and hold more negative views of their parents.[21]

Working with adolescents whose suicide attempts or ideation find their roots at least partially in the family context may be difficult because the situation is often unchangeable or complex. However, the threat of adolescent suicide that comes as a result of family dysfunction and break-ups can be reduced through ministry with parents. Merton Strommen argues that we can assume that a critical factor in preventing adolescent suicide is helping youth to become affiliated with a caring congregation and helping the parents strengthen their marriages through seminars,

---

16. King et al., *Teen Suicide Risk*, 32.

17. Shafii, "Completed Suicide in Children and Adolescents."

18. Peck, "Suicide in Late Adolescence and Young Adulthood," 222.

19. George H. Gallup International Institute, *Gallup Survey on Teenage Suicide*, 72.

20. Queralt, "Risk Factors."

21. Berman and Jobes, *Adolescent Suicide*, 95.

counseling, and retreats.[22] We might add Sunday school classes that address issues such as marital conflict and communication skills to that list. We would also urge Christian educators to take advantage of the variety of audiovisual resources available for instruction and discussion starters in adult Christian education settings

Counselor Jon Harris commends support groups for individuals who are experiencing some degree of family conflict in their lives. The opportunities to see that one is not alone in a particular struggle, to realize the hope presented by those who are more advanced in the healing process, and to be heard and understood by someone else for perhaps the first time are therapeutic and encouraging for many battered, stressed, and hurting people. However, Harris strongly recommends that Christian educators who are going to lead a support group be trained in three areas: small-group dynamics, dysfunctional families, and codependency.[23]

Loss of a Loved One

Another theme related to adolescent suicide or suicide attempts is the loss of a significant person. This may be the dissolution of a love relationship, the death of a parent or sibling, the loss of a parent through divorce or separation, or rejection by one or both parents. The loss of a loved one can be a strong predictor of teenage suicide attempts. Fifty percent of adolescent suicide attempters reported losing a significant other as compared to only 5 percent of non-attempters.[24] Lucy Davidson and colleagues discovered that a powerful stressor preceding suicide was the loss of a girlfriend or boyfriend, or the fear that a relationship would end.[25] In the aforementioned study of Latino adolescents, 50 percent of the victims had divorced or separated parents, compared to 25 percent of those in the non-suicidal control group.[26] In the case of a loss through the death of a loved one, teens sometimes take their own life so that they might be reunited with the individual who so abruptly abandoned them.[27]

---

22. Strommen, *Five Cries of Youth*, 59.

23. Harris, "Dysfunction, Healing and the Family of Origin," 202–6.

24. Morano et al., "Risk Factors for Adolescent Suicidal Behavior."

25. Davidson et al., "Epidemiologic Study."

26. Queralt, "Risk Factors."

27. Klagsrun, *Too Young to Die*, 107; Crook, *Out of the Darkness*, 148.

When an adolescent experiences the loss of a loved one through death, divorce, rejection, or separation, the youth pastor can reduce the possibility of an attempted suicide by sharing in the individual's grief work. This can be accomplished in at least three ways. First, encourage the release of emotions, thoughts, and feelings, both positive and negative. Do not be shocked by the intense rage or anguish that often comes from the mouth of a grieving adolescent. Second, provide empathy and expressions of understanding, caring, and support. At these critical junctures in life, adolescents do not need judgment, correction, or even advice. What they do need is a caring person to listen to them. Compassionate listening and attentive caring are the most effective healing youth workers can provide for a teenager experiencing the loss of a significant person. Third, encourage the adolescent to talk about the loss of the significant person. To talk about the father who has abandoned the family, the sibling who has committed suicide, the boyfriend who has terminated a relationship, or the close friend who was killed in a car accident helps the individual to confront the reality of the devastating experience.[28]

Social Isolation and Loneliness

The landmark study of suicide was done at the end of the nineteenth century by French sociologist Emile Durkheim.[29] Durkheim studied the relationship between society and suicide and concluded that there are three types of suicide that grow out of social conditions. When an individual chooses a group identity and values over individual needs, an individual may be willing to sacrifice his or her life for the community and to commit an *altruistic* suicide. Examples of altruistic suicides are the Jews at Masada, the Japanese kamikaze pilots of World War II, and radical Islamic terrorists. There is also the *anomic* suicide. In this case the individual commits suicide because he or she has experienced great societal and personal upheaval in life and is incapable of adjusting to this radical social change.

Most suicides, however, are *egoistic*. Egotistic suicide occurs when an individual has trouble integrating into society and feels lonely and alienated, disengaged from other people. One of the developmental tasks of adolescence is the achieving of new and more mature relationships

28. Adapted from Olson, *Counseling Teenagers*, 496–500.
29. Durkheim, *Suicide*.

with peers of both sexes. The peer-group and relationships provide support and emotional security to teenagers who are uncertain of themselves and their position in the grand scheme of life.[30]

For some adolescents, however, developing friendships and peer relationships is difficult. The social lives of many teenagers are characterized by interpersonal conflict, social isolation, withdrawal, alienation, and loneliness. For example, Peter Benson and colleagues found that 15 percent of the preadolescents and young adolescents in their study experienced social alienation or estrangement from others.[31] Reginald Bibby and Donald Posterski discovered that 35 percent of Canadian youth were deeply troubled by severe loneliness.[32] Results of a study of adolescent students in two Midwestern schools indicated 66 percent of the youth experienced loneliness. Of sixteen possible survey items, respondents most often identified loneliness as a significant problem in their lives.[33]

We noted earlier that lonely and antisocial people might be more susceptible to suicide and suicide ideation, a hypothesis that is supported by numerous studies. For example, after interviewing Canadian adolescents Marion Crook determined that "social isolation is one characteristic of teens considering suicide; teens who spend a lot of time alone in their rooms or away from home. This isolation increases until they spend very little time with anyone, including the people who use to be their friends. They don't yell, scream, argue, or demand attention; they just quietly withdraw from family and friends, interacting with no one."[34] Shafii discovered that 65 percent of the suicide victims in his empirical study displayed an *inhibited personality*, further characterized as not sharing problems with others, not having close friends, being very quiet, feeling lonely, keeping things inside, and being very sensitive. In contrast, only 24 percent of the nonsuicidal teenagers in the control group were identified as having an inhibited personality.[35] Benson and associates found that preadolescents and young adolescents who experienced social alienation were prone to thoughts of suicide.[36] Similarly, 46 percent of the

30. Guerney and Arthur, "Adolescent Social Relationships," 87.

31. Benson et al., *Quicksilver Years*, 42.

32. Bibby and Posterski, *Emerging Generation*, 60.

33. Culp et al, "Adolescent Depressed Mood."

34. Crook, *Out of the Darkness*, 44.

35. Shafii, "Completed Suicide in Children and Adolescents," 15.

36. Benson et al., *Quicksilver Years*, 42–43.

Latino victims of suicide studied by Magaly Queralt were described as inhibited, uncommunicative, excessively sensitive, or withdrawn.[37]

The link between recurrent loneliness and suicide or suicide ideation is a well-documented fact. Youth ministers are in an ideal position to positively impact the lives of lonely and alienated teenagers who might be experiencing thoughts of suicide. Several suggestions for youth ministry with lonely adolescents are noted as follows:[38]

1. Make special efforts to identify, give special attention to, and spend time with lonely adolescents. For example, give them a phone call, drop them a note, take them out for lunch, or simply talk to them during a youth activity.

2. Foster a sense of inclusiveness and acceptance in the youth group. Include recreational activities in the youth program that are cooperative and noncompetitive in nature. For example, the challenge, difficulty, and hardship of outdoor adventure and wilderness activities such as backpacking or canoeing tend to build camaraderie and teamwork within groups of adolescents.

3. Equip teenagers with social skills and capacities for building friendships, nurturing relationships, and communicating with others. Skills that will help the withdrawn adolescent in relating better to others include listening and attending, conversation, and self-disclosure.

4. Finally, help lonely youth foster or establish a meaningful relationship with God. Often loneliness is spiritual in nature and comes to individuals who are living their lives in separation from the One who created them.

Depression

The most common denominator and hallmark sign of suicide risk for adolescents is depression. Gerald Klerman, a psychiatrist and expert on suicide, reports that there is a complex relationship between depression and suicide. Many depressed patients are suicidal and, conversely, most, but not all, suicidal individuals manifest depressive moods, symptoms,

37. Queralt, "Risk Factors."

38. Specific methods and techniques for carrying out these strategies are described in a special section on loneliness in chapter 6.

or illnesses. He adds that with the alarming increase in youth suicide, there has been a parallel rise in rates of depression.[39] Wade Rowatt argues that depression is without a doubt the greatest single factor in pushing a teenager toward self-destruction.[40]

These conclusions are substantiated by research. For example, one study of sixteen- to twenty-four-year-olds noted that the majority of those who reported suicide ideation also reported high levels of depression.[41] Harry Hoberman and Barry Garfinkle studied suicide victims twenty-five years and under over a ten-year period and found 30 percent of the victims to be suffering from depression at the time of the deaths.[42]

What is depression? Why might teenagers be so susceptible to this emotional state? Depression is a state of prolonged melancholia (sadness or unhappiness) arising either for no apparent reason or as an extreme reaction to a trigger event.[43] Most people, including adolescents, experience mild depression in one form or another; nearly everyone has been "down in the dumps" or feels the "blues" at some time. However, more severe forms of depression, what medical experts call clinical depression, are characterized as mood disorders and can be so devastating that the ability to function in a normal manner is impaired. Usually clinical depression is related to a biochemical imbalance and is best treated under a physician's care by the administration of antidepressant medication.

Depressions occur in various types, the two most familiar forms being endogenous and reactive. *Endogenous* depression, sometimes called psychotic depression, arises from within an individual, sometimes for no reason apparent to the sufferer. For example, there is thought to be an inherited tendency toward neurotic types of depression.[44] Endogenous depression can also be brought about in females by the hormonal changes that occur during premenstruation or the early postnatal period.[45]

Reactive depression occurs as a response to events or circumstances in the individual's life. For example, loss of a loved one is a trigger event that sometimes leads to depression exceeding normal mourning in degree

---

39. Klerman, "Suicide, Depression, and Related Problems," 63.

40. Rowatt, *Pastoral Care with Adolescents in Crisis*, 119–20.

41. Goldberg, "Depression and Suicide Ideation in the Young Adult."

42. Hoberman and Garfinkle, "Completed Suicide in Youth," 28.

43. Shreeve, *Depression*, 23.

44. Gotlib and Colby, *Treatment of Depression*, 81; Shreeve, *Depression*, 25–28.

45. Shreeve, *Depression*, 25–28.

or duration.[46] This is the type of depression most often experienced by adolescents, and the usual treatment includes therapeutic counseling. Depression of any type should be distinguished from discouragement, which is a mild, temporary, and normal mood swing that comes in response to failures, losses, or disappointments of life.

The signs of depression often include the following:[47]

- feelings of sadness, pessimism, despair, and hopelessness
- apathy or lack of interest in things that normally bring interest
- loss of energy and fatigue
- negative self-esteem
- feelings of worthlessness, guilt, and shame
- inability to experience pleasure
- decreased ability to think or concentrate
- sleep disturbance (insomnia, lack of sleep, or too much sleep)
- withdrawal or spending large amounts of time alone
- eating disturbance (loss of appetite or preoccupation with eating)
- stomach and intestinal disorders (indigestion, constipation, or diarrhea)
- tension, muscle aches, and headaches.

Depression is a common occurrence among teenagers and is especially prominent in late adolescence. Ann Culp, Mary Clyman, and Rex Culp found that over half (54 percent) of the adolescents in their empirical study had experienced depression in the past year.[48] Eugene Roehlkepartain and Peter Benson discovered that 40 percent of the adolescents in their study had felt depressed twenty or more times in the previous year.[49] It is generally accepted that adolescent girls experience a greater incidence of depression than boys; levels of depression are higher among girls as well.[50] Four developmental factors help explain why teenagers are susceptible to depression.

---

46. Ibid., 24.
47. Shreeve, *Depression*, 25–28; Gotlib and Colby, *Treatment of Depression*, 2–4.
48. Culp et al., "Adolescent Depressed Mood."
49. Roehlkepartain and Benson, *Youth in Protestant Churches*, 104.
50. Coleman and Hendry, *Nature of Adolescence*, 213.

First, adolescence is a time of life when extreme biological changes occur. The physical changes that take place during puberty are second only to those that occur in infancy. Pubertal changes are often the root of much of the emotional turmoil and moodiness that teenagers experience, with quick shifts in emotions going from feeling great to experiencing sadness, anger, or lousiness.[51]

Second, burgeoning cognitive skills facilitate the ability to think about concepts concerning the self and one's identity. For adolescents introspection becomes intensified, and they often view themselves super-critically.[52] They may be prone to feel inadequate, deficient, unworthy, or incapable of performing tasks effectively. In some cases parents can intensify negative self-perceptions by placing unrealistic expectations on their teenage children or by demanding perfection in performance areas such as sports, music, and academics. Third, physiological and hormonal changes dramatically increase the adolescent's awareness of sexuality. Experimentation with masturbation, homosexuality, sex play, and intercourse can create feelings of guilt that in turn may intensify depression. Sometimes intolerable stress is created when teens cannot talk to their parents about sexual issues or where, as in the case of gay or lesbian teens, they are socially isolated or persecuted.[53]

Finally, adolescence is a stage of the life cycle when the individuation process is intensified. That is, the youth cuts parental ties and becomes a unique, separate individual with his or her own values, personality, interests, and identity. The subconscious may respond to the break with parents as a loss. Coincidentally, the need for peer acceptance, which is central to developing a healthy self-concept, increases with age. Yet many teenagers experience rejection by their age mates and have difficulties nurturing meaningful peer relationships.

It is important to remember that discouragement or even temporary depression is a normal part of the adolescent experience. However, for those teenagers who experience severe depression, when the suffering interferes with the ability to cope with normal living, and when the possibility of suicide or a suicide attempt becomes a reality, intervention is required.

51. Berger, *Developing Person*, 383.

52. Ibid., 416.

53. Crook, *Out of the Darkness*, 48; Coleman and Hendry, *Nature of Adolescence*, 111.

First, the above information can assist the youth pastor in assessing the possibility of depression in the life of a teenager. If the youth worker suspects an adolescent is depressive, referral should be made to a competent psychologist or psychiatrist, especially if the depression appears to be severe enough to warrant medication.

Second, the youth pastor must provide a community in which the depressed teenager can find refuge. Experts agree that if teenagers have a family member or reliable friend they can turn to when they feel depressed or hopeless, then they are most unlikely to attempt suicide. On the other hand, those without such a relationship are at a much-increased risk.[54]

Finally, it is of supreme importance to keep depressed youth from harming themselves. Since depressed people often contemplate killing themselves, the issue of suicide should be addressed directly. The adult youth worker should not hesitate to ask probing question such as, Do you have any thoughts of harming yourself? or Have you ever tried to commit suicide? However, while suicide is the most drastic form of self-harm, young people can harm themselves in other ways as well. Quitting school or a job, leaving home, severing relationships, or quitting the church are ways that depressed teenagers can cause hurt to themselves. There is a tendency to make unwise decisions when one is in a depressed state; therefore, the youth worker must help the teenagers see the possible consequences of unwise decisions, and encourage them to delay making important decisions to a later time.

Substance Abuse

Experts also identify a close connection between substance abuse and adolescent suicide. It is unknown, however, whether alcohol or drug abuse is a cause of suicide or whether the same factors that lead to suicide also lead to the abuse of drugs and alcohol.

In the Suicide Prevention Center sample of adolescents who had committed suicide, Michael Peck found that 40 to 50 percent of the suicide victims were abusing alcohol or drugs at the time of their death.[55] Hoberman and Garfinkle found the majority of adolescent suicide

54. Crook, *Out of the Darkness*, 200.
55. Peck, "Suicide in Late Adolescence and Young Adulthood," 222.

victims in their empirical study abused both drugs and alcohol.[56] The suicide rate for alcoholics is almost sixty times higher than that of the nonalcoholic population, and one out of three suicides in the population as a whole is in some way related to alcohol.[57]

What is the connection between substance abuse and suicide? Klagsbrun suggests that severe drinking or drug use may alienate the teenager from family and friends, and this alienation in turn brings on isolation and depression. Overwhelmed by depression, a troubled teenager may see suicide as only apparent solution.[58] Adolescents who consume drugs can become suicidal during crash periods or coming-down time, when extreme depression can occur. Youth who take hallucinogens may also become suicidal because they lose touch with reality, imagining themselves all-powerful and immune to any form of danger.[59]

CLUSTER SUICIDES

When three or more suicides are grouped together in a particular place or geographical area (such as a community or school district) and occur within a relatively short span of time, they are identified as *cluster* suicides.[60] They are suicides that follow or imitate another. For example, Lucy Davidson and associates investigated two clusters of teenage suicides in Texas between February 1983 and October 1984. Eight of these adolescent suicides made up the first cluster, while six constituted the second. Both clusters included teenagers who were close personal friends and victims who only knew of the other decedents through the media or by word of mouth.[61] According to another study, 1 to 2 percent of all teenage suicides occur within a time or space cluster.[62]

While cluster suicides have been known to occur for a number of years, experts do not entirely understand why this imitation pattern sometimes takes place. One possible explanation is the *contagion* theory. Contagion is the notion that suicide may spread among teenagers who

56. Hoberman and Garfinkel, "Completed Suicide in Youth," 34.
57. Klagsbrun, *Too Young to Die*, 69.
58. Ibid.
59. Ibid.
60. Berman and Jobes, *Adolescent Suicide*, 102.
61. Davidson et al., "Epidemiologic Study of Risk Factors," 2688.
62. Gould et al, "Time-space Clustering of Teenage Suicide."

are exposed to suicide in some manner, either directly (the adolescent actually knew the decedent) or indirectly (the person who committed suicide was known to the teenager only through news accounts or by word of mouth).[63] Either type of exposure may lead a troubled and susceptible teenager to commit suicide, perhaps imitating the initial suicide by employing a similar method in a similar setting. There is much evidence that suggests that the indirect exposure to suicide through printed media, television news stories, and movies about suicide might lead some vulnerable adolescents to commit suicide.[64]

It is also hypothesized that youth have psychological characteristics consistent with greater susceptibility to imitative suicide. Among these imitative factors might be the glorification or romanticization of suicidal behavior. Mass gatherings such as memorial assemblies may nurture the perception that suicide is a powerful act claiming the special attention of one's peers and the public.[65]

Hochkirchen and Jilek provide an exceptionally descriptive quote that helps us understand the way a community reaction to a teenage suicide can trigger further imitative suicides:

> The latest suicide victim may be talked of as a martyred hero. Posthumously he gets attention as never during his lifetime. His entire life is glorified and his 'good old days' are emphasized rather than his more recent, possibly antisocial, behavior. Suicide is seen as the crowning event of his life. His funeral is a big social occasion and the time between death and funeral is filled with memorial services and commemorative gatherings. The attention of the whole community is focused on this particular suicide and on suicide in general, thus making suicidal acts interesting and attractive for predisposed young people.[66]

The incidence of cluster or imitation suicides suggests that one teenager's suicide is a powerful model that influences other youth to also take their lives. Thus follow-up intervention to a successful suicide is essential. Efforts should be made to deromanticize any suicide. In appropriate cases it might be helpful to acknowledge that the deceased was someone who had serious problems that distinguished him or her from most teenagers. For example, if a teenager struggled with substance abuse or mental

---

63. Davidson et al., "Epidemiologic Study," 2687.

64. Ibid.; Phillips et al., "Effects of Mass Media News Stories on Suicide."

65. Davidson et al., "Epidemiologic Study," 2691–92.

66. Quoted in Davidson, "Suicide Clusters and Youth," 92.

illness, it would be important to stress the fact that the problem was related to the death. Furthermore, it should be emphasized that the suicide was an undesirable response and there were, in fact, far better solutions available.

Adult youth workers should be aware of the types of youth who are likely to be at high risk for suicide in a cluster. High-risk adolescents include those in the same social network as the decedent, those who have a history of suicide attempts, and those who are mentally unstable.[67] Once these teens are identified, the youth worker should interview these high-risk teenagers. If the interviewer senses a youth is a suicide risk, the youth worker should refer the teen to a professional counselor.

CONCLUSION

Suicidal behavior such as ideation or threats of taking one's own life can have a devastating effect on the lives of teenagers as well as on the lives of those people around them. Thus, it is essential that youth pastors and other adults who work with teenagers provide intervention in the early stages of suicide ideation. Since youth workers play significant roles in the lives of many adolescents, they must be especially aware of and responsive to the numerous signs of suicide and the steps to take in helping a suicidal youth through the crisis.

67. Davidson, "Suicide Clusters and Youth," 95.

11

Youth, Social Media, and Digital Technology

Anyone who spends even a minimal amount of time with adolescents is cognizant of the fact that media are among the most powerful influences in the lives of contemporary teens. According to a 2010 Kaiser Family report, "Eight- to eighteen-year-olds spend more time with media than in any other activity besides (maybe) sleeping—an average of more than 7½ hours a day, seven days a week."[1] The television shows and movies they watch, the music they listen to, the websites they visit, and the video games they play are a colossal part of their lives. To the viewing and listening media of the past add new communication technology, especially the cell phone (providing text messaging, Instagram, games, and so forth) and the Internet (delivering a multitude of applications such as Facebook, YouTube, and Flickr), and we might say teenager's lives are driven almost entirely by various technologies and platforms. Thus, understanding the role of media and technology in teenagers' lives is absolutely essential for those concerned about promoting the healthy development and spiritual formation of adolescents. As we explore and investigate of media and related technology with all their interconnected platforms and applications, we can easily be overwhelmed. Rather than addressing the traditional media technologies such as television, movies, and even electronic gaming, we will limit this chapter primarily to the impact of social media and related technology devices—still a monumental task.

1. Rideout et al., *Generation M*^{2}, 1.

THE ALLURE OF SOCIAL MEDIA
AND TECHNOLOGY

What is the irresistible allure that draws teenagers to media and media technology? In the recent past (the twentieth century) children, teenagers, and adults alike were attracted to the basic electronic and media technologies such as the telephone, movies, television, and radio for fundamental and obvious reasons—communication, learning, and entertainment. With the relatively recent inventions of the cell phone, electronic gaming devices, and the Internet as well as the rapid evolution of the personal computer, all a major part of the technology explosion of the latter part of the twentieth century and onset of the new millennium, we must look for new and different answers to the question. For example, one of the most striking changes in the media landscape is the cell phone, more specifically the smartphone. Initially the cell phone was used simply for talking to people. Now we can say that some, if not many, teens are addicted to cell phones for text messaging, viewing videos, listening to music, or checking their Facebook accounts. The ready availability of social media on both the smartphone and computer means that teens rarely have a break from a constant stream of electronic stimuli, and to separate them from their technology is to separate them from life itself.

Perhaps one could say that the almost unceasing use of media technology is simply a normal part of the transition from the freedom of childhood to the responsibility of adulthood, part of a natural and unconscious effort to diminish the stresses of their developmental process. Catherine Steiner-Adair offers five helpful suggestions related to that hypothesis:

1. Technology provides ideal tool for the adolescent drive for independence. "Without stepping out of the house," she suggests, "without so much as glancing down as they text, they chat amongst themselves and can roam the world and hang out with anyone they please."[2]

2. Technology offers the perfect collaborator to their adolescent penchant for risk-taking. They can video chat in a dangerous game of truth or dare, arrange hookups with strangers, or steal your identity.

3. Technology provides an ever-present stage for teenage drama. "Texting, video chat, sexting, and social media have created a streaming

2. Steiner-Adair, *Big Disconnect*, 196.

soap opera for teens, a scintillating reality-show subculture in which everyone gets to play both celebrity and paparazzi."[3]

4. Technology offers a quick fix for entertainment and escape. The overwhelming and persistent emotions of inadequacy, loneliness, rejection, emptiness, and hopelessness that plague so many teenagers make them ripe for addiction to their devices.

5. Technology plays to the natural sexual drives of adolescents but removes the critical pause between impulse and deed.

Steiner-Adair insightfully concludes, "There is no app for emotional intimacy, no digital shortcut to the deep, rich knowing of another human being—or of ourselves."[4] Various media provide opportunities for endless interaction but can also foster an unhealthy level of detachment from intimate relationships that are so critical to the emotional health of adolescents.

FROM GROUP SOCIAL LIFE
TO ONLINE ISOLATION

The onset of the twenty-first century has been marked with a breathtaking advancement of personal media technology with foci on information, communication, and entertainment. Thus in the last decade or so we have experienced a paradigm shift in the adolescent world "as the gathering ground for student's social life has shifted from school, sports, after-school playdates, and the neighborhood mall to online and social media."[5] And the amount of time teens spend on various devices is staggering. Ninety-two percent of teens report going online daily, according to a report by the Pew Research Center. The same study indicates that some 88 percent of teenagers have or have access to cell phones, and 90 percent of those with phones text, the typical teen sending and receiving thirty messages a day[6] with some sending and receiving as many as a thousand per day.

The transition from group-oriented social activities to individualized activities such as online gaming, listening to downloaded music,

3. Ibid., 197.
4. Ibid.
5. Ibid., 189.
6. Lenhart, "Teens, Social Media Technology Overview 2015."

watching movies on the computer, texting, Facebooking, and browsing the Internet has the potential to separate adolescents from reality by eliminating in-person socially interactive experiences. To illustrate, consider a group of teens gathered together: they appear to be interacting socially, but in reality each is on their individual devices playing, texting, or checking out their Facebook pages. This is not to say that they are completely isolated, but in actuality are alone in a crowd. One parent tells of the preteen school carpool, teeming with playful giggling and intense conversation. In a matter of weeks three girls in the backseat had all received cell phones, and the talking and laughing ceased. To be fair, teens do not seem to feel isolated in these types of settings. Rather, they feel in contact with each other as they communicate through their devices. The three girls mentioned above were actually interacting with one another and their friends, affording them a level of privacy from the adult world and connection to others outside the car. These types of interactions create a phenomenon that might be described as connected yet disconnected social interaction.

THE IMPACT OF SOCIAL MEDIA AND TECHNOLOGY

Thanks to digital technology we experience life in many enjoyable and comfortable ways. The Internet and various digital devices afford us the privilege of communicating with ease and connecting us to information like never before. No doubt the digital age brings us many benefits. However, Elias Brasil de Souza reminds us in his brilliant essay on "Digital Technology and the Christian Life" that these benefits "come with a price tag because the combination of sophisticated devices with the ever-expanding tentacles of the World Wide Web is reshaping us, our world, and our relationships."[7] Technology of any kind has the potential to be used for the greater good or conversely, the greater harm. Brasil de Souza goes on to remind us that "technology may serve either to plow the land to sustain life or it can be turned into a weapon to destroy life. It can bless humans with devices that save lives, as modern medicine can testify, but it can also produce nuclear bombs to bring destruction and death. However, despite its risks and dangers, technology is a product of human

7. Brasil de Souza, "Digital Technology and the Christian Life, 1.

creativity."[8] Consequently, it is critical that youth workers, parents, and youth themselves reflect on both the benefits and dangers of media technology, and address ways that collectively we might handle our digitally driven world in a manner that pleases God.

The Benefits of Social Media

Some of the benefits of social media and media technology include socialization, creativity, learning opportunities, access to information, staying in touch with friends and parents, and entertainment.[9]

1. *Socialization and communication*: social media make it possible for adolescents to stay connected with friends and family, to share pictures and experiences, to exchange ideas, and to form new friendships and communities otherwise not accessible to them.

2. *Creativity*: social media and devices provide platforms for creativity through the sharing of artistic and musical endeavors and the growth of ideas through the creation of blogs, video presentations, and podcasts. Teens are no longer simply consumers of media but producers as well. YouTube alone has three hundred hours of content uploaded per minute.[10]

3. *Enhanced learning opportunities*: (a) Teens today are most likely to begin research for school assignments on the Internet. (b) Online education provides an alternative for getting class credits. (c) Certain social media programs allow students to collaborate on assignments outside of class. (d) Many schools use blogs as a teaching technique or educational management software that resembles social media platforms like Facebook.

4. *Accessing information*: No doubt one of the greatest benefits of digital media is the availability of information. Teenagers can use the Internet to find out information on nonacademic topics such as music, sports, fine arts, health, and travel.

5. *Staying in touch*: Adolescents use the cell phone to stay in contact with parents.

8. Ibid.
9. O'Keefe et al., "Impact of Social Media," 801.
10. YouTube, Press, "Statistics."

6. *Entertainment:* Media and media devices offer an opportunity for entertainment and escape; teens can play games on their cell phones and computers either as peers together or as individuals.

The Risks and Dangers of Social Media and Media Technology

Without a doubt, every new technology that brings benefits is subsequently accompanied by some problem or detrimental consequence. Parents and youth workers have always been concerned about the effects of media on teenagers. As already indicated, however, new technologies bring new concerns, and social media and related devices present a number of potential dangers for adolescents. Pediatricians Gwenn O'Keefe and Kathleen Clarke-Pearson, along with the Council on Communications and Media propose that "because of their limited capacity for self-regulation and susceptibility to peer pressure, children and adolescents are at some risk as they navigate and experiment with social media."[11] Most risks fall into these categories: individual responsibility (excessive use), peer-to-peer (such as cyberbullying), inappropriate content (such as pornography), online privacy issues, and influences of third-party advertising groups.[12]

Excessive Use and Poor Time Management

An obvious and significant problem for adolescents and use of technology and media is excessive use. As mentioned earlier, teens spend over seven hours a day with media, more than in any other activity except, perhaps, sleeping. Once again we turn to Brasil de Souza as he offers insights as to how excessive use can lead to time waste:

> What starts as a focused digital search may very easily become a distracted, trivial meandering from link to link, checking social media, or updating messages . . . . Wasting time on trivialities with no time for Bible study, reflection, and a healthy devotional life is a major challenge in the digital age . . . So as we use our digital devices, we should be aware that time management may be a serious challenge [for teens] to overcome.[13]

11. O'Keefe et al., "Impact of Social Media," 800.

12. Ibid., 801.

13. Brasil de Souza, "Digital Technology and the Christian Life," 3.

Cyberbullying

The most common online risk for adolescents is the peer-to-peer activity of cyberbullying. Cyberbullying is "deliberately using digital media to communicate false, embarrassing, or hostile information about another person."[14] It includes sending unkind messages or threats to an individual's cell phone or e-mail account, spreading rumors online or through text messages, and posting harmful or threatening messages on social media sites such as Facebook. Online bullying is a serious problem, a form of teen violence that can do enduring harm to young people, even leading at times to suicide or suicide ideation. Over half of adolescents have been bullied online, and about the same number admit to cyberbullying.[15]

Sexting

Another peer-to-peer cyber risk activity is sexting, the "sending, receiving, or forwarding sexually explicit messages, photographs, or images via cell phone, computer, or other digital devices."[16] Sexting is common, involving between 15 and 28 percent of teenagers, and the percentage is growing.[17] There are concerns for Christian parents, youth workers, and teens themselves beyond the obvious inherent morality issue. For example, research indicates that sexting is associated with sexual behavior, and "sexting may precede sexual intercourse in some instances and cement the notion that sexting behavior is a viable indicator of adolescent sexual activity."[18] Consequences for engaging in sexting may include legal charges and school suspensions for perpetrators, as well as emotional distress for victims. An inappropriate selfie to a boyfriend may result in hundreds of peers seeing the picture. This one act may bring shame or bullying to the selfie taker and sex-offender charges against the distributor of the picture.

14. Ibid.
15. Cerullo, "Cyber Bullying Statistics."
16. O'Keefe et al., "Impact of Social Media," 802.
17. Temple and Choi, "Longitudinal Association," 1288.
18. Ibid., 1291.

Technology- and Media-Related Disorders

Psychologists have determined that there are several disorders emerging among adolescents who spend an inordinate amount of time with their devices. These include Facebook depression, sleep deprivation, and anxiety or stress.

- *Facebook Depression*: Researchers have suggested a new psychological phenomenon they have dubbed "Facebook depression," defined as "depression that develops when preteens and teens spend a great deal of time on social media sites, such as Facebook, and then begin to exhibit classic symptoms of depression."[19] The intensity of the online world may be a factor in triggering depression. Like any teens with other forms of depression, adolescents suffering from Facebook depression may be at further risk of social isolation, substance abuse, or self-destructive behaviors.[20]

- *Sleep Deprivation:* Studies indicate that there is a connection between electronic media usage and sleep deprivation. One cause is that teens are often awakened at night by notifications or by software updates flashing.[21] Another cause of sleep deprivation is stimuli overload, as teens may have trouble getting to sleep after excessive hours on their devices. Studies indicate that heavy use of light-emitting screens "between dusk and the time we go to bed at night suppresses release of the sleep-promoting hormone melatonin, enhances alertness and shifts circadian rhythms to a later hour—making it more difficult to fall asleep."[22]

- *Anxiety Disorders:* There may also be a connection between the overuse of media technology and anxiety disorders.[23] One source of anxiety and stress is information overload. Trying to absorb the amount of data made available to teens through the various media is analogous to trying to drink from a fire hose. Furthermore, much of the content (whether news or movies and television shows) is adult-oriented, addressing or reflecting issues that teens often find

19. O'Keefe et al., "Impact of Social Media," 802.

20. Ibid.

21. Cain and Gradisar, "Electronic Media," 735–42.

22. Quoted in National Sleep Foundation, "Annual Sleep in America Poll Exploring Connections with Communications Technology Use and Sleep."

23. Young and Kinnaman, *Hyperlinked Life,* 48.

difficult to deal with. So much exposure to difficult issues and to characters incapable of mastering these tensions presents an emotional threat to adolescents. Either teens respond to this threat by feeling or expressing anxiety over the futility of their struggle, or they respond by projecting a negative identity to the outside world.

Certain tensions are normally not accessible to adolescents without access to the media. Typically, adolescents need three kinds of skills in order to successfully take in adult themes such as war, suicide, sexuality, and so forth. The first is formal operational thought, or the ability to do reflective thinking. The second is the ability to read. The third is the will and interest to digest reading materials written for adults. Obviously a teen could attend to a content-oriented discussion among adults, but this exposure would likely come via the presence of a mediating adult, and would be offered presuming the adolescent's cognitive ability to comprehend and track with the conversation. Now, with the onset of digital and social media, youth are introduced to the realities of the adult world without a mediating adult presence and without the cognitive capacity to deal with adult-oriented issues. Yet these complex realities are presented in a visual language that youth can understand. Adults must talk with teens to reduce the stress and anxiety that might come as adolescence open the Pandora's box of the adult world.

Inappropriate Content

The nature of the content that teens are exposed to is another media-related concern. Teens have always pushed the envelope when it comes to their viewing habits. Much of this may simply be related to the desire to explore the unfamiliar or to rebel against the social and moral norms or rules imposed on them by parents, teachers, and the church. The problem is intensified with today's youth in that all manner of content is available at their fingertips.[24] Pornography that was previously only accessible in certain contexts is now just a click away on their electronic devices. Teenagers are also tempted to upload their own inappropriate content—from provocative pictures on social network sites to pornographic videos on YouTube.

24. Ibid.

Reality versus Fantasy

Younger teens especially lack the ability to distinguish between real life and the fantasy world of cyberspace. Researchers have studied the conflict between virtual and real-world identities and determined this is most notable in the earlier years of transition into the digital world.[25] Many if not most teens find it difficult to make distinctions between the two worlds, believing that they are the same person in both realms. Thus "The Internet has become a new context in which adolescent identity exploration and construction is taking place."[26] When these real-world and created virtual identities are brought into conflict with each other, the teen will often ignore reality and attempt to reinforce their identity by way of the fantasy world that hey have created for themselves. Unfortunately, "such alterations of identity are far more difficult in real life. Because there are few consequences for mistakes, players can experiment more with who they are online than they can in real life."[27]

Privacy Issues

When Internet users visit websites, they leave behind evidence that they have been there. The "digital footprint," it is one of the greatest threats of media sites to teenagers. Teenagers do not always understand that no information that goes onto the online world is truly private. Due to lack of awareness of privacy issues, teenagers "often post inappropriate messages, pictures, and videos without understanding that 'what goes online stays online.'"[28] And since they post a tremendous amount of personal information on their online profiles, it is critical that they learn to use strict privacy settings and are aware of the individuals they allow to view their profiles online. Lack of savvy regarding privacy issues can increase the chances that they will (1) receive a message from a stranger, (2) meet up with a stranger, or (3) be harassed by peers.[29]

25. Gee, *What Video Games Have to Teach.*
26. Calvert, "Behavioral Effects of Media," 65.
27. Ibid, 62.
28. O'Keefe et al., "Impact of Social Media," 802.
29. Enough is Enough, "Dangers of the Social Web."

The Influence of Advertising

Social media sites often inundate users with banner ads and demographi-
cally based advertising that target viewers according to age, gender, education, and so forth. These not only influence teenagers as what to spend
their money on but also help shape what they see to be normal. These ads
function by creating a profile of the user: gathering information and then
targeting the individual by influencing them in their purchasing decisions. Teenagers should be educated in online advertising so that they
can be "media-literate" consumers and understand how easily advertising can manipulate them.[30]

We now see that the meaning of life "is fueled by the successive il-
lusions that purchasing this wardrobe, driving that car, eating this meal,
drinking that beverage will center life and give it coherence."[31] Youth have
become consumers not only of material goods but also of information,
entertainment, communication, and now even of relationships. Our culture has moved from the purchasing of products as impacting identity to
consumerism forming identity and finally to our identity as consumers
of relationships. For example, given that Facebook does not charge for its
service, we might suggest that the users and their relationships are actually the products being sold and consumed.

Deceptive Behaviors

The anonymity that exists within the digital world can lead to deception,
abuse, and lack of inhibitions. Some teens will create false identities for
the purpose of role exploration, sexual gratification, or simply the excite-
ment or high of becoming someone else. This practice finds its way into
the world of online dating and can lead to emotional abuse and disil-
lusionment for those who have been victimized.[32]

---

30. O'Keefe et al., "Impact of Social Media," 802.

31. Peterson, *Reversed Thunder*, 60.

32. One of the authors recently witnessed this type of situation in which a web
of lies surrounding a false identity led to the humiliation of the teen being deceived.

MEDIA AND YOUTH MINISTRY

A priority for youth ministry in the digital age is to equip adolescents with the wisdom and skills to use media technology so that it does not distract from the responsibilities of healthy development and spiritual formation. However, being faithful to God does not demand that youth reject, ignore, or fear digital technology. Rather, it is the responsibility of the youth worker to teach teens how to live their digital lives in a manner that honors God, demonstrates love and respect for their friends and family, and cares for God's creation. "Thus, a godly use of digital devices is one that honors God with the faithful stewardship of our digital resources."[33] With that in mind we offer a few suggestions for addressing media issues to teens and using technology for ministry.

Having a Theology of Media

The first task for youth workers in addressing social media and technology is to develop a theology of media. This theology should be a "deep and livable understanding of how God intends for humans to interact with the tools and information now so readily available."[34] To help the youth worker flesh out a theology of media and ministry we provide a brief outline of the following theological points.[35]

1. Since humankind is created in the image of God (Gen 1:26–27) we have the ability to invent devices and develop technology in ways not possible for other creatures.

2. The initial chapters of Genesis make reference to technological inventions and the use of implements. The first likely allusion to technology is found in Gen 2:15, where God instructs Adam to work the garden of Eden and take care of it: we might presume that he would need some sort of tool (technology) to work the soil. Gen 3:7 indicates that Adam and Eve sewed leaves together and made clothes for themselves, which also presumes a need for simple technology. In Gen 4:17 we find Cain building a city, and in Gen 4:21 we have

---

33. Brasil de Souza, "Digital Technology and the Christian Life," 6.

34. Young and Kinnaman, *Hyperlinked Life*, 32.

35. These theological points are summarized from Brasil de Souza, "Digital Technology and the Christian Life," 1–2.

references to the harp and the flute. (Tools would be necessary to make these.) The following verse refers to Tubal-Cain, who forged all types of tools from bronze and iron. Tools and technology appear to be seen in positive light, used to make life easier and to care for creation.

3. With the entrance of sin into the picture (Gen 3), the products of human creativity (artistic and technological products) are contaminated, and consequently technology, which is value-neutral in and of itself, can be used for good or evil. Technology can be used to till the land or can be turned into a weapon of destruction.

4. Thus we should not ignore, avoid, or reject technology on biblical grounds. Rather we must cautiously embrace it as we have seen God's people so do throughout the Old and New Testament times as well as in the rest of the history of the church.

A theology of media needs to address issues of mission, biblical morality, and ministry strategies. Since the mission of youth ministry is to lead teenagers into a relationship with Jesus Christ and to foster spiritual growth in their lives, the mission of youth ministry must drive not only how we use media but also how we understand youth. "If you want to understand a given culture, pay attention to the methods and tools it uses to communicate."[36] Media are a useful resource for understanding the teenagers and their culture. Media and technology help us to know what our youth are dealing with and often to see how they behave away from church. More importantly, it affords youth workers a window into a culture that most adults are not welcome in and gives youth workers clues about how best to communicate the gospel to that culture, about how to do what missiologists call contextualization. This is exactly what the apostle Paul did in his use of cultural apologetics recorded in Acts 17:19–34.

Teaching and Modeling

Given our previous discussion of media content, it is imperative to teach youth standards of biblical morality as applied to media technology. It is too easy to become desensitized to inappropriate content; thus youth leaders must equip teens to "guard their hearts" (Prov 4:23) against the

36. Ibid.

negative messages social media send them. This also calls for youth work-ers to set an example for teens to follow, including modeling wise and appropriate social media and Internet use in general. Just as adults are peering into the social world of adolescents, we—that is youth workers and other adults—offer them a window into our world of social media and digital technology.

Assisting Parents

Part of the task of working with youth and media-related issues is in-volving parents. Some specific ways in which youth pastors can be of assistance to parents include the following:[37]

1. Counsel mothers and fathers to talk to their teenagers about their online and social media use as well as about some of the issues that today's online adolescents face.

2. Advise parents to improve their own social media and technology awareness by becoming better informed about the many sites and devices their adolescent children are using.

3. Talk with parents about the importance of an online-use strat-egy that involves regular family meetings to discuss online topics, privacy settings, online profiles, and inappropriate posting and conversation.

4. Address the importance of personally supervising online activities with active participation and communication rather than relying on a "net-nanny" program (software designed to monitor Internet activity).

Assisting Youth in Navigating the Digital World

Adolescents are not generally equipped to differentiate and label their media experiences as biased, fictional, inconsistent, or inaccurate. Teens need adult facilitation to in order to successfully navigate their media experiences and to differentiate real life from media creation. Adult me-diation is especially vital considering that most preteens spend no less than 80 percent of their media time accessing material oriented to adults.

37. Adapted from O'Keefe et al., "Impact of Social Media," 803.

Patti Valkenburg suggests, for example, that the reason youth "like to watch adult television programming is that these programs meet their need to orient themselves toward an adult world."[38] Unfortunately teens, as mentioned earlier, lack the cognitive and emotional skills to effectively wrestle with and digest content designed for adults. While some adults can perceive teens as pushing them away, the media world is a place where they often need and subtly invite adult presence and understanding. Every exposure to a media model provides a potential opportunity for an adolescent to learn a behavior or attitude, to identify with someone or something, or to imitate another person. Teens define and construct their identities whether in accordance with the model or explicitly contrary to it, and whether consciously or not.[39] Ultimately dialogue with adults is the key to helping adolescents navigate the adult-oriented waters of the digital world.

There are several ways for the youth worker to enter into dialogue with the teen regarding media and media use, including the following.

1. *Falsity Tags:* Simply helping a teen see a social media comment as potentially false can strip it of its identity-shaping power. Once an idea or image—such as the notion of Santa Claus, to employ an obvious example—is "tagged as false," it is then perceived as fictitious no matter how many times it is presented. These types of tags can considerably minimize the negative effects of media exposure. These "falsity tags" can easily be added through discourse or conversation that encourages critical thinking.

2. *Critical Thinking:* Teens who master the skill of critical and reflective thinking "are less susceptible to media contents that proclaim . . . ideologies."[40] Offering counterpoints and providing a general "running commentary" helps facilitate critical interaction with media. In a group setting the youth worker might show a well-known advertisement, a social media comment, or song lyrics and then lead a discussion about the merits or problems therein.

3. *Meaningful Presence:* Media deprive teens "of a teacher who knows them sufficiently well to reflect back to them their continuity and wholeness as persons. Such reflections help young people attain

38. Valkenburg, *Children's Responses to the Screen,* 5.

39. Huntemann and Morgan, "Mass Media and Identity Development," 310.

40. Valkenburg, *Children's Responses to the Screen,* 11–12.

an integrated sense of identity as adolescents."[41] Meaningful adult presence in the social environment of the teen can counteract many negative media effects on adolescents. When adults enter the world of adolescents, adults have an opportunity to model appropriate behavior and to engage in discourse with the teen. When teens are in the presence of adults, they will usually make wiser decisions, make better selections, and with the help of adult intervention make healthier observations. Giving the history of a situation, offering alternate perspectives, or simply playing devil's advocate are powerful tools in helping youth engage with media.

4. *Modeling:* Parents and youth workers who model higher-order thinking processes of discourse, analysis, and synthesis can fortify their teens against uncritical consumption or against adopting unhelpful exemplars for their identity formation.

5. *Affirmation:* Finally, some of the most powerful comments to an adolescent come not from social media posts but from trusted adults who say something affirming, like "I see you becoming like . . . " or "Your compassion reminds me of Jesus."

In order, then, to help adolescents better perceive the benefits and dangers of the media, the Internet, and related technological devices, youth workers must teach them to make proper and effective use of their intellectual capacities. Technology may be helpful in acquiring data, information, and knowledge, but "no technology can replace the human mind when it comes to understanding and wisdom . . . No machine can replace our brains as we separate the good from the bad and turn knowledge into understanding and wisdom to navigate real life."[42] We must also remind youth (and ourselves) that with the overwhelming and ever-growing amount of information available to us, we must always remember the axiom of Solomon: "The fear of the LORD is the beginning of wisdom, and knowledge of the Holy One is understanding" (Prov 9:10 NIV).[43]

---

41. Elkind, *Hurried Child*, 68.
42. Brasil de Souza, "Digital Technology and the Christian Life," 6.
43. Ibid.

Making Use of Technology in Youth Ministry

With all the distractions and abuses of media and related technology, the astute and tech-savvy youth worker (and most will be in today's world) can make it work for him or her. Some ways the youth worker can use social media and technology is by creating youth ministry social sites, uploading devotional messages or youth talks on these sites, staying connected with youth group members with cellphones and social sites such as Facebook, making announcements and promoting activities. The Internet also provides youth workers with an unlimited amount of ministry and teaching resources such as object lessons, illustrations, movie and YouTube clips, statistics, and stories. Another great benefit of technology for youth ministry is that it provides great equipping opportunities. Many youth ministry organizations offer free or low cost training resources to youth workers and teens via various media types.

CONCLUSION

Like all technological advances and inventions, media and digital technology brings with it certain concerns or dangers. However, rather than rejecting or fearing the digital world, we should be grateful for the variety of opportunities it provides us for ministering to, connecting and communicating with, and teaching adolescents. As such, the role of the youth worker is not so much to mediate the world of digital technology (although that may be part of it), as it is to empower and help teens to form a holistic Christian identity. Two contrasting responses to digital technology must be avoided. Unreflective resignation to the inevitability of teen media consumption is no more helpful than trying to stem the tide of social technology. The youth worker's role is to enter the waters of the digital world as a trusted guide and those who are conversant with the dangers and benefits of this world will find significant influence in the lives of the adolescents with whom they work.

Bibliography

Adams, Jay. *The Christian Counselor's Manual.* Grand Rapids: Baker, 1973.

"Adolescent Sexual Orientation." *Pediatrics and Child Health* 13 (2008) 619–23.

Agras, Stewart W. *Eating Disorders: Management of Obesity, Bulimia, and Anorexia Nervosa.* Psychology Practitioner Guidebooks. New York: Pergamon, 1987.

Aitkins, Jim. *Tough Topics: 600 Questions That Will Take Your Students Beneath the Surface.* Grand Rapids: Zondervan, 2003.

Aldridge, Jerry. "Preadolescence." In *Handbook of Youth Ministry,* edited by Donald Ratcliff and James A. Davies, 97–118. Birmingham, AL: Religious Education Press, 1991.

————. *Self-Esteem: Loving Yourself at Every Age.* Birmingham, AL: Religious Education Press, 1993.

Allman, William. "Science Looks at TV Violence." *U.S. News and World Report,* July 12, 1993.

Allport, Gordon W., and J. Michael Ross. "Personal Religious Orientation and Prejudice." *Journal of Personality and Social Psychology* 5 (April 1967) 432–43.

American Heart Association. "Many Teens Spend 30 Hours A Week On 'Screen Time' During High School." *ScienceDaily.* www.sciencedaily.com/releases/2008/03/080312172614.htm/.

American Psychiatric Association. *Diagnostic and Statistical Manual of Mental Disorders.* 4th ed. Washington, DC: American Psychiatric Association, 1994.

American Psychological Association. In Brief. "Math Test Scores across 29 Nations." http://www.apa.org/monitor/mar05/scores.aspx/.

Andersen, Arnold E. "The Distributions of Eating Disorders." In *Eating Disorders and Obesity,* edited by Kelly D. Brownell and Christopher G. Fairburn, 177–82. New York: Guilford, 1995.

Anderson, Christopher. *Father, the Figure and the Force.* New York: Warner, 1983.

Anderson, Lorin W., et al. *A Taxonomy for Learning, Teaching, and Assessing.* 2nd ed. New York: Pearson, 2013.

Anderson, Neil, and Dave Park. *Stomping Out the Darkness.* Ventura, CA: Regal, 1993.

Anderson, Peter et al. "Impact of Alcohol Advertising and Media Exposure on Adolescent Alcohol Use: A Systematic Review of Longitudinal Studies." *Alcohol & Alcoholism* 44 (2009) 229–43.

Anderson-Fye, Eileen P., and Anne E. Becker. "Sociocultural Aspects of Eating Disorders." In *Handbook of Eating Disorders and Obesity,* edited by J. Kevin Thompson, 565–89. Hoboken, NJ: Wiley, 2004.

Ankerberg, John, and John Weldon. *The Myth of Safe Sex: The Devastating Consequences of Violating God's Plan.* Chicago: Moody, 1993.

Argyle, Michael, and Benjamin Beit-Hallahmi. *The Social Psychology of Religion.* International Library of Sociology. London: Routledge & Kegan Paul, 1975.

Arnett, Jeffrey Jensen. *Emerging Adulthood: The Winding Road from the Late Teens through the Twenties.* New York: Oxford University Press, 2004.

———. *Human Development: A Cultural Approach.* Upper Saddle River, NJ: Pearson, 2012.

Arp, Dave, and Claudia Arp. *60 One-minute Family Builders.* Nashville: Nelson, 1993.

Atkinson, Harley. *The Power of Small Groups in Christian Education.* Nappanee, IN: Evangel, 2002.

Avert. "People Who Inject Drugs (PWID) and HIV/AIDS." http://www.avert.org/professionals/hiv-social-issues/key-affected-populations/people-inject-drugs/.

Bahnsen, Greg. *Homosexuality: A Biblical View.* Grand Rapids: Baker, 1978.

Bailey, Beth L. *From Front Porch to Back Seat: Courtship in Twentieth-Century America.* Baltimore: Johns Hopkins University Press, 1988.

Balswick, Jack O., and Judith K. Balswick. *The Family A Christian Perspective on the Contemporary Home.* 3rd ed. Grand Rapids: Baker Academic, 2007.

———. *The Family: A Christian Perspective on the Contemporary Home.* 4th ed. Grand Rapids: Baker Academic, 2014.

Bandura, Albert. "On the Psychosocial Impact and Mechanisms of Spiritual Modeling." *International Journal for the Psychology of Religion* 13 (2003) 167–73.

———. "The Stormy Decade: Fact or Fiction?" In *Adolescent Behavior and Society: A Book of Readings,* edited by Rolf E. Muuss, 22–31. 3rd ed. New York: Random House, 1971.

Barna, George. *The Future of the American Family.* Chicago: Moody, 1993.

———. *Generation Next.* Ventura, CA: Regal, 1995.

———. *Third Millennium Teens.* Ventura, CA: Barna Research Group, 1999.

Barna Research Group. "Research Examines the Role of Healthy Families in Youth Ministry." https://www.barna.org/barna-update/millennials/565-research-examines-the-role-of-healthy-families-in-youth-ministry#.UuwAl_ldWAg/.

———. *Today's Teens: A Generation in Transition.* Glendale: The Barna Research Group, 1991.

Baucham, Voddie Jr. *Family Driven Faith: Doing What It Takes to Raise Sons and Daughters Who Walk with God.* Wheaton, IL: Crossway, 2011.

Benson, Peter L., *The Troubled Journey: A Portrait of 6th–12th Grade Youth.* Minneapolis: Search Institute, 1993.

Benson, Peter L., et al. *The Quicksilver Years: The Hopes and Fears of Early Adolescence.* San Francisco: Harper & Row, 1987.

Benson, Peter L., and Eugene C. Roehlkepartain. *Youth in Single-Parent Families.* Minneapolis: Search Institute, 1993.

Berger, Kathleen Stassen. *The Developing Person through the Life Span.* 5th ed. New York: Worth, 2001.

Berman, Alan L., and David A. Jobes. *Adolescent Suicide: Assessment and Intervention.* Washington, DC: American Psychological Association, 1991.

Bibby, Reginald W. *Canada's Teens: Today, Yesterday, and Tomorrow.* Toronto: Stoddart, 2001.

Bibby, Reginald W., and Donald C. Posterski. *The Emerging Generation.* Toronto: Irwin, 1985.

———. *Teen Trends: A Nation in Motion.* Toronto: Stoddart, 1992.

Biglan, Anthony et al. *Helping Adolescents at Risk: Prevention of Multiple Problem Behaviors.* New York: Guilford, 2004.

Biller, Henry "The Father and Sex Role Development." In *The Role of the Father in Child Development,* edited by Michael Lamb, 320–35. New York: Wiley, 1981.

Bingham, C. Raymond et al. "An Analysis of Age, Gender and Racial Differences in Recent National Trends of Youth Suicide." *Journal of Adolescence* 17 (1994) 53–71.

Black, David A. *The Myth of Adolescence: Raising Responsible Children in an Irresponsible Society.* Yorba Linda, CA: Davidson, 1999.

Blankenhorn, David. *Fatherless America: Confronting Our Most Urgent Social Problem.* New York: Basic Books, 1995.

The Body. "Fact Sheet: Lesbian, Gay, Bisexual, and Transgender Youth Issues." http://www.thebody.com/content/art2449.html/.

Bokhorst, Caroline L., et al. "Social Support from Parents, Friends, Classmates, and Teachers in Children and Adolescents Aged 9 to 18 Years: Who Is Perceived as Most Supportive?" *Social Development* 19 (2010) 417–26.

Bolen, Patricia. "Abstinence Plan Grows among Youth." *Moody Monthly* (January 1994) 57.

Borgman, Dean. *Hear My Story: Understanding the Cries of Troubled Youth.* Peabody, MA: Hendrickson, 2003.

Bouchey, Heather A., and Wyndol Furman. "Dating and Romantic Experiences in Adolescence." In *Blackwell Handbook of Adolescence,* edited by Gerald R. Adams and Michael D. Berzonsky, 313–20. Blackwell Handbooks of Developmental Psychology. Malden, MA: Blackwell, 2003.

Brandsen, Cheryl Kreykes. *A Case for Adoption: A Guide to Presenting the Option of Adoption to Young Women Experiencing Unplanned Pregnancies.* Grand Rapids: Bethany Christian Services, 1985.

Brasil de Souza, Elias. "Digital Technology and the Christian Life." *Reflections: The BRI Newsletter,* July 2015, 5–10, https://adventistbiblicalresearch.org/sites/default/files/pdf/Digital%20Technology%20and%20the%20Christian%20Life.pdf/.

Braun, Lucy D. *Someone Heard . . . .* Winter Park, FL: Currier/Davis, 1988.

Brittain, Clay. "Adolescent Choices and Parent-Peer Cross-Pressures." In *Adolescent Behavior and Society: A Book of Readings,* edited by Rolf E. Muuss, 224–34. 3rd ed. New York: Random House, 1971.

Brody, Baruch. *Abortion and the Sanctity of Human Life: A Philosophical View.* Cambridge: MIT Press, 1975

Brennan, T. "Adolescent Loneliness: Linking Epidemiology and Theory to Prevention." In *Suicide and Depression among Adolescents and Young Adults,* edited by Gerald L. Klermon, 185–213. Washington, DC: American Psychiatric Press, 1986.

Bronfenbrenner, Uri. "Response to Pressure from Peers versus Adults among Soviet and American Students." In *Adolescent Behavior and Society: A Book of Readings,* edited by Rolf E. Muuss, 433–41. 3rd ed. New York: Random House, 1971.

Brückner, Hannah, and Peter S. Bearman. "After the Promise: The STD Consequences of Adolescent Virginity Pledges." *Journal of Adolescent Health* 36 (2005) 271–78.

Buechner, Frederick. *Wishful Thinking: A Theological ABC.* New York: Harper One, 1993.

Buffardi, Laura E., and W. Keith Campbell. "Narcissism and Social Networking Web Sites." *Personality and Social Psychology Bulletin* 10 (2008) 1303–14.

Bureau of Labor Statistics. *Occupational Outlook Handbook.* 4th ed. Washington, DC: Department of Labor, 1994.

Burgess, Ann. *Youth at Risk: Understanding Runaway and Exploited Youth.* Washington, DC: National Center for Missing and Exploited Children, 1986.

Burgess, Robert L., and Rhonda A. Richardson. "Child Abuse during Adolescence." In *Experiencing Adolescents: A Sourcebook for Parents, Teachers, and Teens,* edited by Richard M. Lerner and Nancy L. Galambos, 119–51. Garland Reference Library of Social Science 201 New York: Garland, 1984.

Burns, Jim, and Mike DeVries. *Partnering with Parents in Youth Ministry.* Bloomigton, MN: Bethany House, 2003.

Busch-Rossnagel, Nancy. "Adolescence and Education." In *Experiencing Adolescents: A Sourcebook for Parents, Teachers, and Teens,* edited by Richard M. Lerner and Nancy L. Galambos, 283–316. Garland Reference Library of Social Science 201. New York: Garland, 1987.

Bushman, John. "Breaking the Ice at the Beginning." In *The Youth Group How-to Book,* edited by Lee Sparks, 13–14. Loveland, CO: Group, 1981.

Bushnell, Horace. *Christian Nurture.* Twin Brooks Series. Grand Rapids: Baker, 1979.

Cain, Neralie, and Michael Gradisar. "Electronic Media Use and Sleep in School-Aged Children and Adolescents: A Review." *Sleep Medicine* 11 (2010) 735–42.

Calvert, Sandra L. "Behavioral Effects of Media: Identity Construction on the Internet." In *Children in the Digital Age: Influences of Electronic Media on Development,* edited by Sandra L. Calvert et al., 57–70. Westport, CT: Praeger, 2002.

Campolo, Anthony. "Christian Ethics in the Sexual Wilderness." *Youthworker* 1 (1985) 13.

———. *Growing Up in America: A Sociology of Youth Ministry.* Grand Rapids: Zondervan, 1989.

———. *101 Ways Your Church Can Change the World.* Ventura, CA: Regal, 1993.

Camus, Albert. *The Plague.* Translated by Stuart Gilbert. New York: Vintage, 1948.

Cannister, Mark. *Teenagers Matter: Making Student Ministry a Priority in the Church.* Youth, Family, and Culture. Grand Rapids: Baker Academic, 2013.

Carter Velma T., and J. Lynn Leavenworth. *Caught in the Middle: Children of Divorce.* Judson Family Life Series. Valley Forge, PA: Judson, 1985.

Center for Parent/Youth Understanding. *Trend Alert October 3 2014.* http://www.cpyu. org/resource/trend-alert-facebook-depression/.

Centers for Disease Control and Prevention. *Diagnoses of HIV Infection in the United States and Dependent Areas.* HIV Surveillance Report 20/2014. http://www.cdc. gov/hiv/pdf/library/reports/surveillance/cdc-hiv-surveillance-report-us.pdf/.

———. "HIV among Youth in the US." *Vital Signs,* November 2012. http://www.cdc. gov/vitalsigns/hivamongyouth/.

———. *National Marriage and Divorce Rate Trends.* http://www.cdc.gov/nchs/nvss/ marriage_divorce_tables.htm/.

———. "NHPC Press Release: HIV Diagnosis." NCHHSTP Newsroom. http://www. cdc.gov/nchhstp/newsroom/2015/nhpc-press-release-hiv-diagnoses.html/.

———. "Same-Sex Couple Households." American Community Survey Briefs. https://www.census.gov/prod/2011pubs/acsbr10-03.pdf/.

———. *Sexually Transmitted Diseases.* "15–24-Year-Olds Account for Half of All New STD Infections." http://www.cdc.gov/std/life-stages-populations/adolescents-YoungAdults.htm/.

———. "STD Trends in the United States: 2010 National Data for Gonorrhea, Chlamydia, and Syphilis." *2010 Sexually Transmitted Diseases Surveillance.* http://www.cdc.gov/std/stats10/trends.htm/.

———. "STDs in Adolescents and Young Adults." *2014 Sexually Transmitted Diseases Surveillance.* http://www.cdc.gov/std/stats14/adol.htm#foot1/.

———. *Teenagers in the United States: Sexual Activity, Contraceptive Use, and Child-bearing, 2002.* http://www.cdc.gov/nchs/data/series/sr_23/sr23_024.pdf/.

———. *Teenagers in the United States: Sexual Activity, Contraceptive Use, and Child-bearing, 2006–2010.* http://www.cdc.gov/nchs/data/series/sr_23/sr23_031.pdf/.

———. *Youth Risk Behavior Surveillance—United States, 2007.* http://www.cdc.gov/mmwr/preview/mmwrhtml/ss5704a1.htm/.

———. *Youth Risk Behavior Surveillance—United States, 2011.* Morbidity and Mortality Weekly Report. http://www.cdc.gov/mmwr/preview/mmwrhtml/ss6104a1.htm#Tab23/.

———. *Youth Risk Behavior Surveillance—United States, 2013.* http://www.cdc.gov/mmwr/preview/mmwrhtml/ss6304a1.htm

Center for Sexual Health Promotion. "National Survey of Sexual Health and Behavior." http://www.nationalsexstudy.indiana.edu/

Center on Education Policy. "Almost Half of U.S. Schools Did not Make Adequate Yearly Progress in 2011, CEP Report Finds." 2011. www.cep-dc.org/cfcontent_file.cfm?Attachment=PressRelease/.

Cerullo, Claudio. "Cyber Bullying Statistics." Teach Antibullying, Inc. http://drclaudiocerullo.com/2011/01/05/cyber-bullying-statistics/

Children's Defense Fund. *The State of America's Children Handbook, 2012.* http://www.childrensdefense.org/library/data/soac-2012-handbook.pdf/.

Christakis, Nicholas A., and James H. Fowler. *Connected: The Surprising Power of Our Social Networks and How They Shape Our Lives.* New York: Back Bay Books, 2011.

Christie, Les John. *Best-Ever Games for Youth Ministry: A Collection of Easy, Fun Games for Teenagers!* Loveland, CO: Simply Youth Ministry, 2015.

———. *What If—? 450 Thought-Provoking Questions to Get Your Kids Talking, Laughing, and Thinking.* Grand Rapids: Zondervan, 1996.

———. *Have You Ever—? 450 Intriguing Questions Guaranteed to Get Teenagers Talking.* Grand Rapids: Zondervan, 1998.

———. *450 Tantalizing Unfinished Sentences: To Get Teenagers Talking & Thinking.* Grand Rapids: Zondervan, 2000.

Clark, Chap. *Hurt 2.0.* Grand Rapids: Baker Academic, 2011.

Clark, Chap, and Kara Powell. *Deep Justice in a Broken World: Helping Your Kids Serve Others and Right the Wrongs around Them.* Youth Specialty Series. Grand Rapids: Zondervan, 2007.

Cline, David W., and Jack C. Westman. "The Impact of Divorce on the Family." *Child Psychology and Human Development* 2 (1971) 78–83.

Clouse, Bonnidell. "Adolescent Moral Development and Sexuality." In *Handbook of Youth Ministry,* edited by Donald Ratcliff and James A. Davies, 178–213. Birmingham, AL: Religious Education Press, 1991.

Cobb, Nancy. *Adolescence: Continuity, Change, and Diversity.* 7th ed. Sunderland, MA: Sinauer Associates, 2010.

Coleman, John C., and Leo B. Hendry. *The Nature of Adolescence.* 3rd ed. London: Routledge, 1999.

Coleman, James S. *The Adolescent Society.* New York: Free Press, 1963.

Coleman, Lyman. *Serendipity Small Group Training Manual: 6 Sessions for Training Leaders.* Littleton, CO: Serendipity, 1991.

Collins, Gary R. *Christian Counseling: A Comprehensive Guide.* Rev. ed. Dallas: Word, 1988.

———. *How to Be a People Helper.* Santa Ana, CA: Vision House, 1976.

Collins, Rebecca L., et al. "Does Watching Sex on Television Influence Teens' Sexual Activity?" Rand Health. http://www.rand.org/pubs/research_briefs/RB9068. html/.

Conger, John J., and Anne C. Petersen. *Adolescence and Youth: Psychological Development in a Changing World.* 3rd ed. New York: Harper & Row, 1984.

Cook, Joanne Valient, and Roy Tyler Bowles, eds. *Child Abuse: Commission and Omission.* Toronto: Butterworths, 1980.

Coopersmith, Stanley. *The Antecedents of Self-Esteem.* Palo Alto, CA: Consulting Psychology Press, 1967.

Costanzo, Philip R., and Marvin E. Shaw. "Parent and Peer Group Influences on Adolescents." In *Adolescent Behavior and Society: A Book of Readings,* edited by Rolf E. Muuss, 246–49. 3rd ed. New York: Random House, 1971.

Crook, Marion. *Out of the Darkness: Teens and Suicide.* Vancouver: Arsenal Pulp Press, 2003.

Csikszentmihalyi, Mihaly, and Jeremy Hunter. "Happiness in Everyday Life: The Uses of Experience Sampling." *Journal of Happiness Studies* 4 (2003) 185–99.

Csikszentmihalyi, Mihaly, and Reed Larson. *Being Adolescent: Conflict and Growth in the Teenage Years.* New York: Basic Books, 1984.

Culp, Anne M., et al. "Adolescent Depressed Mood, Reports of Suicide Attempts, and Asking for Help." *Adolescence* 30 (1995) 827–37.

Cummings, Hope M., and Elizabeth A. Vandewater. "Relation of Adolescent Video Game Play to Time Spent in Other Activities." *Journal of American Medical Association Pediatrics* 161 (2007) 684–89. http://archpedi.jamanetwork.com/article. aspx?articleid=570716/.

Curran, Dolores. *Traits of a Healthy Family: Fifteen Traits Commonly Found in Healthy Families by Those Who Work with Them.* San Francisco: Harper & Row, 1983.

Cutter-Wilson, Elizabeth, and Tracy Richmond. "Understanding Teen Dating Violence: Practical Screening and Intervention Strategies for Pediatric and Adolescent Healthcare Providers." *Current Opinions in Pediatrics* 23 (2011) 379–83. http:// www.ncbi.nlm.nih.gov/pmc/articles/PMC3433035/.

Dausey, Gary. "Communication Killers." In *Parents & Teenagers,* by Jay Kessler and Ronald A. Beers, 226. Wheaton, IL: Victor, 1984.

Dawson, Deborah. "Family Structure and Children's Health and Well-Being: Data From the 1988 National Health Interview Survey on Child Health." *Journal of Marriage and the Family* 54 (1991) 573–84.

Davidson, Lucy E., et al. "An Epidemiologic Study of Risk Factors in Two Teenage Suicide Clusters." *Journal of American Medical Association* 262 (1989) 2687–92.

Davidson, Lucy E. "Suicide Clusters and Youth." In *Suicide among Youth: Perspectives on Risk and Prevention,* edited by Cynthia Pfeffer, 83–100. Washington, DC: American Psychiatric Press, 1989.

Dean, Kenda Creasy. *Almost Christian: What the Faith of Our Teenagers Is Telling the American Church.* New York: Oxford University Press, 2010.

———. *Practicing Passion: Youth and the Quest for a Passionate Church.* Grand Rapids: Eerdmans, 2004.

Dean, Kenda Creasy, and Ron Foster. *The Godbearing Life: The Art of Soul Tending for Youth Ministry.* Nashville: Upper Room, 1998.

DeBard, Robert. "Millennials Coming to College." *New Directions for Student Services* 106 (2004) 33–45.

Derr, Brooklyn C., et al. *Cross-Cultural Approaches to Leadership Development.* Westport, CT: Quorum, 2002.

DeVries, Mark. *Family-Based Youth Ministry.* Rev. ed. Downers Grove, IL: InterVarsity, 2004.

Dowd, Frances Smardo. *Latchkey Children in the Library & Community: Issues, Strategies, and Programs.* Phoenix: Oryx, 1991.

Downs, Perry G. "Faith Shaping: Bringing Youth to Spiritual Maturity." In *The Complete Book of Youth Ministry,* edited by Warren S. Benson and Mark H. Senter III, 49–60. Chicago: Moody, 1987.

———. *Teaching for Spiritual Growth.* Grand Rapids: Zondervan, 1994.

Dryfoos, Joy G. *Adolescents at Risk: Prevalence and Prevention.* New York: Oxford University Press, 1990.

Dunn, Richard R. *Shaping the Spiritual Life of Students: A Guide for Youth Workers, Pastors, Teachers & Campus Ministers.* Downers Grove, IL: InterVarsity, 2001.

Durkheim, Emile. *Suicide: A Study in Sociology.* New York: Free Press, 1951.

Dykstra, Craig. "Faith Development and Religious Education." In *Faith Development and Fowler,* edited by Craig Dykstra and Sharon Parks, 251–71. Birmingham, AL: Religious Education Press, 1986.

Dykstra, Craig, and Sharon Parks, eds. *Faith Development and Fowler.* Birmingham, AL: Religious Education Press, 1986.

Edwards, Maria. *Total Youth Ministry: An Approach for Parish Workers.* Winona, MN: St. Mary's, 1980.

Edwards, Shawn, et al. *Name Your Favorite . . . : 700 Rapid-Fire Ice Breakers to Get Teenagers Talking.* Youth Specialties. Grand Rapids: Zondervan, 2002.

Elkind, David. *All Grown Up & No Place to Go.* Rev. ed. Cambridge: Perseus, 1998.

———. *The Hurried Child: Growing Up Too Fast Too Soon.* 3rd ed. Cambridge: Perseus, 2001.

———. *A Sympathetic Understanding of the Child: Birth to Sixteen.* 3rd ed. Boston: Allyn and Bacon, 1994.

Ellison, Craig W. *Loneliness: The Search for Intimacy.* Chappaqua, NY: Christian Herald, 1980.

Employment and Social Development Canada. "Learning—School Dropouts." http://well-being.esdc.gc.ca/misme-iowb/.3ndic.1t.4r@-eng.jsp?iid=32#M_1/.

Enough Is Enough. Internet Safety 101. "The Dangers of the Social Web." http://internetsafety101.org/snsdangers/.

Erikson, Erik H. *Identity, Youth, and Crisis.* New York: Norton, 1968.

———. *Identity and the Life-Cycle.* New York: Norton, 1980.

———. *The Life Cycle Completed.* New York: Norton, 1982.

———. "Youth and the Life Cycle." In *Adolescent Behavior and Society: A Book of Readings,* edited by Rolf E. Muuss and Harriet D. Porton, 252–60. 5th ed. Boston: McGraw-Hill, 1999.

Feinberg, John S., and Paul D. Feinberg. *Ethics for a Brave New World.* Wheaton, IL: Crossway, 1993.

Field, David. *The Homosexual Way—A Christian Option?* Downers Grove, IL: Inter-Varsity, 1979.

Fine, Mark, and Lawrence Kurdek. "The Adjustment of Adolescents in Stepfather and Stepmother Families." *Journal of Marriage and the Family* 54 (1992) 725–36.

Finkelhor, David. "Psychological, Cultural and Family Factors in Incest and Family Sexual Abuse." In *Child Abuse: Commission and Omission,* edited by Joanne Valiant Cook and Roy Tyler Bowles, 263–69. Toronto: Butterworths, 1980.

Ford, Kevin. *Jesus for a New Generation: Putting the Gospel in the Language of Xers.* Downers Grove, IL: InterVarsity, 1995.

Foster, Timothy. *Called to Counsel.* Nashville: Oliver Nelson, 1986.

Foubert, John. "Supporting a Campus Culture Free from Title IX Violations." http://slideplayer.com/slide/7455560/.

Fowler, James W. "Faith and the Structuring of Meaning." In *Faith Development and Fowler,* edited by Craig Dykstra and Sharon Parks, 15–42. Birmingham, AL: Religious Education Press, 1986.

———. *Stages of Faith: the Psychology of Human Development and the Quest for Meaning.* San Francisco: Harper & Row, 1981.

Francke, Linda Bird. *The Ambivalence of Abortion.* New York: Random House, 1978.

The George H. Gallup International Institute. *The Gallup Survey on Teenage Suicide.* Princeton: George H. Gallup Institute, 1991.

Gallup, George, and Robert Bezilla. *The Religious Life of Young Americans: A Compendium of Surveys on the Spiritual Beliefs and Practices of Teen-agers and Young Adults, with Commentary and Analysis by George H. Gallup.* Princeton: George Gallup International Institute, 1992.

Garber, Steven. *The Fabric of Faithfulness: Weaving Together Belief & Behavior during the University Years.* Downers Grove, IL: InterVarsity, 1996.

Garland, Diana S. Richmond. "Developing and Empowering Parent Networks." In *The Church's Ministry with Families,* edited by Diana S. Richmond Garland and Diane L. Pancoast, 91–109. Dallas: Word, 1990.

Garvin, Vicki, and Ruth H. Striegel-Moore. "Health Services Research for Eating Disorders in the United States: A Status Report and a Call to Action." In *Eating Disorders: Innovative Directions in Research and Practice,* edited by Ruth H. Striegel-Moore and Linda Smolak, 135–52. Washington, DC: American Psychological Association, 2001.

Gee, James Paul. *What Video Games Have to Teach us about Learning and Literacy.* Rev. ed. New York: Palgrave Macmillan, 2007.

Geisler, Norman L. *Ethics: Alternatives and Issues.* Grand Rapids: Zondervan, 1971.

Gelles, Richard. "Violence toward Children in the United States." In *Child Abuse: Commission and Omission,* edited by Joanne Valiant Cook and Roy Tyler Bowles, 35–48. Toronto: Butterworths, 1980.

Gil, David G. *Violence against Children: Physical Child Abuse in the United States*. A Commowealth Fund Book. Cambridge: Harvard University Press, 1970.

Gillespie, V. Bailey *The Experience of Faith*. Birmingham, AL: Religious Education Press, 1988.

Gilligan, Carol. *In a Different Voice: Psychological Theory and Women's Development*. Cambridge: Harvard University Press, 1982.

Glasser, William. *Schools Without Failure*. New York: Harper & Row, 1969.

Gluck, Samantha. "Self-Injury, Self Harm Statistics and Facts." http://www.healthyplace. com/abuse/self-injury/self-injury-self-harm-statistics-and-facts/.

Goldberg, E. "Depression and Suicide Ideation in the Young Adult." *American Journal of Psychiatry* 138 (1981) 35–40.

Gordon, Thomas. *Parent Effectiveness Training: The Tested New Way to Raise Children*. New York: Wyden, 1970.

Gotlib, Ian H., and Catherine A. Colby. *Treatment of Depression*. New York: Pergamon, 1987.

Gould, Roger. *Transformations*. New York: Simon & Schuster, 1978.

Gould, Madelyn S., et al. "Time-space Clustering of Teenage Suicide." *American Journal of Epidemiology* 131 (1990) 71–78.

Grabove, Valerie. "The Many Facets of Transformative Learning Theory and Practice." *New Directions for Adult and Continuing Education* 74 (1997) 89–96.

Grant, Carol Lee, and Iris Goldstein Fodor. "Adolescent Attitudes toward Body Image and Anorexic Behavior." *Adolescence* 21 (1986) 269–82.

Greenberger, Ellen, and Laurence Steinberg. *When Teen-agers Work*. New York: Basic Books, 1986.

Greene, A. L., and Michelle Denise Grimsley. "Age and Gender Differences in Adolescents' Preference for Parental Advice: Mum's the Word." *Journal of Adolescent Research* 5 (1990) 396–413.

Griffith, Brian, and Julie Griggs. "Religious Identity Status as a Model to Understand, Assess, and Interact with Client Spirituality." *Counseling and Values* 26 (2001) 14–25.

Grudem, Wayne. *Systematic Theology*. Grand Rapids: Zondervan, 1994.

Guerney, Louise, and Joyce Arthur. "Adolescent Social Relationships." In *Experiencing Adolescents, A Sourcebook for Parents, Teachers, and Teens*, edited by Richard Lerner and Nancy Galambos, 87–118. Garland Reference Library of Social Science 201. New York: Garland, 1984.

Guiness, Os. *In Two Minds*. Downers Grove, IL: InterVarsity, 1976.

Gullotta, Thomas P., et al. *The Adolescent Experience*. 4th ed. San Diego: Academic Press, 2000.

Guttmacher Institute. "U.S. Teenage Pregnancies, Births and Abortions: National and State Trends and Trends by Race and Ethnicity," by Kathryn Kost and Stanley Henshaw. http://www.guttmacher.org/pubs/USTPtrends.pdf/.

———. "U.S. Teen Pregnancy, Birth and Abortion Rates Reach Historic Lows." http://www.guttmacher.org/media/nr/2014/05/05/

Hall, G. Stanley. *Adolescence: Its Psychology and Its Relations to Physiology, Anthropology, Sex, Crime, Religion and Education*, vol. 1. New York: Appleton, 1904.

Hansen, Jane, and Sandra McIntosh. "New Sex Abuse Trend: Kids Attacking Kids." *Atlanta Journal-Constitution*, October 15, 1989, A1 and A18.

Hardy, Kenneth V., and Tracey A. Laszloffy. *Teens Who Hurt: Clinical Interventions to Break the Cycle of Adolescent Violence*. New York: Guilford, 2005.

Harris, Jon. "Dysfunction, Healing and the Family of Origin." In *Handbook of Family Religious Education*, edited by Blake J. Neff and Donald Ratcliff, 202–6. Birmingham, AL: Religious Education Press, 1995.

Harrison, Beverly Wildung. *Our Right to Choose: Toward a New Ethic of Abortion*. Boston: Beacon, 1983.

Havinghurst, Robert J. *Developmental Tasks and Education*. 2nd ed. New York: Longmans, Green, 1952.

Hendrick, Bill. "Youth's Suicide Highlights its No. 3 Rank as Killer of Teens." *Atlanta Journal–Constitution*, March 26, 1994, n.p.

Herrman, Judith. "The Teen Brain as a Work in Progress: Implications for Pediatric Nurses." *Pediatric Nursing* 31 (March April 2005) 144–48.

Hersey, Paul H., et al. *Management of Organizational Behavior*. 10th ed. Englewood Cliffs, NJ: Pearson, 2012.

Hoberman, Harry M., and Barry D. Garfinkle. "Completed Suicide in Youth." In *Suicide among Youth: Perspectives on Risk and Prevention*, edited by Cynthia R. Pfeffer, 21–40. Contemporary Issues Companion. Washington, DC: American Psychiatric Press, 1989.

Hoffman, Lee. "The ABCs of Eating Disorders." In *Eating Disorders*, edited by Myra H. Immell, 33–40. San Diego: Greenhaven, 1999.

Hoge, Dean R., and Gregory H. Petrillo. "Determinants of Church Participation and Attitudes among High-school Youth." *Journal for the Scientific Study of Religion* 17 (1978) 359–79.

———. "Youth and the Church." *Religious Education* 74 (May-June 1979) 305–12.

Hollander, Michael. *Helping Teens Who Cut: Understanding and Ending Self-Injury*. New York: Guilford, 2008.

Hovell, Mel, et al. "Family Influences on Latino and Anglo Adolescents' Sexual Behavior." *Journal of Marriage and the Family* 56 (1994) 973–86.

Hughes, Philip E. *Christian Ethics in Secular Society*. Grand Rapids: Baker, 1983.

Hurst, Ed. *Overcoming Homosexuality*. Elgin, IL: David C. Cook, 1988.

Huntemann, Nina, and Michael Morgan. "Media and Identity Development." In *Handbook of Children and the Media*, edited by Dorothy G. Singer and Jerome L. Singer, 303–20. 2nd ed. Los Angeles: Sage, 2012.

Hyde, Kenneth E. "Adolescents and Religion." In *Handbook of Youth Ministry*, edited by Donald Ratcliff and James A. Davies, 119–61. Birmingham, AL: Religious Education Press, 1991.

———. *Religion in Childhood and Adolescence*. Birmingham, AL: Religious Education Press, 1990.

Ingersoll, Gary M. *Adolescents in School and Society*. Lexington, MA: Heath, 1982.

Issler, Klaus, and Ron Habermas. *How We Learn: A Christian Teacher's Guide to Educational Psychology*. Grand Rapids: Baker, 1994.

Jackson, Edgar. *Understanding Loneliness*. Philadelphia: Fortress, 1980.

Jesse R., et al. *Interpersonal Effects of Alcohol Abuse*. Center City, MN: Hazelden, 1978.

Johnson, James R. "Toward a Biblical Approach to Masturbation." *Journal of Psychology and Theology* 10 (1982) 137–46.

Johnston, Ray. *Developing Student Leaders*. Grand Rapids: Zondervan, 1992.

Jones, Timothy Paul, and Randy Stinson. "Family Ministry Models." In *A Theology for Family Ministries*, edited by Michael Anthony and Michelle Anthony, 155–80. Nashville: B&H Academic, 2011.

K12 Academics. "History of School Shootings in the United States." http://k12academics. com/school-shootings/history-school-shootings-united-states#.VpQT2FJjRrZ/.

Kachur, S. Patrick, et al. *Suicide in the United States, 1980–1992*. Atlanta: Centers for Disease Control and Prevention, 1995.

Kalodner, Cynthia R. *Too Fat or Too Thin? A Reference Guide to Eating Disorders*. Westport: Greenwood, 2003.

Kaplan, Paul S. *Adolescence*. Boston: Houghton Mifflin, 2004.

Kempe, C. Henry. "Sexual Abuse, Another Hidden Pediatric Problem." In *Child Abuse: Commission and Omission*, edited by Joanne Valiant Cook and Roy Tyler Bowles, 97–108. Toronto: Butterworths, 1980.

Kempe, Ruth S., and C. Henry Kempe. *Child Abuse*. Developing Child. Cambridge: Harvard University Press, 1978.

King, Cheryl A., et al. *Teen Suicide Risk*. New York: Guilford, 2013.

Kinnaird, Keri L., and Meg Gerrard. "Premarital Sexual Behavior and Attitudes toward Marriage and Divorce among Young Women as a Function of Their Mothers' Marital Status." *Journal of Marriage and the Family* 48 (1986) 757–65.

Kinnaman, David. *You Lost Me: Why Young Christians Are Leaving Church—and Rethinking Faith*. Grand Rapids: Baker, 2011.

Kirkpatrick, Jim, and Paul Caldwell. *Eating Disorders: Everything You Need to Know*. Rev. ed. Buffalo: Firefly, 2004.

Kirsh, Steven J. *Media and Youth: A Developmental Perspective*. Chichester, UK: Wiley-Blackwell, 2010.

Klagsbrun, Francine. *Too Young to Die: Youth and Suicide*. New York: Pocket Books, 1981.

Klerman, Gerald. "Suicide, Depression, and Related Problems among the Baby Boom Cohort." In *Suicide among Youth: Perspectives on Risk and Prevention*, edited by Cynthia Pfeffer, 63–81. Washington, DC: American Psychiatric Press, 1989.

Koh, Me Ra. *Beauty Restored*. Ventura, CA: Regal, 2001.

Koh, Me Ra. "13 Characteristics of a Date Rapist: A List You Need to Share." http:// www.babble.com/relationships/13-characteristics-of-a-date-rapist-a-list-you-need-to-share/.

Koteskey, Ronald L. *Understanding Adolescence*. Wheaton, IL: Victor, 1987.

————. "Adolescence as a Cultural Invention." In *Handbook of Youth Ministry*, edited by Donald Ratcliff and James A. Davies, 42–69. Birmingham, AL: Religious Education Press, 1991.

Kreider, Rose M., and Renee Ellis. "Living Arrangements of Children: 2009." http:// www.census.gov/prod/2011pubs/p70-126.pdf/, 3.

Kuntsche, Emmanuel, et al. "Why Do Young People Drink? A Review of Drinking Motives." *Clinical Psychology Review* 25 (June 2005) 841–61.

Lamb, Michael. "Fathers and Child Development: An Integrative Overview." In *The Role of the Father in Child Development*, edited by Michael Lamb, 1–70. Wiley Series on Personality Processes. New York: Wiley, 1981.

Landau Elizabeth. "Obesity, Politics, STDs Flow in Social Networks." Why Do I Do That? Your Brain and Your Behavior. CNN. http://www.cnn.com/2009/TECH/10/08/social.networks.connected/

Larson, Scott, and Larry Brendtro. *Reclaiming Our Prodigal Sons and Daughters: A Practical Approach to Connecting with Youth in Conflict.* Bloomington, IN: National Education Service, 2000.

Lee, James Michael. *The Content of Religious Education.* Birmingham, AL: Religious Education Press, 1985.

————. *The Flow of Religious Education.* Birmingham, AL: Religious Education Press, 1973.

LeFever, Marlene D. *Creative Teaching Methods.* Elgin: Cook, 1985.

Lehmann, N., and H. Sullinger. *The Document: Declaration of Feminism.* Minneapolis: Powderhorn Station, 1972.

Lenhart, Amanda. "Teens, Social Media & Technology Overview: 2015." Pew Research Center website. Internet and Tech. April 9, 2015. http://www.pewinternet.org/2015/04/09/teens-social-media-technology-2015/.

Levinson, Daniel, et al. *The Seasons of a Man's Life.* New York: Ballantine, 1978.

Lisak, David, and Paul M. Miller. "Repeat Rape and Multiple Offending among Undetected Rapists." *Violence and Victims* 17 (2002) 73–84.

Livermore, David, and Terry Linhart. *What Can We Do? Practical Ways Your Youth Ministry Can Have a Global Conscience.* Grand Rapids: Zondervan, 2011.

Llewellyn-Jones, Derek. *Herpes, AIDS, and Other Sexually Transmitted Diseases.* London: Faber & Faber, 1985.

Luce, Ron. *Battle Cry for a Generation.* Colorado Springs: NextGen, 2005.

Luster, Tom, and Stephen A. Small. "Factors Associated with Sexual Risk-Taking Behaviors among Adolescents." *Journal of Marriage and the Family* 56 (1994) 622–32.

Lutes, Chris. *What Teenagers Are Saying about Drugs & Alcohol.* Wheaton, IL: Tyndale House, 1987.

Maccoby, Eleanor E., and Carol N. Jacklin. *The Psychology of Sex Differences.* Stanford: Stanford University Press, 1974.

Marcia, James. "Identity and Psychosocial Development in Adulthood." *Identity: An International Journal of Theory and Research* 2 (2002) 7–28.

Martin J. A., et al. "Births: Final Data for 2013." *National Vital Statistics Reports* 64/1. http://www.cdc.gov/nchs/data/nvsr/nvsr64/nvsr64_01.pdf/.

Mason, W. Alex, and Michael Windle. "Family, Religious, School, and Peer Influences on Adolescent Alcohol Use." *Prevention Researcher* 9 (2002) 6–7.

Maynard, Rebecca A., ed. *Kids Having Kids: Economic Costs and Consequences of Teen Pregnancy.* Washington, DC: Urban Institute Press, 1997.

Mazanec, Jana. "Birth Rate Soars at Colorado School." *USA Today,* May 19 1992, 3-A.

McDowell, Josh, and Dick Day. *Why Wait? What You Need to Know about the Teen Sexuality Crisis.* San Bernardino: Here's Life, 1987.

McGinnis, Alan Loy. *The Friendship Factor.* Minneapolis: Augsburg, 1979.

McNeely, Clea, and Jayne Blanchard. *The Teen Years Explained: A Guide to Healthy Adolescent Development.* Baltimore: John Hopkins Bloomberg School of Public Health, 2013. http://www.jhsph.edu/research/centers-and-institutes/center-for-adolescent-health/_includes/_pre-redesign/Interactive%20Guide.pdf/.

McWhirter, J. Jeffries et al. *At-Risk Youth: A Comprehensive Response.* Pacific Grove, CA: Brooks/Cole, 1993.

Meier, Paul D. et al. *Introduction to Psychology and Counseling.* 2nd ed. Grand Rapids: Baker, 1991.

Meyers, Chet, and Thomas B. Jones. *Promoting Active Learning*. San Francisco: Jossey-Bass, 1993.

Mezirow, Jack. *Transformative Dimensions of Adult Learning*. San Francisco: Jossey-Bass, 1991.

———. "Transformative Learning: Theory to Practice." *New Directions for Adult and Continuing Education* 7 (1997) 5–12.

Miles, J. Herbert. *Sexual Understanding before Marriage*. Grand Rapids: Zondervan, 1971.

Miller, B., et al. "Dating Age and Stage as Correlates of Adolescent Sexual Attitudes and Behavior." *Journal of Adolescent Research* 1 (1986) 361–71.

Miller Brent C., and C. Raymond Bingham. "Family Configuration in Relation to the Sexual Behavior of Female Adolescents." *Journal of Marriage and the Family* 51 (1989) 499–506.

Moore, Kristin A., et al. "Parental Attitudes and the Occurrence of Early Sexual Activity." in *Journal of Marriage and the Family* 48 (November 1986) 777–82.

Morano, Christopher D., et al. "Risk Factors for Adolescent Suicidal Behavior: Loss, Insufficient Familial Support, and Hopelessness." *Adolescence* 28 (1993) 851–65.

Morganthau, Tom. "It's Not Just New York . . . " *Newsweek,* March 9, 1992, 29.

Mortimer, Jeylan T. "The Benefits and Risks of Adolescent Employment." *Prevention Researcher* 17 (2010) 8–11. http://www.ncbi.nlm.nih.gov/pmc/articles/PMC2936460.

Morton, Tom. "Assessing True Love Waits." *Youthworker* 11 (1994) 54–60.

Mueller, Walt. "Culture Watch: From Athens to Main Street; the Seven Steps of Engaging Culture." *Youth Worker*, December 3, 2011. http://www.youthworker.com/youth-ministry-resources-ideas/youth-culture-news/11659535/.

———. *Understanding Today's Youth Culture*. Wheaton, IL: Tyndale, 1994.

Mulford, Carrie, and Peggy C. Giordano. "Teen Dating Violence: A Closer Look at Adolescent Romantic Relationships" (2008). http://www.nij.gov/journals/261/pages/teen-dating-violence.aspx/.

Munro, Harry C. *Protestant Nurture*. Englewood, NJ: Prentice Hall, 1956.

Muuss, Rolf E. "Marcia's Expansion of Erikson's Theory of Identity Formation." In *Adolescent Behavior and Society: A Book of Readings,* edited by Rolf E. Muuss and Harriet D. Porton, 260–70. 5th ed. Boston: McGraw-Hill, 1999.

———. *Theories of Adolescence*. 6th ed. New York: McGraw-Hill, 1996.

Narramore, Bruce. *You're Someone Special*. Grand Rapids: Zondervan, 1978.

Natale, Samuel M. *Loneliness and Spiritual Growth*. Birmingham, AL: Religious Education Press, 1986.

National Center for Education Statistics. The Condition of Education. "Status Dropout Rates." http://nces.ed.gov/programs/coe/indicator_coj.asp/.

National Center on Addiction and Substance Abuse at Columbia University. "National Survey of American Attitudes on Substance Abuse XII: Teens." http://www.casacolumbia.org/addiction-research/reports/national-survey-american-attitudes-substance-abuse-teens-2012/.

National Commission on Educational Excellence. *A Nation at Risk*. Washington, DC: The National Commission on Excellence in Education, 1983.

National Institute of Mental Health. *The Teen Brain: Still under Construction*. http://www.nimh.nih.gov/health/publications/the-teen-brain-still-under-construction/index.shtml/.

National Sleep Foundation. "Annual Sleep in America Poll Exploring Connections with Communications Technology Use and Sleep." https://sleepfoundation.org/media-center/press-release/annual-sleep-america-poll-exploring-connections-communications-technology-use-/.

Neff, Blake J. "Communication and Relationships." In *Handbook of Youth Ministry,* edited by Donald Ratcliff and James A. Davies, 162–77. Birmingham, AL: Religious Education Press, 1991.

Nel, Malan. "The Inclusive Congregational Approach to Youth Ministry." In *Four Views of Youth Ministry and the Church,* edited by Mark H. Senter, 1–22. Youh Specialties Series. Grand Rapids: Zondervan, 2001.

Nelson Bryan, and Timothy Paul Jones. "Introduction." In *Trained in the Fear of God: Family Ministry in Theological, Historical, and Practical Perspective,* edited by Randy Stinson and Timothy Paul Jones, 13–29. Grand Rapids: Kregal, 2011.

Nelson, Hapt M., and Raymond H. Potvin. "Gender and Regional Differences in the Religiosity of Protestant Adolescents." *Review of Religious Research* 22 (March 1981) 268–85.

Newcomer Susan F., and J. Richard Udry. "Mothers' Influence on the Sexual Behavior of Their Teenage Children." *Journal of Marriage and the Family* 46 (1984) 477–85.

———. "Parental Marital Status Effects on Adolescent Sexual Behavior." *Journal of Marriage and the Family* 49 (1987) 235–40.

Newman, Barbara, and Phillip Newman. "Group Identity and Alienation." *Journal of Youth and Adolescence* 30 (2001) 515–38.

———. *Adolescent Development.* Columbus: Merrill, 1986.

Novella, Antonia C. *Surgeon General's Report to the American Public on HIV Infection and Aids.* Washington, DC: Public Health Service, 1994.

Ogilvie, Lloyd John. *God's Best for My Life.* Eugene, OR: Harvest House, 1981.

O'Keeffe, Gwenn Schurgin, et al. "The Impact of Social Media on Children, Adolescents, and Families." *Pediatrics* 127 (2011) 800–804. http://pediatrics.aappublications.org/content/127/4/800.

Olson, Keith. *Counseling Teenagers.* Loveland, CO: Group Books, 1984.

Olson, Richard. *A Job or a Vocation?* Youth Forum Series. Nashville: Thomas Nelson, 1973.

Painter, Kim. "Fewer Kids Save Sex For Adulthood." *USA Today,* March 5 1991) 1D.

Pancoast, Diane L., and Kathy A. Bobula. "Building Multigenerational Support Networks." In *The Church's Ministry with Families: A Practical Guide,* edited by Diana S. Richmond Garland and Diane L. Pancoast, 171–83. Dallas: Word, 1990.

Papalia, Diane E., et al. *A Child's World: Infancy through Adolescence.* 13th ed. New York: McGraw-Hill, 2014.

Papolos, Demetri, and Janice Papolos. *Overcoming Depression.* New York: Harper & Row, 1987.

Pardun, Carol A., et al. "Linking Exposure to Outcomes: Early Adolescent's Consumption of Sexual Content in Six Media." *Mass Communication and Society* 8 (2005) 75–91.

Parker, Jullia. *Women and Welfare: Ten Victorian Women in Social Service.* London: Palgrave Macmillan, 1989.

Parks, Sharon. *The Critical Years: Young Adults and the Search for Meaning, Faith, and Commitment.* New York: HarperCollins, 1991.

Parrott, Les. *Helping the Struggling Adolescent: A Guide to Thirty-Six Common Problems for Counselors, Pastors, and Youth Workers.* Rev. ed. Grand Rapids: Zondervan, 2000.

Pasupathi M., and T. Hoyt. "The Development of Narrative Identity in Late Adolescence and Emergent Adulthood: The Continued Importance of Listeners." *Developmental Psychology* 45 (2009) 558–74.

Patty, Steven. *Impact: Student Ministry That Will Impact a Generation.* TruthQuest. Nashville: B&H 2005.

Pearl R., T. Bryan, T. and A. Herzog. "Resisting or Acquiescing to Peer Pressure to Engage in Misconduct: Adolescents' Expectations of Probable Consequences." *Journal of Youth and Adolescence* 19 (1990) 43–44.

Peck, Michael L. "Suicide in Late Adolescence and Young Adulthood." In *Suicide: Assessment and Intervention,* edited by Corrine Loing Hatton and Sharon McBride Valente, 220–30. 2nd ed. Norwalk, CT: Appleton-Century-Crofts, 1984.

Pendered, David. "Sex: Teens More Open, Active." *Atlanta Journal and Constitution* (January 13 1991) D1.

Penner, Clifford L. "A Reaction to Johnson's Biblical Approach to Masturbation." *Journal of Psychology and Theology* 10 (1982) 147–49.

Peterson, Eugene H. *Reversed Thunder: The Revelation of John and the Praying Imagination.* San Francisco: Harper & Row, 1988.

Phillips, David P., et al, "Effects of Mass Media News Stories on Suicide, with New Evidence on the Role of Story Content." In *Suicide among Youth: Perspectives on Risk and Prevention,* edited by Cynthia R. Pfeffer, 101–6. Washington, DC: American Psychiatric Press, 1989.

Place, Michael D. "Masturbation." In *The HarperCollins Encyclopedia of Catholicism,* edited by Richard P. McBrien, 841. San Francisco: HarperSanFrancisco, 1995.

Posterski, Donald C., *Friendship: A Window on Ministry to Youth.* Scarborough: Project Teen Canada, 1985.

Potard, C., et al. "The Influence of Peers on Risky Sexual Behavior During Adolescence." *European Journal of Contraception and Reproductive Health Care* 13 (2008) 264–70.

Primack B. A., et al. "Association between Media Use in Adolescence and Depression in Young Adulthood: A Longitudinal Study." *Arch Gen Psychiatry* 66 (2009) 181–88. http://www.ncbi.nlm.nih.gov/pubmed/19188540/.

Prinstein, Mitchell J., and Kenneth A. Dodge. *Understanding Peer Influence in Children and Adolescents.* Duke Series in Child Development and Public Policy New York: Guilford, 2008.

Queralt, Magaly. "Risk Factors Associated with Completed Suicide in Latino Adolescents." *Journal of Adolescence* 17 (1993) 832–50.

Radcliff, Donald, and James A. Davies, eds. *Handbook of Youth Ministry.* Birmingham, AL: Religious Education Press, 1991.

Reardon, David C. *Aborted Women: Silent No More.* Westchester, IL: Crossway, 1987.

Rees, Jane Mitchell. "Eating Disorders during Adolescence: Nutritional Problems and Interventions." http://staff.washington.edu/jrees/ch1edado.html/.

Reidy, Thomas. "The Aggressive Characteristics of Abused and Neglected Children." In *Child Abuse: Commission and Omission,* edited by Joanne Valiant Cook and Roy Tyler Bowles, 471–77. Toronto: Butterworths, 1980.

Reid, Alvin L. *Raising the Bar: Ministry to Youth in the New Millennium.* Grand Rapids: Kregel, 2004.

Rekers, George Alan. *Shaping Your Child's Sexual Identity.* Grand Rapids: Baker, 1982.

Rice, Wayne. *Up Close & Personal: How to Build Community in Your Youth Group.* Youth Specialties Series. Grand Rapids: Zondervan, 1989.

Rice, Wayne, et al. *Creative Learning Experiences.* Winona, MN: Saint Mary's Press, 1981.

Rice, Wayne, and Mike Yaconelli. *Play It! Over 400 Games for Groups.* Youth Specialities. Grand Rapids: Zondervan, 1986.

Richards, Lawrence O. *A Theology of Christian Education.* Grand Rapids: Zondervan, 1975.

Rideout, Victoria J., et al. *Generation M²: Media in the Lives of 8- to 18-Year-Olds.* A Kaiser Foundation Study. Menlo Park, CA: Kaiser Family Foundation, 2010. http://files.eric.ed.gov/fulltext/ED527859.pdf/.

Rissover, Fredric, and David Birch. *Mass Media and the Popular Arts.* 3rd ed. New York: McGraw-Hill, 1983.

Robbins, Duffy. *Building a Youth Ministry That Builds Disciples.* Youth Specialties Grand Rapids: Zondervan, 2012.

———. *The Ministry of Nurture.* Youth Specialties Series. Grand Rapids: Zondervan, 1990.

Roehlkepartain, Eugene C. *The Teaching Church: Moving Christian Education to Center Stage.* Nashville: Abingdon, 1993.

———. "The Thinking Climate: A Missing Ingredient In Youth Ministry." *Christian Education Journal* 15 (Fall 1994) 53–63.

Roehlkepartain, Eugene C., and Peter L. Benson. *Youth in Protestant Churches.* Minneapolis: Search Institute, 1993.

Root, Andrew. *The Children of Divorce: The Loss of Family as the Loss of Being.* Grand Rapids: Brazos, 2010.

Rosenblaum, Emil, and Denise B. Kandel. "Early Onset of Adolescent Sex and Drug Use." *Journal of Marriage and the Family* 52 (1990) 783–98.

Rothman, Jack. *Runaway & Homeless Youth: Strengthening Services to Families and Children.* New York: Longman, 1991.

Rowatt, G. Wade. *Pastoral Care with Adolescents in Crisis.* Louisville: Westminster John Knox, 1989.

Rowley, William J. *Equipped to Care.* Wheaton, IL: Victor, 1990.

Sadker, Myra Pollack, and David Miller Sadker. *Teachers, Schools, and Society.* 3rd ed. New York: McGraw-Hill, 1994.

Santrock, John W. *Adolescence.* 12th ed. New York: McGraw-Hill Higher Education, 2008.

Schein, Edgar H. *Organizational Culture and Leadership.* 4th ed. San Francisco: Jossey-Bass, 2010.

Schiffrin, Holly H., et al. "Helping or Hovering? The Effects of Helicopter Parenting on College Students' Well-Being." *Journal of Child and Family Studies* 23 (2014) 548–57.

Schlegel, Alice, and Herbert Barry III. *Adolescence: An Anthropological Inquiry.* New York: Free Press, 1991.

Schwadel, Phil, and Christian Smith. *Portraits of Protestant Teens*. Chapel Hill, NC: National Study of Youth and Religion, 2005. http://youthandreligion.nd.edu/assets/102510/portraitsprotteens.pdf.

Sebald, Hans. *Adolescence: A Social Psychological Analysis*. 3rd ed. Englewood Cliffs, NJ: Prentice-Hall, 1984.

———. "Adolescent's Shifting Orientation towards Parents and Peers." *Journal of Marriage and the Family* 48 (1986) 5–13.

Seem, S. R. and Clark, M. D. "Healthy Women, Healthy Men, and Healthy Adults; An Evaluation of Gender Role Stereotypes in the Twenty-First Century." *Sex Roles* 55 (2006) 247–58.

Sell, Charles M. *Family Ministry*. 2nd ed. Grand Rapids: Zondervan, 1995.

Senter, Mark H., III. "Response from a Stratigic Perspective." In *Four Views of Youth Ministry and the Church*, edited by Mark H. Senter, 31–34. Grand Rapids: Zondervan, 2001.

Setran, David P., and Chris A. Kiesling. *Spiritual Formation in Emerging Adulthood: A Practical Theology for College and Young Adult Ministry*. Grand Rapids: Baker Academic, 2013.

Sexuality and U.ca. Sexual Health. "Statistics on Canadian Teen Pregnancies." http://www.sexualityandu.ca/sexual-health/statistics1/statistics-on-canadian-teen-pregnancies/.

Shafii, Mohammed. "Completed Suicide in Children and Adolescents: Methods of Psychological Autopsy." In *Suicide among Youth: Perspectives on Risk and Prevention*, edited by Cynthia R. Pfeffer, 1–19. Washington, DC: American Psychiatric Press, 1989.

Shedd, Charlie. *The Stork Is Dead*. Waco: Word, 1968.

Sheehy, Gail. *Passages*. New York: Bantam, 1974.

Shreeve, Caroline M. *Depression: Its Causes and How to Overcome It*. Life in Crisis Book. Wellingborough, UK: Thorsons, 1984.

Siegel, Michele, et al. *Surviving an Eating Disorder: New Perspectives and Strategies for Family and Friends*. New York: Harper & Row, 1988.

Simons, Ronald L., et al. "The Effect of Social Skills, Values, Peers, and Depression on Adolescent Substance Use." *Journal of Early Adolescence* 11 (1991) 466–81.

Slaikeu, Karl A. *Crisis Intervention*. 2nd ed. Boston: Allyn & Bacon, 1990.

Small, Stephen A., et al. "Adolescent Autonomy and Parental Stress." *Journal of Youth and Adolescence* 17 (October 1988) 377–91.

Smith, Christian. *Soul Searching: The Religious and Spiritual Lives of American Teenagers*. New York: Oxford University Press, 2005.

Smith, Christian, and Patricia Snell. *Souls in Transition: The Religious and Spiritual Lives of Emerging Adults*. Oxford: Oxford University Press, 2009.

Smolak, Linda, and Sarah K. Murnen. "Gender and Eating Problems." In *Eating Disorders: Innovative Directions in Research and Practice*, edited by Ruth H. Striegel-Moore and Linda Smolak, 91–110. Washington, DC: American Psychological Association, 2001.

Solomon, Theo. "History and Demography of Child Abuse." In *Child Abuse: Commission and Omission*, edited by Joanne Valiant Cook and Roy Tyler Bowles, 63–68. Toronto: Butterworths, 1980.

Sorensen, Robert. *Adolescent Sexuality in Contemporary America*. New York: World, 1972.

Staal, Stephanie. *The Love They Lost: Living with the Legacy of Our Parents' Divorce*. New York: Random House, 2000.

Statistic Brain Research Institute. "High School Dropout Statistics." http://www.statisticbrain.com/high-school-dropout-statistics/.

———. "Illiteracy Statistics." http://www.statisticbrain.com/number-of-american-adults-who-cant-read/.

———. "Teenager Consumer Spending Statistics." http://www.statisticbrain.com/teenage-consumer-spending-statistics/.

Statistics Canada. "Crude Birth Rate, Age-specific and Total Fertility Rates (Live Births), Canada, Provinces and Territories." http://www5.statcan.gc.ca/cansim/a26?lang=eng&id=1024505&p2=46/.

Steele, Les. "Identity Formation Theory and Youth Ministry." *Christian Education Journal* 9 (Autumn 1988) 91–99.

———. *On the Way: A Practical Theology of Christian Formation*. Grand Rapids: Baker, 1990.

Steinberg, Laurence, et al. "Negative Impact of Part-Time Work on Adolescent Adjustment: Evidence from a Longditudinal Study." In *Adolescent Behavior*, edited by Elizabeth Aries, 452–74. New York: McGraw-Hill /Dushkin, 2001.

Steiner-Adair, Catherine. *The Big Disconnect: Protecting Childhood and Family Relationships in the Digital Age*. New York: Harper, 2013.

Stevens, Richard. *Erik Erikson: An Introduction*. New York: St. Martins, 1983.

Stewart, Kathryn. "Preventing Underage Alcohol Access: Policy and Enforcement." *The Prevention Researcher* 9 (2002) 8–11.

Straus, Murray, et al. *Behind Closed Doors: Violence in the American Family*. Garden City, NY: Anchor, 1980.

Strommen, Merton P. *The Five Cries of Youth* 2nd rev. ed. San Francisco: Harper and Row, 1993.

Strommen, Merton P., and A. Irene Strommen. *Five Cries of Parents*. San Francisco: Harper & Row, 1985.

Sullivan, Erin et al. "Suicide Trends among Persons Aged 10–24 Years–United States, 1994–2012." Morbidity and Mortality Weekly Report. Centers for Disease Control and Prevention. http://www.cdc.gov/mmwr/preview/mmwrhtml/mm6408a1.htm/.

Sundene, Jana L., and Richard R. Dunn. *Shaping the Journey of Emerging Adults: Life-Giving Rhythms for Spiritual Transformation*. Downers Grove, IL: IVP Books, 2012.

Super, Donald. E. "A Life-span, Life-space Approach to Career Development." *Journal of Vocational Behavior* 16 (1980) 282–98.

Sutton, Jan. *Healing the Hurt Within: Understand Self-Injury and Self-Harm, and Heal the Emotional Wounds*. 3rd ed. Begbroke, UK: How To Books, 2007.

Suziedelis, Antanas, and Raymond H. Potvin, "Sex Differences in Factors Affecting Religiousness among Catholic Adolescents." *Journal for the Scientific Study of Religion* 20 (March 1982) 38–51.

Teen Health and the Media. Media Literacy. "Fast Facts." http://depts.washington.edu/thmedia/view.cgi?section=medialiteracy&page=fastfacts/.

Teen Sex Survey in the Evangelical Church. Dallas: Josh McDowell Ministry, 1987.

Temple, Jeff R., and HyeJeong Choi. "Longitudinal Association." *Pediatrics* 134 (2014) 1287–92. http://pediatrics.aappublications.org/content/134/5/e1287/.

Temple, W. "Perspective Transformation among Mainland Chinese Intellectuals Reporting Christian Conversion while in the United States." PhD diss., Trinity International University, 1999.

Tennant, Mark. "Perspective Transformation and Adult Development." *Adult Education Quarterly* 44 (1993) 34–42.

Thornburg, Hershel D. *Development in Adolescence.* 2nd ed. Monterey: Brooks/Cole, 1982.

Thorton, Arland, and Donald Camburn, "Religious Participation and Adolescent Sexual Behavior and Attitudes." *Journal of Marriage and the Family* 51 (1989) 641–53.

Tobin-Richards, Maryse H., et al., "Puberty and Its Psychological and Social Significance." In *Experiencing Adolescents: A Sourcebook for Parents, Teachers, and Teens,* edited by Richard M. Lerner and Nancy L. Galambos, 17–50. Garland Reference Library of Social Science 201. New York: Garland, 1984.

Toch, Thomas. "Violence in Schools." *U.S. News and World Report,* November 8, 1993, 34.

Turkle, Shelly. *Life on the Screen: Identity in the Age of the Internet.* New York: Simon & Schuster, 1995.

Ungar, Michael T. "The Myth of Peer Pressure." *Adolescence* 35 (2000) 167–80.

United States Census Bureau. "Living Arrangements of Children: 2009." https://www.census.gov/prod/2011pubs/p70-126.pdf/.

———. "Families and Living Arrangements." 13 Nov 2012. http://www.census.gov/hhes/families/.

———. "Statistical Abstract of the United States: 2009." http://www.census.gov/compendia/statab/2012/tables/12s1337.pdf/.

United States Department of Health and Human Services. "Child Maltreatment 2013." http://www.acf.hhs.gov/sites/default/files/cb/cm2013.pdf.

———. Office of Adolescent Health. Reproductive Health. "Trends in Teen Pregnancy and Childbearing." http://www.hhs.gov/ash/oah/adolescent-health-topics/reproductive-health/teen-pregnancy/trends.html/

United States Department of Labor. "Employment Projections." http://data.bls.gov/projections/occupationProj/.

———. "Labor Force Statistics from the Current Population Survey." http://www.bls.gov/cps/cpsaat03.htm/.

Valkenburg, Patti M. *Children's Responses to the Screen: A Media Psychological Approach.* Mahwah, NJ: Erlbaum, 2004.

Van Pelt, Rich. *Intensive Care: Helping Teenagers in Crisis.* Youth Specialty Series. Grand Rapids: Zondervan, 1988.

Varenhorst, Barbara B. *Training Teenagers for Peer Ministry.* Loveland, CO: Group, 1988.

Vigeveno H. S., and Anne Claire. *Divorce and the Children.* Glendale, CA: Regal, 1979.

Vondracek, Fred, and John Schulenberg "Adolescence and Careers." In *Experiencing Adolescents: A Sourcebook for Parents, Teachers, and Teens,* edited by Richard M. Lerner and Nancy L. Galambos, 317–59. Garland Reference Library of Social Science 201. New York: Garland, 1984.

Waggoner, Brad. *The Shape of Faith to Come: Spiritual Formation and the Future of Discipleship.* Nashville: B&H, 2008.

Wallerstein, Judy S., and Sandra Blakeslee. *Second Chances: Men, Women, and Children a Decade after Divorce.* New York: Ticknor and Fields, 1989.

Wallis, Claudia. "The Nuclear Family Goes Boom!" *Time,* Fall Special, 1992, 42–44.

Westerhoff, John. *Will Our Children Have Faith?* San Francisco: HarperCollins, 1976.

Whitbeck, Les B., et al. "The Effects of Divorced Mothers' Dating Behaviors and Sexual Attitudes and Behaviors of Their Adolescent Children." *Journal of Marriage and the Family* 56 (1994), 615–21.

White, David F. "The Social Construction of Adolescence." In *Awakening Youth Discipleship,* edited by Brian J. Mahan et al., 3–20. Eugene, OR: Cascade Books, 2008.

Williams, Lena. "U.S. Teens Increasingly View Sex as a Personal Right, Experts Say." *Atlanta Journal and Constitution,* February 27 1989 C4.

Willits Fern K., and Donald M. Crider. "Church Attendance and Traditional Religious Beliefs in Adolescence and Young Adulthood: A Panel Study." *Review of Religious Research* 31 (September 1989) 68–81.

Windle, Michael, "Alcohol Use among Adolescents." *Prevention Researcher* 9 (2002) 1–3.

Wong, Sui. "The Effects of Adolescent Activities on Delinquency: A Differential Involvement Approach." *Journal of Youth and Adolescence* 34 (2005) 321–33.

Worick, Wayne, and Warren Schaller. *Alcohol, Tobacco and Drugs.* Englewood Cliffs, NJ: Prentice-Hall, 1977.

Wright, H. Norman. *Crisis Counseling.* Ventura, CA: Regal, 1993.

Wright, Steve. *ReThink: Is Student Ministry Working?* Wake Forest, NC: InQuest, 2007.

Yaconelli, Mike, and Jim Burns. *High School Ministry.* Grand Rapids: Zondervan, 1986.

Yaconelli, Mike, and Dave Lynn. *Tension Getters Two.* Grand Rapids: Zondervan, 1985.

Yarhouse, Mark A. *Understanding Sexual Identity: A Resource for Youth Ministry.* Grand Rapids: Zondervan, 2013.

Young, A., et al. "Adolescents' Experiences of Sexual Assault by Peers: Prevalence and Nature of Victimization Occurring in and out of School. *Journal of Youth & Adolescence* 38 (2008) 1072–83.

Young, Jun, and Kinnaman, David. *The Hyperlinked Life: Live with Wisdom in an Age of Information Overload.* Grand Rapids: Zondervan, 2013.

Yount, William R. *Created to Learn: A Christian Teacher's Introduction to educational Psychology.* 2nd ed. Nashville: B&H Academic, 2010.

YouTube. Press. "Statistics." https://www.youtube.com/yt/press/statistics.html/.

Zuck, Roy B., and Gene A. Getz, *Christian Youth, an In-Depth Study.* Chicago: Moody, 1968.

Index

people increasingly more interested in, 136

placing a high priority on, 153

used to live out Christian community and hospitality, 164

religion

fathers having impact, 123

influence of on lives of teenagers, 189

marginal for young people, 190

young people ambivalent toward, 163

religiosity or faith, as perceived by identity-diffused youth, 31

religious activity, 190

religious faith, 22, 187

religious groups, enjoyment from, 189

religious organizations, involvement in, 22

religious participation, importance in determining sexual behavior, 209

remarried family, radically different from the original intact family, 91

remembering (recalling information), 77, 78

repressiveness, of the church, 197

residential programs, rehabilitating substance-abusing adolescents, 253–54

resistance to authority, indicating alcohol abuse, 245

retaliation, against a parent, 94

Rice, Wayne, 36, 161

Richards, Lawrence, 33

"right-now" sensation, providing, 32

rigid authoritarianism, 106–7

risk-taking, technology and, 283

rites of passage, going through, 45

Robbins, Duffy, 76

rock and pop music, as synonymous with sex, 211–12

"rock" form, of cocaine, 249

Roehlkepartain, Eugene, 22, 80, 193, 194, 209–10, 276

Rogalski, Kelly, 265

role models, 47–48, 71–72

role-playing, 82–83

Roman Catholic Church, on the subject of masturbation, 216

romantic relationship, ending in a breakup, 167

romantic relationships, as a central aspect of the adolescent social world, 166

Root, Andrew, 21

Rothman, Jack, 117

Rowatt, Wade, 12, 275

Rubbins, Duffy, 81

runaways

caused by communication problems, 108–9

characteristics of, 120

homes of, 107

identifying new, 121

linked to physical abuse, 117

reaching alarming proportions, 120

reasons for leaving home, 120–121

serious argument with one or both parents, 109

sexual abuse linked to, 115

working with, 121

"running commentary," providing to facilitate critical interaction, 296

sacred and the secular, false dichotomy between, 196

sadness, of two or more weeks, 19

safe context, providing for doubts, 79

safe environment, creating, 198

safe sex, abstinence as the only, 262

safety

concerns keeping students home, 178

in a group, 140

provided by the community of faith, 47

same-sex attraction, 62, 63

Sartre, Paul, 162

Saul, changed his name to Paul after his conversion, 143

scaffolding, 44–48

school environment, social change in, 9

school performance, deterioration in, indicating alcohol abuse, 245

service projects
  heading up, 40
  ideas for, 34
service sector, increase of the low-
    paying, 183
Setran, David, 163
setting, comfortable and conducive to
    sharing, 138
severe depression, experiencing, 277
severe drinking or drug use, effects
    of, 279
sex
  as a personal right or choice, 200
  portrayed as a casual activity on
      television, 210–211
sex act
  masturbation as perversion of, 216
  not defining one's sexual orienta-
      tion, 62
sex and sexuality, contrasting views
    of, 197
sex before marriage, consequences
    for, 200
sex offenders, adolescent, 229–30
sex roles, modification of traditional,
    65
sexting, 288
sexual abstinence, teenagers commit-
    ing to, 212
sexual abuse. See also abuse
  by adolescents, 230
  of children by other children and
      adolescents, 229
  as a common occurrence in the
      United States, 114–16
  as a criminal act, 116
  crossing all social strata, 115
  defined, 113
  effects of, 115
  enhancing the prevention of, 116
  youth workers legal responsibility to
      report, 116
sexual activity
  as an accepted and integral part of
      adolescent dating, 171
  alcohol use associated with, 241–42
  illicit drugs increasing the risk of,
      249

not central to dating in early adoles-
    cence, 166
permissive clearly commonplace,
    200
television promoting, 211
sexual behaviors and attitudes,
    200–222
sexual content, of television and other
    electronic media, 210
sexual development, anxiety from
    delayed, 60
sexual drives of adolescents, technol-
    ogy playing to, 284
sexual experience, including homo-
    sexual acts or feelings, 218
sexual identity, 62, 63
sexual intercourse
  adolescents from single-parent
      families and, 97
  engaging in at younger and younger
      ages, 201
  forced, 19, 168
  never having or with four or more
      individuals, 20
  sexting preceding, 288
  significant decline in its occurrence
      among teenagers, 201
sexual media world, teenagers living
    in, 210
sexual orientation, 61, 62–63
sexual pressure, knowing how to resist,
    203
sexual promiscuity, indicating alcohol
    abuse, 245
sexual purity, fortifying the message
    of, 213
sexual revolution, among American
    youth, 201–2
sexual self-control, importance of, 222
sexual sin, skit portraying the conse-
    quences of, 213
sexual talk, having the same impact as
    actual depictions of sex, 211
sexual violence, during dating, 168
sexuality. See also adolescent sexuality
  adolescent's awareness of, 277
  closely related to identity formation,
      59

Youth Specialties, 193n76
youth teachers
  avoiding spoon-feeding youth, 77
  modeling a thinking faith, 81
youth workers. *See also* adult youth
    workers; youth pastors
  assessing risk for contracting AIDS,
    261
  assisting in the adoption process,
    228
  being aware of youth likely to be at
    high risk for suicide, 281
  checking own attitudes concerning
    homosexuals, 220
  concentrating on being available to
    teenagers or parents, 109
  counseling youth in achieving
    vocational and occupational
    goals, 59
  demonstrating to teenagers how to
    behave or live, 33
  discovering high-risk adolescents,
    115
  doing informal counseling helping
    the potential dropout, 177
  earning the right to be heard by
    teenagers, 135–36
  empowering and helping teens
    to form a holistic Christian
    identity, 298
  encouraging adoption as an option
    for pregnant teenagers, 227
  encouraging participation in recov-
    ery groups, 253
  encouraging participation of teenag-
    ers from single-parent homes,
    191
  entering into dialogue with a teen,
    296
  explaining parental regulations, 107
  having an impact on teenagers who
    work, 186
  helping adolescents struggling with
    doubts, 79
  helping adolescents turn crises into
    opportunities, 6
  identifying indicators of physical
    abuse and neglect, 118

  ill-equipped to deal with critical
    issues, 3
  impacting how adolescents respond
    to parents and peers, 50–51
  impacting teenagers with the gospel
    of Christ, 134
  implications for, 76
  involved with teenagers in treat-
    ment, 254
  levels of intervention efforts for
    prevention of substance use
    and abuse, 250
  making the youth group a safe place
    to doubt, 198
  male, needed by teenagers experi-
    encing father absenteeism, 103
  nurturing adolescents, 39
  offering teens a window into social
    media and digital technology,
    295
  organizing exploration groups,
    58–59
  placing a priority on building com-
    munity, 133, 136
  promoting Christian community,
    160
  reaching below-average students,
    193
  recognizing the impact adolescents
    have on one another, 151
  referring depressive adolescents, 278
  reporting child abuse, molestation,
    or rape, 230
  responsibility in responding to
    physical abuse, 118
  setting an example for teens to fol-
    low, 295
  spending time with teens outside the
    formal instructional setting, 33
  teaching teens how to live their digi-
    tal lives in a manner honoring
    God, 293
  using social media and technology,
    298
  working with adolescents from
    divorced homes, 93
YouTube, content of, 286

Zuck, Roy, 129